STUDIES ON MEDIEVAL AND EARLY MODERN WOMEN 4

In the same series

1 Christine Meek & Katharine Simms (eds), *'The fragility of her sex'? Medieval Irish women in their European context*

2 Christine Meek (ed.), *Women in Renaissance and early modern Europe*

3 Christine Meek & Catherine Lawless (eds), *Studies on medieval and early modern women: pawns or players?*

4 Christine Meek & Catherine Lawless (eds), *Studies on medieval and early modern women 4: victims or viragos?*

Studies on medieval and early modern women 4

VICTIMS OR VIRAGOS?

Christine Meek &
Catherine Lawless

Editors

FOUR COURTS PRESS

Typeset in 10.5 pt on 12.5 pt Ehrhardt by
Carrigboy Typesetting Services, County Cork for
FOUR COURTS PRESS LTD
7 Malpas Street, Dublin 8, Ireland
e-mail: info@four-courts-press.ie
and in North America for
FOUR COURTS PRESS
c/o ISBS, 920 N.E. 58th Avenue, Suite 300, Portland, OR 97213.

A catalogue record for this title is available
from the British Library.

ISBN 1–85182–888–5 hbk
1–85182–889–3 pbk

Printed in England by
MPG Books, Bodmin, Cornwall

Contents

Illustrations

Introduction

In June 2004 the British Sunday newspaper *The Observer* was moved to publish a supplement entitled 'Men uncovered: the state they're in.' This is just one example of a plethora of debates both in the popular media and in academia. In a neat reversal of the Aristotelian idea that women were deformed men, scientists today discuss the importance of the SRY element of the Y chromosome in the formation of maleness within the womb, that which stops the foetus remaining female.[1] To paraphrase Joan Scott, gender is not only a tool for historical enquiry, but is also a topic of daily popular debate.[2] Transexuality, same sex parenthood, the fluidity of sexual identities, all of these are factors which, in fact, show the continuing importance of historical enquiries into gender identity and construction. It appears that never before in the western world have the biological characteristics of humankind been less deterministic of gender identity than today. Masculinity seems no longer to be an unquestioned given, with femininity its problematic 'other', but is now itself a focus of anxiety and questioning. Today the validity of 'women's history' as a category in itself is frequently seen as inadequate. Increasingly the category 'women' is replaced by the category 'gender' in academic disciplines and publishing.

So why do we have a book entitled *Studies on Medieval and Early Modern Women*? We have the title partly, it must be admitted, to ensure continuity with previous volumes. This is the fourth volume of essays which has arisen from the

---

1 Steve Jones, *Y: the descent of men*. In 1990 geneticists Robin Lovell-Badge and Peter Goodfellow discovered that women lacked the SRY, the sex-determining region of the Y-chromosome and this lack was the sole cause of a woman's femaleness. 'The Y-chromosome is a scrappy little thing, and yet for the rest of a man's life it directs his body to one crucial goal: that of preventing him from reverting to his natural sexual state – of being female': Robin McKie, 'The Y Chromosome', *The Observer*, 27 June 2004, supplement, '*Men uncovered: the state they're in*,' p. 33. 2 Joan W. Scott, 'Gender: a useful category of historical analysis', *American Historical Review* 91 (1986), pp. 1053–75. 3 See Lucy Irigaray, interviewed by Alice Jardine and Anne Menke in 'Writing as a woman' in *Je tu nous: towards a culture of difference*, trans. A. Martin (London, 1993), pp. 52–8, reprinted in Hilary Robinson (ed.), *Feminism-art-theory: an anthology, 1968–2000* (Oxford, 2003), p. 44: 'At the present time, there aren't that many women working in institutions. Those that do are often restricted in how far they can go in their career.

now annual conference on the history of women in the medieval and early modern periods in Trinity College, Dublin. This volume, compiled in 2004, coincides with the centenary of women's admission to Trinity. We thus acknowledge a century of women's achievements in higher education, but we also remember that such a privilege is only a century old.[3] It is less than a century old elsewhere: Oxford, although it admitted women in 1878, only awarded them full degrees in 1920.[4] In Ireland, a study published in 1999 by Ruane and Sutherland found that women constituted 28% of those holding faculty posts in third level institutes, with just over 5% at professorial level. Yet approximately half of all undergraduate and postgraduate students in Ireland are female.[5] In Britain and Ireland female high performance in final school examinations has contrasted in recent years with poor performance by males, leading to a perceived crisis and suggested curriculum revision to accommodate the under-achieving males.[6] Although it is to be desired that all children perform to the best of their ability, it must be observed that, when males outranked females in educational performance, no crisis was perceived; in fact, it was so normal that it was hardly commented on. In many parts of the world basic education is still unavailable to many because of poverty, but is unavailable to others simply because they are women.[7] According to figures published by UNESCO, 'more than 56 percent of the 104 million out of school children are girls and over two-thirds of the world's 860 million illiterates are women'.[8]

'Women' has not been replaced by 'gender' in the title of this book, partly because such a title may mislead, as many of the essays are not explicitly concerned with gender theory but rather with women as historical subjects in medieval and early modern Europe, but also partly because the need for women's history still exists:

Very few women reach the highest posts and they pay very dearly for it, in one way or another. That this is true is shown by the debates concerning names for occupations ... It's quite possible that many of the women who are allowed into institutions talk about a culture that has already passed and not about what will remain as a trace of the elaboration of the present and the future.'   4 http://www.ox.ac.uk/aboutoxford/women.shtml   5 F. Ruane and J.M. Sutherland, *Women in the labour force* (Dublin, 1999). For a comparison of these figures with European and American institutions and analysis of them, see Pat O'Connor, 'A bird's eye view ... resistance in academia', *Irish Journal of Sociology* 10 (2001), pp. 86–104.   6 See the debates carried on in the letters page of the *Irish Times*, August–September 2004, mirrored in the letters pages and editorials of the British newspapers upon the release of A-level results.   7 See Jerry A. Jacobs, 'Gender inequality and Higher Education', *Annual Review of Sociology* 22 (1996), pp. 153–85. Figures for women's participation in higher education globally are given on pp. 158–9.   8 UNESCO EFA Global Monitoring Report , 2003/4. Available at http://portal.unesco.org/education.   9 Scott, 'Gender: a useful category', p. 1056. Scott goes on to say: 'But only one facet. "Gender" as a substitute for "women" is also used to suggest that information about women is necessarily information about men, that one implies study of the other. This

Whereas the term 'women's history' proclaims its politics by asserting (contrary to customary practice) that women are valid historical subjects, 'gender' includes but does not name women and so seems to pose no critical threat. This use of 'gender' is one facet of what might be called the quest of feminist scholarship for academic legitimacy in the 1980s.[9]

This volume, while cognizant of the dangers of using the term 'women' as, to quote Biddick, a 'foundational category',[10] shows the number of stories that can still be told by scholars from different disciplines using various methodologies.[11] In this study, while masculinity and femininity are not seen as binary oppositions – indeed, the very term *virago* is often associated with *virility* – our starting point is how *women* behaved, how they saw themselves, and how they were seen by others. How did women operate within institutions that were created by men, albeit men raised by women? How was power seen and held by women? Did women see themselves as an inferior opposite to men, or did they, as Caroline Bynum Walker suggests, see themselves as on a continuum with men?[12]

This book consists of essays concerned with individual women such as Emma of Normandy, Matilda of Tuscany, Blessed Chiara of Montefalco and Adela of Blois; with female networks of power such as those found at the French and Spanish courts of the seventeenth century; with how women were affected by and participated in the wars in seventeenth-century Ireland and the medieval Crusades; and with how the perennial 'women's issues' of marriage and the family and their contribution to [male] civilization were discussed and debated by Protestant reformers, the eighteenth-century Scottish Enlightenment

usage insists that the world of women is part of the world of men, created in and by it.' As the title of the article suggests, 'gender' is seen as a more useful category than 'women'. 10 Kathleen Biddick, 'Genders, bodies, borders: technologies of the visible', *Speculum* 68 (1993), pp. 389–418. 11 Perhaps the most unifying methodology present here is that of Natalie Zemon Davis: 'It seems to me that we should be interested in the history of both women and men, that we should not be working only on the subjected sex any more than an historian of class can focus entirely on peasants. Our goal it so understand the significance of the *sexes*, of gender groups in the historical past. Our goal is to discover the range in sex roles and in sexual symbolism in different societies and periods, to find out what meaning they had and how they functioned to maintain the social order or to promote its change': Natalie Zemon Davis, 'Women's history in transition: the European case', *Feminist Studies* 3 (1975–6), p. 90, quoted in Joan W. Scott, 'Gender: a useful category', p. 1054. 12 Caroline Bynum Walker, *Fragmentation and redemption: essays on gender and the human body in medieval religion* (New York, 1992), p. 109; see also p. 220. 13 'Because, on the face of it, war, diplomacy, and high politics have not been explicitly about those relationships, gender seems not to apply and so continues to be irrelevant to the thinking of historians concerned with issues of politics and power. The effect is to endorse a certain functionalist view ultimately rooted in biology and to perpetuate the idea of separate spheres (sex or politics, family or nation, women or men) in the writing of history': Scott, 'Gender: a useful category', p. 1057.

and the well-known men and the less well-known women of the French Revolution. The hierarchy of historical subjects, from constitutional, diplomatic and military history 'down' to social, religious, economic and cultural history has firmly placed 'women's history' in the lower genres of historical research. Yet, in accordance with the views expressed by Scott and Zemon Davis, 'women's history' can inform these soi-disant higher spheres.[13]

Kimberley LoPrete's essay is a fitting opening to the volume. LoPrete discusses the term *virago* and removes it from its modern context of 'shrew' or 'harridan', replacing it with its medieval connotation, according to Jerome, Isidore of Seville and others, as a lordly woman who wielded powers that were generally conceived of as male. LoPrete points out that the binary gender oppositions of male/female are largely modern constructions, and that medieval views saw men and women as having gendered elements in different proportions. She demonstrates that in the medieval period female lordship was a not unusual occurrence in the dynastic life cycle, and that in an era of crusade, pilgrimage and war, women rulers, acknowledged by their peers as 'viragos', exercised political power. She also shows that medieval writers used the word *virago* in the sense of women behaving in a manlike (*viriliter*) fashion as rulers of lands. She points out that this was not freakish behaviour but an extension of the role of domestic custodian in an era where there was no conceptual boundary between the domestic and the public. However, these powers were largely restricted to aristocratic women, and not all aristocratic women could expect to have them: 'Manly women' were not men, but neither were they average women. Female political power was not accepted as an equal substitute for male, but as something that might be expedient in hard times.

Maia Sheridan shows the importance of Emma of Normandy in the complicated dynastic politics of eleventh-century England. In an attempt to procure power for her sons by Cnut, she manipulated her image through the work she commissioned from a Flemish monk, the *Encomium Emmae Reginae*. Sheridan shows that the author of the *Encomium* written in honour of Emma of Normandy does not omit her active exercise of power as frequent regent during her husband's absence, but emphasizes the traditional role of a pious mother passively awaiting her sons' assumption of power, an account which contradicts the likely involvement of Emma in the affairs of England. In the hands of the encomiast, in order to achieve the propagandistic purpose of the work, the powerful woman, or *virago*, must become an innocent victim, forced to flee England. Although the *Encomium* compares Emma with the biblical heroine Esther in the role of drawing together two divided peoples, English and Danish, her promotion of the Danish line appears to have been unwelcome to her Anglo-Saxon son Edward, who dispossessed her. Her influence and power demonstrates 'the ephemeral nature of female power in the Middle Ages', and like many other lordly women discussed in this volume, depended upon both her life cycle and the dynastic life cycle of which she was a part.

Patrick Healy demonstrates that Matilda of Tuscany could be described not only as a *virago* but as a crusader. He looks at the influence of Matilda of Tuscany on the Gregorian reform movement. Referred to as a *virago* by Hugh of Flavigny, Matilda was, in her military and political championship of Gregory VII and his reform, likened to the biblical heroines Deborah and Judith. Following the example of her mother Beatrice in an earlier imperial-papal contest, Matilda attempted to mediate between the Emperor Henry IV and Pope Gregory VII; this was briefly successful with the famous meeting at Matilda's castle of Canossa. When warfare was resumed, the court of Matilda offered not only sanctuary to the leaders of Gregorian reform but a centre for intellectual debate. The protection and encouragement given to such figures as Anselm of Lucca, John of Mantua and Bonizio of Sutri led to innovative writings on the role of Christian warfare.

Conor Kostick uses a range of sources to show that women participated in the Crusades in a greater number than previously thought. He finds that the women on crusade were not just nuns and camp followers, but many other varieties of medieval women also. The problems of source material are raised, as women's voices are absent. While the motivations of aristocratic women are shown, albeit in male-authored material, the reasons for other women to go on Crusade are rarely mentioned by the sources. Some women were probably of marginal status, such as the former concubines of priests, cut adrift from such relationships by the clerical reforms of the eleventh century. Kostick also contrasts the topos of women dressing as men in contemporary hagiography and poetry with the criticism levelled by churchmen at women who did so on the Crusades. Such women were not seen as *viragos* but as betrayers of their sex and offenders against not only social mores, but scriptural tradition.

Richard Sims' examination of legal cases looks at how crime, and female participation in it, was perceived in medieval law. He finds that there is no reason to suppose that either society or the courts looked at female thieves any differently from male ones, although this was not necessarily the case with other crimes. Robbery, defined as theft with violence, was usually masculine. Infanticide was seen as predominately female. Female killers rarely acted alone, unlike their male counterparts. Systems of kinship and spatial confinement formed an important framework for criminals of both sexes, but was more important for women. Sims points out that, although the numbers of women accused of crime were large enough to merit study, the role of women in crime was very different from that of men; often women's crime could be argued to have benefited others (the family) and even in cases of homicide or suicide, less violent techniques were generally used.

Cordelia Warr's essay examines the world of late medieval piety and devotional iconography. This was a period in which female piety and the experience of the *imitatio Christi* through the female body challenged traditional religious structures and practices. Warr looks at the role of the image, not only in the devotions of holy women, but also in the very construction of their *vitae*. Using the case of the Beata Chiara de Montefalco, Warr shows how Chiara's heart was cut open by her fellow nuns after her death in an unusual, and secret, procedure and how the instruments of the Passion (a popular image in late medieval religion) were found inscribed upon it. The internalization of such imagery and the affective piety of Chiara which led to her body effectively becoming a reliquary are analysed here and shown as a fleshly, and female, echo of the stigmata of Saint Francis. The attempts made by her fellow sisters and followers to have her canonized as a saint failed, but the importance of imagery and its mediation through a female body is shown through the canonization procedure and the testimony of the nuns and the male ecclesiastics present.

Helga Robinson-Hammerstein looks at the position of nuns in the Protestant Reformation. Using visual as well as documentary sources, she shows how women were a crucial prop in reformation ideas of the family. She also shows how Luther's dismantlement of religious vows as anti-gospel led to the disbanding of convents and the removal of a long-established alternative to marriage. Old female kinship networks were broken and some nuns found their roles as teachers outside the convents less rewarding and prestigious than their old roles as choir sisters. Women's role in the family was closely equated with the good of society. Marriage was seen as the only reasonable prospect for a woman in reformation Germany. With the only place for women being marriage and motherhood, some wives of pastors, such as Catherina von Bora, the wife of Luther, adopted a 'semi-spiritual' role in helping to care for the congregation. Robinson-Hammerstein also examines the interesting case of Caritas Pirckheimer and her nuns in Nuremberg, who resisted all attempts to close their convent.

Three essays concern women in the seventeenth century, those of Bernadette Whelan, Linda Kiernan and Alistair Malcolm. Bernadette Whelan shows how women were affected by and participated in warfare in seventeenth-century Ireland. As in the medieval period looked at by LoPrete and Kostick, women in Ireland exercised power over their households in a natural extension of authority. Such households made obvious targets and women were the main victims who bore the brunt of soldiers' activities in Ireland. Women also participated, both as members of mobs, motivated by politics but also sometimes by economic necessity, and served as soldiers on the battlefield dressed as men, to the disapproval of male authorities. Some women, such as Margaret, dowager countess of Orrery, smuggled papers belonging to her husband and nephew. Women also participated in more traditional nurturing roles, as the wives and mistresses of serving soldiers. Such women, if widowed, often faced destitution and isolation and legislation was enacted in order to deal with this social problem. Whelan argues that war involved all of society, not just male society, and thus military history is not just concerned with the history of men.

Linda Kiernan and Alistair Malcolm, instead of using traditional court records such as inventories and notarial accounts, demonstrate the usefulness of journals and private correspondence, showing that access to the centres of power was often mediated by women. This was known and understood by contemporaries and the effort to secure advantageous court positions for women was intense. The women discussed by Linda Kiernan in seventeenth-century France held a certain type of power that was utterly dependent upon their biological sex. Kiernan examines the role of women at court, in this case the court of Louis XIV in France. She looks at how marriage legislation fitted with the desires of the French monarchy and the nobility and how networks of kinship were arranged in order to facilitate access at court. She examines the importance of the privileged position of the king's mistress, the *maîtresse-en-titre*, and indeed sometimes her husband. However, the marriage of Madame de Maintenon to the king revealed the adroit skills with which a woman managed to be first mistress and then wife.

Alistair Malcolm examines the importance of women in the court machinery of seventeenth-century Spain. The role women played at court, both as courtier and as queen, is a facet of power which has been overlooked in diplomatic history until recently. Unlike France, there was no position of chief mistress, or *maîtresse-en-titre*, in seventeenth-century Spain, but female courtiers, the *Meninas* depicted by Velazquez, could, through their access to the royal centre, exercise certain degrees of diplomacy and power. The queen herself could also exercise power through traditional methods of cultural and religious patronage and, as in the case of Emma of Normandy, considerable political power during the normal dynastic life cycle. The cultural patronage of the queen in Spain was a legitimate arena of power, as was her regency. However, Malcolm demonstrates that in the case of Mariana of Austria, she excelled in the first role, but in the second her lack of training and neglect of a traditionally female role, that of mother, paved the way for the decline of the Spanish monarchy.

Two essays examine eighteenth-century thought and society, those of Michael Brown and Colm Ó Conaill. Brown looks at the writings of the Scottish philosopher and Jacobin sympathizer John Millar, and in particular, at a revealing footnote in his *The Origin of the Distinctions of Ranks*. Brown locates Millar's work within the tradition of 'stadialism' and points out that Marxist historians are the few who, until recently, saw the importance of Millar's writings. Under the influence of Hume's empirical philosophy, Millar traced human beings' capacity to act in a predictable fashion, to form habits and then customs, and placed the evolution of marriage within this paradigm. The progress of a society, according to Millar, could be seen in the rights afforded to women within that society. Chivalric society, by elevating women removed them from normal life, whereas an economically progressive society loosened those restraints. For Millar, virtue began in the home and domestic harmony contributed to political and social well-being. In this the role of women was of paramount importance.

The next essay deals with social reality rather than economic or philosophical query. Colm O Conail looks at divorce legislation in the French revolutionary period. Although there was no question of women's equal participation in all levels of society, divorce and marriage legislation was seen as important for both sexes. Proponents of the divorce law of 1792 argued that society could not function without female equality in the home. The importance of this law can be seen by the fact that 70% of divorce petitions were initiated by women. Nor was the participation of women restricted to those who petitioned for divorce. Women such as Etta Palm d'Ælders played an important part in the pamphlet literature discussing marriage and divorce. The revolutionary language of rights, duty and liberty was used by women in their divorce petitions and writings such as those of Girod, who argued for refinements to be made to the law on the basis of equality between rich and poor women. O Conail demonstrates that divorce was a social demand, which was enacted into law by the French Revolution, and that women, although denied access to much of the political apparatus of the republic, were able to play an important role in framing and responding to divorce legislation.

These essays are varied in many ways, in period, geography, methodology, discipline and conclusions. However, the agency of women themselves and the perception, by both men and women, of what it meant to be female provide a unifying link between the female lords of medieval France and Tuscany, the queens of medieval England and seventeenth-century Spain and France, whose power was largely defined by their life cycle and those of their menfolk, of those women who are found on the margins of traditional medieval history, those who committed or were accused of committing crimes, of those women whose devotion and power was manifested, at least in the minds of their followers, in the female body, of the women who formed so important a part in the Lutheran reformation and those nuns who resisted some of the demands issued by the male reformers, and lastly, the women imagined by John Millar in his prescriptions for an ideal society, and the French Revolutionary women who, having fought for such a society, were determined to be heard within it.

Gendering viragos: medieval perceptions of powerful women

Kimberly A. LoPrete

The aim of this essay is straightforward: to underscore the need to avoid anachronism when assessing the lives and powers of aristocratic women during the Middle Ages.[1] When we classify evidence and gauge the impact of cultural discourses on peoples' experiences, we must not assume uncritically that our analytic categories or core definitions will comprehend phenomena in the same way as medieval people perceived them. Even in the wake of concern to avoid universalizing what are in effect culturally determined categories of modern western scholarship, there has been little sustained examination of the extent to which 'modern' concepts fundamental to the study of women correspond to their 'medieval' counterparts. Notions meriting a closer look include, most notably, the cognate categories of sex and gender, public and domestic spheres, and official and unofficial powers.

Medieval and modern portrayals of the sexually active and socially marked women of the aristocratic elite, frequently represented as somehow 'manlike', point to significant disjunctions alongside obvious overlaps in such core concepts. If care is not taken to account for differences over time in discourses of sexuality and political power, an anachronistic analytical prism will cause us to minimize unjustly both the numbers of politically active women in the pre-modern world and the range of lordly powers they wielded as they played out their gendered social roles. Perhaps more important, we risk misconstruing how

1 Earlier versions of this paper, drawn from an on-going research project examining the significance of the term virago in a range of medieval and modern contexts, have been presented at the Medieval Academy of America (Austin, Texas, April 2000) and to the Medieval, Renaissance & Early Modern Association at the National University of Ireland, Galway (April 2002); some aspects were developed in papers presented in April 2002 at the Denys Hay and Medieval Studies seminars at the universities of Edinburgh and St Andrews, respectively. I thank both the participants at those fora for their stimulating queries and Mark Stansbury for his knowledge of classics and computers. Because it is a work in progress, references to secondary literature are not compre-hensive and primary texts are occasionally cited in widely available editions rather than

17

male contemporaries of female lords perceived and valued such powerful women in their midst – the issue that is the main focus of this paper.

According to prevailing opinion, a handful of politically powerful women may have existed in the Middle Ages. But they were individual rule-proving exceptions, especially after the year 1000. Indeed, because of the very exceptionality of their position and the dearth of their interventions in the 'male' domain of public power, such *dominæ* were perceived as, and treated like, surrogate men. Hence, on the one hand, they can be dismissed from the history of women; on the other, they were rare to the point of being uncanny, arousing intense anxiety in their male contemporaries, who viewed them as scandalous aberrations if not outright monsters.[2] They were transgressors of the natural order and usurpers of powers legitimately belonging only to men.

To quote Georges Duby, whose eloquent essays have done much to popularize such views: 'to assume this command [beyond the confines of a feminine domestic sphere] a woman must cease to be a woman, must take on masculinity, must change in gender'; and again: 'the [male] authors [discussed] generally regarded such a situation, that of the *domina* effectively dominating, as abnormal. Indeed, such a woman figured … as virtually a usurper'.[3] In other words, in those rare cases when the powers of a woman could not be denied, they could be contained: simply label her a virago and cart her off the historical stage. No longer performed by a real woman, her powers are rhetorically explained away. At the same time, other women are warned that the exercise of such powers is at best an ambivalent claim to fame.

The swelling stream of document-based studies devoted to the particular lives of individual noblewomen is fast confirming the view that powerful women were not exceptional in the Middle Ages.[4] Indeed, as Marc Bloch aptly reminded us over half a century ago, because prevailing political structures were rooted in the domestic sphere of the dynastic family and lordly household, women – in particular as wives and mothers – could find themselves at the centre of the public stage while playing out their traditional, prescribed, and 'feminine' household roles.[5] Just how many women and with what frequency

current critical editions.   2 For disjunctions between medieval and modern notions of the uncanny that merit consideration in this context, see Caroline Walker Bynum, 'Wonder', in her *Metamorphosis and identity* (Cambridge, Mass., 2001), pp. 37–75 at pp. 40–7 (first published, *American Historical Review* 102 (1997), pp. 1–26).   3 Georges Duby, 'Women and power' in Thomas N. Bisson (ed.), *Cultures of power: lordship, status, and process in twelfth-century Europe* (Philadelphia, 1995), pp. 69–85, at pp. 78, 75.   4 See, for example, the essays and works cited in Theodore Evergates (ed.), *Aristocratic women in medieval France* (Philadelphia, 1999) and Christine Meek and Catherine Lawless (eds), *Studies on medieval and early modern women: pawns or players?* (Dublin, 2003).   5 Marc Bloch, *Feudal society*, trans. L.A. Manyon, 2 vols (Chicago, 1961), first published in French in 1940. This insight also underlay the pioneering work of Marion Facinger, 'A study of medieval queenship: Capetian France, 987–1237', *Studies in Medieval and*

they acted authoritatively in political affairs would depend on personal, familial, and wider political circumstances. Nonetheless, medieval demographic trends, combined with the growing popularity of crusading after 1095, indicate that the numbers of, and opportunities for, noblewomen to wield lordly powers were greater than is generally appreciated.[6] The dynamic interplay between the life-cycles of dynastic families and the domestic base of their power assured that, throughout the Middle Ages, the number of women exercising lordly authority at any one time was consistently high enough for most elite men to have treated with at least one female lord during his lifetime, irrespective of either the relatively modest (though always significant) proportion of aristocratic women who came to wield authoritative powers of command over lands and men, or the percentage of women among all medieval lords.[7]

Renaissance History 5 (1968), pp. 1–48; JoAnn McNamara and Suzanne Wemple, 'The power of women through the family in medieval Europe, 500–1100', *Feminist Studies* 1 (1973), pp. 126–42, rvsd. rpt. in Mary Erler and Maryanne Kowaleski (eds), *Women and power in the Middle Ages* (Athens, Ga., 1988), pp. 83–101; and Pauline Stafford, 'Sons and mothers: family politics in the early Middle Ages', in Derek Baker (ed.), *Medieval women: essays presented to R.M.T. Hill*, Studies in Church History, subsidia 1 (Oxford, 1978), pp. 79–100. **6** Note Jack Goody's discussion of the proportion of families in present-day 'traditional' societies which, for several reasons that also apply to medieval Europe, fail to produce male heirs or which see daughters inherit in the absence of sons: *The development of the family and marriage in Europe* (Cambridge, 1983), pp. 240–61, at p. 257. Aristocratic women tended to marry significantly older husbands: see, e.g., Duby, 'The structure of kinship and nobility: northern France in the eleventh and twelfth centuries' in Cynthia Postan (trans.), *The chivalrous society* (Berkeley, CA, 1977; first published in French in 1967), pp. 134–48; Robert Hajdu, 'Family and feudal ties in Poitou, 1100–1300', *Journal of Interdisciplinary History* 8 (1977–8), pp. 123–4; Dominique Barthélemy, 'Kinship' in P. Ariès and G. Duby (eds), *A history of private life*, trans. A. Goldhammer (Cambridge, Mass., 1988), vol. 2, pp. 96–104; and James C. Holt, 'Feudal society and the family in early medieval England, IV: the heiress and the alien', *Transactions of the Royal Historical Society*, 5th ser., 35 (1985), pp. 26–8; while aristocratic men, as a result of their military and related pursuits, tended to predecease their wives: see, for case studies, Hajdu, 'The position of noblewomen in the *pays des Coutumes*, 1100–1300', *Journal of Family History* 5 (1980), pp. 129–30; David Herlihy, *Medieval households* (Cambridge, Mass., 1985), pp. 102–9; Karl J. Leyser, *Rule and conflict in an early medieval society: Ottonian Saxony* (Oxford, 1979), pp. 51–8; Suzanne F. Wemple, *Women in Frankish society: marriage and the cloister, 500 to 900* (Philadelphia, 1981), pp. 101–2, and Evergates, 'Aristocratic women in the county of Champagne', pp. 76–85, 87–9, 97–103. **7** Lack of evidence makes it impossible to determine the overall proportion of women at any one time among those persons who exercised jurisdiction over non-knightly tenants, who served as either feudal lords or feudal tenants, or who acted with the authority of regents, guardians, or household heads, but the proportion does not appear ever to have been significantly lower than 10% and may well have been of the order of 20% or more in some regions or at some times; for a summary and critique of earlier quantitative studies of women property holders see Penny Schine Gold, *The lady and the Virgin: image, attitude, and experience in twelfth-century France*

Furthermore, medieval people could account for this consistently significant 'anomaly' in prevailing gender structures – those construed in the mind as well as on the ground – in any number of ways short of viewing powerful lordly women as either 'unnatural' or socially 'transgressive' (or both). Some of the ways medieval people could reckon powerful women to be 'natural' and 'normal' in certain circumstances are revealed in the following examination, perforce selective rather than comprehensive, of medieval conceptions of the term *virago*. Once the word's medieval connotations are known, historians can better grasp how medieval people perceived the sexually active aristocratic women who were so described.

Even though the term is increasingly evoked with the disclaimer, 'but of course virago meant something different in the Middle Ages', most recent scholarly attention focuses on religious viragos: those perpetual virgins whose absolute renunciation of 'female' carnality freed them for man-like contemplation of the divine.[8] Little effort has been devoted to tracing the term's connotations when applied to lay women active in the world. Nor is it always realised that many women dubbed 'viragos' by modern historians were not so labeled in the medieval sources cited. When the term is not evoked specifically to describe a woman warrior, modern male historians most frequently deploy it in a transgressive sense, in order to marginalise, if not condemn, the woman under discussion, assuming that the medieval authors they quote felt likewise.[9]

(Chicago, 1985), pp. 117–41. For telling figures that belie the notion that female lords were structural anomalies perceived as 'once-off' exceptions (and that no doubt could find parallels elsewhere), it should be noted that during the 133-year history of the county of Champagne (1152–1285), regent countesses ruled for about one-third of the time, while for at least 110 of those years, 20% of the counts' fiefholders were women (Evergates, 'Aristocratic women', pp. 76–104); and that during Ivo of Chartres' twenty-five years as bishop of Chartres (1095–1115), for about a third of his tenure the three leading lay lords in town were women: for seventeen years he dealt with a widowed countess (Adela of Blois, who continued to be active after Ivo's death), for ten–twelve years he treated with a widowed viscountess (Alice of Le Puiset), and for about eight years his episcopal advocate, or *vicedomina*, was the twice-widowed Helisende (who was succeeded by her daughter, Elizabeth).   8 Among the growing literature see the comments of Barbara Newman, *From virile woman to WomanChrist: studies in medieval religion and literature* (Philadelphia, 1995), pp. 3–6, 22–8; and Joan F. Ferrante, *To the glory of her sex: women's roles in the composition of medieval texts* (Bloomington, Ind., 1997), pp. 14–18, 94–6, 113–14, 159–70.   9 Compare, on Constance of Arles, Jean Dhondt, 'Sept femmes et un trio de rois', *Contributions à l'histoire économique et sociale* 3 (1964–65), pp. 40–2, and Georges Duby, *Le chevalier, la femme et le prêtre: le mariage dans la France féodale* (Paris, 1981), p. 85 (trans. by Barbara Bray, *The knight, the lady and the priest: the making of modern marriage in medieval France* (New York, 1983), p. 77); check also against the cited sources the instances given by Duby, 'Women and power', pp. 72, 79–81; and Marie-Louise Portmann, *Die Darstellung der Frau in der Geschichtschreibung des früheren Mittelalters* (Basel, 1958), pp. 8–12, 19–23. Régine Le Jan, correctly

The argument presented here is that the term virago, in fact infrequently evoked, was used most often by medieval authors to praise lordly women who wielded authoritative powers that were generally conceived as male. The accolade did not detract from the fundamental 'femininity' and child-bearing value of those women in the eyes of their male contemporaries; that is, they were still expected to adhere to the same behavioural standards as all other lay women and were judged largely in terms of traditionally 'female' virtues. Nor did the label imply that such women's jurisdictional authority or political powers were in any way unnatural or usurped.

Although the term *virago* is 'quite rare' in medieval sources,[10] it is undeniable that powerful women frequently were described as acting 'manfully' (*viriliter*) in some way, or with some kind of 'manly' (*virilis*) verve, spirit, or strength (whether physical, emotional, or intellectual). But did such 'manly' traits or behaviour turn strong women into men or into an unnatural hybrid species of 'man-woman'? As Thomas Laqueur intimated and Joan Cadden has comprehensively explained, fundamental ancient and medieval notions about the psychophysical constitution of men and women are quite different from modern ones.

perceives the more positive sense of 'virago' when applied to widowed mothers, even though the term is not used by all the tenth-century authors she cites and her claim that the term became even rarer after the year 1000 is without foundation (*Famille et pouvoir dans le monde franc, VIIe-Xe siècle: essai d'anthropologie sociale* (Paris, 1995), pp. 375–7). Patrick Corbet wisely does not reduce the 'manly women' of the Saxon aristocracy to their male attributes, but nonetheless presents 'the Virgin' and 'the Virago' as contrasting ideal types in the minds of medieval men to which 'real' women were meant to conform and understands both as being in some way a- (if not anti-) maternal, and hence 'unfeminine' (*Les saints ottoniens: sainteté dynastique, sainteté royale et sainteté féminine autour de l'an Mil* (Sigmaringen, 1986), pp. 108–9, 154, 262–3). William of Tyre never calls Melisende of Jerusalem – or any other women – a virago in his *Historia rerum in partibus transmarinis gestarum*, ed. R.B.C. Huygens, Corpus Christianorum Continuatio Mediaevalis [henceforth *CCCM*], vols 63–63A (Turnhout, 1986), while the only contemporaries to call Matilda of Tuscany a virago were, perhaps surprisingly, Hugh of Flavigny (see below, n. 54) and John of Mantua, both with a praiseworthy import and in textual contexts (passing references in a lengthy chronicle and a letter, respectively) analogous to those in which the term is applied to Matilda's contemporary, Adela of Blois, who is discussed below.   10 The quotation is from Margaret Howell, *Eleanor of Provence: queenship in thirteenth-century England* (Oxford, 1998), p. 222, in relation to the one reference to Eleanor as a virago; see also the works cited in the previous and next notes. The mother-in-law of Eleanor's elder sister was Blanche of Castile, the regent-mother of Louis IX, who was dubbed, as the height of praise, a *tota virago* yoking *femineae cogitationi ac sexui masculinum animum* (cf. 2 Mac. 7.21, with *ac sexui* added), by at least one near contemporary, Louis' confessor Geoffrey of Beaulieu, first writing in 1272–3 (*Vita ... Ludovici*, ch. 4, ed. *RHF*, 20: 4d). As Ferrante remarked, 'It may seem demeaning to compliment women by calling them 'manly', but in a culture which assumes the male as the norm, to recognize maleness in a woman, particularly when encouraging her in a male role in the male world, can be a positive affirmation' (*To the glory*, p. 15).

Modern views presuppose two incommensurable and sexed natures – male and female – primordially and teleologically distinguished by reproductive function as impressed definitively into the fundamentally different material components of men's and women's bodies. The earlier approach posited a single set of gendered elements – both anatomical features of the body and intangible psychological traits – that would be distributed in varying proportions to the material and immaterial components of individual persons through the processes of sexual reproduction. And in the pre-modern world, women, as well as men, were often deemed to play an active (albeit subordinate) role in the conception of offspring, even after Aristotle's theories were reintroduced and gained authoritative status in a range of university disciplines.[11] In other words, that some women, in physiological terms, would be born with some 'male' or 'masculine' attributes that in certain combinations enabled them to perform in some capacities as well as, or even better than, some men, was built into the order of things – or, 'only natural'.[12]

   In late antiquity and the early Middle Ages classical and Christian views on viragos creatively cross-fertilized in a number of literary contexts, thanks to the erudition of Jerome, who translated the Bible into Latin. Looking for a Latin word to capture the Hebrew pun in the name given by Adam to the woman (*mulier*) created from his flesh and bone, Jerome chose virago: 'Let her [says Adam, using a feminine pronoun] be called wo-man (*vir-ago*)'.[13] The aural connection to Adam, the man (*vir*), is obvious; the deeper significance of the

11 Thomas Laqueur's widely-read *Making sex: body and gender from the Greeks to Freud* (Cambridge, Mass., 1990), oversimplifies the complex skeins of medieval medical thought, though his insight about fundamental ancient ideas that endured is useful; Joan Cadden, *Meanings of sex difference in the Middle Ages* (Cambridge, 1993), in particular pp. 93–7, 117–30, 201–8, is essential for explicating the complexity and co-existence of various views, whereby, for example, aspects of so-called 'two-seed' theories of conception continued to be held alongside 'one-seed' theories, even after the reintroduction of Aristotelian texts in western Europe in the later twelfth and thirteenth centuries; John W. Baldwin, *The language of sex: five voices from northern France around 1200* (Chicago, 1994), pp. 43–8, 173–210, confirms that theories of conception stressing women's participation were not fully displaced by 'newer' (i.e., revived) Aristotelian notions. Core 'post-modern' views of sex/gender relations, ironically, mirror medieval ones more than is generally realized, even if the explanatory scientific rationales for them are radically different. 12 Note Cadden, *Meanings*, p. 205: 'the masculine woman, especially when honored with the title 'virago' took on the glow of manly virtues, although she was unambiguously on the female side of the anatomical spectrum and thus clearly distinguished from a hermaphrodite'; see also her 'It takes all kinds: sexuality and gender differences in Hildegard of Bingen's "Book of Compound Medicine"', *Traditio* 40 (1984), pp. 149–74. 13 Gen. 2.23: 'Dixitque Adam: Hoc nunc, os ex ossibus meis, et caro de carne mea: haec vocabitur Virago, quoniam de viro sumpta est' (though some medieval biblical manuscripts read *mulier*, repeating the term used at Gen 2:22); the Hebrew terms are *ish* and *ishshah*. Jerome's choice of the neologism *virago* (most frequently used in classical texts for divine or semi-divine females) over the more

relationship was left tantalizingly vague with the phrase *quoniam de viro sumpta est*: 'for she was taken from man'. Exegetes, drawing on an array of ancient usages and developing any number of 'senses' in the scriptural verse, were soon elaborating on Jerome's cryptic tag-line. From commentaries on Genesis evocations and amplifications of the term *virago* migrated to discussions of other scriptural passages, and, indeed, to a variety of texts by authors steeped in the Bible and biblically-related works.[14]

Isidore of Seville's seventh-century discussion of viragos in book eleven of his *Etymologies* is of particular importance.[15] Not only did Isidore weave together several classical and Christian exegetical traditions, but his definitions also circulated widely, both through the popularity of his own encyclopedia and the verbatim adoption of his comments in other oft-copied compilations. These include Hrabanus Maurus' widespread *De universo* of the ninth century, as well as several anonymous discussions of the 'ages of man' in works produced in the eleventh and twelfth centuries.[16]

Embedding his discussion of viragos into his commentary on the words *mulier* and *femina*, Isidore opens by explaining that *mulieres* are named for their 'feminine sex' rather than for any bodily corruption because the *mulier* Eve was formed from the side of man, rather than from physical contact with one. Proffering next several possible origins for the word *virgo* (virgin), he includes what had become an exegetical commonplace; namely, that the word virgin came from a word meaning 'lack of corruption' – as if a virago – since 'female passions' are unknown to virgins. Viragos, however (as Isidore learned from Servius), are so named 'because they act as men do'; that is, they 'perform manly deeds and have masculine vigor'.[17] Thus the ancients called them strong

classical *vira* may well reflect his use of the Septuagint.   **14** See, for example, Isidore of Seville's seventh-century *De differentiis verborum*, 2.21.80, ed. *PL*, 83:82: 'feminae vero virgines vel viragines dicuntur. Dicta autem virago, vel quod a viro sumpta sit, vel quod sit masculini vigoris'; Andrew of St Victor in the twelfth century (who preferred the nuances of meaning found in other widespread late antique and early medieval texts like Servius and Isidore's *Etymologies*, discussed below, over against Jerome's own gloss): 'Proprius, si latinitas pateretur, "uiram" dixisset, quia *virago* non significat de uiro sumptam, sed potius uiriliter se agentem feminam' (*Expositio super Heptateuchum*, ed. C. Lohr and R. Berndt, *CCCM*, 53 (Turnhout, 1986), p. 34); and, reflecting traditions that preferred virginal viragos, Peter Comestor, when discussing how Adam's wife took her name and her matter from him, noted that virago, becoming *virgo* by syncopation, is the generic term for all women during the years they keep intact the physical integrity with which they are born, though they are called *mulieres* after it is broken (*Historia scholastica*, Genesis, ch. 18, ed. *PL*, 198:170–1).   **15** Isidore, *Etymologiarum sive originum, libri xx*, 11.2, ed. W.M. Lindsay, 2 vols (Oxford, 1911), 2:18–24; this section of book 11 is devoted to *de aetatibus hominum*.   **16** Hrabanus' text, also known as *De rerum naturis*, 7.1 ('*De aetatibus hominis*'), ed. *PL*, 111:184; note also the encyclopedic compilation published with the works of Hugh of St Victor, 3.68, ed. *PL*, 177:133.   **17** Isidore, *Etymologiarum*, 2:11.ii, 18–24: 'Alias [virgo] ab incorruptione, quasi virago,

women: *fortes feminas* (a tag linking them to the *mulier fortis* of Proverbs
31:10–31, as more than one later commentator would note). Then, in contrast to
Augustine and other Fathers, Isidore asserts that virgins are not properly called
viragos, since they do not typically fulfill the office or duty of men (like viragos do).
A woman (*mulier*) who performs virile deeds is fittingly called a virago: like the
Amazons, for example. (This example is in fact rare amongst late antique Latin
authors; Isidore may well have gleaned it from Lactantius.)[18] Making his transition
by echoing Festus, Isidore explains that the ancients named the person now called
a *femina* a *vira*, on the model of how *serva* was derived from *servus*.[19] He concludes
his remarks with further discussion of the word *femina*.

   Three points need to be underscored about this passage. First, as Cadden has
concluded in her discussion of Isidore and an array of medieval medical writers,
viragos were seen to lie 'unambiguously on the female side of the anatomical
spectrum'.[20] They were construed and viewed as women, and – as we will see –
spent most of their lives playing traditional 'women's roles'. Second, quoting
Servius' well-known commentary on Vergil's *Aeneid*, Isidore clearly distinguishes
viragos from most virgins. Viragos are women who fulfill male duties or offices;
that is, they perform social functions traditionally gendered male – like Virgil's
divine Juturna driving her brother's chariot through the ranks of Aeneas' army.[21]
Nonetheless, virgins are virago-like because the strength that they muster to
master their carnal female desires is unquestionably conceived as 'male'.[22] In the

quod ignoret femineam passionem. Virago vocata, quia virum agit, hoc est opera virilia
facit et masculini vigoris est. Antiqui enim fortes feminas ita vocabant. Virgo autem non
recte virago dicitur, si non viri officio fungitur. Mulier vero si virilia facit, recte virago
dicitur, ut Amazona'. For Servius, see n. 21 below.   **18** Lactantius, *Divinarum
institutionum*, 1.9.2,5, ed. P. Monat, *Institutiones divines*, Sources chrétiennes, no. 326
(Paris, 1986), 1:96/8.   **19** Sextus Pompeius Festus, *De verborum significatu* as
abbreviated by Paul the Deacon, ed. W.M. Lindsay (Leipzig, 1913; rpt. 1978), p. 314,
though Isidore does not mention Festus' linking of such *vira* with wise women or seers.
20 Cadden, *Meanings*, pp. 201–8, as quoted above at n. 12.   **21** Maurus Servius
Honoratus, *Servii grammatici qui feruntur in Vergilii carmina commentarii*, 12.468, ed. G.
Thilo, (Leipzig, 1878–87; rpt. New York, 1986), vol. 1, glossing Virgil's evocation of
'*Juturna virago*': *virago dicitur mulier quae virile implet officium*, with a further addition
found in a ninth-century Tours manuscript (probably from a gloss made at Fleury), *id
est mulier quae viri animum habet, has antiqui viras dicebant*). Juturna is the only virago in
Virgil's text, and, as a non-human creature, actually takes on the voice, bodily form and
arms of Turnus' charioteer, though she is then compared to a swallow feeding its young.
(I have found no historical women dubbed viragos by medieval authors who are also
represented in the same text as cross-dressing.) Yet Isidore is silent about Servius' most
prominent virago, Dido, whose name, Servius asserts three times, is simply the
Phoenician word for virago (see the commentary on *Aeneid*, 1.340, ed. 1:120; 4.335, ed.
1:523; 4.674, ed. 579–80, and note 4.36, ed. 1:468, where the precise gloss connecting
the terms is a later addition); Dido merits the accolade for casting herself onto the flames
of her funeral pyre in order to avoid an unwanted second marriage.   **22** Note also
Isidore's comments in his *De differentiis verborum*, 1.5.590, ed. *PL*, 83:68: 'Virgo est quae

medieval world, the fact that women, playing out their traditional household roles, could perform vigorously and intelligently the same tasks as their male counterparts, made them not honorary *men*, but women of distinction.

Two issues need to be clarified before we turn to a discussion of some historical women who actually were dubbed viragos. First, what attributes and allegorical valences were granted to that pre-lapsarian Virago in the earlier Middle Ages? And which 'manly duties' were viragos called on to perform? First of all, the *Ur*-virago was immortal; created not only from man's side, but from a strong rib-bone, she was a perfect prefiguration of the church, headed by her male husband Christ.[23] Yet that rib, and even that man's fleshy side, had implications for ordinary women and real wives as well.

When commentators faced philosophical dualists, as did Augustine and some of his medieval heirs, they drew out those implications by bringing a mediating, tripartite, model of the human person to discussions of the prelapsarian pair. Such 'trinitarian' schemata limited the risk that mistaken metaphysical conclusions would be reached by those who made a strong conceptual alignment between the first Man as strong, immaterial reason and the Wo-man as weak, fleshy passions. In contrast, in the tripartite view all human persons are composed of immaterial masculine spirits or minds (*animus* or *mens*) and very material feminine flesh (*caro/carnis*), but the grammatically feminine soul (*anima*) was then harnessed – either as an appetitive soul or the inferior part of the spirit – to mediate between spirit and body. As Augustine explained when commenting on Genesis to combat Manicheans, the *Ur*-virago, 'bone of my bones and flesh of my flesh',

---

virum nescit, virago autem quae virum agit, hoc est opera virilia facit. Non autem solum virgines viragines, sed et corruptae mulieres, quae virilia faciunt, viragines recte dicuntur'.   **23** For the immortality of the virago made from Adam's rib see, for example, the mortuary roll, most probably for Bruno the Carthusian, poem 141, ed. *PL*, 152:592; for the *Ur*-virago as the church, see, for example, the commentary on Genesis published with the fifth-century works of Eucherius of Lyons, bk 1.23, ed. *PL*, 50:909; Isidore's mystical commentary on Genesis, 3.10, ed. *PL*, 83:218; Ambrosius Autpertus' eighth-century *Expositio in Apocalypsin*, 3.5, lines 201–3, ed. R. Weber, *CCCM*, 27 (Turnhout, 1975); the Pentateuch commentary attributed to Bede by the ninth century, at Gen. 2, ed. *PL*, 91:210 (also with an explicit link to the *mulier fortis* of Proverbs); the homilies attributed to Haymo of Halberstadt (d. 853), no. 68, ed. *PL*, 118:442–3 (with an explicit connection made also to 'Eve', the first woman and mother of men); the twelfth-century Psalm commentary published with the works of Gerhoch of Reichersberg, at Psalm 21(22).18, ed. *PL*, 193:1024; and Christmas sermons of Martin of León at the end of the twelfth century, ed. *PL*, 208:213. Another positive valence to the label virago arose when it was used to describe a powerful virgin Mary, as, for example, in the later eleventh century by Folcard of St Bertin in his verses on St Vigor, bishop of Bayeux, ed. *PL*, 147:1179, as copied in the earlier twelfth century by Hariulf of Oudenburg in his chronicle of St Riquier, 4.20, ed. *PL*, 174:1333; the twelfth-century account of Marian miracles performed for William Crispin, ed. *PL*, 150:740; and the twelfth-century verse-prayer to the Virgin published with the works of Marbod of

acquired some strength from Adam's rib – she was neither pure weakness or nor totally feeble – and from the first man's flesh she acquired enough innate temperance to temper her own carnal passions. In other words, she had access to some immaterial sources of strength through the soul animating her body.[24]

In the late-eleventh and early-twelfth centuries reforming churchmen as diverse as Guibert of Nogent, Bruno of Segni, and Rupert of Deutz, drawing on a variety of sources, independently amplified these notions in their explorations of the moral sense of scripture. The matter, both flesh and bone, shared by Adam and his companion in paradise, naturally brought men and women together: in love and marriage where each partner would have the spiritual strength to moderate those lusty urges of the flesh that assailed husband and wife alike. Distinguishing 'the nature of Woman' (inferior to that of Man) from individual women (who could be good or bad), these clerics deployed the term virago for those women, married to men, who had the inner strength to control their bodies and sexuality. Good women because modest wives (as Rupert underscored by quoting 1 Peter 3:5–6), such strong, wifely, viragos could be found in all eras. Yet men's equals they are not and, however 'manly' their capacities or deeds, they are to remain obedient to their husbands.[25]

Rennes, no. 8, ed. *PL*, 171:1652.   **24** Augustine, *De Genesi contra Manichaeos*, 2.13 (quoting Gen. 2.23), ed. D. Weber, Corpus Scriptorum Ecclesiasticorum Latinorum [*CSEL*], 91 (Vienna, 1998); Augustine expresses similar views in greater detail (though without reference to viragos) in *De vera religione*, c. 41, ed. K.-D. Daur, Corpus Christianorum Series Latina [*CCSL*], 32 (Turnhout, 1962). A similar combination of ideas, drawing also on Isidore and pointing to future exegetical trends, can be found in Rather of Verona's *Praeloquia*, 2.3, ed. P.L.D. Reid, *CCCM*, 46A (Turnhout, 1984), p. 47: 'Virago enim, id est fortis mulier, uocata es in principio, ut et fortem te contra uitia et flexibilem in subiectione Domini preceptorum esse debere memineris omnino. Vir atque mente, mulier carne, insurgentes et tu aduersus spiritum insanos uitiorum uoluptatumque tumultus forti mentis uigore stude deuincere, perpendens plurima tibi in Scripturis diuinis huius operis exempla suppeditare ...; et in Nouo innumerabiles femineam oblitas infirmitatem, uirili peracto hostibus deuictis certamine, cum triumpho gloriae palmam uictoriae et coronam meruisse insignem'. The heyday of debates about whether or not women had souls was long after the Aristotelian revival (i.e., in the years of transition to what is often construed as the early modern period).   **25** Guibert of Nogent, *Moralia in Genesim*, 2.23, ed. *PL*, 156:70, writing by 1084 (see his *Monodiae*, or *De vita sua*, 1.17, ed. E.-R. Labande (Paris, 1981), p. 142, and the comments in John F. Benton's translation, *Self and society in medieval France: the memoirs of abbot Guibert of Nogent* (1064?-c.1125) (New York, 1970), p. 236); Bruno of Segni, *Expositio in Pentateuchum*, Gen., ch. 2, ed. *PL*, 164:164–5 (see further at Reginald Grégoire, *Bruno de Segni: Exégète médiéval et théologien monastique* (Spoleto, 1965)); and Rupert of Deutz, *Commentarius in librum Ecclesiastes*, 7.27, ed. *PL*, 168:1268–9 (see further at John H. Van Engen, *Rupert of Deutz* (Berkeley, CA, 1983), esp. pp. 67–94, 228–31). All of the authors, Benedictine monks at some stage in their careers, stress women's inferiority to men but nonetheless appear to instance the budding concern to develop a theology of marriage based on wives as legally competent and morally responsible human persons (at least in

That such ideas, articulated in an exegetical context, could be carried into other literary domains is clear from Geoffrey Malaterra's 'Deeds of count Roger of Sicily and duke Robert Guiscard' written at the end of the eleventh century. After recounting in prose how Roger married his daughter Matilda to count Raymond of Provence, he burst into verse to praise chaste and legitimate marriage based on spousal affection and the desire for offspring – as divine law directed when the first virago was joined in loving affection (*sociatur*) to the first man.[26]

What manly offices did viragos – wifely or otherwise – fill in other textual contexts? In addition to informing generations of students about the goddess Juturna driving a war-chariot in Vergil's *Aeneid*, Servius transmitted the tradition (still tapped by Christine de Pizan and other writers in the later Middle Ages) that Dido was simply the Phoenician word for virago: a name bestowed upon this able founder and ruler of Carthage because of her manly death. After saving her people from attack, Servius' virago (though not Virgil's Dido) planned a startling suicide in order simultaneously to avenge and to remain faithful to her murdered first husband.[27] Another ancient virago was the goddess of wisdom, Minerva; one of her best known medieval manifestations was in Martianus Capella's didactic allegory, *The Marriage of Philology and Mercury*, in which she merited the appellation because she presided over the counsels of men.[28] A well-known ninth-century compilation of astrological lore (indicating – among other things – that viragos, like adulterers, will always be with us) transmitted the view that women born at certain stellar conjunctions would be inclined to pursue agriculture, warfare, and construction; though such viragos might be neglectful

certain situations).   **26** Geoffrey's work is also known as the *Historia Sicula*, 3.21–2, ed. *PL*, 149:1168; a Benedictine monk when writing, he has no more to say about Matilda beyond the details he provides about her marital assigns, the wedding festivities, and how she travelled to them.   **27** For Servius, see n. 21 above. The Middle Ages knew multiple Didos, often influenced by Servius, as discussed by Mary Louise Lord, 'Dido as an example of chastity: the influence of example literature', *Harvard Library Bulletin* 17 (1969), pp. 22–44, 216–32; and Marilynn Desmond, *Reading Dido: gender, textuality, and the medieval 'Aeneid'*, Medieval Cultures, no. 8 (Minneapolis, 1994), most notably, pp. 15–16, 57–69, 81–3, 105–27, 215–24, though at least three of her claims need to be reconsidered in light of the analysis in this paper: that Servius uses virago to encapsulate Dido's 'masculine identity' (p. 83), that endowing a woman with a 'masculine spirit' was a way to represent her refusal to perform sexually (p. 62), and that medieval women who served as political leaders transgressed their gender roles (p. 108). Servius also kept alive the image of the immortal warrior Juturna as a true virago who peformed men's deeds (see, for example, the sixteenth-century Scottish author, Gavin Douglas see Desmond, p. 193).   **28** Martianus Capella, *De nuptiis philologiae et mercurii, libri viiii*, bk 6.575–7 (on geometry), ed. A. Dick and J. Préaux (Stuttgart, 1969), p. 286; in the ninth century, virago was glossed: *id est mulier viriliter agens* (Remigius of Auxerre, *Commentum in Martianum Capellam, libri i–ix*, bk 6.286.16, ed. Cora E. Lutz, 2 vols, (Leiden, 1965),vol. 2, p.125; and John Scottus Eriugena, *Annotationes in Marcianum*, bk 6.286.16, ed. *eadem* (Cambridge, Mass., 1939), p. 134. Medieval authors would also personify some of the

of women's scents, fine sandals and clothing when seeking what is more
common to men, their husbands would not reprove them.²⁹

And from the biblical camp came the chaste widow Judith. In an anonymous
twelfth-century verse epitome of human history she appears as an '*honesta*'
(honorable and respectable) virago, a 'warrior and prudent counselor' (*bellatrix
et prudens consiliatrix*), astute enough to deploy a woman's sexual charms as
weapons in single combat with an unrighteous prince. Fortified by the crown of
her own strong mind, she emerges victorious in her fight to the death –
presented in this text as a judicial duel absolving her of any imputation of sin or
crime in her deed. On her return, the people she has saved hail – on bended
knee – Judith as their leader, or duke.³⁰

Active in the spheres of deliberative counsel, battle, justice, governance,
public works and other outdoor physical labours, these married or widowed
viragos lost little of their femininity as they moved into socio-political arenas
traditionally conceived as male in order to perform tasks more frequently done

liberal arts as viragos.   **29** *Pseudo-Bede: 'De mundi celestis terrestrisque constitutione': A
treatise on the universe and the soul*, 421, ed. and trans. Charles Burnett (London, 1985),
p. 54.   **30** The text is published with the works of the poet-prelate Hildebert of
Lavardin, *PL*, 171:1229–30. Like many medieval versifiers, the author uses the
masculine *dux* rather than the clumsy feminine *ducatrix*, arguably more for metrical
reasons than for making gender claims about ruling women, since prose writers tend to
use the *dux* and *ducatrix* interchangeably (see n. 36 below), and are scrupulous in
documents when using the more typical formal title *comitissa* (rather than *comes*, though
that will occasionally be used of women in more literary texts). Referring to Judith as a
virago is rare, though Dracontius, in his poetical *De laudibus Dei* of the closing decades
of the fifth century, was perhaps the first to do so and may well have inspired some later
writers (bk 3, ed. *PL*, 60:882). Later in the twelfth century Guibert of Gembloux
compared the Rhineland recluse, Jutta, to her biblical namesake, dubbed a mighty virago
(*instar Iudith viraginis fortissime; ep.* 38, ed. Albert Derolez, *CCCM*, 66A (Turnhout,
1989), p. 376), and presented the death of Holofernes in moral terms, as the victory of
virtue over vice (an interpretation popularized in patristic times). During the Middle
Ages overwhelmingly positive and desexualized (rather than erotic) images of Judith as
a pious and chaste heroine predominate in both verbal and visual representations,
whether she is vanquishing the public-political enemy of her people or personal vices;
see, for example, Ambrose, *De viduis*, c. 7, ed. *PL*, 16:245–7; John of Salisbury,
Policraticus, 18.20, ed. C.C.J. Webb , 2 vols (Oxford, 1909); Judith, bearing Holofernes'
head in triumph to the people assembled on her city's walls on a nave capital from
Vézelay of the earlier twelfth century, published as pl. 27 in H. Kraus, *The living theatre
of medieval art* (Philadelphia, 1972), pp. 50–2 (with further examples); and Judith
conquering vice in the *Speculum virginum* of the second quarter of the twelfth century,
from London, British Library, Arundel MS. 44, fo. 34v, published as fig. 15 of pl. 7 in
A. Katzenellenbogen, *Allegories of the Virtues and Vices in medieval art* (rpt., New York,
1964). For bibliography on the medieval iconography of Judith see E. Ciletti,
'Patriarchal ideology in the Renaissance iconography of Judith' in M. Migiel and J.
Schiesari (eds), *Refiguring women: perspectives on gender and the Italian Renaissance*, (Ithaca,

by men. Although Dido could be evoked as both a positive and a negative exemplar, she is dubbed a virago in overwhelmingly positive portrayals of the ruling, chaste, widow who saved her people – like the honourable yet still seductively charming widow Judith.[31] In the fourth century Ambrose perhaps consciously avoided the term *virago* in his catalogue of virtuous widows; yet his account of the judge Deborah is worthy of note because it was echoed by later writers.[32] Her deeds, Ambrose explains, show not only that widows can success-fully assume men's duties and take authoritative decisions without men's help; they also stand as an example to other women who might be deterred from performing virtuous acts by claiming the infirmity of their sex (*sexus*). The widow Deborah ruled her people, led the army, appointed generals, organized battles and commanded triumphs. She thus demonstrates that a woman is by nature neither always fickle nor forever bound to commit sinful deeds: the 'virtue' (i.e., the power) of one's soul (*virtus animae*), not one's sex, makes a person strong.[33] The image of the married or widowed virago who was strong yet attractive, modest yet a leader of men, was readily available to those medieval authors who wanted to praise the lordly wives and mothers in their midst.

This background allows historical women called viragos by their contem-poraries to be evaluated according to medieval standards. The space remaining will be devoted to them, starting with a brief summary of my more general findings about the textual contexts in which the term is deployed. Then, since the age of ruling viragos is often held to have ended around the year 1000, I will discuss a few later eleventh- and twelfth-century aristocratic women who were granted that accolade.

One curious general observation is that the word virago appears more frequently in poetry than in prose – and metrical considerations for its use merit further examination. Epitaphs and tomb inscriptions comprise the greatest number of such verses; the others are short praise poems found either in longer prose chronicles or in dedicatory epistles placed at the head of other texts.[34]

1991), pp. 35–70 at p. 38 n.4.   **31** See above, nn. 27, 30.   **32** Ambrose perhaps avoided the term because in the classical texts on which he was raised, most viragos are divine or semi-divine figures; not only are they frequently cast in raging, destructive roles, but, as goddesses still worshipped by many of his contemporaries, they could only be condemned as demonic by a Christian bishop.   **33** *De viduis*, c. 8, ed. *PL*, 16:247–50; these notions are also expressed in c. 7 (*PL*, 16:245–7), where Judith's strength to rise above the customary weakness of her sex is attributed to her mental devotion and wisdom (*sapientia*). Yet Ambrose depicts both of these strong widows in their domestic settings, acting in relation to fathers and sons (they were once sexually active), and judges them according to virtues he deems of peculiar importance to women *qua* females.   **34** See, for example, the epitaph for the *generosa virago* Heloise, 'duchess of Orleans' and founder of St Georges in Pithiviers (André Duchesne ed., *Histoire généologique de la maisone royale de Dreux et quelques autres familles illustres* (Paris, 1631), pt. 5, p. 57); the cleric Garin's dedication in the copy of Odilo of Cluny's *Epitaphium*

The context is clearly laudatory and virago meant as a compliment, evoked frequently to commend the woman being memorialized for the strength of mind that she employed to control her sexuality – the direct extension of using the term to praise perpetual virgins. But these viragos are applauded for exercising lordly powers as well, most often when they are commemorated for having established or endowed a monastery. In addition to any personal piety of the donors, these viragos, as monastic patrons or protectors, had the authority to alienate property over which they exercised rights, always assumed and sometimes described in the poems.

As will be seen in the examples, the range of 'manly' deeds performed by viragos depicted in prose works is greater than in poems, and their 'manly' vigour is deployed in a wider arena of 'public'-political activities. Although the actions of such viragos are not always presented in a favourable light, the reasons for which a few were condemned depend more on authors' general political views than on the gender of the actors.[35] And in all cases the viragos are clearly marked as sexually-active women, playing customary domestic roles as wives and mothers, or meriting praise for traditionally feminine virtues, such as beauty, modesty, and religious devotion.

My first case comes from a long letter directed to the 'duke' (*dux/ducatrix*) Adelaide (d. 1091) by the eloquent schoolmaster turned hermit and church reformer Peter Damian. Adelaide was the thrice-widowed heiress to the march of Turin and countess of Savoy by marriage, who, in 1064 when Peter wrote, was ruling the combined lordships even though her eldest son had come of age.[36] After praising her several times for her manly strength, the churchman requests that Adelaide become a 'virago of the Lord'. Like Deborah and her

Adelheide he made at the behest of Adela of Flanders (d. 1079), ed. *MGH,SS* 4:635 (for the empress as a virago); Fulcois of Beauvais' epitaph for William the Conqueror's wife Matilda (d. 1083), ed. Henri Omont, 'Épitaphes métriques en l'honneur de différents personnages du XIe siècle composées par Foulcoie de Beauvais, archidiacre de Meaux', no. 9, in *Mélanges Julien Havet* (Paris, 1895), pp. 211–36, at 223–4; Henry of Huntingdon's twelfth-century poem in praise of Æthelflæd in his *Historia Anglorum*, 5.17, ed. Diana Greenway (Oxford, 1966), p. 308 (a virago who is by nature a *puella*). 35 Implicit contrasts between 'good' and 'bad' viragos are drawn when they are described as either *prudens* or *imprudens*, a distinction with roots in classical representations and analyzed in an early modern context by Natalie Zemon Davis in her now classic discussion of vicious and virtuous viragos: 'Women on top' in *Society and culture in early modern France* (Stanford, CA, 1975), pp. 133–48. 36 Peter Damian, ep. 114, ed. Kurt Reindel, *Die Briefe des Petrus Damiani* vol. 3:488–502, MGH, *Die Briefe der deutschen Kaiserzeit*, no. 4³ (Munich, 1989). For Adelaide see G. Sergi in *Lexikon des Mittelalters* (Munich, 1980–99) 1:147a, with bibliography, and the discussion in Ferrante, *To the glory*, pp. 14–17. Another praiseworthy virago and *excellentissima dux* in Peter's letters is Beatrice of Tuscany, Matilda's mother (*ep.* 141, to her husband's chaplain in 1066, ed. Reindel, 3:488–502 at 490d), on whom see Elke Goez, *Beatrix von Canossa und Tuszien: Eine Untersuchung zur Geschichte des 11. Jahrhunderts* (Sigmaringen, 1995).

general Baruch, she is to campaign alongside the bishop of Turin, with the cross for her weapon as Jael used a tent stake, and with the God-given strength of the widow Judith: Peter explictly evokes three biblical exemplars who put vacillating or depraved men to shame. The fight, ironically, is to compel priests to live celibately, safe from the corrupting power of women and sex. The stakes are high because Peter equates priestly unchastity with heresy and God destroys heretics; thus, a lord who enforces divine law will not only save her people, but also see her earthly power extended. The reformer must enlist a woman, because, even though he has one bishop firmly in his camp, the duchess's authority as protector of the church runs through several dioceses.

By the letter's end Peter has offered an opinion on how Adelaide will relate to her several husbands in paradise, advised her to act as a generous and just advocate to the monasteries she has founded, and counseled this female lord on how to reach just judgements when hearing disputed cases. Men like the saintly king David, as well as a veritable catologue of biblical wise women, are presented to the duchess for emulation. The fact that Adelaide is enlisted where men have failed reveals Peter's belief in fundamental gender asymmetry, but casts no cloud on either the legitimacy or the extent of this widowed mother's lordly authority – authority she acquired and wielded in the natural course of a dynastic family's life cycle.

Overtones of Dido's manly suicide appear in the case of Gunhild, sister of Swein (the future Danish king of England), as reported by William of Malmesbury in his *Deeds of the Kings of the English* (written by *c.* 1126). A 'not unattractive virago', she and her husband, a powerful count, came to England in the opening years of the second millennium, where they converted to Christianity. When Anglo-Danish hostilities resumed about a decade later, Gunhild offered herself to the English as a hostage for peace. Prophesying the bloodbath to come after she and the other Danes are ordered beheaded, she watches unflinchingly the execution of her husband and comely son as she dispassionately awaits her own death with great 'presence of mind'.[37] A king's sister, count's wife, and mother of an heir pierced by lances before her very eyes, this virago was cast by William as a political martyr with a prophetic voice. Yet for all the publicly active wives or mothers glimpsed in William's lengthy narrative, Gunhild is one of only three viragos, all of whom merited praise for the political powers they wielded as sisters, wives, and mothers.[38]

37 William of Malmesbury, *Gesta regum Anglorum*, 2.177.1, ed. and trans. R.A.B. Mynors, R.M. Thomson, and M. Winterbottom, 2 vols (Oxford, 1998–9), 1:300; William's *non illepidae formae uirago* was translated by Mynors as 'a woman of some beauty and much character'. William is the sole source for Gunhild's death, according to the editors (2:161), and all his details may not be accurate reflections of actual events. His account is reminiscent of the martyrdom of the seven Maccabees and their mother (2 Mac. 7:20–22, 41).   38 See Ferrante's discussion of William, *To the glory*, pp. 100–104; the other viragos are Adela of Blois, discussed below, and Æthelflæd, a *virago*

From across the channel comes the case of Bertrada of Montfort, 'an eloquent and most learned virago' (*virago faceta et eruditissima*), according to her political adversary, the abbot Suger, who refused to grant this sometime countess and stepmother of his hero, the French king Louis VI, her title of queen.[39] To preface his account of a contest in 1109–10 over castles in whose devolution Bertrada had earlier played a decisive role, Suger portrays this virago plying her sexual charms, together with the most amazing of woman's artifices, so audaciously that she could bend to her will all the men who defined her life. Manifestly more powerful than any or all of them (*his omnibus potentior*), they were her brother, Amaury of Montfort; her royal bed mate and eldest son by him (both named Philip); her stepson (the ever obedient Louis VI – though other sources reveal his relations with Bertrada could be stormy);[40] her son by her first marriage (the young count Fulk V of Anjou, whose succession, we know from other sources, Bertrada arranged after his older half-brother's untimely death);[41] and even her ex-husband (count Fulk IV le Réchin), who, according to Suger, continued to sit worshipfully at Bertrada's feet long after she had banished him from their marriage bed.

potentissma, king Alfred's married daughter who advised her royal brother, built cities, and remained chaste after the difficult birth of her first child (William of Malmesbury, *Gesta Regum*, 2.125.4, ed. 1:198; see also n. 34, above). The praiseworthy Empress Matilda – the rightful ruler and *domina* of the English, according to William – is also dubbed a virago in his *Historia novella*, a work written for her leading supporter (and half-brother), Robert of Gloucester, and that is silent about any 'character' problems that Matilda's detractors emphasized – if they did not invent them (*Historia novella*, 1.21, 3.52, ed. Edmund King (Oxford, 1998), pp. 42, 98); in other words, Matilda was not called a virago by William because of any supposed imperiousness towards the Londoners in 1141 (or at any other time). As with Bertrada of Montfort (n. 40, below) and Matilda of Tuscany (n. 9, above), representations of the empress, whether as a virago or no, must be analyzed text by text.   **39** Suger, *Vita Ludovici Grossi regis*, ch. 18, ed. and trans. Henri Waquet (Paris, 1929), pp. 122/8, at 122/4; see also chs. 1, 8, 13, ed. pp. 10, 36, 82.   **40** Images of Bertrada are as legion as the authors writing about her; her contemporaries and near-contemporaries cast her in diverse (and discordant) roles; in addition to Suger's promiscuous *femme fatale* intent on destroying the realm, she has been cast in the role of the archetypical wicked stepmother (Orderic Vitalis, *The ecclesiastical history of Orderic Vitalis* [hereafter cited as OV],13 books in 6 vols, 8.14, ed. Majorie Chibnall (Oxford, 1969–80),11.9, ed. Chibnall, 6:50/54); of the social-climbing seductress trading in her count for a king (William of Malmesbury, *Gesta regum*, 3.325.5; 3.257.1; 4.345.5, and 5.404.1, ed. 1:348, 474, 596, 730–310); of a sexually beguiling peace weaver (OV, 8.20, ed. Chibnall, 4:260/62); and even in the role of a tearful merciful intercessor (William of Tyre, 14.1 (using earlier sources emanating from Angevin circles), ed. Huygens, 63A:31).   **41** Maurice Prou (ed.), *Recueil des actes de Philippe Ier, roi de France (1059–1108)* (Paris, 1908), pp. 391–6, nos. 157–58 and notes, datable to 11 October 1106; Fulk IV's eldest son, Geoffrey Martel, Junior, had been killed in May. Bertrada's documented actions, however, carry no implication that she actually arranged for Geoffrey's death, as alleged in later narratives (*Gesta Ambaziensium*

The staunch Capetian loyalist and active supporter of Louis the Fat ascribes Bertrada's scheming to her misplaced personal desire to benefit her own blood relatives at the expense of the realm and the overtones of virago's 'modern' meaning as a domestic scold are perceptible in Suger's vignette.[42] But to reduce Bertrada to just another 'clever shrew', as have the recent American translators, or even to an amiable sexual *dominatrix* ('*maîtresse femme*'), as in the standard French translation, is to overlook the medieval tradition gendering eloquence and learning as 'manly' traits oft-praised in lords of both sexes.[43] More important, it is to minimize the complex power-political agenda Bertrada was so skillfully pursuing (to Suger's great displeasure). If she was not striving ultimately to place one of her own sons on the French throne, as the abbot would have us believe, at least she was working to increase, though association with the royal court, the profiles of both her natal family and her son by her first marriage. Ironically from Suger's perspective, king Louis' alliance with Bertrada's son by the count of Anjou – count Fulk V – soon proved crucial to his own political success; fortunately for the new king (as other commentators freely admitted and charters clearly attest), his so-called 'conniving stepmother' had prepared the ground by renewing contacts with her relations by her first husband.[44]

dominorum, in Chroniques des comtes d'Anjou et des seigneurs d'Amboise, ed. Louis Halphen and René Poupardin (Paris, 1913), p. 66, a passage with verifiable inaccuracies written in the 1150s; and, in the thirteenth century, the so-called Tours chronicle, ed. *Recueil des Historiens des Gaules et de la France*, 12:468). **42** According to the *Oxford English Dictionary*, 2nd edn., *s.v.* Virago, 3, the seventeenth century saw the first uses of virago with the meaning of a termagant or a scold (after Chaucer labeled Semiramis a virago in the traditional medieval sense of an *imprudens virago*, glossed by the compilers as meaning a bold, impudent [or wicked] woman); that usage doubtless increased with renewed reading of Plautus' comedies in the sixteenth century, where such domestic scolds appear, e.g., in his *Mercator* (see F. Brünholzl, 'Plautus im Mittelalter', *Lexikon des Mittelalters*, 7:16–17). Note also, *s.v.* Virago 2, that the term's meaning as a vigorous and heroic woman is 'now rare'. **43** See *The Deeds of Louis the Fat*, trans. Richard C. Cusimano and John Moorhead (Washington, D.C., 1992), p. 80, and Waquet, ed. p. 122. For *facetia* and *eruditio*, see C. Stephen Jaeger, *The origins of courtliness: civilizing trends and the formation of courtly ideals, 930–1210* (Philadelphia, 1985), pp. 165–68, 213–26; note also representations of Minerva and the liberal arts (see n. 28 above), and Theodulf of Orleans' verse depiction of the learned virago Liutgard, Charlemagne's daughter (Peter Godman (ed. and trans.), *The poetry of the Carolingian Renaissance*, no. 15, lines 83–90 (London, 1985), pp. 150–63 at 154–5). **44** See above, nn. 40, 41. Among the most notable charters see Olivier Guillot, *Le comte d'Anjou et son entourage au XIe siècle*, 2 vols (Paris, 1972), 2:272, no. 441 (19 May 1106–14 April 1109; Bertrada's remunerated intervention in a dispute between a castellan and a nunnery in Angers); Paris, BNF, Collection de Touraine et d'Anjou [*olim* Collection Housseau], vol. 4, fol. 130, no. 1307 (1110; a pious bequest made by Fulk V, *consilio et admonitione Bertradae reginae matris ejusdem comitis*); Jean Dufour (ed.), *Recueil des actes de Louis VI, roi de France (1108–37)*, 4 vols (Paris, 1992–4), 1:317–18 n. 1 (= Augustin Fliche, *Le règne de Philippe Ier, roi de France (1060–1108)* (Paris, 1912), p. 75 n. 1) (1115: Bertrada's donation to Marmoutier

However much Suger disapproved of the eloquent Bertrada's goals in this contest to control castles, he set her astute political-alliance building in its typically medieval context: the domestic spaces of lordly households where wives and mothers actively coordinated the agendas of two (or more) dynastic families, which they served as pivotal, yet vital, power brokers. Bedroom politics were public politics in Bertrada's day; to take decisive political action, learned and persuasive viragos crossed no 'denaturing' or 'delegitimising' conceptual thresholds between domestic and public spheres. At the same time, the powers Suger claims Bertrada abused were the sexual powers thought natural to all women. By casting this virago in the role of a seductive *femme fatale*, the abbot of St Denis deployed deeply entrenched gender stereotypes simultaneously to defame one particular woman and to deride Bertrada's political agenda, even as he laid bare the socio-political structures that made any aristocratic sister, wife, and mother a potential player in medieval power politics.[45]

As a concluding example I would like to shift approach in order to draw together several themes of this essay. Instead of analyzing one author's depiction of an historical virago, I will discuss the term's use in a case where I am familiar with all the extant sources concerning one politically active female lord: Adela, the youngest daughter of William the Conqueror (b. *c.*1067) and, by marriage, countess of Blois, Chartres, and Meaux in the decades straddling 1100. In the one hundred and seventy-five sources comprising the 'Adela dossier', the countess was called a virago a mere four times: in one charter (of over ninety), in one letter (of over forty), and in two narrative histories (of about fifteen) – though in no poems (of six). In other words, 'virago' was not a frequent accolade for this woman who is exceptional more for the fact that no gender-based criticism of her actions survives than for the lordly powers she wielded as wife, mother, widow – and even as a nun.[46]

of certain dower properties, adjoining land her son Fulk had granted (in 1110), that she had 'bought' from Louis VI and then granted precarially to a cleric; although Fliche argued that Louis' 'sale' of the land implied hostility towards his stepmother, as Dhondt points out ('Sept femmes', p. 69, n. 102) dower properties normally could not be alienated freely; Louis was short of cash during this decade of conflict and Bertrada may well have offered to pay him, perhaps even generously, for the right to alienate dower properties Philip had bestowed on her; according to A. Luchaire, *Louis VI le Gros: annales de sa vie et de son règne (1081–1137)* (Paris, 1890), pp.79–80, no. 154, the grant would have been made in the year she retired to Haute-Bruyères. See also LoPrete, 'Adela', pp. 33–8, for further discussion of events.)   **45** For a thirteenth-century Capetian queen mother and regent (Blanche of Castile) cast positively as a virago, see n. 10 above.   **46** For a full discussion of how Adela was represented in these sources see K.A. LoPrete, 'The gender of lordly women: the case of Adela of Blois' in C. Meek and C. Lawless (eds), *Studies on medieval and early modern women: pawns or players?* (Dublin, 2003), pp. 90–110; and for her political activities, LoPrete, 'Adela of Blois: familial alliances and female lordship' in T. Evergates (ed.), *Aristocratic women in medieval France* (Philadelphia, 1999), pp. 7–43, 180–200.

The charter, written by monks of Marmoutier, records how the countess, ruling during her husband's absence on crusade, negotiated a settlement in the monks' quarrel with neighbouring canons over tithes and then formally reconciled the disputing parties in the canons' chapter house at Blois.[47] For her authoritative deployment of several lordly powers (the contested tithes were on dower properties she had alienated several years before), the monks hailed Adela as a virago, though in a second charter documenting the same events they gratefully praised the countess who championed their claims as their 'most fervent lover' (*amatrix ferventissima*) as well.[48]

The letter dates from after Adela's death (d. 1137) and was an attempt by the prior of Westminster abbey to win support from her sons, king Stephen and Henry, the bishop of Winchester (the missive's recipient). Flattering the sons by praising their parents, prior Osbert calls Adela a 'splendid and distinguished virago' worthy of such acclaim because she – daughter of that 'most victorious' king William – mothered a bishop, king, and counts before 'laying aside the purple of secular glory' to conquer both 'the world and her sex' in a convent.[49] To a celibate churchman, a ruling mother who gave birth to, and moulded, leading lords of the next generation would only increase her merit by choosing to renounce her earthly powers and become a nun – a context in which the lordly and the virginal connations of virago coalesce.

William of Malmesbury economically combined these themes with the laconic comment he devoted to this daughter of William the Conqueror and wife of count Stephen: she was 'a virago of praiseworthy power in the world [who] recently has donned a nun's habit'.[50] Writing a history of the English kings, William had several reasons not to elaborate upon Adela's activities, though he later noted in passing her diplomatic contributions to the peace negotiated on the eve of her monastic retirement.[51] All the same, even his passing observations disclose that the countess's political power arose from her traditional domestic roles as wife and mother.

The most loquacious chronicler to call Adela a virago was Hugh, the chanter of York cathedral. Hugh actually met Adela in 1120 while he and his exiled

47 E. Mabille (ed.), *Cartulaire de Marmoutier pour le Dunois* (Châteaudun, 1874), p. 62, no. 68 [hereafter *MD*]; the document is technically a third-person notification dated to 1101.   48 *MD*, pp. 60–2, no. 67; see further at LoPrete, 'Gender', pp. 103–4. 49 Osbert of Clare, ep. 15, ed. E.W. Williamson, *The letters of Osbert of Clare* (Oxford, 1929), pp. 83–5, at 84–5 (datable to early 1139): 'praefatus autem victoriosissimus princeps Adelam genuit, quae pretiosa et insignis virago ex Stephano comite [p]alatino sponso suo liberos suscepit, pontificesque et reges et consules in lucem temporalis ortus effudit. Haec, depositis inflatae carnis fastibus et purpura gloriae saecularis abiecta, apud Marciniacum et saeculum vicit et sexum'.   50 My translation; William of Malmesbury, *Gesta regum*, 3.276, ed. 1:504, devoted to William's children: 'Adela, Stephani Blesensis comitis uxor, laudatae in seculo potentiae uirago, nouiter apud Marcenniacum sanctimonialis habitum sumpsit'.   51 William of Malmesbury, *Gesta regum*, 5.419.2, ed.

archbishop shuttled between the countess's household, the papal entourage, and the French royal court, mediating resolutions to two international conflicts – one involving Adela directly, the other indirectly. Praising the countess as a lord (*domina*) who received the archbishop joyfully and honourably, and with whom he could discuss the greatest affairs of state in all confidence, the historian then described her decision to renounce the wealth and pomp of the world to become a nun. His concluding assessment: 'by the testimony of king Louis [VI] and the princes (*principes*) of all France, there has been no wiser (*prudencior*), better looking (*melius composita*) or more virile virago (*magis uirilis uirago*) in all Gaul for many an age'.[52] That was indeed a fitting tribute to the countess who helped reconcile the author's archbishop to her own brother, king Henry I, as she had instigated Henry's reconciliation to Anselm of Canterbury fifteen years earlier.[53]

It is also a tribute that shows Adela was not unique as a woman performing the duties of a man. She may have been *more* 'virile' (powerful) than most other politically-active *dominae* of her day, but then not all lordly women were the daughters of kings married to leading princes and thus as well-placed as she was to intervene in the international politics of both 'church' and 'state'.[54] (Indeed, the countess of Blois, Chartres, and Meaux had more political power than most lordly men.) Nonetheless, historians can document significant numbers of other noblewomen who, like Adela, could come to exercise lordly powers and play power politics through the same channels as she did.

They could be married to politically powerful noblemen who were nonetheless their wives' social inferiors (a situation that accorded wives greater social prestige than their mates and hence potentially greater influence). Noblewomen also could control land and have access to liquid and other revenues from their dowries and dowers – properties on which they wielded lordly powers over servile tenants as well as any knightly ones, and could owe a vassal's services to other lords (even if these *dominae* were not themselves heiresses or did not perform military services personally). Or they simply could be women married to older men whom they could well outlive – or rule on behalf of – should their husbands either predecease them or depart from the home front for any extended period.[55] The political powers of aristocratic women were woven into

1:758 (events of 1120).   **52** Hugh the Chanter, *The history of the church of York, 1066–1127*, ed. Charles Johnson, rvsd. by M. Brett, C.N.L. Brooke and M. Winterbottom (Oxford, 1990), pp. 152/4; see also LoPrete, 'Gender', p. 107.   **53** LoPrete, 'Adela', pp. 30–3, 38–9. **54** Cp. her contemporary, Matilda of Tuscany, depicted as a virago by Hugh of Flavigny in his lengthy *Chronicon*, bk 2, ed. *PL*, 154:333: 'At vero Mathildis comitissa, Romanae aecclesiae filia, virilis animi constantiam tenens, tanto ei fortius resistebat, quanto magis hujus astutias et papae innocentiam noverat. Sola enim tunc temporis inventa est inter feminas, quae regis potentiam aspernata sit, quae calliditatibus ejus et potentiae etiam bellico certamine obviaverit, ut merito nominetur virago, quae virtute animi etiam viros praeibat'. **55** See above, nn. 4, 6, 7.

the texture of a society in which 'domestic' household management included what we might consider public political duties: commanding armed warriors and organizing the defence of lands and tenants; adjudicating disputes among fief-holding knights and other dependents, as well as their monastic neighbours; managing revenues from entire lordships, as well as disbursing them – not only to purchase day-to-day necessities, but also to buy political favours and armed allies, in addition to spiritual support for both the living and the dead.

In other words, whether she was commanding household cooks, household clerics or household knights, the *domina*, or 'lady', of the castle, was as much a lord – *dominus* – as her husband was. When she controlled lands, honours and revenues in her own right (whether as inheritances or marital assigns or both), or when she acted as regent-guardian for an absent husband or minor son, her lordly powers and political impact would often expand. But those activities were natural extensions, not transgressions, of her traditionally 'feminine' and domestic social roles.

Yet the very infrequency with which clerical authors called lordly women viragos – even when they were ready enough to praise them for the occasional 'manly' deed or courageous act – reveals the ambivalent lineage of the term.[56] Viragos, like all powerful people, could use their powers for good or ill. They could be 'prudent' or 'imprudent', 'virtuous' or 'vicious', and the line between the two depended largely on the perspective of the commentator, just as the same king could be one author's 'lion of justice' and another's 'tyrant'.[57] But the gender cards were stacked against lordly women as they were against all women. Whereas all aristocratic men might reasonably expect to command others in some authorized capacity during their lifetimes, many aristocratic women would not, and those who did would have more limited opportunities to wield lordly powers than did their male peers. Moreover, such female lords would be expected to behave like all other lay women, even as they commanded men in 'male' domains – a tricky tightrope to walk at the best of times.[58]

'Manly women' were not men, but neither were they average women. To eliminate all doubt on both counts, some clerical commentators were quite scrupulous when describing the activities of lordly men and women. One of these was the monk-chronicler of mixed Anglo-Norman parentage, Orderic Vitalis, who depicted in positive terms several lordly deeds of the countess Adela.[59] Not all female lords merited praise, however: they could loot monasteries as well as protect them, poison political rivals as well as aid allies on the battlefield, act for personal gain as well as for the greater good of church or

---

56 See, e.g., Cadden, *Meanings*, pp. 208–9.   57 See n. 35 above; though tyrant is always a negative epithet, in the Middle Ages virago needs a modifying adjective to give it a negative valence; otherwise it is almost always a positive term of praise.   58 I have found no historical women dubbed viragos by medieval authors who are also represented in the same text as cross-dressing.   59 LoPrete, 'Gender', pp. 97–9, 109.

realm.[60] But common to all these women in Orderic's narrative is the fact that they come to exercise lordly authority in the ordinary life course of the noble family: a natural progression that regularly produces heiresses, wives acting for absent husbands, and widow-regents. Yet not one is described by Orderic as acting as a man; the one hundred or so people acting *viriliter*, or performing virile deeds in his history are all men. The rare Amazon appears, actually bearing arms herself, and one lone virago: a nameless wife bravely speaking out in court against her husband's unjust conviction.[61] She slipped in from Orderic's source, an English hagiographic narrative in which several otherwise unknown wives and mothers are given that accolade (while the male saint performs the miracles). Orderic normally was quite careful both to demarcate and to gender the deeds of men and women[62] – even as he did not distinguish between public and domestic spheres of political action. Yet even to him, such a modest yet forthright virago merited more praise than censure for her courageous attempt to save her husband.

Several important conclusions result from this glance at connotations of the word virago as it was deployed to depict lay women in the Middle Ages. First, it must be recalled that to act authoritatively beyond the inner chambers of castles, lordly women crossed no conceptual threshold separating domestic from public spheres. Nor by performing their traditional women's roles with mental fortitude, resolute strength, and decisive energy did they become men. Lay viragos in the Middle Ages were neither monstrous, hybrid, 'men-women', nor otherwise 'unnatural' women usurping men's 'natural' places and powers in the world – even as they routinely performed men's deeds in 'male' domains when familial circumstances required. More often than not such sexually-active viragos were praised for the lordly deeds they performed, usually as wives and mothers, and such deeds were recorded with appreciation by their male peers. If modern historians ignore or downplay the lasting contributions of such female lords both to their wider worlds and to significant historical events, it is in large part because of the distorting lenses we wear when approaching a world in which writers relished in paradox while simultaneously eschewing a strictly determinist, either/or, logic based on binary oppositions.

60 See, e.g., Marjorie Chibnall, 'Women in Orderic Vitalis'. *Haskins Society Journal* 2 (1990), pp. 105–22.   61 The Amazon, Isabel of Conches: OV, 8.14, ed. Chibnall, 4:212/4; Bricstan's nameless wife: OV, 6.10, ed. Chibnall, 3:346/52.   62 Henry Platelle, 'Le problème du scandale: les nouvelles modes masculines aux XIe et XIIe siècles', *Revue Belge de Philologie et d'Histoire* 53 (1975), pp. 1071–96.

Mothers and sons: Emma of Normandy's role in the English succession crisis, 1035–42

Maia Sheridan

This paper discusses the representation of Emma of Normandy and her relationship with her sons in the work she commissioned from a Flemish monk, the *Encomium Emmae Reginae*, which I believe she used as a weapon in the succession crisis in England after the death of Cnut in 1035, to demonstrate the kingworthiness of her sons over all other rivals.

Emma of Normandy was twice queen of England, and mother of two English kings. She was the daughter of Richard I, duke of Normandy, though her mother was Danish. She was married to the ageing Anglo-Saxon king, Aethelred II, in 1002, when she may have been as young as twelve. She undoubtedly had little choice in the marriage; Aethelred was forty years her senior, with six adult sons from his first marriage. Emma produced two more sons, Edward and Alfred. The succession was thus likely to be disputed between her sons and her stepsons. However, events were further complicated by the conquest of England by the Danish royal house of Swein Forkbeard and his son Cnut. Aethelred's elder sons were all dead or had disappeared by the time Cnut married the now widowed Emma. They produced another royal heir in Harthacnut, but Cnut already had two sons, Harald and Swein, with his concubine, Aelfgifu of Northampton.

The succession should have been limited to Emma's sons, through hereditary right, designation and legitimacy, but when Cnut died, none of them was immediately able to put this title into practice. Obtaining the English throne for one of her sons was vital to Emma. As queen, she was the king's wife or the king's mother. In exile she was nothing, not even a proper dowager, since we must assume her dower lands in England had been confiscated. She had little to lose in fighting tooth and nail to restore her fortunes via one of her sons; she had much to gain if she could only back the right one. Serial monogamy, or even polygamy, of kings had greatly confused the succession issue. Hereditary succession had been accepted but primogeniture was slow to follow in Anglo-Saxon England. With two dynasties vying for the English throne, with brothers and half-brothers all eligible, the role of the mothers of these contenders would be a powerful one. Emma was also up against Danish inheritance practices which usually recognized sons of concubines as legitimate and had no order of preference for succession. Cnut may even have set up his sons as rulers of his overseas kingdoms during his lifetime, so acknowledging all of them as kingworthy.[1] Harthacnut received Denmark, the patrimony, which was usually reserved for the eldest or most favoured son, while Swein was sent to the new acquisition of Norway. Perhaps Harald remained in England by design, waiting to take over from Cnut. There was thus a hierarchy of legitimate and illegitimate sons, but all received a share. Cnut's own father had divided his kingdoms; Swein left the patrimony to Cnut's brother Harald, and the new conquest of England to Cnut.[2]

This situation created insecurity for wives and potential heirs; succession to the throne would always be in doubt while the rules were not fixed and all sons were eligible. Such faction fights and power struggles gave unusual opportunities to the mothers of royal heirs to attain and wield power in the interests of their sons.[3] It could come down to the relative strengths of the maternal kin and their allies on each side. Emma had become very wealthy, obtaining dower lands on both her marriages; she would have been one of the greatest land-holders in England.[4] Political connections at court, patronage links, support of the church and the strength of the resources available to the queen could be vital in getting her child on to the throne.[5] Emma was in a strong position in all these respects but still lost ground initially, for the power struggle within the royal family had wider implications. It brought out other ambitions and rivalries; Mercia and Wessex supported different candidates in the succession disputes of the tenth and eleventh centuries.[6] The church supported Emma, probably influenced by her generous patronage. Archbishop Aethelnoth refused to crown Harald or anyone else: 'while the sons of Queen Emma lived he would approve or consecrate no other man as king'.[7] But Aelfgifu of Northampton had followers in the north, and was busy bribing and persuading others to join her son's cause.[8]

1 P. Stafford, *Unification and conquest* (1989), p. 77.   2 Saxo Grammaticus, *Danorum Regum Heroumque Historia*, books x–xvi, trans. E Christiansen, 3 vols, British Archaeological Reports, International Series, 118 (Oxford, 1980), p. 34.   3 L.L. Huneycutt, 'Images of high medieval queenship', *Haskins Society Journal* 1 (1989), p. 61.   4 P. Stafford, *Queen Emma and Queen Edith* (London, 1997), pp. 128–30. Emma received lands in Rockingham Forest, Northamptonshire, Winchester, Exeter, East and West Suffolk, Bury, Ipswich.   5 P. Stafford, *Queens, concubines and dowagers: the king's wife in the early Middle Ages* (Athens, GA, 1983), p. 12.   6 P. Stafford, 'The reign of Aethelred II: a study in the limitations on royal policy and action' in D. Hill (ed.), *Aethelred the Unready: papers from the Millenary Conference*, British Archaeological Reports, British Series, 59 (Oxford, 1978), p. 24.   7 *Encomium Emmae Reginae*, ed A. Campbell, Camden Third Series 72 (London, 1949), III.2, p. 42 [hereafter cited as EE].   8 W.H. Stephenson, 'An alleged son of Harold Harefoot', *English Historical Review* 28 (1913),

Emma had to make the most of opportunities to secure her position, and the *Encomium* was her method of attack. It purports to be a panegyric of Emma, although she does not appear until the end of the second book; the author omits her numerous pious works, donations to churches, and her holy life, which would usually be reported in secular and royal biographies. Instead he tells us that glorifying her family will reflect glory on her.[9] However, his account is selective and partisan, for the family he tells us about is not Anglo-Saxon but Danish: Swein, Cnut and Harthacnut. The final book tells the story of Emma, her three sons and their attempts to wrest the throne from the usurper Harald. The work contains several important errors and omissions which may have been deliberate. The reasoning behind these misrepresentations can help us to understand Emma's motives in producing the *Encomium*. The author's image of Swein Forkbeard differs markedly from that of later chroniclers. William of Malmesbury says Swein 'oppressed England with rapine and with slaughter', and was 'not a lawful sovereign, but a most cruel tyrant'.[10] Orderic Vitalis reports him as 'the fierce idolater Swein'.[11] In astonishing contrast, the Encomiast portrays Swein as a model Christian king, to whom 'divine power granted such great favour', even exhorting Cnut on his deathbed to 'the zealous practice of Christianity' as if Emma needed to establish that divine grace favoured Cnut's family.[12]

The most glaring distortion of the *Encomium* is the omission of Emma's first marriage to Aethelred II. Emma was not ashamed of her Anglo-Saxon associations, which she played up when she needed to, but her first marriage was inconvenient to the narrative; in order to be seen as a loving wife and mother she could not be portrayed so readily marrying the conqueror of her first husband and abandoning the claims of her first children. Although the Encomiast did not deny the legitimacy of her two eldest sons, their parentage was obscured; he implies they were 'other legitimate sons' of Emma and Cnut.[13]

The seminal event of her life which Emma seeks to illustrate is her marriage to Cnut, and its consequences for his legitimacy as king of England and thus the succession of their son Harthacnut. Cnut saw the advantage in legitimating his position through marriage to the widow of the last Anglo-Saxon king; as well as keeping some continuity with the old regime, he would benefit from her experience of English administration, while underlining his conquest. Upon her marriage to Aethelred, Emma had taken on the Anglo-Saxon name of his saintly grandmother, Aelfgifu; she kept the name and the association when she married Cnut, acting as a bridge to the West Saxon royal house. Cnut could be seen as symbolically restoring the old regime by marrying her. Her offspring by Cnut were all given Danish names, just as her first family had been given Anglo-

pp. 115–16.   9 EE, Prologue, p. 5.   10 William of Malmsbury, *Chronicle of the kings of England before the Norman Conquest* trans. J. Stephenson (Lampeter, 1989), p. 164. 11 Orderic Vitalis, *The ecclesiastical history of Orderic Vitalis*, ed. and trans. M. Chibnall (Oxford, 1980), vol. 4, p. 245.   12 EE, II.1, p. 9; EE, II.5, p. 15.   13 EE, II.18, p. 35.

Saxon names; her Norman roots were subsumed by both her royal marriages. The Encomiast tries to persuade us to see Emma as Esther, as the means of reconciling two bitterly divided peoples, English and Danish, and restoring peace to England after the terrible havoc of the 'accursed and loathsome troubles of war'.[14] Her marriage to Cnut 'should lay the disturbances of war to rest', because although she was Norman by birth, she was playing at being Anglo-Saxon. The image is continued later in the *Encomium* in Emma's efforts to bring peace to her kingdom, saving England from the tyranny of Harald through her sons, though she was fully prepared to wage war to achieve this peace. We can imagine that Emma was glad to be able to return to prominence after her sudden eclipse on the death of Aethelred. The Encomiast writes of the difficulty of finding a worthy bride for Cnut to flatter Emma; in reality she may even have been his prisoner. Cnut had 'to obtain her hand lawfully', so the marriage would be properly sanctified and could not be contested later. But it seems unlikely that she would have had sufficient control over her circumstances to set any conditions for her second marriage; the Encomiast's claim that Cnut swore 'that he would never set up the son of any wife other than herself to rule after him, if it happened that God should give her a son by him' was probably fabricated to strengthen Harthacnut's claims over those of Harald. Emma had heard that 'the king had had sons by some other woman', presumably Aelfgifu of Northampton. In 'the delightful hope of future offspring' and in 'wisely providing for her offspring' the *Encomium* shows her sagely anticipating both the birth of Harthacnut and the ensuing problems.

Cnut would 'make her the partner of his rule'; the Encomiast implies that Emma was to be no mere figurehead but an active participant in the rule of England. Charter evidence suggests she had little political influence at first, as her name appears less frequently in the witness lists than under Aethelred. By 1020, however, after the birth of Harthacnut perhaps, she had obtained her former position, subscribing just after the king, or even jointly with him.[15] She and Godwine, earl of Wessex, became the most prominent people at Cnut's court.[16] After all she had more experience of government and of England than Cnut did, and he was frequently away in Scandinavia; it seems reasonable to suppose Emma took on some form of regency role in his absence. Although she may have had the marriage forced upon her, she was rapidly able to exert power within it.

Book III focuses on the succession crisis after the death of Cnut. Emma was the grieving widow, 'sorrowing for the death of her husband', but she was also the concerned mother, 'alarmed at the absence of her sons'.[17] Harthacnut was detained in Denmark by the threat of Magnus Olafson, king of Norway; the others were in Normandy.[18] Harald, putative son of Aelfgifu and Cnut, was the only man on the

14 EE, II.16, p. 33. 15 S. Keynes, 'The Aethlings in Normandy', *Anglo-Norman Studies* 13 (1991), pp. 175, 185. 16 P. Stafford, 'The king's wife in Wessex, 800–1066', *Past and Present* (1981), p. 26. 17 EE, III.1, p. 39. 18 M. Lawson, *Cnut: the Danes in*

spot, and 'certain Englishmen … preferred to dishonour their country than to ornament it, and deserted the noble sons of the excellent queen Emma'.[19] Emma's background would suggest to her that the sanctity of marriage in the eyes of the church, and her special status as consecrated queen should mean that her son was more kingworthy that anyone else's. This means that Edward and Alfred must be especially kingworthy too, as Emma was also Aethelred's consecrated queen.[20] To be formally recognized as queen was of great benefit to her, setting her above other wives or concubines by divine approval, and to her sons, who would have enhanced kingworthiness. She was the anointed and consecrated queen, unlike Aelfgifu, and she was the one with the promise from Cnut that her son would be king. She could also use the same claims against Harald that Aelfthryth had used against Edward the Martyr; he had been born before his father was anointed king, and his mother had never been anointed or officially recognized as queen.[21] Emma may also have been thinking of parallels with the intercessory role of the Virgin Mary as the Queen of Heaven; this ideal model for queens elevated their status and position in relation to kingship. A picture of Cnut and Emma presenting a magnificent cross to the New Minster at Winchester depicts a familiar literary and artistic parallel between the heavenly queen, and an earthly queen, Emma.[22] There was a Marian cult at Winchester, Emma's power base, which specialized in iconographic representation of Mary as *Maria Regina*.[23] What could be more useful to a potential queen mother than an association with the queen of Heaven?

The Encomiast tries to undermine Harald by casting doubts on his paternity and even his maternity; he reports rumours that Harald was the son of a servant smuggled into the bed of the concubine.[24] Emma was probably the source of those rumours, later repeated in the *Anglo-Saxon Chronicle*.[25] Emma had to prove that Harald had not been designated by the previous king, and that he did not have a hereditary right to rule. He had to be shown as illegitimate, a usurper, a tyrant and 'indeed even turned from the whole Christian religion', the antithesis of the good Christian king model that the Encomiast sets up for Cnut.[26] This castigation has usually been explained as possible because Harald was dead; what if he were not dead but the one person Emma feared most and had to vilify throughout the document, to prove that her sons were the only ones with legitimate title to the crown?

England in the early eleventh century (London, 1993), p. 113. **19** EE, III.1, p. 41. **20** Stafford, *Queen Emma and Queen Edith*, p. 174; a charter of 1004 mentions Emma's consecration. **21** J. Nelson, 'Inauguration rituals' in P. Sawyer and I. Wood (eds), *Early medieval kingship* (Leeds, 1977), p. 67; A. Williams, 'Some notes and considerations on problems connected with the English royal succession, 860–1066', *Proceedings of the Battle Conference on Anglo-Norman Studies* 1 (1978), p. 156. **22** C.R. Dodwell, *Anglo-Saxon art* (Manchester, 1982), plate 47, p. 177. **23** D.A. Bullough, 'The continental background of the reform' in D. Parsons (ed.), *Tenth-century studies* (London, 1975), p. 36; Stafford, 'The king's wife', p. 23. **24** EE, III.1, p. 41. **25** *Anglo-Saxon Chronicle*, ed. and trans. M. Swanton (London, 1996), 'C' 1035, p. 158. **26** EE, III.1, p. 41.

Emma wanted to be seen as having supported all her sons as much as she could, but the account is riddled with hints and attempts to bolster Harthacnut's claim to the throne at every turn. He was given an especially kingworthy name, claims the Encomiast, and his Christian baptism is emphasized, to contrast with Harald's apostasy.[27] As soon as Harthacnut was born he was designated future ruler, as 'the heir to the kingdom'. Cnut later 'pledged to him the whole realm which was subject to his command', another mark against Harald, who seems to have been older, but was not only illegitimate, he had not been designated as heir. The author spends some time extolling Harthacnut's kingly virtues, 'for he excelled all the men of his time by superiority in all high qualities'.[28] Emma's relationship with Harthacnut is always shown as harmonious, the loving mother with 'unparalleled love for this child', and the dutiful son who is ever obedient; their relationship has a different quality from that of Emma with Edward and Alfred. Emma and Cnut had packed 'their other legitimate sons' off to Normandy, ostensibly for their education. She could not ignore her sons by Aethelred, but they were hard to explain. On the death of Alfred, Emma of course was 'dazed beyond consolation with sorrow for her murdered son', as any natural mother would be, and her desolation is often commented upon, but the text's portrayal of her relationship with Edward and Alfred lacks the sense of intimacy and shared actions that she seems to have had with Harthacnut. When Alfred was killed, she appears almost as concerned for 'her own life and her position' as for his fate.[29]

Both Harald and Godwine were implicated in the murder of Alfred, Harald directly and Godwine more covertly. The long description of the 'martyrdom of Alfred' may be to arouse sympathy for the bereaved mother and deflect attention from her part in it, for the letter which the author claims was forged by Harald, to lure Edward and Alfred to their deaths in England, may in fact have been genuine.[30] Harald had little to fear from them while he was supported by the majority of the English nobles; once they were in England, however, he would have to deal harshly with any rivals. Emma, afraid that Harthacnut would never come, had selfishly turned to her other offspring to help restore her position, although there could be little support for them in England, where they had not been for twenty years and where few people would know them. The *Encomium*'s lengthy discussion of this episode may indicate the guilt Emma felt over causing the death of Alfred, and the bitterness of her betrayal by Godwine, as well as providing useful propaganda to blacken the name of Harald. The Encomiast is the only contemporary writer to mention the cult of the martyred *aethling* Alfred at Ely, claiming that miracles occurred around his tomb.[31] The twelfth-century *Liber Eliensis* agrees that 'in that place wonderful and beautiful visions of light and virtue frequently occurred'.[32] It may have been Emma's

27 EE, II.18, p. 35; EE, III.1, p. 41.   28 EE, II.18, p. 35.   29 EE, III.7, p. 47.   30 EE, III.3, pp. 41–3.   31 EE, III.6, p. 47.   32 *Liber Eliensis*, ed. E. O. Blake, Camden Third

invention to promote the cult of Alfred, but it failed to become anything more than a local phenomenon. Other royal saint cults were prevalent in Anglo-Saxon times, including that of Edward the Martyr, the murdered elder brother of Aethelred II. Emma would have been familiar with the resonance that such a cult could add to the family prestige, while the designation of sanctity would show God's favour for that dynasty.[33] It would also be a constant reminder to the perpetrators of the murder, usually a rival family or a branch of the royal dynasty, and would restate the inviolability of kingship.[34]

The *Encomium* does include what appear to be Emma's answers to various criticisms made of her, especially in regard to her treatment of her sons: the murder of Alfred and her subsequent conduct in fleeing to Flanders, her neglect of Edward. Either she felt guilty about her role or criticisms had already been expressed when the *Encomium* was being written. Her part in the murder of Alfred must have weighed upon her; this is the most detailed story in the work, despite the author's protestations that he can write only briefly upon such a crime. The Encomiast pleads that would be 'wrong and abominable ... if a matron of such reputation had lost her life through desire for worldly dominion'. Her grasping for power had cost the life of one of her sons; now she must defend and justify herself against accusations of pursuing power at any cost, using the image of a helpless woman, a victim, a grieving widow and mother. Women were frequently made scapegoats for turning against their stepsons, or even their own sons, to save their own position, and it shows the reputation of Emma that this could be written about her; in particular her overarching ambition to get a son on the throne is reflected by the perception that she would do this at any cost. Thietmar of Merseberg's account of her role in the siege of London in 1016 has her accepting the harsh terms of having to hand over either her own two sons or two of her stepsons to be killed, though in the meantime 'the two brothers escaped in the silence of the night'. By the twelfth century clerical attitudes towards women wielding power had hardened. William of Malmesbury thought it a disgrace for Emma to marry Cnut and 'to share the nuptial couch of that man who had so cruelly molested her husband and driven her children into exile'.[35] The twelfth-century French historian Gaimar paints her as the archetypal evil stepmother, claiming that it was Emma who urged Cnut to exile the two sons of Edmund Ironside, telling him that: 'These are the right heirs of the land, If they live they will make war'.[36] To protect her own sons' inheritance, 'She devised an evil plan' to have Edmund's children maimed or killed when they became the focus of opposition to Danish rule. Gaimar

Series, 91 (London, 1962), p. 160.   **33** D. Rollason, 'Relic-cults as an instrument of royal policy, *c.*900–*c.*1050', *Anglo-Saxon England* 15 (1986), p. 92.   **34** S. Ridyard, *The royal saints of Anglo-Saxon England* (Cambridge, 1988), p. 239.   **35** William of Malmesbury, *Chronicle*, p. 164.   **36** Geffrei Gaimar, *L'Estoire des Engleis*, ed. A. Bell, Anglo-Norman Text Society, vols 14–16 (Oxford, 1960), p. 142.

demonstrates that Emma was considered to be capable of any extreme to support her own sons. In a similar attribution of ambition, Snorri Sturlason in *Heimskringla* reports a story about Emma's determination to get Harthacnut declared as king of Denmark by stealing Cnut's official seal and forging letters to Ulf, regent of Denmark.[37] It may hint at some sort of conflict between Emma and Cnut, perhaps over the appointment of Swein as king of Norway.[38] Did Emma demand a similar honour for her own son?

Even the Encomiast shares the misogynistic tendencies of the later chroniclers about politically active women so he conspires with Emma to portray her as passive and obedient to traditional gender roles. He skilfully presents Emma as a model wife, loving mother, and as the ideal queen, using conventional imagery to describe these accepted female roles. Emma is concerned for the rightful inheritance of her children, but without any masculine ambitions to force the issue. She is shown in the prescribed female role, passive, pious, innocent, while Harald was scheming with 'fraudulent men' and 'secretly laying traps for the queen'. The Encomiast says she, 'silently awaited the outcome of the matter', 'daily gaining God's help by prayer'.[39] In reality, she was doing much more than that, taking active measures to help whichever of her sons she felt most likely to regain the throne. As queen she had run the royal household and been in charge of patronage and distribution of offices. She also had an official, public role to play; within the tradition of queenly power she could sit in judgement, give counsel, she could even be regent.[40] In an age of personal rule, she had intimate access to the centre of power and the decision-making process. She must have taken advantage now of her contacts and influence, built up over the years in power, but the Encomiast does not depict her actively intervening in the crisis. He makes her powerless, dependent entirely on the actions of her sons, while her actions from 1035 to 1037, when she propped up Harthacnut's claim to England by acting as regent of Wessex with Godwine, using her housecarls to seize the treasury at Winchester, are nowhere mentioned. Queens wielding power were accepted during a succession crisis, but Emma did not want to be criticized for transgressing any boundaries. The Encomiast probably had no language in which to describe a politically active woman, and had to resort to conventional family roles. This suited Emma admirably for these were the areas where she could attack Harald, through the irregular union of his mother and his illegitimate birth. She appears to do nothing that would contravene the position of a woman, even a queen, in medieval Christian society. She even

37 Snorri Sturlason, *Heimskringla, or Lives of the Norse Kings*, trans. A.H. Smith, ed. E. Monsen (Cambridge, 1932, reprinted New York, 1990), pp. 389–90. 38 M.W. Campbell, 'Queen Emma and Aelfgifu of Northampton, Cnut the Great's women', *Medieval Scandinavia* 4 (1971), p. 72. 39 EE, III.2, p. 41. 40 P. Stafford, 'The portrayal of royal women in England, mid-tenth to mid-twelfth centuries' in J.C. Parsons (ed.), *Medieval queenship* (New York, 1993), p. 146.

becomes an innocent victim, forced to flee England in fear for her life at the hands of a murderous tyrant.

In Bruges she received the hospitality of the count of Flanders, Baldwin V, a friend to later exiles from England as well, and with family connections to Emma. While there she called both Edward and Harthacnut to her and they both dutifully obeyed her summons – she still had plans for the re-conquest of England. Edward sportingly declined to invade, the Encomiast claims, because the English nobles had not sworn any oath of allegiance to him; this claim may have inspired the author of the later *Vita Edwardi Regis* to invent such an oath sworn to Edward *in utero*.[41] In reality Edward must have been aware of the limited resources the troubled duchy of Normandy could provide during the minority of William, and the lack of an influential party backing Edward in England. While Edward could do nothing, Harthacnut was the one who 'burned in his heart to go and avenge his brother's injuries', as if Alfred had been his own full brother, and of course 'to obey his mother's message' to re-conquer England.[42] So while Edward was inactive, unable or unwilling to help, Harthacnut rose to the occasion like a true Danish hero. And it was in Harthacnut's face that Emma saw 'the face of her lost one in his countenance', associating the visage of a saint with Cnut's son rather than Alfred's full brother.[43]

However, Harthacnut came when he was ready and not before. He first dealt with the problems in Denmark, by making a treaty in 1039 with Magnus Olafson. Then, at last, he was free to look to England, and to answer his mother's demands. England after all was still the richest country in Northern Europe, and the Danish economy depended on it. He raised an invasion fleet but Harald's timely death saved them the trouble. God had intervened to remove Harald before Harthacnut needed to use his fleet.[44] Harald had turned against his faith and so could not be allowed to rule; Emma's pious sons would restore the Christian faith as it should be. Harthacnut was now the obvious successor, having the arms to back up his claim. The Encomiast depicts the English nobles obsequiously inviting Harthacnut and his mother back home. Emma must have revelled in yet another restoration of her fluctuating fortunes. The exaggerated wailing scene on her departure from Flanders made a fitting contrast with her lonely flight from England. Hers was a triumphant return.[45]

The last chapter deals with the invitation to Edward to come and share the English throne in some form of power-sharing agreement. Was this voluntary or forced? The author has Harthacnut 'gripped by brotherly love', but there is some suggestion that Harthacnut's reign was unpopular. His redundant invasion fleet had to be paid for; the *Anglo-Saxon Chronicle* complains of heavy taxation and harsh rule, claiming 'all those who had hankered for him before,

---

41 *Life of King Edward who rests at Westminster*, ed. F. Barlow (2nd edition, Oxford, 1992), pp. 6–8.   42 EE, III.8, p. 49.   43 EE, III.10, p. 51.   44 EE, III.9, p. 49.
45 EE, III.13, p. 53.

were then disloyal to him' and 'he never accomplished anything kingly for as long as he ruled'.[46] With another adult rival just across the water, Harthacnut and Emma had to be careful; it may have been better to have Edward in England where he could be watched, than able secretly to foster rebellion in Normandy. Saxo asserts that Harthacnut associated Edward with him in the kingship to forestall his ambition, 'to prevent him from seeking the whole kingdom by giving him half', not from brotherly affection, but 'because he suspected his popularity and the authority of his father's family'.[47] The criticisms which the Encomiast seems to be trying to answer could conceivably have been made by Edward himself, who was likely to know more about Emma's role in the death of Alfred than anyone else.

Emma portrays her ideal kingship at the end of the *Encomium*, where 'there is loyalty among sharers of rule, here the bond of motherly and brotherly love is of strength indestructible'.[48] The frontispiece shows a remarkable sub-servience of Harthacnut and Edward to their mother, who is crowned and enthroned in a reprise of the *Maria Regina* parallel.[49] The reality was probably quite different. Harthacnut seems to have been willing to rely on his mother's counsel but Edward's immediate dispossession of Emma when he came to the throne suggests long-standing grievances against her. Her disgrace was only temporary but she never recovered her influence at court. She was buried at Winchester with Cnut and Harthacnut, not with Edward's father, Aethelred.

Emma illustrates the ephemeral nature of female power in the Middle Ages. Her ability to act and influence people depended on her life cycle, as daughter, wife, widow and mother, and as queen and queen mother. She was always dependent on the status of her male relatives, and the *Encomium* emphasizes her dependency. Deprived of any military means for action while in exile, Emma had no other avenue for expressing her opinions than through literature. The Encomiast conducts a campaign of defamation against Aelfgifu and Harald through the female concerns of marriage and birth. The 'faithful mother' image stood in accusation against Emma, so she turned it round to defend herself, to show herself through the *Encomium* as loyal to the cause of all her sons, while discrediting the claims of her rival. He establishes Emma's credentials as mother of the rightful heir to the throne through her marriage, consecration, designation as queen, and the oath Cnut took for her sons. The legitimacy of Harthacnut as heir to England is the dominant theme of the *Encomium*, but her other sons were also worthy heirs, although secondary to Harthacnut. Only Harald was excluded from the succession.

---

46 ASC, 'C' 1040, p. 160, p. 162   47 Saxo Grammaticus, p. 47.   48 EE, III.14, p. 53.
49 J. Backhouse, 'Literature, learning and document sources' in J. Backhouse, D.H. Turner, L. Webster (eds), *The Golden Age of Anglo-Saxon art* (London, 1984), no.148, p. 144.

Merito nominetur virago: Matilda of Tuscany in the polemics of the Investiture Contest*

Patrick Healy

In one of the more dramatic events of the 'Investiture Contest', King Henry IV of Germany entered Rome on 21 March 1084. His bitter enemy, Pope Gregory VII, could only watch from his impregnable fortress of the Castel S. Angelo as, on Easter Sunday, the king had himself crowned emperor by his antipope Wibert of Ravenna.[1] The disastrous defeat for the pope was compounded when Gregory VII's seal fell into the hands of the German king. At this moment of crisis for the 'Gregorian' party, Countess Matilda of Tuscany wrote to all the faithful in Germany, warning them not to trust any papal pronouncements issued under the stolen seal. Anyone purporting to use the papal seal without her corroboration was to be considered a 'false witness'. She also alluded to Henry IV and his antipope, the latter being referred to allegorically as 'Barrabas the thief'.[2] Matilda's warning to the faithful, preserved in the chronicle of Hugh of Flavigny, is the only surviving letter in her name. I propose to take Matilda's letter as the starting point for the two themes of this paper: the role of Matilda as military protector of the reform papacy, and Matilda's influence on the biblical exegesis and polemical literature of the 'Investiture Contest'.

Matilda was of the very highest nobility, holding extensive possessions in Tuscany and in Lotharingia. Her father, Boniface, had been margrave of Tuscany. Her mother Beatrice was the daughter of Duke Frederick II of Upper Lotharingia. After the death of Matilda's father, Beatrice married Duke Godfrey 'the Bearded' of Lotharingia. Matilda was not the first woman of her family to assist the reform papacy. According to a historian in Matilda's

* The author would like to acknowledge the generous support and funding of the Irish Research Council for the Humanities and Social Sciences for the research and writing of this essay. 1 H.E.J. Cowdrey, *Pope Gregory VII, 1073–1085* (Oxford, 1998), pp. 228–9. 2 *Chronicon Hugonis Monachi Virdunensis et Divinionensis et Abbatis Flaviniacensis*, ed. G.H. Pertz, *MGH SS* 8, 463.5–12.

entourage, Bonizo of Sutri, Beatrice played an important part in opposing the antipope Cadalus of Parma ('Honorius II') in 1061–2.[3] Beatrice thus helped to establish the candidate of the 'reform' movement, Alexander II, on the papal throne. From the very inception of his pontificate in 1073, Pope Gregory VII seems to have envisaged a similar role for Matilda. In 1074, both Beatrice and Matilda were central to Gregory's plans to discipline his Norman vassal Robert Guiscard. The pope also hoped that the countesses would participate in an expedition to relieve the eastern Christians at Constantinople.[4] These plans proved abortive as Gregory was distracted by his worsening relations with Henry IV of Germany. Here again, Matilda emerged as a central figure. Gregory had excommunicated Henry IV at his Lenten synod of 1076 and had declared the king to be deposed. The two were famously reconciled at Matilda's castle of Canossa in January 1077. At this point in her career, Matilda, although a fervent supporter of the pope, should be considered as a mediator between pope and king.[5]

However, Matilda's ability to act as mediator between pope and king was extinguished by events in the year 1080. Gregory VII again excommunicated the king and declared him deposed. Henry's response was to summon a synod of bishops loyal to him at Brixen in June 1080. At this synod, Pope Gregory was declared deposed and an anti-pope, Wibert of Ravenna, was raised up in opposition to him. Wibert took the name 'Clement III'. At this point, Matilda took up arms to defend the papacy in battle, but suffered a devastating defeat at Volta (near Mantua) in October 1080 at the hands of Henry IV's Lombard supporters.[6] In 1081 Henry IV accused her of treason and sentenced her to forfeiture of all her lands.[7] Despite these setbacks Matilda remained steadfastly loyal to Gregory VII and procured an important military victory against a royalist army at Sorbaria on 2 July 1084. This victory would have done much to revive the morale of the 'Gregorian' party after Henry IV's entry into Rome in March 1084 and Gregory's subsequent flight to Salerno.[8]

Matilda's military activity in defence of the papacy is all the more striking when one considers that she had once wanted to escape the cares of secular life. She had been married to her stepbrother, Duke Godfrey 'the hunchback' of Lotharingia, but the union had failed from the start. This experience must have disillusioned Matilda as Pope Gregory VII in 1074 wrote to dissuade her from her apparent intention of taking the veil as a nun.[9] Entry into a monastery or

---

3 Bonizo, *Liber ad Amicum* 6, *MGH Libelli* 1, 595, 596, 598.   4 Cowdrey, *Pope Gregory VII*, p. 300. *Das Register Gregors VII*, ed. E. Caspar, *MGH Epistolae Selectae* 2 (Berlin 1920–23) 1.46, 1.72, 2.9, 2.30, pp. 69f., 103f., 138f., 163f.   5 Donizo of Canossa, *Vita Mathildis* 1.19, vv.1350–54, *MGH SS* 12, 378: *hae mediatrices* (sc. Beatrice and Matilda) *inerant et regis amicae*; Paul of Bernried, *Vita Gregorii VII*. c. 59, ed. J. M. Watterich, *Vitae pontificum Romanorum* 1 (Leipzig, 1862), p. 506: *inter Dominum Papam et regem mediatrices fuerant*.   6 Cowdrey, *Pope Gregory VII*, p. 301 n. 139.   7 ibid p. 302 n.140. 8 ibid p. 302 n.144.   9 *Register Gregors VII*, 1.47, 1.50, pp. 71f., 76f.

nunnery was a traditional aristocratic route for the expiation of sin. However, Gregory discouraged this practice. He wanted a politically active aristocracy who would act as agents of papal policy. In short, Gregory exhorted the high nobility to engage with the world in a *vita activa* rather than retire from it in a *vita contemplativa*.[10] In this spirit, the pope wrote to Abbot Hugh of Cluny in January 1079, rebuking him because the abbot had accepted Duke Hugh I of Burgundy as a monk at Cluny. He bemoans that 'those who seem to fear and to love God flee from Christ's war, disregard the safety of their brothers and, loving only themselves, seek peace ...'[11] Gregory VII's vision of Christ's war encompassed the violent rejection of simoniacal clergy in Germany,[12] the Patarine rebellion in Milan, and the proposed crusade to Constantinople. Gregory needed magnates like Matilda of Tuscany to serve as 'vassals of St Peter' (*fideles beati Petri*).[13] Moreover, although Gregory denied the nobility the monastic route to salvation, he did not deprive them the opportunity to expiate their sins. As we shall see, Gregory offered to Matilda and his other secular allies the opportunity to practise a new kind of 'Christian warfare' that brought its own spiritual rewards. In the words of a grammarian in her entourage, John of Mantua, Matilda should complete with the secular sword what is missing from the sword of the word.[14] Her warfare against the opponents of Pope Gregory VII would complement the spiritual warfare of the clergy against the devil.

It should be emphasized that Matilda's military activity in defence of Gregory VII posed many problems in a feudal society guided by scripture. Matilda's vassals refused to fight against their feudal overlord, Henry IV in 1075 and 1080[15], and Matilda herself had scruples about making war against Christians. For example, John of Mantua composed his *Tractatus* on the Old Testament *Song of Songs* at the request of the countess of Tuscany. The urgent tone of this work betrays the doubts that Matilda must have had about the validity of warfare in the name of St Peter.[16] In a polemic now lost,[17] the anti-pope Wibert

10 I.S. Robinson, 'Gregory VII and the soldiers of Christ', *History* 58 (1973), pp. 190–1. 11 *Register Gregors VII*, 6. 17, pp. 423–4. 12 *Register Gregors VII*, 2. 45, p. 182f., to the South German dukes. 13 *Register Gregors VII*, 9.3, p. 574 (March 1081) where Gregory wrote concerning Welf IV of Bavaria, Matilda's future father-in-law. The pope sought to raise an army of 'knights of St Peter' (*fideles beati Petri*) offering his recruits 'remission of sins': Robinson, 'Gregory VII and the soldiers of Christ', p. 177; Carl Erdmann, *Die Entstehung des Kreuzzugsgedankens* (Stuttgart, 1935), pp. 185–211. 14 *Iohannis Mantuani In Cantica Canticorum et de Sancta Maria Tractatus ad Comitissam Matildam*, ed. B. Bischoff and B. Taeger (*Spicilegium Friburgense* 19, Freiburg, 1973), p. 52: 'just as St Peter himself punished with the heavenly sword, do you with the material sword exercise vengeance on the heresy that is springing up and subverting the greater part of the world'. 15 Kathleen G. Cushing, *Papacy and law in the Gregorian revolution: the canonistic work of Anselm of Lucca* (Oxford, 1998), pp. 133–138. 16 Robinson, 'Gregory VII and the soldiers of Christ', p. 185. 17 The arguments of this polemic can be inferred from the reply framed in the *Liber Contra Wibertum* of

of Ravenna, a kinsman of Matilda, criticized the Gregorian concept of 'Christian warfare'. His reproof was clearly aimed at detaching Matilda from her 'Gregorian' allegiance. Wibert could point to the New Testament text John 18:11, where Christ commanded to Peter on the night of his arrest : 'Put up thy sword into the sheath.' This seemed to be a literal and definitive biblical injunction against the use of military force. To refute it, John of Mantua depended on an allegorical interpretation of the Bible. This allowed him to show that the biblical text in question meant the opposite of what it appeared to mean. According to John, the command 'put up thy sword into thy sheath' in fact means 'do not fling it away but return it to its place'. John concludes that 'the place of the sword is the righteous power which is not divided from the authority of St Peter'.[18] In this interpretation, the pope, as the vicar of St Peter, wields both the spiritual and the material sword. Such a statement amounts to a revolution in medieval political theory and anticipates the highly important 'two swords theory' of Bernard of Clairvaux in his letter to Pope Eugenius III in 1146.[19]

John of Mantua was not the only intellectual in the circle of Matilda of Tuscany who developed new and important arguments to justify the Gregorian concept of 'Christian warfare'. Many others sought refuge at her court, exiled from cities that maintained a royalist allegiance to Henry IV. Among these were numbered Heribert, who became bishop of Reggio in Emilia in 1085 with Matilda's help[20], the saintly Bishop Anselm II of Lucca, Gregory VII's legate in Lombardy, and the polemicist Bonizo of Sutri. The career of Bonizo indicates the importance of sanctuary at Matilda's court. Sometime between March 1086 and the early summer of 1088, Bonizo left the entourage of Matilda and was elected bishop of Piacenza by a pro-papal faction in that city. However, in 1090 Bonizo was attacked and mutilated by a royalist faction at Piacenza. According to Rangerius of Lucca, Bonizo's tongue was cut out, as were his eyes, and his nose and ears cut off.[21] A horrific attack of this kind invalidated the unfortunate victim for the exercise of sacerdotal office.[22] Chapter 21 of the Old Testament book of Leviticus prescribed that the priests of Israel were to be without physical blemish and this stricture was maintained in the Middle Ages. The mutilation of Bonizo, serves as a potent reminder of the passions engendered by the 'Investiture Contest', and illustrates why so many reform-minded intellectuals sought Matilda's protection.

Anselm of Lucca, MGH Libelli 1, 527, and in fragments preserved in Wido of Ferrara, *De Scismate Hildebrandi, MGH Libelli* 1, 554.   18 John of Mantua,*Tractatus*, p. 41. 19 Bernard of Clairvaux, *Epistola* 256, *PL* 182, 463–4; Robinson, 'Gregory VII and the soldiers of Christ', p. 186.   20 Bernold of St Blasien, *Chronicon sub anno* 1085, *MGH SS* 5, 443.   21 Rangerius of Lucca, *Vita metrica Anselmi episcopi Lucensis, MGH SS* 12, 1299; cf. the account in Bernold of St Blasien, *Chronicon sub anno* 1089, *MGH SS* 5, 449.   22 For example, the mutilation of the patarine priest Liudprand in Milan in 1075 by the faction of the *Capitanei*: Landulf Junior de Sancto Paulo, *Historia Mediolanensis* c. 3, 35, 36, *MGH SS* 8, 21–1, 35. Landulf was the nephew of Liudprand.

Matilda's court provided more than mere protection from physical attack: it became a powerhouse of intellectual inquiry in support of the tenets of Gregorian reform. In his letters, Gregory VII made wide-ranging and radical claims but often they were not supported with reference to canon law and the church Fathers. In an age deeply hostile to novelty, the opponents of the pope accurately perceived that his programme of reform was fundamentally inno-vatory. It was left to the supporters of Gregory VII to supply the 'authorities' necessary to legitimize his ideas. Matilda's entourage was the key centre which elaborated the principles of 'Gregorian reform', an especially vital function after Gregory VII's death in 1085. The above mentioned Bishop Heribert of Reggio wrote an *Exposition on the Penitential Psalms* which compared the contem-porary plight of the Church at the hands of Henry IV with the persecution of the early Church by Nero and Diocletian.[23] Heribert quotes Matthew 16: 18 to assert that 'the gates of hell shall not prevail against [the Church]', that is, although apparently victorious, Henry IV would not triumph. Bonizo of Sutri, like John of Mantua, sought to justify 'Christian warfare' with an allegorical interpretation of the Bible. He referred to Genesis 21:10 where Isaac received his inheritance at the expense of Ishmael who was driven out. According to the traditional patristic exegesis, Isaac signified the catholic faithful whereas Ishmael signified the heretics. In Genesis 26: 21 Isaac did not resist the attempts of the Philistines to seize his wells, and his attitude was taken to signify the patient suffering of Christians when oppressed by infidels. Thus far Bonizo has relied upon the traditional interpretation of these passages of the Bible. Now he makes his innovation. Bonizo claims that there are two kinds of persecution. He says 'when persecution is inflicted by those who are outside, it must be overcome by suffering ... when it is inflicted by those who are within ... it must be fought with all our strength and weapons'.[24] Thus Matilda was clearly justified in resisting Henry IV, whose actions fell under the rubric of 'persecution from within'.

It can be seen that John of Mantua, Heribert of Reggio and Bonizo of Sutri all interpreted the Bible in the light of contemporary events. Their figurative style has been called 'political allegory' and it is clear that the cultivation of this style was peculiar to the ambience surrounding Matilda of Tuscany. It is in the context of 'political allegory' that the only surviving letter of Matilda of Tuscany should be understood. Matilda refers to the anti-pope Wibert of Ravenna as 'Barrabas the thief', with the clear implication that the deposed Gregory VII stands in the place of Christ. The same comparison is made by Matilda's adviser Bishop Anselm II of Lucca in his treatise on the Psalms.[25] Anselm explored the meaning of Psalm 2:2: 'the kings of the earth stood by and

---

23 Heribert of Reggio, *Expositio in VII psalmos poenitentiales*, PL 79, 626D.   24 Bonizo, *Liber ad Amicum, MGH Libelli* I, 572; I. S. Robinson, '"Political allegory" in the biblical exegesis of Bruno of Segni', *Recherches de Théologie Ancienne et Moderne* 50 (1983), p. 81 n. 57.   25 Partially preserved in c. 112 of Paul of Bernried's *Vita Gregorii Septimi*.

the princes gathered together'. This passage was traditionally given a chris-
tological interpretation. 'The kings' were understood to signify Pontius Pilate
while 'the princes' of the Psalm were understood to signify the priests and
Pharisees who delivered Christ to him.[26] However, Anselm expanded upon this
traditional interpretation. Christ signified 'St Peter and his vicar Gregory',
Pilate signified Henry IV, while the priests and Pharisees were the Henrician
bishops who supported the antipope Wibert. This expanded interpretation
allows Anselm to exclaim 'Is not Barrabas chosen again and Christ given up to
death by Pilate, when Wibert of Ravenna is elected and Pope Gregory rejected?'
The characterization of Wibert as Barrabas here is thus a form of 'political
allegory' occurring with precisely the same meaning in the letter of Matilda of
Tuscany. It may even be conjectured that Matilda's only surviving letter was in
fact composed by Bishop Anselm II of Lucca. This hypothesis is corroborated
by Matilda's warning that anyone using the stolen seal of Gregory VII should
be considered a 'false witness'. In Anselm's exegesis on Psalm 2:2 he intones
'Does it not seem to you that they are holding a council in the house of Pilate to
deliver up Christ to death, when Henry has provided so many false witnesses
against the supreme pontiff'. The 'false witnesses' here probably refer to the
council of Brixen on 15 June 1080 when Henry IV and the bishops loyal to him
set up Wibert of Ravenna as anti-pope 'Clement III'. At the very least, the
'political allegory' of Bishop Anselm had a profound influence on the one
surviving letter of Matilda of Tuscany, and shows the degree to which she had
come to identify with the ideology of 'Gregorian' reform.

The exegetes in the circle of Matilda had to find biblical allegories not only
for Pope Gregory VII but also for the countess herself. They tried to find
examples of strong, assertive women from the Bible who could be considered
analogous to Matilda of Tuscany. The *Vita* of Anselm II of Lucca says of
Matilda that 'it was granted to her in remission of her sins, that like another
Deborah, she should judge the people, practice warfare and resist the heretics
and schismatics'.[27] Deborah was the female prophet and judge of the Old
Testament Book of Judges. Moreover she received military instructions directly
from God concerning a pending battle with Canaanites under their leader
Sisera. Logically, if Matilda was analogous to the victorious prophet Deborah,
then Henry IV was analogous to the defeated Canaanite general Sisera. In a
eulogy to Matilda at the end of his *Liber ad Amicum*, Bonizo invoked a second
heroine from the Book of Judges, Jael, who actually assassinated Sisera. He
wrote: 'for we believe it is into her hands that Sisera is sold'.[28] Another female
biblical figure is introduced in the polemic of Anselm of Lucca against Wibert
of Ravenna. Perhaps writing in the aftermath of Matilda's victory at Sorbaria in

26 Cassiodorus, *Expositio in Psalmos*, PL 70, 36D–37A. 27 *Vita Anselmi Lucensis* c.11,
MGH SS 12, 16; cf. *Anselmi episcopi Lucensis Vitae primariae fragmenta, MGH SS* 20,
694. 28 Bonizo, *Ad Amicum* 9, *MGH Libelli* 1, 620.11–12.

1084, Anselm comments that Matilda was prepared 'to struggle even to the shedding of her own blood … until the Lord delivers his enemy into the hands of a woman'.[29] The biblical allusion here is to the Old Testament book of Judith (16: 7) where the eponymous heroine leads the Israelites to victory against the Assyrians and their general Holofernes. Biblical allegories of this kind served a number of purposes: to validate 'Christian warfare' and to present it in the context of the Israelite struggle for liberation, to prophesy the inevitable defeat of Henry IV that was prefigured in the grisly deaths of Sisera and Holofernes, and finally to present Matilda in a biblical tradition of strong female leadership.

This last point needs to be emphasized. Many royalist polemics focused on Matilda's gender as an important component in the escalation of hostilities between Henry IV and Gregory VII. The anonymous polemicist of Hersfeld wrote in 1093 that Matilda, because of her secret conversations with Gregory VII, was 'now impossible to restrain, animated by female passions so that she prefers war to peace'.[30] The close relationship between Pope Gregory and Matilda from the start of his pontificate provided much scope to slander the pope. When the royalist bishops of Germany abjured Gregory VII at Worms in 1076, they alleged that he had filled the whole church with the stench of scandal 'by his intimacy and cohabitation with a strange woman'.[31] Gregory VII was mindful of the danger of this kind of accusation and from 1077 on, in his correspondence at least, there is a perceptible coolness in his salutations to the countess.[32] Despite the biblical allegories that might be posited by Anselm of Lucca or Bonizo, the medieval church was fundamentally hostile to women who were politically active. As part of their attack on Gregory VII, the royalist bishops of Worms fulminated that the universal church was governed by 'this new senate of women'.[33] Matilda and her mother Beatrice were implicated in this complaint, as was Dowager-Empress Agnes, the mother of King Henry IV.

Writing in the 1090s the Lotharingian chronicler Hugh of Flavigny said of Matilda 'justly might she be called *virago* [because] her virtue made her a leader of men'.[34] Matilda's fame was not simply confined to a circle of intellectuals in Tuscany: her defence of the 'Gregorian' papacy had won renown throughout

---

29 Anselm of Lucca, *Liber contra Wibertum*, MGH *Libelli* 1, 527.   30 *Liber de Unitate Ecclesiae Conservanda* 2.36, MGH *Libelli* 2, 263.   31 *Quellen zur Geschichte Kaiser Heinrichs IV. (Ausgewählte Quellen zur deutschen Geschichte des Mittelalters* 12, Darmstadt 1963) ed. F.–J. Schmale and I. Schmale-Ott, Anhang A, p. 474.10–15. Lampert of Hersfeld knew and rebutted the allegation of impropriety: *Annales* a. 1077, MGH *SS* 5, 400.10–20; cf. Cowdrey, *Pope Gregory VII*, p. 300.   32 Cowdrey, *Pope Gregory VII*, p. 301.   33 *Quellen zur Geschichte Kaiser Heinrichs IV.* (as note 31); this phrase echoes the definition of Peter Damian that the college of cardinals acted as the 'senate' of the Roman Church.   34 *Chronicon* (as note 2) 462.15: … *ut merito nominetur virago, quae virtute animi etiam viros praeibat.* For the concept of the *virago* in the Middle Ages see J.M.H. Smith, 'The problem of female sanctity in Carolingian Europe *c.*780–920', *Past and Present* 146 (1995), pp. 19ff., and also the essay of Kimberly LoPrete in this volume.

Europe. This was recognized even by her enemies. In 1103, the Lotharingian
royalist Sigebert of Gembloux denounced the 'Gregorian' notion of 'Christian
warfare'. His criticisms directly mention Matilda, and like many contemporaries Sigebert lucidly perceived Matilda's influence on the debate. He says:
'It was Pope Hildebrand alone who originally laid his hands on the sacred
canons. Of him we read that he commanded Margravine Matilda for the
remission of her sins to make war on Emperor Henry.'[35] The remission of sins
or *remissio peccatorum* was perhaps the most important concept supporting the
incipient crusading movement. Crucial to the 'Gregorian' party in the
'Investiture Contest', it would soon be employed even more dramatically to
absolve the warriors of the First Crusade. The ideology of crusade, being a
righteous military venture under the aegis of the pope, was developed with the
help of devout nobles like Matilda. Hugh of Flavigny says that Matilda could
justly be called a *virago*. In her military assistance to Pope Gregory VII, she
could with equal justice have been called a crusader.

---

35 Sigebert of Gembloux, *Epistola Leodicensium adversus Paschalem* c. 13, *MGH Libelli*
2, 464.

Women and the First Crusade: prostitutes or pilgrims?

Conor Kostick

The general view of the first crusade is that it was an entirely male affair, and this is not surprising given that even eminent experts in the history of the crusade can begin articles by saying that 'the history of the First Crusade is, in large part, the history of mass movements of men'.[1] Yet the sources for the crusade give ample and overwhelming evidence that 'innumerable'[2] numbers of women joined the movement. A typical, if rather salacious, comment for example occurs in the history of Albert of Aachen as he talks about the setting forth of the crusade:

> Crowds from different kingdoms and cities gathered together, but in no sense turning away from illicit and sexual intercourse. There was unbridled contact with women and young girls, who with utter rashness had departed with the intention of frivolity; there was constant pleasure and rejoicing under the pretext of this journey.[3]

Albert of Aachen was a monk, who wrote a history of the first crusade in the early 1100s.[4] His description of the immorality and licentiousness of the

1 J.A. Brundage, *The crusades, holy war and canon law* (Aldershot, 1991), II, p. 380. An unfortunate beginning to his 1960 article, which is more than redressed in the path-breaking 'Prostitution, miscegenation and sexual purity in the First Crusade', ibid., XIX, pp. 57–65.   2 Bernold of Constance, *Chronicon*, 1096, *Die Chroniken Bertholds von Reichenau und Bernolds von Konstanz 1054–1100*, ed I.S. Robinson, MGH SRG (Hanover, 2003) p. 529: *innumerabiles*.   3 Albert of Aachen. *Historia Hierosolymitana*, ed. S.B. Edgington (unpublished PhD thesis, University of London, 1991) I.25, p. 125 (Recueil des Historiens des Croisades [henceforward RHC] 4, p. 291): *Hiis itaque per turmas ex diversis regnis et civitatibus in unum collectis, sed nequaquam ab illicitis et fornicariis commixtionibus aversis, inmoderata erat commessatio cum mulieribus et puellis, sub eiusdem levitatis intentione egressis, assidua delectatio, et in omni temeritate sub huius vie occasione gloriatio.* I am grateful to Dr Edgington for permission to quote from her dissertation.   4 Susan Edgington suggests a date soon after 1102 for the completion of the first six books of the *Historia Hierosolymitana*. S.B. Edgington, 'The First Crusade:

Crusade is coloured by the morality of a celibate male infused with the characteristic misogyny of monasticism. But it is nevertheless a striking passage that
raises interesting questions. What motivated women to join the first crusade?
Was the undertaking an opportunity for them to escape a sexually restrictive
society? Did they see themselves as participants or were they camp followers?

Firstly, to establish that there were indeed thousands of women involved in
the crusade, and that their presence is well attested, the sources can quickly be
surveyed. Orderic Vitalis, who wrote his *Ecclesiastical History* between 1125 and
1141, noted that the determination to either go to Jerusalem or to help others
who were going there affected 'rich and poor, men and women, monks and
clerks, townspeople and peasants alike. Husbands arranged to leave beloved
wives at home, the wives, indeed, sighing, greatly desired to journey with the
men, leaving children and all their wealth.'[5] That many women acted on this
inclination is clear. Guibert, abbot of Nogent, is an important source for the
first crusade, writing his history with the anonymous work of an eyewitness
before him (the *Gesta Francorum*) and adding in information from returned
crusaders. His own history, written to provide the monastic reader with a set of
moral standards[6] is full of (usually derogatory) references to women and is an
important source more generally for the theological and moral view of women
in the early twelfth century. Guibert was an eyewitness to the setting forth of
people on the expedition and described how 'when the beginning of this
journey of Christian peoples was spread abroad and not without divine will
proclaimed throughout the Roman Empire, the meanest most common men and
even unworthy women were appropriating to themselves this miracle [the mark
of the cross].'[7] Ekkehard, abbot of Aura and crusader on the 1101 expedition
alongside many of those who had participated in 1096, wrote that of the
common people, 'a great part of them were setting out with wives and offspring
and laden with the whole household.'[8] The Anglo-Saxon chronicler, writing in
Peterborough, had very little to say about the crusade, but he did think it

reviewing the evidence' in J. Phillips (ed.), *The First Crusade: origins and impact*
(Manchester, 1997), pp. 57–77 at p. 61.   5 Orderic Vitalis, *The ecclesiastical history*,
trans. and ed. M. Chibnall (Oxford, 1975), p. 17: *Diuitibus itaque et pauperibus, uiris et
mulieribus. monachis et clericis, urbanis et rusticis, in Ierusalem eundi aut euntes adiuuandi
inerat uoluntas mirabilis. Mariti dilectas coniuges domi relinquere disponebant, illae uero
gementes relicta prole cum omnibus diuitiis suis in peregrinatione uiros suos sequi ualde
cupiebant.*   6 J.G. Schenk, 'The use of rhetoric, biblical exegesis and polemic in Guibert
of Nogent's Gesta Dei per Francos,' unpublished M Phil thesis, Trinity College Dublin,
2001.   7 Guibert of Nogent, *Gesta Dei per Francos*, ed. R.B.C. Huygens (Turnhout,
1996) p. 330: *Viae enim huius cum christianarum ubique gentium percrebruisset initium et id
non sine divina fieri uoluntate per Romanum clameretur imperium, quilibet extremae
vulgaritatis homines et etiam muliebris indignitas hoc sibi tot modis, tot partibus usurpavere
miraculum.*   8 Ekkehard of Aura, *Chronica*, ed. F-J Schmale and I Schmale-Ott
(Darmstadt, 1972), p. 140: *magna quippe pars eorum cum coniungibus ac prole totaque re*

noteworthy that countless people set out, with women and children (*wifan and cildan*).⁹ The near contemporary Annals of Augsburg say that along with warriors, bishops, abbots, monks, clerics and men of diverse professions, 'serfs and women' (*coloni et mulieres*) joined the movement.¹⁰ The Annals of St Giles of Brunswick state that in 1096 'many nobles, kings and also the commoners of both sexes began to strive for Jerusalem with armed might.' The reference to 'kings' is inaccurate, but the brevity of the entry does indicate that the annalist found the presence of both sexes as particularly noteworthy.¹¹

The epic poem, the *Chanson d'Antioche*, which, it is generally accepted, contains eyewitness material, has the lines: 'There were many ladies who carried crosses, and the (freeborn) French maidens whom God loved greatly went with the father who begat them.'¹² Anna Comnena, the daughter of the Byzantine emperor, Alexius I, writing in the 1140s gave a brief description of the People's Crusade whose unusual make-up must have been a striking feature. She remembered seeing 'a host of civilians, outnumbering the sand of the sea shore or the stars of heaven, carrying palms and bearing crosses on their shoulders. There were women and children too, who had left their countries.'¹³ In his description of the disastrous aftermath of the battle of Civetote, 21 October 1096, Albert of Aachen wrote of the Turks who came to the camp of the crusaders, 'entering those tents they found them containing the faint and the frail, clerks, monks, aged women, young boys, all indeed they killed with the sword. Only delicate young girls and nuns whose faces and beauty seemed to please the eye and beardless young men with charming expressions they took away.'¹⁴ This description by Albert is particularly important in that it draws attention to the previously barely noticed fact that nuns (*moniales*) came on the crusade.

Even after the slaughter at Civetote, many women were assimilated into the Princes' Crusade. It is clear, indeed, that large numbers of women were travelling with the princes' contingents. In Brindisi on 5 April 1097 the first ship of those sailing with Robert of Normandy capsized, and Fulcher, a cleric in the

---

familiari onusti proficiscebantur. **9** *The Anglo-Saxon Chronicles*, ed. Michael Swanton (London, 2000), p. 323. **10** *Annales Augustani*, MGH SS 3, p. 134. **11** *Annalium S. Aegidii Brunsvicensium Excerpta.* 1096, MGH SS 30, p. 10: *Eodem anno multi nobilium, regum quam eciam vulgi utriusque sexus armata manu Iherosolimam tendere ceperunt.* **12** *Chanson d'Antioche*, II.2, lines 9–12, ed. P. Paris (Geneva, Slatkine Reprints, 1969 of the edition of 1832–48), p. 72: *Des dames i ot maintes qui ont les crois portées; Et les frances pucieles que Diex a moult amées O lor pères s'en vont quit les ont engenrées.* See also Susan B. Edginton, '*Sont çou ore les fems que jo voi la venir?* Women in the *Chanson d'Antioche*' in S.B. Edginton and S. Lambert (eds.), *Gendering the Crusades* (Cardiff, 2001), pp. 154–62, at p. 155. **13** Anna Comnena, *The Alexiad*, X.5, trans. E.R.A. Sewter (London, 1979), p. 309. **14** Albert of Aachen. *Historia Hierosolymitana*, I.21 p. 119 (RHC 4, 228): *tentoria vero illorum [omitted by Ms. A] intrantes quosquos repererunt laguidos ac debiles, clericos, monachos [omitted by Ms. A], mulieres gradeuas, pueros, sugentes, omnen vero etatem gladio extinxerunt. Solummodo puellas teneras et moniales quarum facies et forma*

chaplaincy of count Baldwin of Bouillon, wrote of the incident that four hundred 'of both sexes' perished by drowning.[15] Fulcher describes the united army at Nicea as containing women and children.[16] The *Chanson d'Antioche* indicates that the camp of the crusaders had a particular women's section, which was raided by the Turks shortly after the siege of Nicea:

> Firstly, turning their violence on the ladies,
> Those who attracted them they took on horseback,
> And tearing the breasts of the old women,
> When the mothers were killed their children cried out,
> The dead mothers suckled them, it was a very great grief,
> They climbed up on them seeking their breasts,
> They must be reigning [in heaven] with the Innocents.[17]

The anonymous author of *Gesta Francorum* says that at the battle of Dorylaeum, on 1 July 1097: 'the women in our camp were a great help to us that day, for they brought up water for the fighting men to drink, and bravely always encouraged them, fighters and defenders.'[18] Of this incident the *Chanson d'Antioche* says:

> The baronage was thirsty, it was greatly oppressed;
> The knights of Tancred strongly desired water.
> They were greatly served by them who were with them.
> The ladies and maidens of whom there were numerous in the army;
> Because they readied themselves, they threw off their cloaks,
> And carried water to the exhausted knights,
> In pots, bowls and in golden chalices.
> When the barons had drunk they were reinvigorated.[19]

During the battle, Turkish horsemen were sent to cover a possible line of retreat, and the near contemporary *Historia Vie Hierosolimitane* records that they 'cruelly put to the sword almost a thousand men, women, and unarmed,

oculis eorum placere videbatur, iuvenesque inberbes et vultu venustos adbuxerunt.
15 Fulcher of Chartres, *Gesta Francorum Iherusalem Peregrinantium*, RHC 3, 330: *utriusque sexus.*   **16** Ibid., p. 332.   **17** *Chanson d'Antioche*, III.4, lines 15–21, pp. 152–3: *Premièrment aus Dames vont leur regne tournant, Celes qui lor contequent es sieles vont montant, Et aus vieilletes vont les mamelles torgant. Quant les mères sont moretes, si crient li enfant, Sor les pis lor montoient, les mameles querant, La mère morte alaitent; ce fu dolor moult grant, El regne aus innocents doivent estre manans.* See also Susan B. Edginton, 'Women in the *Chanson d'Antioche*', p. 155.   **18** *Gesta Francorum*, ed. R. Hill (Oxford, 1962) p. 19: *feminae quoque nostrae in illa die fuerunt nobis in maximo refugio, quae afferebant ad bibendum aquam nostris preliatoribus, et fortiter semper confortabant illos, pugnantes et defendentes.*   **19** *Chanson d'Antioche*, III.11, lines 3–10, p. 159–60: *Li barnages ot soif, si fu moult oppressés; Forment desirent l'aigue li chevalier Tangrés. Mestier lor ont éu*

common folk.'[20] Further along the march in the arid stretches of Asia Minor, in July 1097 William of Tyre noted the presence of women on the crusade, and their suffering, 'Pregnant women, because of the rigours of both thirst and of the intolerable heat were forced to expel the foetus before the time decreed by nature. Through sheer mental distress they cast them out in coverlets, some of them alive, some half dead. Others with more humane feelings embraced their offspring. They fell down along the route and forgetful of their feminine sex exposed their secret parts. To a great extent they were more apprehensive about the immediate risk of death than that about the preservation of the reverence that was due to their sex.'[21] Albert of Aachen refers to there being thousands of women and children at the siege of Antioch that began 21 October 1097.[22] The *Gesta Francorum* has a description of a woman in the camp of Bohemond being killed by an arrow during that siege.[23] In the plague that followed the capture of the city women were notably more likely to be victims.[24] At the climactic denouement of the first crusade, the capture of Jerusalem, 13–15 July 1099, women were still present in considerable numbers, sharing the work and bringing water and words of encouragement to the men. Indeed, according to William of Tyre, 'however even women, forgetful of their sex, and having grown heedless of frailty, presumed to take up the use of arms, they played a manful role above their strength.'[25]

This by no means exhaustive selection of references to women on the crusade, from a range of sources, establishes without a doubt that women were present in large numbers. But is it possible to focus more closely on the women present in the first crusade and indicate something of their motivation?

celes de leur regné, Les dames et pucieles dont il i ot assés; Quar eles se rebracent, les dras ont jus jetés, Et portèrent de l'aigue aus chevaliers lassés, As pos et as escueles et as henas dorés: Quant ont bu li baron tout sont resvigorés. See also Susan B. Edginton, 'Women in the *Chanson d'Antioche*', p. 155.   **20** Gilo of Paris and a second, anonymous author, *Historia Vie Hierosolimitane*, ed. C.W. Grocock and J.E. Siberry (Oxford, 1997). pp. 86–7: *crudeliter ense necauit, Mille viros ferme, mulieres, vulgus inerme.*   **21** William of Tyre, *Chronicon*, III.17 (16), ed. R.B.C. Huygens, Corpus Christianorum 63 (Turnhout, 1986), pp. 217–18: *pregnantes pre sitis angustia et caloris intemperie ante tempus a natura decretum fetus edere compellerentur, quos pre anxietate spiritus quosdam vivos, extinctos quosdam, alios etiam semineces in strate proiciebant; alie, ampliore habundantes humanitate proles suas circumplexe, per vias volutabantur et sexus oblite feminei archana denudabant, magis pro instante mortis periculo sollicite quam ut sexui debitam conservarent reverentiam.*   **22** Albert of Aachen, *Historia Hierosolymitana*, III.37, p. 252 (RHC 4, pp. 93–133): *absque sexu femineo, et pueris sequentibus quorum milia plurima esse videbantur.*   **23** *Gesta Francorum*, p. 29: *Exibant quidem alii de civitate, et ascendebant in quamdam portam, et sagittabant nos, ita ut sagittae eorum caderent in domini Boamundi plateam; et una mulier occubuit ictu sagittae.*   **24** William of Tyre, *Chronicon*, VII.1, p. 344.   **25** William of Tyre, *Chronicon*, VIII.13, p. 403: *sed et mulieres, oblitae sexus, et inolitae fragilitatis immemores, tractantes virilia, supra vires, armorum usum apprehendere praesumebant.*

One group of women whose presence and role is most easily understood are those who were members of the aristocracy.[26] Because the sources are largely written for the benefit of the aristocracy, and because historians such as William of Tyre, are interested in the genealogy of the leading noble families in Outremer, we are in a position to name some of the aristocratic women involved in the crusade. Raymond of Toulouse brought with him on the crusade his third wife, Elvira, daughter of Alfonso VI of Castile by his mistress, Ximene.[27] Baldwin of Boulogne, later count of Edessa, also brought his wife, Godehilde of Tosny, 'an illustrious lady of high rank from England' says William of Tyre.[28] Interestingly Godehilde's first cousin, Emma of Hereford, came on the crusade with her husband Ralph I of Gael – which, as J. Riley-Smith observes, is a good example of the fact that many of the aristocratic crusaders were connected by kinship ties.[29] Bohemund brought his sister with him on crusade and once he and his nephew[30] Tancred had obtained their impressive landholdings in Outremer, he sought and received suitably prestigious marriage partners. Bohemund married Constance and Tancred her half-sister Cecilia, both daughters of Philip I of France. It is likely that count Baldwin du Bourg brought at least one of his sisters with him as she later (12 September 1115) married Roger, prince of Antioch.[31] Walo II, lord of Chaumont-en-Vexin brought his wife, Humberge, daughter of Hugh Le Puiset and sister of the crusader Everard.[32] On the death of Walo, Humberge is described as being supported by a band of mature ladies (*matres*).[33] Many other lesser nobles, intending to stay in the newly won crusader states were, in all likelihood, accompanied by their wives and sisters. A charter from St Martin des Champs allows us to name Emeline, wife of Fulcher a knight of Bouillon for example.[34] These women seem to have played no independent role in the crusade. Their actions or words are not mentioned. This is hardly surprising given that for an aristocratic woman to have a measure of authority *c.*1100 she would have had to be a widow with a

---

26 For a full discussion of their presence on the crusade see S. Geldsetzer, *Frauen auf Kreuzzügen 1096–1291* (Darmstadt, 2003), esp. Appendix 2, pp. 184–7.　27 Guibert of Nogent, *Gesta Dei per Francos*, p. 134.　28 William of Tyre, *Chronicon*, X.1, p. 453: *uxorem ex Anglia duxit, illustrem et nobilem dominam Gutueram nomine.*　29 J. Riley-Smith, *The First Crusaders, 1095–1131* (Cambridge, 1997), p. 91 (Emma), p. 93 (Godehilde).　30 The relationship that historians have generally reached consensus upon, see R.L. Nicholson. *Tancred: A study of his career and work in their relation to the First Crusade and the establishment of the Latin states in Syria and Palestine* (Chicago, 1940), pp. 3–15, who opts, based on a discussion of the contemporary evidence, for Tancred being the son of Bohemund's half-sister Emma, whereas she is shown as a full sister to Bohemund but without supporting evidence in the Hauteville family tree in E. van Houts, *The Normans in Europe* (Manchester, 2000), p. 298.　31 William of Tyre, *Chronicon*, XI.3, p. 498.　32 Gilo of Paris and a second, anonymous author, *Historia Vie Hierosolimitane*, p. 127.　33 Or *neruis* in version D *m. pr.*, Gilo of Paris and a second, anonymous author, *Historia Vie Hierosolimitane*, p. 126.　34 J. Riley-Smith, *The First*

sizeable patrimony or a mother with significant influence over powerful sons. It was the next generation of aristocratic women who controlled property in the kingdom of Jerusalem who were able to wield some political power, or indeed those women left behind by their noble husbands. The women of the nobility present on the initial expedition were brought to generate families should the conquest be successful and were not in a position to play an independent political role during the campaign. Indeed if their male guardian died on the crusade such aristocratic women could be placed in a difficult position; Humberge is given a speech on the death of Walo which includes the question: 'other than with a man, can a woman live following the camp?'[35] Although dependent on Ovid for the phrase, Gilo posed the question in the contemporary setting of the crusade, using the classical reference to indicate the dependency of the position of aristocratic women on their guardians.

Beyond the aristocratic women there were far greater numbers of women of the other social orders. There is no possibility of finding out their names or much detail concerning their backgrounds. However, eyewitness descriptions of the gathering of forces for the first crusade have important information to offer. It is clear, first of all, that women from the social order of *pauperes*, both urban and rural poor, came with their husbands and children on the crusade. Guibert of Nogent, for example, was amused at the setting forth of entire families of the poor from southern France: 'you were seeing extraordinarily and plainly the best of jokes; the poor, for example, tied their cattle to two-wheeled carts, as though they were armoured horses, carrying their few possessions, together with their small children, in the wagon. And these infants, when coming to a castle or a city, enquired eagerly if this were the Jerusalem to which they strained.'[36]

From Pope Urban II's letter to the clergy and people of Bologna of September 1096, it is clear that the unexpected departure of large numbers of non-combatant forces was a concern and a development to be restrained.[37] But it is hardly surprising that peasants undertaking the crusade with the expectation of finding a better life moved in entire families. As Ekkehard disapprovingly observed, 'the farmers, the women and children, roving with unheard of folly, abandoned the land of their birth, gave up their own property and yearned for that of foreigners and go to an uncertain promised land.'[38] There can be no

Crusaders, p. 201.   **35** Gilo of Paris and a second, anonymous author, *Historia Vie Hierosolimitane*, pp. 128–9: *Absque viro uiuet femina castra sequens?*   **36** Guibert of Nogent, *Gesta Dei per Francos*, p. 120: *Videres mirum quiddam et plane ioco aptissimum, pauperes videlicet quosdam, bobus biroto applicitis eisdemque in modum equorum ferratis, substantiolas cum parvulis in carruca convehere et ipsos infantulos, dum obviam habent quaelibet castella vel urbes, si haec esset Jherusalem, ad quam tenderent rogitare.*   **37** Urban II, letter to the clergy and people of Bologna, in H. Hagenmeyer (ed.), *Epistulae et Chartae ad Historiam Primi Belli Sacri spectantes quae supersunt aevo aequales ac genuinae* (repr.: Hildesheim, 1973), pp. 137–8.   **38** Ekkehard of Aura, p. 140: *Chronica, ruricolarum, feminarum ac parvulorum quasi inaudita stulticia delirantes subsannabant,*

question of describing such women as prostitutes or camp followers. These married women were non-combatant participants like the elderly, the clergy and the children on the crusade.

In addition to married women of urban and rural poor families, there is also evidence that unattached women participated in the Crusade. For this there are five important and interesting sources. The first has already been presented: Albert of Aachen's fury that what should be been a chaste undertaking in the manner of all pilgrimages was contaminated by licentiousness.[39]

The second is a description of the recruiting activities of Peter the Hermit by Guibert of Nogent. Peter was an enormously influential figure in generating support for the crusade and headed the 'People's Crusade' that preceded the 'Princes' Crusade': '[the] commoners [...] slender in possessions but most abundant in number, clung to a certain Peter the Hermit ... we saw him circulating through cities and townships for the purpose of preaching, surrounded by such numbers, being given such great gifts and being praised for such saintliness that I remember no one to be held in such high honour. For he was liberal towards the poor showing great generosity from the goods that were given to him, making wives of prostitutes [*prostitutae mulieres*] through his gifts to their husbands.'[40]

Guibert's use of the term *prostitutae* needs to be put in context. In contemporary ideology, particularly that of a monk, for a woman to fail to give an appearance of modesty, let alone for her to engage in sexual activity outside the bonds of marriage, meant she was considered a prostitute.[41] In fact canonists found it very difficult to define prostitution. A letter by Jerome (*c*.342–420) contained the definition that 'a whore is one who lies open to the lust of many men'. In the same letter Jerome clarifies this by saying that 'a women who has been abandoned by many lovers is not a prostitute.'[42] It was the first formulation that was to be used by Gratian for his widely distributed *Decretum* (*c*.1140).[43] In other words, the early twelfth-century concept *prostitutae* was far broader and much more detached from financial exchange than the modern term prostitute. For example, the term was used by reformers to refer to priests' wives, women

---

utpote qui pro certis incerta captantes terram nativitatis vane relinquerent, terram repromissionis incertam certo discrimine appeterent, renunciarent facultatibus propriis, inhiarent alienis.   **39** See above, note 3.   **40** Guibert of Nogent, *Gesta Dei per Francos*, p. 121: *tenue illud quidem substantia sed numero frequentissimum vulgus Petro cuidam Heremitae cohesit ... urbes et municipia predicationis obtentu circumire vidimus, tantis populorum multitudinibus vallari, tantis muneribus donari, tanto sanctitatis preconio conclamari, ut neminem meminerim simili honore haberi: multa et enim fuerat ex his quae sibi dabantur dilargitione erga pauperes liberalis, prostitutas mulieres non sine suo munere maritis honestans.*   **41** As summarised in J.A. Brundage, *Sex, law and marriage in the Middle Ages* (Aldershot, 1993), I, p. 378.   **42** Jerome, *Epistula*, 64.7, *PL* 22, col. 611: *Meretrix, quae multorum libidini patet*; col. 612: *Non meretricem, quae multis exposita est amatoribus.* **43** Gratian, *Decretum*, C.XVI. See J.A. Brundage, *Sex, law and marriage in the Middle*

who would have considered themselves entirely respectable. Given this context, it seems reasonable to understand Guibert's *prostitutae mulieres* as wandering women – his sense of proper place being offended in a manner similar to his attitude towards runaway monks – rather than their literally being 'prostitutes'.

In an article unrelated to the crusade G. Duby made a comment that is extremely helpful in analysing the description given by Guibert of the activities of Peter the Hermit. In discussing the consequences of the drive to reform the church from 1075–1125, Duby wrote: 'Prostitution flourished in the rapidly expanding towns, thronging with uprooted immigrants. Above all, there were those women without men that the reform movement had itself thrown out onto the street, the wives abandoned by husbands because they were priests, or if laymen, because they were bigamists or had contracted an incestuous union. These women were to be pitied, but they were also dangerous, threatening to corrupt men and lead them astray …'[44]

The fact that Peter the Hermit was providing dowries to 'prostitutes' has been noted by E.O. Blake and C. Morris as showing that his was an urban audience.[45] But it seems possible to draw a further conclusion, that Peter the Hermit was using his gifts to gather a following amongst marginalized women. Those who accompanied him on crusade should therefore, once more, not be considered camp followers in the conventional sense. In the period of the first crusade these women were *prostitutae* only in the sense that they were unmarried and as such a cause for concern, particularly to the clergy who were anxious at the potential social disorder they might cause and the contamination of the purity of the pilgrimage. The reforming concept of pilgrimage was closely related to that of the Truce of God, a clerically-led peace movement that emphasized chastity and abstinence during the period of peace.

The third source, Raymond of Aguilers, gives very detailed accounts of the speeches of peasant visionaries, from which it is possible to detect elements of the political programme of the poor crusader. In one vision of St Andrew to Peter Bartholomew, 30 November 1098, we have evidence that the body of unmarried women was still a cause for concern, as the saint says 'amongst your ranks is a great deal of adultery, though it would please God if you all take wives.'[46] This idea seems remarkably similar to the aims of Peter the Hermit who was closely linked to the *pauperes*, for whom, in part, Peter Bartholomew was speaking. Guibert of Nogent, writing for the edification of his congregation

Ages, p. 827.   **44** G. Duby, *Women of the twelfth century*, I: *Eleanor of Aquitaine and six others*, trans. J. Birrell (Cambridge, 1997), p. 36.   **45** E.O. Blake and C. Morris, 'A hermit goes to war: Peter and the origins of the First Crusade', *Studies in Church History* 22 (1984), pp. 79–107.   **46** Raymond d'Aguilers, 'Historia Francorum qui ceperunt Iherusalem', ed. John France, (unpublished PhD thesis, University of Nottingham, 1967), p. 171 (RHC 3, 269): *Inter vos caedes et … plurima adulteria: quum Deo placitum sit, si uxores vos omnes ducatis.* I am grateful to Prof. France for permission to quote from

of monks, says that the measures taken on the Crusade against unmarried
women were far more severe than desiring they be married off. Having made the
point that those requiring the protection of God should not be subject to lustful
thoughts, he wrote that 'it happened there that neither a mention of harlot or
the name of a prostitute was tolerated ... because if it was found that any of
those woman was found have become pregnant, who was proven to be without
husbands, she and her procurer were surrendered to atrocious punishments ...
Meanwhile it came to pass that a certain monk of the most famous monastery,
who had left the cloister of his monastery and undertaken the expedition to
Jerusalem, being inspired not by piety but by shallowness, was caught with
some woman or other. If I am not mistaken he was found to be guilty by the
judgement of red-hot iron, and finally the bishop of Le Puy and the others
ordered that the miserable woman with her lover be led naked through all the
corners of the camps and be most fearfully lashed by whips, to the terror of the
onlookers.'[47] That Guibert is particularly vehement on this point is
unsurprising given his purpose. As Brundage has noted, the incident is likely to
have some basis in fact given that Albert of Aachen tells a similar story.[48]

Fourthly, a more precisely observed episode of relevance occurred at a
moment of great strain for the crusade, January 1098, during the siege of
Antioch, when famine was causing the movement to disintegrate. During this
crisis the higher clergy managed to gain an influence over the movement, which
they were not subsequently able to maintain. Their argument that to weather
the crisis particularly devout behaviour was required carried the day and
therefore their hostility to the presence of unmarried women on the crusade
surfaced in the form of a decision that women should be driven from the camp.
Fulcher – at the time in Edessa – wrote that 'the Franks, having again consulted
together, expelled the women from the army, the married as well as the
unmarried, lest perhaps defiled by the sordidness of riotous living they should
displease the Lord. These women then sought shelter for themselves in
neighbouring towns.'[49] William of Tyre describes the same incident as being a
more limited purge of solely 'light foolish women' (*leves mulierculae*).[50] This

his thesis.   **47** Guibert of Nogent, *Gesta Dei per Francos*, p. 196: *Unde fiebat ut ibi nec
mentio scorti nec nomen prostibuli toleraretur haberi ... quod si gravidam inveniri constitisset
aliquam earum mulierum, quae probantur carere maritis, atrocibus tradebatur cum suo lenone
suppliciis. Contigit interea quemdam predicatissimi omnium coenobii monachum, qui
monasterii sui claustra fugaciter excessarat et Iherosolimitanam expeditionem non pietate sed
levitate provocatus inierat, cum aliqua femina ibi deprehendi, igniti, nisi fallor, ferri iudicio
convinci ac demum Podiensis episcopi ceterorumque precepto per omnes castrorum vicos miseram
illam cum suo amasio circumduci et flagris nudos ad terrorem intuentium dirissme verberari.*
48 Albert of Aachen, *Historia Hierosolymitana*, III.46, pp. 261–2 (RHC 4, 370–1).
49 Fulcher of Chartres, *Gesta Francorum Iherusalem Peregrinantium*, RHC 3, 340: *tunc facto
deinde consilio, ejecerunt feminas de exercitu, tam maritatas quam immaritatas, ne forte luxuriae
sordibus inquinati Domino displicerent.*   **50** William of Tyre, *Chronicon*. IV.22, p. 264.

incident reveals the presence of significant numbers of unmarried women on the crusade and that given the opportunity the senior clergy moved to drive them away and give the movement a character more in keeping with the reforming military pilgrimage that pope Urban II had envisaged.

Finally, I wish to consider the fifth piece of direct evidence for the presence of large numbers of unmarried women on the crusade, an excerpt from the chronicle of Bernold of St Blaisen. 'At this time a very great multitude from Italy and from all France and Germany began to go to Jerusalem against the pagans in order that they might liberate the Christians. The lord pope was the principal founder of this expedition … an innumerable multitude of poor people leapt at that journey too simple-mindedly and they neither knew nor were able in any way to prepare themselves for such danger … It was not surprising that they could not complete the proposed journey to Jerusalem because they did not begin that journey with such humility and piety as they ought. For they had very many apostates in their company who had cast off their monastic habits and intended to fight. But they were not afraid to have with them innumerable women who had criminally changed their natural clothing to masculine clothing with whom they committed fornication, by doing which they offended God remarkably just as also the people of Israel in former times and therefore at length, after many labours, dangers and death, since they were not permitted to enter Hungary they began to return home with great sadness having achieved nothing.'[51]

The importance of Bernold's work is that it is the most contemporary eyewitness account of the setting forth of the crusade. He did not wait for the end of the year to write up his chronicle and therefore it is particularly valuable in recording the immediate response to events. It is notable that he shares with Guibert of Nogent a sense that women leaving their allocated social position are similar to monks casting off their habits. Bernold's description of women dressing as men in order to go on crusade is supported by an entry in the Annals of Disibodenberg, which states that news of the expedition depopulated 'cities of bishops [and] villages of dwellers. And not only men and youths but even the greatest number of women undertook the journey. Wonderful indeed was the

---

51 Bernold of Constance, *Chronicon*, 1096, pp. 527–9: *His temporibus maxima multitudo de Italia et omni Gallia et Germania Ierosolimam contra paganos, ut liberarent christianos, ire cepit. Cuius expeditionis domnus papa maximus auctor fuit… Nimium tamen simpliciter innumerabilis multitudo popularium illud iter arripuerunt, qui nullomodo se ad tale periculum praeparare noverunt vel potuerunt… Non erat autem mirum, quod propositum iter ad Ierosolimam explere non potuerent, quia non tali humilitate et devotione, ut deberent, illud iter adorsi sunt. Nam et plures apostatas in comitatu suo habuerunt, qui abiecto religionis habitu cum illis militare proposuerunt. Sed et innumerabiles feminas secum habere non timuerunt, quae naturalem habitum in virilem nefarie mutaverunt, cum quibus fornicati sunt; in quo Deum mirabiliter, sicut et Israheliticus populus quondam offenderunt. Unde post multos labores, pericula et mortes, tandem, cum Ungariam non permitterentur intrare, domum inacte cum magna tristicia ceperunt repedare.*

spirit of that time in order that people should be urged on to this journey. For women in this expedition were going forth in manly dress and they marched armed.'[52]

It is possible to see women taking men's clothing as a form of protection for their journey. Their action could also be a form of social statement, indicating a desire to be considered pilgrims. Both ideas are present in a twelfth-century saint's life, that of St Hildegund, who is disguised by her father, a knight, during their travels on crusade to Jerusalem and who retains her garb to become a famous monk whose secret is only revealed upon her death.[53]

The prescriptions against women wearing men's clothes would have been well known at the time of the first crusade, for example that in Burchard of Worms' widely disseminated *Decretum*: 'if a woman changes her clothes and puts on manly garb for the customary female clothes, for the sake, as it is thought, of chastity, let her be anathema.'[54] Guibert of Nogent also tells an interesting story in his autobiography in which men and women overcome their fear and distaste of cross-dressing in order to disguise themselves for an escape.[55] Nevertheless by this time there was an almost respectable tradition of pious women disguising themselves as men to escape persecution or to live like monks, for example, Pelagia, Thecla, Anastasia, Dorothea, Eugenia, Euphrosyne, Marina and Theodora.[56] Whether these tales had any influence over the cross-dressing crusaders is entirely speculative, but it is possible to draw at least one unambiguous conclusion from the description in Bernold and the Annals of Disibodenberg, which is that these women did not attach themselves to the movement as prostitutes – male attire and the bearing of arms being completely inappropriate for such a role.

Insofar as historians have considered the role of women on the first crusade they have tended to make the assumption that the majority of women were associated with the movement as camp followers, prostitutes. A closer examination of the evidence suggests that this is an error and that the thousands of women who went on the crusade – to find a promised land, or to get away from the towns in which many of them had been abandoned – did so as participants, as pilgrims.

---

52 *Annales s. Disibodi*, MGH SS 17, p. 16: *regna rectoribus, urbes pastoribus, vici vastantur habitatoribus; et non tantum viri et pueri, sed etiam mulieres quam plurimae hoc iter sunt aggressae. Mirabilis enim spiritus illius temporis homines impulit ad hoc iter aggrediendum. Nam feminae in hanc expeditionem exeuntes virili utebantur habitu et armatae incedebant.*   53 A. Butler, *Butler's lives of the Saints, April* (London, 1999), pp. 141–2. See also V.L. Bullough and B. Bullough, *Cross dressing, sex and gender* (Philadelphia, 1993), p. 54.   54 Buchard of Worms, *Decretum*, VIII.60, *PL* 140, col. 805A: *Si qua mulier propter continentiam quae putatur, habitum mutat, et pro solito muliebri amictu virilem sumit, anathema sit.*   55 Guibert of Nogent, *De Vita Sua*, *PL* 156, cols. 930D–931A: *Vir plane muliebrem non verebatur, nec mulier virilem.*   56 D. Farmer, *Oxford dictionary of saints* (Oxford, 1997), p. 396 (Pelagia), p. 462 (Thecla). J. Coulson (ed.), *The saints: a concise biographical dictionary* (London, 1958), p. 28 (Anastasia), p. 160 (Eugenia), p. 177 (Euphrosyne), p. 300 (Marina), p. 428 (Theodora). See also V.L Bullough and B. Bullough, *Cross-dressing, sex and gender*, p. 51.

Secondary offenders? English women and crime, c.1220–1348[*]

Richard J. Sims

Crime has been a boundless source of fascination in the western world through the ages, from antiquity to the present day. This interest has extended beyond the realms of reality and broken into fiction, but it is fair to say that scholarly thought has followed this trend at a slow pace and, despite the emergence last century of the discipline known as 'criminology', historians have lagged behind. Despite the abundance of legal records in England, both legal and social historians have tended to ignore crime in the Middle Ages, as they see few interesting developments with regard to its place in the legal framework, a viewpoint exemplified by S.F.C. Milsom:

> The miserable history of crime in England can be shortly told … Nothing worth-while was created. There are only administrative achievements to trace.[1]

In fact, a great deal more attention has been devoted to the mechanism of the medieval criminal justice system than to the individuals actually committing the crimes. Even those writers who have devoted time to studying the behavioural patterns of medieval criminals have concentrated on the activities of members of the nobility, rather than the peasantry, and largely on organized crime.[2] They have also consistently ignored the role played by the female sex. Indeed, it was only the pioneering work of Barbara Hanawalt in the 1970s which sought to address these voids.[3] This study follows on from Hanawalt, but uses records

* I am most grateful to Dr Janet S. Loengard of Moravian College, Pennsylvania, for taking time to provide comments and suggestions. 1 S.F.C. Milsom, *Historical foundations of the common law* (London, 1981), p. 403. 2 E.L.G. Stones, 'The Folvilles of Ashby-Folville, Leicestershire, and their associates in crime', *Transactions of the Royal Historical Society*, 5th series, 7 (1957), pp. 91–116; J.G. Bellamy, 'The Coterel gang: an anatomy of a band of fourteenth-century criminals', *English Historical Review* 79 (1974), pp. 698–714. 3 B.A. Hanawalt, 'The female felon in fourteenth-century England', *Viator* 5 (1974), pp. 253–68; *Crime and conflict in English communities, 1300–1348* (Cambridge, Mass., 1979).

from the south and south-west, rather than the eastern parts of England, and in a slightly earlier period.

THE LEGAL FRAMEWORK

Medieval English law recognized a distinction between felonies (grave criminal offences whose perpetrators met with execution) and trespasses (lesser offences resulting in a fine, imprisonment, or another milder form of punishment).[4] In later years, as the distinction between crime and tort widened, trespasses became known as misdemeanours to avoid confusion with civil law.[5] The significance of this distinction only waned in England in very recent times[6] and still applies in the United States. The 'crimes' discussed herein are felonies and, in particular, the two most common felonies of the medieval period, homicide and the various forms of theft.

Felonies all attracted the death penalty, but for those prepared to make the sacrifice, it was possible to avoid a capital sentence by seeking sanctuary in a church. The accused could remain there undisturbed for forty days, and would be supplied with food and drink. When these forty days had elapsed, he or she could choose to abjure the realm. In this event, the accused would be required first to confess before the coroner, after which he or she would be assigned a port, usually the nearest, sent there dressed as a pilgrim and carrying a wooden cross and told to leave England, never to return. Any deviation from this route was punishable by hanging. As well as this legal penalty, there was the obstacle of aggrieved victims and their relatives, who might try to avenge the abjurer, if he or she were to return. The other obvious way to avoid the death penalty was to flee justice, or simply to refuse to appear. This would result in the forfeiture of chattels, and the accused – if male – would be 'exacted and outlawed'. Because of their inferior legal position, women could not be outlawed in the same way. As Bracton explains:

> a woman ... cannot be outlawed because she is not under the law, that is, in frankpledge or tithing, as is a male of twelve years and upwards; thus, she cannot be outlawed, but when she has taken flight for a felony she may well be waived and regarded as one abandoned, for waif is that which no one claims.[7]

Such legal technicalities would have provided little comfort to the female fugitive. She too could expect to be hanged if caught and, despite their inferior

4 F. Pollock and F.W. Maitland, *The history of English law*, 2 vols (London, 1956), vol. 2, p. 466.   5 J.H. Baker, *An introduction to English legal history* (London, 1979), p. 572. 6 Criminal Law Act 1967.   7 *Bracton de Legibus et Consuetudinibus Angliae*, ed. G. Woodbine, trans. S.E. Thorne, 4 vols (New Haven, 1968), vol. 2, pp. 353–4.

legal status, ordinarily women were accorded no special treatment merely on account of their sex.

The only occasion on which women were able to use the peculiarities of their sex to their advantage was when they became pregnant. Canon law protected the unborn child of the convicted woman, and provided that she could enjoy a stay of execution at least up to the birth of the child. A body of women known as a 'jury of matrons' was selected to determine the validity of the defendant's claim, a practice which continued for centuries in both criminal and civil trials.[8] In later times, once they had given birth, women were often reprieved and given a lighter sentence, perhaps transportation.[9] In the medieval world, though, expectancy would do nothing more than delay the inevitable and, as a result, few women would have feigned pregnancy. It is true that prisons of the time were mixed institutions, but we should be wary of Hanawalt's idea that repeated pregnancies were 'impossible to avoid'. She does cite one individual, a Matilda Hereward of Northamptonshire, who found herself pregnant on numerous occasions while in gaol, even many months after her husband had been hanged.[10] Undoubtedly, such occurrences would have been commonplace if male prisoners were not deprived of the company of the fairer sex, but this is an unlikely scenario. Starting with York castle in 1237, there was segregation of the sexes within gaols, just as there was segregation between petty offenders and more serious criminals.[11] Opportunities for any social interaction were probably minimal in most gaols, and it is unlikely many women were able to rely on a state of perpetual pregnancy to help them dodge the gallows.

General defences against accusations of felony were available in a primitive form in the thirteenth century. The one of most interest, as far as women were concerned, was marital coercion. Agnes le Folur appeared before the courts charged with larceny, arson, harbouring criminals and other offences.[12] Although found guilty, it was held that she should be acquitted, as she was called on by her husband to carry out unlawful deeds. Bracton tells us that, as a rule, a wife was subservient to her husband but she 'need not be obedient in heinous deeds'.[13] In other words, it was not necessary to take part in wrongdoing to prove obedience, but the law was sympathetic to women who did take their loyalty to felonious ends. In modern English law, the defence of coercion by a husband is still available[14] but

8 The last recorded use is believed to be *Blakemore v Blakemore* (1845) 71 ER 769. J.Oldham, 'Jury research in the English Reports in CD-ROM', in J.W. Cairns and G. McLeod (eds), *The dearest birth right of the people of England: the jury in the history of the Common Law* (Oxford and Portland, 2002), pp. 131–53 at p. 134.   9 J. Oldham, 'On pleading the belly: a history of the jury of matrons', *Criminal Justice History* 6 (1985), pp. 1–64.   10 Hanawalt, *Crime and conflict*, p. 43.   11 R.B. Pugh, *Imprisonment in medieval England* (Cambridge, 1968), p. 352.   12 C.A.F. Meekings (ed.) *Crown pleas of the Wiltshire eyre of 1249* (Wiltshire Archaeological and Natural History Society, 16, Devizes, 1961), pl. 146, p. 180.   13 Woodbine, *Bracton De Legibus*, vol. 1, p. 151. 14 Criminal Justice Act 1925, s.47.

is seldom used and has become so rare that it has an uncertain future.[15] Although in its embryonic stage seven centuries ago, it arguably afforded wives much greater protection than is possible now. Then, unlike now, the defence covered homicide. Secondly, it may have been applied more generously. A mere sense of love or duty is no longer seen as a valid basis for claiming coercion.[16] This *did* seem to be sufficient in the late Middle Ages. Despite her role in a criminal act, the law was prepared to recognize Agnes' extenuating circumstances arising from the institutionalized male control over women that existed in the thirteenth century, and to concede that, while there should be a limit to uxorial obedience, this was difficult to enforce. Moreover, it was prepared to do so without the need to show that her husband had applied threats or motivated her in any specific way. The mere fact that he had enlisted his wife's help was apparently enough to convince the court that there were sufficient grounds. This sympathetic attitude was enhanced in the sixteenth century, where the mere existence of husband/wife collaboration was often enough for coercion to be inferred.[17] What better example could there be of the development of criminal law reflecting changes in society?

CRIMES AGAINST THE PERSON

The most serious felony in medieval England, as is the case with most societies, was homicide.[18] Unlike property crimes, its victims are seldom selected at random, nor are they always chosen by using materialistic criteria. Antagonism, whether long-standing or immediate, is the prime motivation and, because of this, the culprit and the victim are more likely to be reasonably well-acquainted. There is no reason to suppose that women in thirteenth-century England should have broken with this trend, especially as their social circles were small, and opportunities to develop relationships outside the normal run of everyday life were more restricted than in the modern age. More often than not, the records neglect to mention how the two parties knew each other, but we cannot assume this meant they were strangers. Indeed, the relationship with the victim may have been very close indeed.

Infanticide has long been perceived as being almost exclusively in the female domain and for this reason is a form of familial homicide which deserves special attention. It has become fashionable among historians to play down the

---

15 The Law Commission (Law Com. No. 83) has recommended its abolition.   16 *R v. Richman* [1982] Crim. LR 507.   17 C.Z. Wiener, 'Is a spinster an unmarried woman?', *American Journal of Legal History* 20 (1976), pp. 27–31; V.C. Edwards, 'The case of the married spinster: an alternative explanation', *American Journal of Legal History* 21 (1977), pp. 260–5.   18 Treason, the most serious offence of all, was classed separately and its definition set down in the Treasons Act 1351.

prominence of infanticide in the Middle Ages, but determining how widespread it actually was is difficult, as there is a great variance in the records.[19] Hanawalt's figures show that, from her sample of coroners' rolls, only four out of 4,000 homicides (0.1%) could be described as infanticide.[20] Elsewhere, she claims that just three out of 5,000 (0.06%) fall into that category.[21] Her methodology is somewhat misleading, though, insofar as her figures play down the relative regularity of homicides involving older children. The complications arise in part because of the law's failure to provide a strict definition of infanticide, before the 1624 statute clarified matters.[22] Hanawalt herself proceeds to explain that 247 out of 1,409 violent deaths (17.5%) from her counties involved children under the age of twelve.[23] This statistic suggests rather dramatically that the killing of young people was much more common than her argument would at first imply. The numbers of infants killed under the age of one year might have been even higher, but the widespread phenomenon of secret births prevents an easy assessment. Moreover, it is widely accepted that courts would pass off a case or two of homicide as misadventure. In one particular instance, a woman named Agnes Tuppel struck a six-month-old boy, William son of Michael the vintner 'so that he died at once'. The fact that she did so with an axe lends some credibility to C.A.F. Meekings'[24] view that coroners often turned a blind eye to unlawful and deliberate killing.[25] This was especially true for children. Although they were more likely than adults genuinely to encounter accidental death, through folly and curiosity, this also meant that their killings were potentially easier to disguise. If women had a greater ability to conceal crimes, as many have suggested, then infanticide was an ideal opportunity for them to exercise this gift. There was huge scope for disposal of the bodies, and for creating excuses. Killing of one's own offspring was still uncommon and the particular distaste expressed today might well have been shared by our ancestors[26] but, then as now, children were at risk on account of both their physical vulnerability and the stress of child-rearing.

Much is made of the fact that infanticide was 'culturally alien' and an abomination to the deeply cherished concept of the family as the essential and

19 G. Brucker, *The society of renaissance Florence* (New York, 1971), p.147; R.C. Trexler, 'Infanticide in Florence: new sources and first results', *History of Childhood Quarterly* 1 (1973–4), pp. 98–116 at pp. 103ff.; B.A. Kellum, 'Infanticide in England in the later Middle Ages', *History of Childhood Quarterly* 1 (1973–4), pp. 367–88; R. Helmholz, 'Infanticide in the province of Canterbury during the fifteenth century', *History of Childhood Quarterly* 2 (1975), pp. 382–89; Hanawalt, *Crime and conflict*, p. 154. 20 Hanawalt, *'Of good and ill repute': gender and social control in medieval England* (New York, Oxford, 1998) , p. 168.   21 Hanawalt, *Crime and conflict*, p. 154.   22 Infanticide Act 1624. Discussed in J.A. Sharpe, *Crime in early modern England, 1550–1750* (London and New York, 1999), p. 88.   23 Hanawalt, *Crime and conflict*, p.155.   24 *Wiltshire eyre of 1249*, pl. 322, p. 213.   25 Ibid., introduction, pp. 67–9.   26 J. Given, *Society and homicide in thirteenth-century England* (Stanford, 1977), p.61, provides several examples

sacred unit of medieval society.[27] There is a danger that this view will blinker the historian's efforts in trying to elucidate the true incidence of child-killing. Nonetheless, it cannot be denied that medieval peasant life revolved to a very large extent around the home and this raises the puzzling question of whether that setting would increase or decrease the likelihood of women killing other members of their family. The fact that domestic life was treated so seriously suggests there would have been a strong revulsion to killing members of their family. Evidence of homicide between blood relations is extremely rare, and accounted for around 6.5% of all killings.[28] This compares very favourably to 18.95% in eighteenth-century Wiltshire[29] and 24.79% in modern-day America.[30] The discrepancy is even more striking when one considers the close proximity in which peasant families lived, and the forced intimacy they had to endure as a result of living conditions. Houses were small, on average between 25 and 50 ft. in length and 12 and 16 ft. in width.[31] Any which were substantially larger than this would probably accommodate some animals as well, so an average family of five would enjoy no more than about 90 sq. ft. per person. If any atmosphere is conducive to conflict, it must have been that suffered by medieval English peasants. Hanawalt agrees that spatial confinement was no guarantee of security for either women or men.[32] Elsewhere, though, she argues that homicides at this time were motivated by a desire for "dominance in the community", and that killing one's own family did not meet such an end.[33] Some may well have been motivated by power but there is nothing to suggest that thirteenth-century homicides were not also motivated by envy, anger, lust, or a multitude of other timeless sins. The only acceptable explanation for the increase in homicide within the family in subsequent centuries must be one which acknowledges the crucial role of this institution in medieval society, and the importance attached to kinship. When women *did* kill members of their household or their family, the victim was most likely to be the husband. Bearing in mind that much greater domestic tension flourished here than with blood relations, this should not be surprising. However, we are given no sense that the murder of husbands was a regular occurrence. In the entire Devon Eyre of 1238, there is not a single case of a woman killing her husband,[34] although two aided and abetted such deeds.[35] In the past it has been held that spouses seldom killed each other, because of the

using largely anecdotal evidence.   27 Trexler, 'Infanticide in Florence', p.103. 28 Given, *Society and homicide*, p. 55.   29 R.F. Hunnisett (ed.), *Wiltshire coroner's bills, 1752–1796* (Wiltshire Record Society, 36, Devizes, 1981), introduction, pp. xlviii-xlix. 30 M.E. Wolfgang, *Patterns in criminal homicide*, (Philadelphia, 1958).   31 C.C. Dyer, (ed.), *Everyday life in medieval England* (London and Rio Grande, 1994), p. 155. 32 Hanawalt, *Good and ill repute*, p. 82.   33 Hanawalt, *Crime and conflict*, pp. 167–8. 34 Although two were acquitted of such a charge. H. Summerson (ed.), *Crown pleas of the Devon eyre of 1238* (Devon and Cornwall Record Society, n.s. 28, Torquay, 1985), pl. 291, p. 53 and pl. 756, p. 121.   35 Ibid., pl. 184, p. 37 and pl. 579, p. 95.

severity of the reaction, both judicial and social. After all, technically speaking, the murder of a husband was petty treason against her lord. However, the example Summerson cites from Devon in 1281, where a woman was burned on these grounds, is almost certainly exceptional.[36] In reality, it was much more usual for murderous wives to face hanging, as criminals rather than traitors.

James Given, in his heavily statistical work, claims that homicide at this time had a distinctly collective nature because of what he terms 'bonds of mutual dependence' among peasants.[37] Records from the west of England defy this trend, though, and his theory is certainly not borne out in Devon where, in 1238, only six killings were the work of more than two men, and the vast majority committed by individuals acting alone.[38] Women, however, were different. Even in the West Country they sought (or were asked to provide) assistance and it was rare to find them participating alone. In the 1239 Devon Eyre there was not a single case of a woman acting alone and in Wiltshire a woman was three times more likely to act in company than a man was.[39] Very often, she acted in collaboration with her husband and, as we have seen, sometimes she would be *forced* to assist him. At other times, the cooperation would have been more willing. Lone female killers were few and far between in the Middle Ages. They constituted a mere 16.7% in the east and the Midlands, according to Given's figures[40] and 20% in Wiltshire.[41] Sadly, Given's figures are less than helpful as he records all *suspected* women rather than those actually convicted. But, by and large, it is fair to say women throughout the land preferred to commit homicide with somebody else, be it a husband, a lover, a brother or another woman.

Although records are often unhelpful in this respect, we know that killers employed various methods to dispatch their victims, and a variety of weapons were used. Scythes and the like were vital tools in tending the land, and men and women alike would have had easy access to knives, as they were used not only in performing agricultural tasks, but also by all classes of society in eating.[42] Dean has brushed aside the significance of the ubiquitous nature of these dangerous implements and has asked why, if knives were so commonplace, they were so seldom used as weapons, by both men and women, being employed in 'only a third of homicides'.[43] Aside from the obvious response, that this is actually quite a high proportion (much higher indeed than today), the answer must surely lie in the fact that alternatives were equally accessible. These other weapons of destruction did not involve much imagination: everyday items such

---

36 *Devon eyre of 1238*, introduction, p. xxix. JUST. 1/86, m. 5d.   37 Given, *Society and homicide*, pp. 43, 100.   38 *Devon eyre of 1238*, introduction, p. xxx.   39 Eight out of ten cases, *Wiltshire eyre of 1249*.   40 Given, *Society and homicide*, pp. 41–54.   41 In Wiltshire, a mere two homicide cases were committed by women alone, *Wiltshire eyre of 1249*.   42 P.W. Hammond, *Food and feast in medieval England* (Stroud, 1993), p. 58. 43 T. Dean (ed.), *Crime in medieval Europe* (London, 2001), p. 22.

as rocks and sticks were used with deadly intent. However, more obvious weapons such as axes and hatchets were also popular. This helps us to understand why so many homicides were spontaneous. Because they were carried about the person, spur-of-the-moment attacks would have been possible in a way that could not occur in modern western society, in environments where weapons, even in the United States, are not carried legitimately on such a regular basis.

We have already discussed the fallibility of legal records of the Middle Ages, so to what extent can these figures provide an accurate reflection of patterns of criminality? Many historians and sociologists have espoused the theory that women are more adept at concealing criminal activity.[44] While this is based on rather dubious psychology, it is a theory which is hard to disprove on the evidence. If women *were* truly successful in concealing crimes, they would leave no trace. Not all killings were violent. Sometimes, more subtle techniques are evident, and nearly always it was women who employed them. Poisoning, for example, was not only less violent but less likely to lead a trail to the killer. There are a few cases of women who tried to divest themselves of unwanted husbands in this manner.[45] There is virtually no evidence, on the other hand, of male killers going to the trouble of using 'clever' methods such as these, perhaps lending some credibility to the idea that women, if not actually more cunning, were more understated.

For every deliberate killing, committed with independence of mind, there were other cases where the apportioning of blame was less clear-cut. As well as general defences to crimes modern common law (and now, also statute) recognizes specific homicide defences, and these were apparent in some form in the thirteenth century.[46] As we have seen, the law of pardons recognized the importance of the *mens rea* of killing and this led to a distinction between criminal and excusable homicide, but the distinction between different degrees of felonious homicide did not come about until 1390 and the term 'manslaughter' was not used until 1510.[47] One must ask whether the law's failure to recognize manslaughter may have had an effect on the conviction rate for homicides, with equitable 'not guilty' or 'misadventure' verdicts being recorded instead, in the absence of any intermediate plea.

Insanity was another common law defence which cropped up occasionally in the medieval period. Although a general defence, which was sometimes used by those accused of theft or arson,[48] it has usually been associated with homicide and, poignantly, it was most likely to be employed by women when they were accused of killing their own children. It seems appropriate, then, to discuss the plea of insanity and the crime of homicide together. In an age where much

---

44 O. Pollak, *The criminality of women* (Philadelphia, 1950), p. 10.   **45** F. Pedersen, *Marriage disputes in medieval England* (London, 2000), pp. 197–8.   **46** T.A. Green, 'Societal concepts of criminal liability for homicide in medieval England', *Speculum* 47 (1972), pp. 669–94.   **47** Baker, *English legal history*, p. 601.   **48** Pathological arsonists are discussed in J.E.D. Esquirol, *Mental maladies: a treatise on insanity* (New York, 1965).

research has been carried out into mental illness, it is difficult to imagine the complications this would have caused in the thirteenth century. Even today, the fate of the criminally insane is a controversial one. Although it was agreed that the insane should be spared the gallows, the law was unclear as to the alternatives. It would have been neither legally appropriate, nor politically prudent, to allow a madwoman to return to the community whence she came, although Bracton seems to imply that any other course of action would amount to wrongful punishment, as lack of *mens rea* must necessarily entail acquittal:

> ... for a crime is not committed unless the will to harm be present.[49]

The declaration was prophetic, as the sixteenth century proved, when it became common practice to acquit, rather than grant a pardon to, the insane killer.[50] Thirteenth-century justices saw the dangers in such measures and, once a pardon had been granted, it was the responsibility of the madwoman's family to ensure future good behaviour.[51] In the absence of suitable medical provisions, it was about the only option available. There was still some element of paternalism, though. The crown would confiscate the chattels of the insane woman and, from that money, provide a living for her, being as Pollock and Maitland put it 'morally bound to maintain the idiots out of the income of their estates'.[52] Upon recovery, the chattels would be returned to the rightful owner.[53]

The Middle Ages had a surprisingly sophisticated understanding of what insanity entailed, and certainly there was a belief from a very early date that those of an unsound mind should enjoy special treatment.[54] Theories abounded as to the cause of mental illness, ranging from the scientific to the superstitious.[55] At one end of the scale, there seemed to be a primitive understanding of manic depression and melancholia. At the other, there was a belief that the crescent moon had a debilitating effect on one's mental state, whence the word 'lunatic' derives, although this may not have been in common usage at the time.[56] In several cases, the records simply state that there was a crescent moon in the sky, or refer to the waxing of the moon, as if this alone was enough to explain the

49 Woodbine, *Bracton De Legibus*, vol. 2, pp. 340–41. 50 N.D. Walker, *Crime and insanity in England* (2 vols, Edinburgh, 1973), vol. 1, p. 26; N.D. Hurnard, *The King's pardon for homicide before A.D. 1307* (Oxford, 1969), p.159. 51 T.A. Green, *Verdict according to conscience: perspectives on the English criminal trial jury, 1200–1800*, (Chicago, 1985), pp. 86–93. 52 Pollock and Maitland, *History of English law*, vol. 1, p. 481. 53 Walker, *Crime and insanity*, vol. 1, pp. 24–25. 54 A most interesting recent study of this matter traces the plea of insanity back to Ancient Greece. D.N. Robinson, *Wild beasts & idle humans: the insanity defence from antiquity to the present* (Cambridge, Mass., 1998). 55 T.F. Graham, *Medieval minds: mental health in the Middle Ages* (London, 1967); Hanawalt, *Crime and conflict*, p. 146. 56 *Piers Plowman*, Prologue to version B. The adjective 'lunatic' was used from about 1300. *Chambers Dictionary of Etymology* (Edinburgh and New York, 1998), p. 615.

behaviour of the culprit: *res ipsa loquitur*.[57] Debilitating physical illness was also an acceptable basis for madness, as in the case of Margery Martyn, suffering from an acute fever, who took a knife and killed her husband.[58] However, in the same way that it was not deemed necessary to explain the motives of criminals, it was not usually considered important to try to explain the nature of the madness, but we cannot infer from this that there was no concept of the distinction between its different forms. With regard to the killing of children, there were clearly two kinds of susceptible women, suffering from distinct types of madness. The traumatic psychological effects of childbirth were understood sufficiently to allow recommendations for pardons to be granted to mothers who committed neonaticide, that is to say, those who killed their offspring in the immediate aftermath.[59] Secondly, there were women suffering from what we would today recognize as manic depression, who killed their children to save them from the horrors of the world around them. Quite clearly, the latter was not caused by the immediate consequences of the pains of childbirth, so jurors must have attributed such behaviour to other reasons.

The seventeenth century saw a torrent of pleas of insanity, leading Sir Matthew Hale to suppose that many were not genuine, and that a change in the law was necessary.[60] Four hundred years before, it seems, no such 'counterfeiting' took place. The defendant's eccentric behaviour would have been a rich source of gossip among villagers, and this was often enough to convince juries of madness. The admissibility of hearsay evidence ensured that juries could be more confident in their own evaluation. A sane defendant would have had an uphill struggle in convincing his peers otherwise. While its definition may be far-reaching in everyday parlance, insanity is in legal terms defined today very narrowly and, in the words of Radzinowicz, should 'not occupy more than one chapter of the whole range of cases covered by the term "mental illness"'.[61] Certainly, those involved in the administration of justice in the thirteenth century did not have such an acute understanding of these matters, but they were able to distinguish between different types of 'insanity', and they did adopt a sympathetic approach to women who used that defence.

In one Norfolk case, the behaviour of one allegedly insane man led his victim to employ a different defence. Late one night in 1312, with the moon (significantly in its cresent stage) providing the only light, Sybel Climne was walking home along the alleys of Middlegate in her hometown, Great Yarmouth. Suddenly, she encountered a strange man who took her hood and pulled it around her neck in an attempt to strangle her. Fearful for her own life and in a desperate bid

---

57 B.A. Hanawalt (ed.), *Crime in East Anglia in the fourteenth century: Norfolk gaol delivery rolls, 1307–16* (Norfolk Record Society, 44, 1976), pl. 244, pp. 50–1.   58 KB 27/327, m.36, cited in Hanawalt, *Crime and conflict*, p. 147.   59 Hurnard, *King's pardon for homicide*, p.169.   60 Baker, *English legal history*, p. 598.   61 L. Radzinowicz and J.W.C. Turner (eds), *Mental abnormality and crime* (London, 1944), introduction, pp. viii–ix.

to escape, Sybil took a small knife and plunged it into her assailant's stomach, killing him instantly. This was the story she told the court and she was able to produce a witness, Matilda Arnald, to testify.[62] The jurors believed her and a pardon from the king was sought.[63] Killing by self-defence (*se defendendo*) was pardonable but uncommon. Since the Statute of Gloucester in 1278, the application for a pardon for self-defence had become a more straightforward affair, with the judge reporting directly to the king without need for an enquiry.[64] Although the killing still theoretically incurred forfeiture of chattels, this was not put into practice and, in subsequent years, to avoid the confusion, straight verdicts of 'not guilty' were passed without the need for a pardon.[65]

Suicide (*felonia de se ipsa* was the usual Latin tag) was classed as a felony, and killing oneself was treated no differently from killing anybody else.[66] Although suspects could obviously not face trial in a physical sense, they were tried post-humously and, if found guilty, their chattels confiscated just like any other convict. Just as with every other felony, it entailed the confiscation of lands and chattels and consequently it was inevitable that some suicides would be disguised, thus making it difficult to determine how many deaths by misadventure were really cases of suicide. From the point of view of the townships or the tithings, there was no reason for them not readily to attribute deaths to misadventure rather than suicide. After all, their surviving inhabitants were in no danger, nor had any harm been caused to them.

Typically, accounts of suicide in legal records are brief, and little is divulged aside from names and, for women, marital status. Can we attribute certain common characteristics to murderers and suicides? One theory suggests that aggression cannot be directed both inward and outward at the same time.[67] This seems to be based on the Freudian notion that homicide and suicide are opposites. As a consequence, it is argued, different types of individuals were capable of the two acts. In the twentieth century, this has divided along socio-economic lines. Such conclusions can also be reached from evidence in the thirteenth and fourteenth centuries where on average suicides were five times richer than murderers.[68] Of course, this far-reaching theory fails to account for the many cases where murderers ended up taking their own lives.

62 This may not have been helpful. Witnesses for the defence were not sworn and there seemed to be some doubt surrounding their validity at all: Baker, *English legal history*, pp. 581–2.   63 Hanawalt (ed.), *Crime in East Anglia*, pl. 244, pp. 50–1. See above n. 57.   64 Baker, *English legal history*, p. 601.   65 J.M. Beattie, *Crime and the courts, 1600–1800* (Oxford, 1986), p. 87; Green, *Verdict according to conscience*, pp. 56–7.   66 It ceased to be criminal in England and Wales only with the Suicide (Decriminalization) Act 1961.   67 A. Henry and J. Short, *Suicide and homicide* (Glencoe, 1954).   68 £3 3s. for suicides and 13s. 2d. for homicides. These calculations are this author's, based on all cases from M. Clanchy (ed.), *Roll and writ file of the Berkshire eyre of 1248* (Selden Society, 90, London, 1973) and *Wiltshire eyre of 1249*.

Hanawalt's assertions that the two sexes committed suicide with 'equal frequency' and that females 'showed no preference for one form of death over another'[69] are not borne out by evidence from the printed sources from the western counties in the thirteenth century, where numbers of men resorting to suicide *did* outnumber women by fifteen to three (83.3%).[70] As well as showing greater reluctance, females were more consistent when they undertook the task. The methods by which self-killings were carried out tells us much of the tough nature of individuals of the time. There was no room for squeamishness in an age where instant and painless methods were not obvious. Probably one method which would have caused minimal suffering, if carried out with diligence, was hanging. This was an approach favoured by all three women in the above cases, while men chose more theatrical ways to end their lives, either by stabbing, cutting their throats, drowning or, in one especially gruesome incident, disembowelling. A direct comparison with the modern age would be unhelpful thanks to the introduction of firearms and other technological developments, but a female preference for non-violent means remains.[71] Drowning, starvation and so on may well have been more imaginative and dramatic, but if any gender-based psychological explanation can be deduced from these cases, it must surely be that women, when they did choose to kill themselves, were keen to do so in the least painful, quickest and most sensible manner. This sort of mentality conflicts with the stereotype of the female 'cry for help'. An alternative explanation is that men were more aware of the leniency with which suicides tended to be treated. Hanging could not possibly be construed as accidental in the same way that drowning could and perhaps the unusual methods were often attempts at disguise to save face but also, of course, to preserve one's chattels for the next generation. This brings to the fore the debate over the extent to which knowledge of the law and legal procedure could be found among the peasantry. While there has been much discussion on this matter by legal historians, there is nothing to indicate that women were in the dark any more than men. Finally, juries may have looked favourably upon male suicides who had contributed positively to the community, to enable them to keep their property within the family. At law, married women at least had no chattels.

At the heart of Given's argument seems to be the notion that the society of the time disapproved of calculated violence enacted both *by* and *against* women. Nonetheless, recent research seems to show that women participated in violent behaviour to the same degree as men, and that this was a pan-European phenomenon. This need not have anything to do with crime. There is evidence to suggest that women were as likely as men to use violence as a method of

69 Hanawalt, *Crime and conflict*, p.103.   **70** C.E.H. Chadwyck Healey (ed.), *Somerset pleas Richard I–41 Henry III* (Somerset Record Society, 11, Frome and London, 1897); *Devon eyre of 1238; Berkshire eyre of 1248; Wiltshire eyre of 1249.*   **71** L.I. Dublin, *Suicide: a sociological and statistical study* (New York, 1963), pp. 40, 221–2.

defending their honour.[72] Secondly, and more importantly from our point of view, if thirteenth-century English society was really so concerned with feminine fragility, is it not paradoxical that rape, the very embodiment of criminal masculinity, should have been treated with such apparent indifference? The reluctance of juries to convict, the number of appeals which were withdrawn mysteriously without reason, and the all-too-common 'compromise' reached between suspect and victim are all indicative of this attitude. A further impediment to justice was created by medical orthodoxy of the time, especially the idea that if a child was conceived, the woman must have consented to the intercourse.[73] This was a theory that outlived the Middle Ages, and remained the accepted wisdom throughout Europe for years to come.[74] Crucially, rape was not prosecutable by the crown prior to 1275 so the burden of proof rested with an individual, usually the victim, and it was not classed as a felony until 1285.[75] Late medieval society was brutal by our own sensitive standards and was governed by a different set of values. This brutality, alongside the ready availability of weapons, would frequently manifest itself in violence, supporting the school of thought that pre-industrial cultures which are yet to undergo a process of urbanization have a higher rate of violent crime.[76] This is a phenomenon which affected both sexes alike.

CRIMES OF PROPERTY

Theft took three forms: in ascending order of severity, larceny, burglary and robbery. Larceny (*latrocinium*) was the simple taking and carrying off of goods. Although the most common felony, there were certain legal restrictions. Land could not be appropriated through larceny, nor could wild beasts (*ferae naturae*) nor, in later centuries, could a host of other items.[77] Crucially, the offence could be of two kinds: grand larceny and petty larceny and, in the thirteenth century, the theft of anything whose value was less than a shilling was petty larceny, and not punishable by death. The threshold of a shilling was fixed because this was the sum deemed sufficient to keep a person alive for a week.[78] Burglary (usually *burglaria*) was the act of breaking into a building with felonious intent (*felonice*). There was no requirement for an intention to steal anything, as remains the case

72 N. Gradowicz-Pancer, 'De-gendering female violence: Merovingian female honour as "an exchange of violence"', *Early Medieval Europe* 11 (2002), pp. 1–18, cited in Dean, *Crime in medieval Europe*, p. 77.   73 R. Kittel, 'Rape in thirteenth-century England: a study of the common law courts' in D. Kelly Weisberg (ed.), *Women and the law: the social historical perspective* (Cambridge, Mass., 1982), vol. 2, pp. 104–05.   74 O. Hufton, *The prospect before her: a history of women in Western Europe* (London, 1995), p. 54.   75 3 Edw. I.   76 R. Quinney, 'Suicide, homicide and economic development', *Social Forces* 43 (1965), p. 224.   77 By the seventeenth century, it also included dogs, cats, singing birds and diamonds. Baker, *English legal history*, p. 606.   78 *Devon eyre of 1238*, introduction, p. xxxiv.

today.[79] Finally, robbery was the illegal acquisition of property through the use of violence, or the threat of violence.

Larceny was very much a crime of the times. The simple carrying off of unguarded property is not something which occurs today. Items of value are carefully protected, and theft of livestock is rarer, largely because of the declining dependence on agriculture. This perhaps helps to explain why, in twentieth-century America, where the historic definitions still exist, burglary has become more common than grand larceny.[80] In the Middle Ages, larceny was an activity which attracted a large number of females: in Wiltshire, eight out of 25 (32%) of all female-perpetrated crimes involved theft.[81] Of course, in absolute terms, women were still outnumbered and, even in this county, only made up eight of the 124 total thieves (6.5%) similar to the four of 76 cases (5.3%) in Berkshire.[82] Other nearby counties show similar patterns: six out of 92 (6.5%) in Devon and two out of 66 (3.3%) in Somerset.[83] This does not seem to have affected the likelihood of their conviction. In the year 1249 in Wiltshire, 12 out of 25 women tried were convicted (48.0%) compared with 188 out of 313 men (60.1%).[84] Allowing for a reasonable margin of error, these statistics cannot be said to conflict with Hanawalt's assertion that male and female conviction rates were roughly in line with each other.[85] There is little reason to suppose that either the law or society at large looked at female thieves any differently from their male colleagues. Those women who took it upon themselves to steal without assistance or collaboration were in a minority. As the status of married women and widows was usually reported, we can assume that they were mostly single.[86] Perhaps it was the financial insecurity of spinsterdom that led them down a path of crime.

The markets and fairs of medieval England were a vital element of the economy. They also provided excellent stamping grounds for petty theft and, to try to maintain order at a period of heightened turmoil, the institution of the fair court was established, with jurisdiction over all fairgoers. Mostly offences were committed by strangers, that is to say, those who were unknown both to the local community and very often to their fellow-merchants. There were some exceptions, such as Alice Tanner, a resident of St Ives, who was gaoled for theft in 1291.[87] Alice would certainly have been well-known locally. She was a long-term resident in the town, a prolific brewer of ale, and the wife of a juror,

79 Theft Act 1968, s. 9. Intention to commit rape or grievous bodily harm will suffice. 80 In 1963, there were 324.3 larcenies and 517.6 burglaries per 100,000 people. By the following year, larceny had increased by 13% and burglary by 16%. W.A. Lunden, *Facts on crime and criminals* (Ames, Iowa, 1961), p. 19.   81 *Wiltshire eyre of 1249.* 82 *Berkshire eyre of 1248.*   83 *Devon eyre of 1238; Somerset pleas Richard I–41 Henry III.*   84 *Berkshire eyre of 1248; Wiltshire eyre of 1249.*   85 Hanawalt, *Crime and conflict*, p.59.   86 This is true of all cases of lone female larcenists in Wiltshire, *Wiltshire eyre of 1249.*   87 E.W. Moore, *The fairs of medieval England* (Toronto, 1995), pp. 183, 345.

Nicholas Tanner. However, few well-known figures, especially those who relied on the custom of local people, would risk the blemish of a criminal record.

The divide between the two forms of larceny, grand and petty, is traditionally believed to have been established at the Second Statute of Westminster.[88] Roger Groot presents a most convincing argument that there existed a distinction between grand and petty larceny long before the Second Statute of Westminster.[89] He goes on to suggest that some juries manipulated the value, so as to allow a lesser punishment. In borderline cases, an artificially low value could be placed on an item or a set of items, to ensure that the thief was found guilty of petty, rather than grand, larceny, thus sparing her the ultimate penalty. Although this would have been an easy measure to take, evidence of such mercy is relatively scarce. On the contrary, the authorities seemed reluctant to settle for lesser charges. The first indication is the small number of petty larceny cases. In Berkshire of 1248, there were fifty-nine charges of grand larceny, compared with only three of petty larceny (a ratio of 19.6:1). Items stolen in the latter category included geese and hens and 'petty things' (*parvis rebus*).[90] At any rate, many women were forced to pay a higher price than the law demanded, and the argument put forward by European historians that women were punished less severely does not hold weight in England, with regard to theft or any other felony.[91] In one case, the original decision was overruled, but the news came rather too late, as the suspect had already packed her bags and departed the country:

> A certain Helen put herself in St Thomas' church in Salisbury and confessed to stealing a rochet.[92] The coroners and bailiffs of Salisbury city made her abjure the realm. Because Helen by [their] compulsion abjured the realm for so small a crime it is held that the bailiffs and coroners be in mercy.[93]

The fact that the coroner was amerced suggests a recognition that small thefts should not result in death (or in this case abjuration) but the failure to provide any details of specific value may lead one to wonder if in fact the twelve pence threshold was already as firmly established as Groot suggests. If it was a 'rule', how widespread was it, and how flexible? Certainly, it seems to have caused some confusion in this case. However, the practice of transforming a felony into a petty larceny or a trespass became more common as the years progressed. Groot is correct to point out the existence of some jury lenity as far back as the 1220s. There are cases of women avoiding the gallows after stealing goods of

88 3 Edw. I, c.15.   89 R.D. Groot, 'Petit larceny, jury lenity and Parliament' in Cairns and McLeod, *Dearest birth right*, pp. 47–61.   90 *Berkshire eyre of 1248*, pl. 725, p. 300; pl. 747, p. 306; pl. 891, p. 52.   91 C. Gauvard, *De Grace especial: crime, état et société en France à la fin du moyen âge* (Paris, 1991), pp. 300–28, cited in Dean, *Crime in medieval Europe*, p. 78.   92 Most likely this is any close-fitting vestment, although Groot specifies a smock. Groot, 'Petit larceny', p. 57.   93 *Wiltshire eyre of 1249*, pl. 557, p. 256.

little value in the early part of the thirteenth century, although even these sometimes resulted in harsh repercussions. In Plympton, Alice, a Cornish weaver, stole two pairs of shoes and had an ear cut off for her efforts (*absciditur eius auricula*).[94] Fifty years later, though, it was not unusual to see a relaxation of punishments and, by the turn of the century, very short terms of imprisonment were meted out regularly and a mere three weeks in gaol was often deemed suitable.[95] However, whatever the punishment, it was a step down from execution, and a sign that minor forms of theft were recognized in law. One must question, though, how strict this pre-Westminster "rule" was, and there is nothing to suggest that *parvis rebus* was a technical term with a precise meaning. After all, even in the years following Westminster, the twelve pence threshold cannot be said to have remained rigid. In the Kent Eyre of 1313, two men who stole a little over a shilling *between them* were executed.[96]

Another interesting point which emerges from this discussion is the new way in which gaols began to operate. For various misdemeanours, prison was starting to serve as a punishment in itself, and gaols were acting as more than the glorified waiting-rooms of the past. The evidence from Wiltshire brings into question the traditional view that incarceration was not a usual form of punishment until many centuries later, and Foucault's identification of the "birth of the prison" as being in the first half of the nineteenth century now seems a little incredible.[97]

Burglary differed from larceny, in that it involved the forceful entry into a building, with an intent to commit a felony. Usually, a phrase was used which referred to the breaking and entering, such as *felonice fregit domum*, but some complications are encountered. There was a marked lack of clarity and consistency, stemming from what seem to have been regional differences in the definition of the crime and this makes it difficult to produce any comparisons across England. There is also some confusion over whether it was necessary for the houseowner to be present in the building at the time.[98] In one Berkshire case, concerning what was initially described as burglary (*burglaria*), the actual conviction was for larceny. (*latrocinium*).[99] Because of the tendency for women to steal items of domestic utility, it was quite natural that they should try to break into houses to procure them. Hanawalt tells us that, in the thirteenth and fourteenth centuries, 'no particular talents were necessary to break into most medieval houses'.[100] Although it was primitive even by Tudor standards, we

---

94 *Devon eyre of 1238*, pl. 555, p. 91.   **95** R.B. Pugh (ed.), *Gaol delivery and Trailbaston trials, 1275–1306* (Wiltshire Record Society, 33, Devizes, 1978), passim.   **96** W.C. Bolland, F.W. Maitland and L.W. Vernon Harcourt (eds), *The eyre of Kent of 6 and 7 Edward II (1313–14)* (Selden Society, 24, London, 1909), p. 90.   **97** M. Foucault, *Discipline and punish: the birth of the prison* (London, 1979), pp. 23–5.   **98** Baker, *English legal history*, pp. 604–5.   **99** *Berkshire eyre of 1248*, pl. 786, p. 317 and pl. 855, p. 340.   **100** Hanawalt, *Crime and conflict*, p. 80.

must be careful not to underestimate the level of security employed by house-owners to deter unwelcome visitors. According to archaeological evidence, houses were not the flimsy structures that Hanawalt describes. The doors them-selves, hung on iron hinges, were no push-over, and were provided with iron locks.[101] An enormous amount of force would have been required to break these down. Wooden shutters, again with iron hinges, were also a common feature of windows in even the most modest peasant homes in the thirteenth century.[102] Such physical obstacles created huge difficulties for the would-be burglar and only the most cavalier house-breaker would attempt a forced entry without either a large dose of brute strength or careful planning beforehand. However, it seems that the women of the time were able to overcome these difficulties.

As well as the hindrance of security, there was the added worry of how to transport the appropriated goods. Again, women did not allow their sex to deter them from performing a successful getaway. When Isabel Avenaunt of Norfolk broke into the house of John Herbert, she was able to carry away a variety of goods useful for food and warmth with apparent ease: a tunic worth 3*s.*, two bushels of barley, and a large roll of canvas, in total amounting to 13*s.* 3*d.*[103] To smuggle all these items from the house single-handedly was no mean feat. Again, we must remind ourselves of the likely physical strength of the medieval peasant woman, and not dismiss her ability to undertake heavy tasks. The image in the popular imagination of the medieval peasant woman living a life of drudgery may be exaggerated, but the economy of the time relied strongly on heavy physical labour and women were often to be found in back-breaking work: mowing, haymaking and even mending roads.[104] Harvesting of grain was another common activity, and it was only in subsequent centuries that they were exempt from such heavy-duty work.[105]

Burglary sometimes took place in conjunction with another felony, arson. Although a relatively rare crime in the thirteenth century, arson was one which could arise from many motives. It could be used to conceal another crime, either *before* a theft to remove the inhabitants and avoid identification by witnesses, or *after* a theft or homicide to obliterate any traces. Such an arrangement lent itself to an obvious, if potentially hazardous, distribution of labour: one person would set fire to the premises while the other ransacked them. In Wiltshire, Agnes le Folur and Isabel of Bradford were accused of just this.[106] Many other reasons could usually be offered for burning houses, shops and barns.

> Mariota daughter of Philip the carpenter burned Stephen the smith of Pangbourne's house, and fled. She is suspected, so she is to be exacted and

101 Dyer, *Everyday life*, pp. 156–57. **102** Ibid, p. 157. **103** JUST 3/48, m.2d. **104** H. Leyser, *Medieval women: a social history of women in England 450–1500* (London, 1997), p. 148. **105** W. Rosener, *Peasants in the Middle Ages* (Cambridge, 1992), pp. 184–5. **106** *Wiltshire eyre of 1249*, pl. 146, p. 180. See above, n. 12.

waived ... Later it is attested that Mariota was captured and imprisoned
at Reading ... and escaped.[107]

Personal grievances would often result in revenge attacks, or would perhaps be
the culmination of a violent argument, but again the historian is frustratingly
deprived of any scandalous details, and the background behind crimes such as
Mariota's is usually left to the reader's imagination. Secondly, arson could be
used as part of an extortion scheme by gangs intent on terrorising householders,
but such cases are probably unreported due to the complex nature of such
rackets, which often involved a long chain of individuals.[108]

Robbery was a crime of terror, in which the perpetrator was prepared to act
in a physically aggressive manner and, if necessary, even take part in violent
skirmishes. Although it is true that some burglars were prepared to kill, this was
really only done *in extremis* and spontaneously when they were challenged by a
householder. The robber, on the other hand, used the threat of death as a tool
of the trade. The clearest characteristic of robbery was its masculinity, and it
attracted even fewer women to its ranks than other felonies. This fits in with the
general trend of women shying away from acts of calculated violence. Robbery was
an activity whose nature ensures that it has always been dominated by young men,
physically athletic, with no roots to bind them to one geographical area, and this is
certainly the trend in the modern era.[109] In all ages, the robber has needed to travel
to carry out his deeds and only a very few confined themselves to the locality. The
reasons for this do not need spelling out: carrying out robberies on one's doorstep
is certain to arouse suspicion before long. In the Berkshire and Wiltshire Eyres, few
were parochial in their outlook and only two robbers out of 34 (5.8%) lived in the
same hundred as their victim and committed the crime there.[110] The social
restrictions imposed on medieval women in terms of physical space and travel
prevented the freedom of movement necessary for such a life. That is not to
suggest that women were *never* involved in robbery or even in gangs but, when
they were, their most likely target was other women, as in the case of Alice de
Bruges. Accused of breaking into the chamber of a wealthy local lady, Philippa of
Reading, and taking a bag of money through force, she managed to escape justice
for the usual reason, because the victim failed to appear in court. Intimidation of
both victims and witnesses was unlikely to cause great problems, either moral or
practical, to hardened robbers. Terrorism was their trademark, and this was just as
likely to be applied after one of their number had been brought to trial. Even if,
according to the juries, they were innocent of committing any crime themselves, it
is perhaps not surprising that some women would follow robbers in their villainous

107 *Berkshire eyre of 1248*, pl. 1019, p. 389.   **108** J.G. Bellamy, *Crime and public order in
England in the later Middle Ages* (London and Toronto, 1972), pp. 75–7.   **109** F.H.
McClintock and E. Gibson, *Robbery in London: an enquiry by the Cambridge Institute of
Criminology* (London, 1961).   **110** *Berkshire eyre of 1248*; *Wiltshire eyre of 1249*.

pursuits. In Wiltshire, a woman by the name of Alice (daughter of Thomas of the reeve) followed the notorious robber William le Escot and on one occasion was accused of aiding and abetting him.[111]

The masculinity of the crime is more obvious when we see the extent to which it was connected to the rape of the female victim, as happened with some 14.7% of robberies in Berkshire and Wiltshire.[112] Indeed, the two crimes appear to be so intertwined that it is seldom clear which was the primary motivation, but the monetary rewards were potentially so magnificent that robbery is unlikely ever to have been far from the culprit's mind. Maud of Sundon, who was thrown from her horse, raped and then imprisoned for three days, also claimed that her ordeal involved the theft of her three gold rings and 20s. in cash.[113] Such a find was of enormous value, the money alone totaling more than half a year's wages for an unskilled labourer,[114] and was surely more than a chance discovery on the part of her assailant.

CONCLUSION

Medieval women were indicted (and subsequently convicted or acquitted) for fewer crimes than men. Despite the fact that the position of women has changed so dramatically in legal (and of course social) terms, this statement is as true in the England of the twenty-first century, as in the thirteenth and fourteenth. This study shows that a little under 10% of felonies were committed by women, not too distant from the seventeenth and eighteenth centuries where a lot more work has been carried out[115] and roughly in line with modern Britain (11.9%).[116] The only offence where women outnumbered men was in the counterfeiting of coins, which was a treason not a felony.

Rather than asking why so few females were involved in felonies, we should perhaps ask why, given their social situation, they were involved in so *many*. Today, women have time and opportunity. Their ancestors, by contrast, were isolated, spending most of their time at work, and nearly always confined to their homes. The social life of the European female peasant was virtually non-existent, yet she still managed to commit the same proportion of offences as her modern-day descendant. Of course, not all felonies required social interaction, but many did require planning. There are some cases of the medieval woman

---

111 *Wiltshire eyre of 1249*, pl. 311, pp. 210–11.   112 Five out of thirty-four cases. *Berkshire eyre of 1248*; *Wiltshire eyre of 1249*   113 *Berkshire eyre of 1248*, pp. 381–2. 114 C. Dyer with S.A.C. Penn, 'Wages and earnings in late medieval England: evidence from the enforcement of the labour laws' in Dyer (ed.), *Everyday life*, p. 167.   115 M. Feeley and D. Little, 'The vanishing female: the decline of women in criminal proceedings 1687–1912', *Law and Society Review* 25 (1991), pp. 719–57.   116 H. Mannheim, *Comparative criminology* (London, 1965), pp. 596–7, 677.

being coerced into wrongdoing by her master and lord which, as we have seen, sometimes resulted in acquittal. But there must have been other cases where she was obedient even to the gallows. The real solution lies in the fact that women were responsible for feeding their families and furnishing their houses and, when resources ran low, as they did in the early fourteenth century, they often resorted to theft and their involvement was far from peripheral. At first sight, this may seem to conflict with Hanawalt's theories of spatial confinement.[117] However, despite the tendency for women to stray from their own dwelling-places in search of food and clothing, their crimes were still committed within the village, and largely in neighbours' houses.

If we accept that the participation of women was large enough to merit curiosity, we must also accept that their role was very different from that of men. It is too sweeping simply to declare that they 'avoided homicide and preferred petty theft'.[118] Women were less aggressive in committing crimes, but not because they were deterred by some overpowering societal disdain for feminine violence, as has been suggested in the past. Medieval peasants were immersed in a tough culture and womenfolk were very much a part of it. Rather, it was because such felonies as larceny and burglary usually required no personal contact and could be undertaken with greater anonymity. Moreover, these were crimes whose rewards would benefit their family as well as them-selves on a very practical level. Even the techniques used by women in homicide and suicide were less violent. Again, though, it would be unwise to attribute this to the perceived public opprobrium of the time.

---

117 Hanawalt, *Of good and ill repute*, pp. 70–87.   118 Dean, *Crime in medieval Europe*, p. 23.

Representation, imitation, rejection: Chiara of Montefalco (d. 1308) and the passion of Christ*

Cordelia Warr

The visualization and imitation of Christ were central to thirteenth- and fourteenth-century spirituality. Saints and holy people increasingly focused their spirituality through the bodily re-enactment or re-presentation of Christ's Passion. Images, and thus the sense of sight, were central in religious practice. Representations of the Passion, in the form of paintings or sculptures, led to its imitation on the part of the viewer. Visual stimuli, real or imagined, provoked physical reactions.

A number of different strategies were used to ensure that the focus on Christ's suffering was maintained at the greatest possible pitch. The Franciscan author of the *Meditationes Vitae Christi*, written in the second half of the thirteenth century, advised his reader to 'be present at the same things that it is related that Christ did and said, joyfully and rightly, leaving behind all other cares and anxieties'.[1] 'Being present' during the Passion of Christ meant suffering with Christ. For many, this involved ensuring that every aspect of their lives was centred on the Passion. One means of doing this was to use the body as a means of inducing a mental state which would facilitate meditation on Christ's Passion.[2] Praying with arms extended in the form of a cross was a common monastic practice.[3] *De modo orandi*, a thirteenth-century prayer manual, describes the ways in which St Dominic (d. 1221) used to pray. Dominic's sixth mode of praying is described as follows:

* I would like to thank the Leverhulme Trust for a Research Fellowship (2002–2003) during which I completed research on this paper. Thanks also to Christine Meek and Catherine Lawless for their encouragement and patience.   1 Isa Ragusa (trans. and ed.) and Rosalie B. Green (ed.), *Meditations on the Life of Christ, an illustrated manuscript of the fourteenth century* (Princeton, NJ, 1961), p. 5.   2 William Hood, *Fra Angelico at San Marco* (New Haven and London, 1993), p. 200.   3 G. Penco, 'La preghiera a forma di croce', *Vita Monastica* 21 (1967), pp. 131–6.

Our holy father Dominic was also seen praying with his hands and arms
spread out like a cross, stretching himself to the limit and standing as
upright as he possibly could.[4]

It is clear from the text that, in assuming this position, Dominic intended to
imitate Christ on the cross:

And this was how the Lord prayed when he hung on the cross, his hands
and arms stretched out, when, with great cries and weeping, his prayer
was heard because of his reverence.

Visual stimuli also helped to induce imitation of Christ's Passion, especially
through meditation in front of a cross or crucifix.[5] According to *De Modo
Orandi*, Dominic's fourth way of prayer involved fixing 'his gaze on the
Crucifix, looking intently at Christ on the cross'.[6] The Blessed Margherita da
Cortona (d. 1297) also spent many hours praying in front of the cross in San
Francesco, Cortona, and, like St Francis, heard Christ speaking to her whilst
meditating before the image.[7] Representations of Christ and the saints were
regularly used in order to focus and encourage the prayers of the faithful who,
it is implied, needed these images as an aid to meditation and contemplation. In
1448, only eight years after the death of Francesca Bussa dei Ponziani, men and
women were reported as praying in front of an image of the Blessed Francesca
in Santa Maria in Trastevere, Rome.[8] For both boys and girls, images were
recommended instruments of religious education. Writing his *Regola del
governo di cura familiare* in the early fifteenth century, Cardinal Giovanni
Dominici advised that, 'The first thing is to have in the house paintings of holy
boys and young virgins'.[9] One version of the life of Catherine of Alexandria has
her going with her mother to visit a hermit who gave the young girl an icon of
the Virgin and Child.[10] Paintings and sculptures affected the behaviour of those

---

4 Simon Tugwell OP (ed.), *Early Dominicans: selected writings* (London, 1982), p. 98.
5 The Dominican friar Girolamo Savonarola (d. 1498) recommended meditation in
front of the crucifix. See Sixten Ringbom, *Icon to narrative: the rise of the dramatic close-
up in fifteenth-century devotional painting* (Doornspijk, 2nd ed., 1984), p. 20.   6 Tugwell,
Early Dominicans, p. 96.   7 Joanna Cannon and André Vauchez, *Margherita of Cortona
and the Lorenzetti: Sienese art and the cult of a holy woman in medieval Tuscany*
(University Park, PA, 1999), pp. 4, 23–24. See also Fortunato Iozelli (ed.), *Iunctae
Bevegnatis: Legenda de Vita et Miraculis Beatae Margaritae de Cortona* (Biblioteca
Franciscana Ascetica Medii Aevi 13, Grottaferrata, 1997), pp. 181, 253–4, 271, 275, 286,
396, 433.   8 Giovanni Brizzi, 'Contributo all'iconografia di Francesca Romana', in *Una
Santa tutta Romana: Saggi e ricerche nel VI centenario della nascità di Francesca Bussa dei
Ponziani*, ed. Giorgio Picasso (Siena, 1984), pp. 267–362 at p. 268.   9 See Catherine
King, *Renaissance women patrons: wives and widows in Italy, c. 1300–1550* (Manchester
and New York 1998), p. 24.   10 Dominique Rigaux, 'Women, faith and image in the late

who came into contact with them.[11] St Francis' encounter with the speaking crucifix at San Damiano demonstrates the suggestive power invested in images.[12] Images not only spoke, they also bled and cried.[13] Images – painted, sculpted, or in wax – did not only remind the viewer of the object of their meditations, induce certain mental or physical states, or form the focus of visions or other spiritual experiences; they were also used in order to record and commemorate miracles or visions. A vow made to the Franciscan Gerard Cagnoli (d. 1345) during a duel in 1346 resulted in an image of the saint being presented at his tomb.[14]

The use of images by holy women as foci for their religious devotions appears to have been widespread. The Blessed Aldobrandesca of Siena (d. 1309) was known to have meditated on Christ's Passion in front of a crucifix. Having received a vision resulting from the intensity of her meditations, she then proceeded to commemorate it by commissioning a painting.[15] Other holy women carried images around with them in order to aid their devotions. Jeffrey Hamburger has noted that the 'lives of holy women testify vividly to the use of images as instruments of affective piety'.[16] These women commissioned images on parchment or paintings on panel which aided their meditations and recorded their visions. They kept images with them at all times, tying them to their body, ensuring that they touched their skin, kissing them.[17] For some, images, especially those of the Passion, had a powerful effect. According to Angela of Foligno (d. 1309);

> Whenever I saw the Passion of Christ depicted, I could hardly bear it, and I would come down with a fever and fall sick. My companion, as a result, hid paintings of the Passion or did her best to keep them out of my sight.[18]

The reaction to paintings of the Passion described here may appear to be exaggerated. Nevertheless it exemplifies opinions held by theologians such as

Middle Ages', in Lucetta Scaraffia and Gabriella Zarri (eds), *Women and faith. Catholic religious life in Italy from late antiquity to the present* (Cambridge, Mass. and London, 1999), pp. 72–82 at pp. 72–3. See also Millard Meiss, *Painting in Florence and Siena after the Black Death* (Princeton, NJ, 1951), p. 107.   **11** See the discussion by Ringbom, *Icon to narrative*, pp. 13–19.   **12** St Bonaventure, *The Life of Saint Francis of Assisi*, ed. Cardinal Manning (Rockford, IL, 1988; first edition 1867), pp. 17–18.   **13** Michael E. Goodich, *Violence and miracle in the fourteenth century: Private grief and public salvation* (Chicago and London, 1995), pp. 142–3.   **14** Goodich, *Violence and miracle*, p. 35.   **15** Discussed by Chiara Frugoni in, 'Female mystics, visions, and iconography' in Daniel Bornstein and Roberto Rusconi (eds), *Women and religion in medieval and renaissance Italy*, trans. M.J. Schneider (Chicago and London, 1996), pp. 130–64, at p. 137.   **16** Jeffrey Hamburger, *Nuns as artists: the visual culture of a medieval convent* (Berkeley, Los Angeles and London, 1997), p. 177.   **17** Hamburger, *Nuns as artists*, p. 178.   **18** Quoted by Chiara Frugoni in 'Female mystics, visions, and iconography', p. 137.

the Franciscan St Bonaventure (d. 1274) and the Dominican St Thomas
Aquinas (d. 1274), who thought that images were the most effective means of
arousing the emotions.[19] This conviction about the power of images had a long
history in Christian thought, going back at least to Pope Gregory the Great
(d. 604).[20] Gregory's instruction that 'images are to be employed in churches,
so that those who are illiterate might at least read by seeing on the walls what
they cannot read in books'[21] was particularly relevant to mystics and women
viewers, who were held to be more susceptible to visual imagery and who were
also more easily affected by the emotions.[22]

Visual references informed the ways in which holy women were understood
by their contemporaries and the ways in which their *vitae* were constructed.
The life of Chiara of Montefalco, written by Berenger of Saint-Affrique shortly
after her death in 1308, contains descriptions of various visions, a number of
which were experienced by Berenger himself.[23] Chiara Frugoni has demonstrated
the extent to which these visions were interconnected and intertwined with
visual imagery.[24] Visual literacy was important in relation to the instruments of
the Passion found in Chiara's heart after her death on 17 August 1308.[25] An
early eighteenth-century woodcut accompanying an extract from Battista
Piergili's *Vita della Beata Chiara, detta della Croce di Montefalco*, which had first
been published in Foligno in 1640, shows the interior of Chiara's heart (fig. 1).
In a series of macabre events, some of which took place in the dead of night,[26]
the nuns of Chiara's convent eviscerated her body. They removed the heart and
entrails and then proceeded to cut open the heart. News soon circulated
through Montefalco that they had found the symbols of the Passion.[27] The
crown of thorns, the whip and the column, the rod and the sponge and the nails

---

19 Anne Derbes, *Picturing the Passion in late medieval Italy: narrative painting, Franciscan
ideologies and the Levant* (Cambridge, 1996), p. 188, n. 41. See also, David Freedberg, *The
power of images: studies in the history and theory of response* (Chicago and London, 1989), pp.
162–3.   **20** See, for example, Catherine King, 'Effigies: human and divine' in Diana
Norman (ed.), *Siena, Florence and Padua: art, society and religion, 1280–1400*. Volume 2:
Case Studies, (New Haven and London, 1995), pp. 105–27 at pp. 125–6.   **21** Quoted by
Freedberg in *The power of images*, p. 163.   **22** Ringbom, *Icon to narrative*, p. 18.
23 Michele Faloci-Pulignani, 'La vita di Santa Chiara da Montefalco scritta da Berengario
di Sant'Africano', *Archivio Storico per le Marche e per l'Umbria* 1 (1884), pp. 557–625 and
2 (1885), pp. 193–266.   **24** Chiara Frugoni, '"Domine, in conspectu tuo omne desiderium
meum": visioni e immagini in Chiara da Montefalco' in Claudio Leonardi and Enrico
Menestò (eds.) *Chiara da Montefalco e il suo tempo* (Florence, 1985), pp. 155–82.
25 Frugoni, '"Domine, in conspectu tuo omne desiderium meum"', p. 171.   **26** It was not
uncommon to deal with the bodies of saints, or those popularly revered as saints, in the
middle of the night in order to avoid undue commotion. St Dominic's translation, for
example, took place at night (23–24 May 1233). See Anita Fiderer Moskowitz, *Nicola
Pisano's Arca di San Domenico and its legacy* (University Park, PA, 1994), p. 7.   **27** Silvestro
Nessi, 'I processi per la canonizzazione di Santa Chiara da Montefalco', *Bollettino della
Deputazione di Storia Patria per l'Umbria* 65/2 (1968), pp. 103–60, at p. 103.

VERO RITRATTO DEL CUORE
DELLA B. CHIARA
DA MONTEFALCO, DETTA DELLA CROCE.

Con una succinta narrativa delli Misterj in esso ritrovati, cavata dalla di lei Leggenda.
dal Reverendissimo Signor BATTISTA PIERGILJ di Bevagna.

CVM CLARA PECTVS EXPLICAT

FVLGET CRVCIS MISTERIVM

PONE ME VT

SVPER COR TVVM

CANT. C.

SIGNACVLVM

Nacque la B. CHIARA l'anno del Signore 1268, nella Terra di Montefalco Diocese di Spoleto; Di anni cinque quasi avestela l'uso perfetto di ragione, entrò in Congregazione con alcune Serve di Dio, dove cominciò, e poi sotto la Regola di S. Agostino proseguì una vita santissima, & austerissima sopra ogni credere, fregiata d'ogni virtù in grado eroico. Fù favorita dal Signore di doni eminenti, come della Scienza Infusa, Spirito Profetico, cognizione de' Soprani Misterj, singolarmente della Santissima Trinità, significato nelle tre Palle (✱) trovate nel sete, non solo per esser queste a tutto simili nella grandezza, nella figura, nel colore, ma di peso eguale, e quel che cagiona singolar meraviglia, tanto pesa una sola, quanto le tre insieme, o le due, e contraposte nel bilancio una a due, pure si trovano in equilibrio. Contemplando fin la Fanciulla l'eccesso dell'amore Divino, mostrato a noi del patir di Gesù Redentore, e corrispose col più eccellente amore, che potesse avere in quella vita. Nè potea pensare ad altro, che alla di lui amara Passione, si che sagri Misterj, siccome ella con l'intelletto gli veniva contemplando, nel suo Cuore il Signore l'andava formando, lavorandoli in vera carne; come si vidde dopo il suo felice transito, seguito li 17. Agosto 1308. e dell'età sua li 40. quando aperto il suo Verginco Corpo, fu trovato il Cuore pieno di Miracoli. Primo; Perche era grande più assai del naturale, somigliando di grandezza la testa di un Putto. Secondo; Di dentro non era congiunto, o unito, ma diviso come un Reliquiario in due parti, le quali parti erano unite solo nella circonferenza, che poi fu diviso con un solo taglio di Rasojo. Terzo; Li Misterj erano di rilievo formati di materia carnofa, o più sotto nervosa; ciascuno di essi stava riposto dentro la carne del Cuore nella sua proporzionata concavità, dalla quale era disgiunto in ogni parte, eccetto nello stipide, che con un sol filo di carne era unito alla carne del Cuore, acciò si vedesse, ch'era opera Divina, e per tale fu riconosciuta da più Testimonj, e singolarmente da due Cardinali Giacomo Colonna, e Napolione Orfino, & altri Prelati di qualità. Per tanto si deve mirare questo ritratto non occhio più materiale, che corporale, e esercare d'imprimersi nel cuore quelli sacri Misterj, come erano scolpiti in quello della Beata, nel quale (✱) l'Imagine del Crocefisso era di lunghezza simile al Police di una Donna, alla quale s'aggionge lo stipide della Croce proporzionata, estremità dell'istessa Croce fuori delle Breccia, le quali corrispondendo al corpo con debita proporzione si vedevano elevate, e stese in alto. Un picciolo globo di

carne, che rappresenta la Testa, stava piegato verso il braccio destro, e grossamente vi si conoscevano li suoi delineamenti. La grossezza del Corpo era nel petto della grossezza del Police di Donna, comprensavi anco fa Croce, restringendosi a proporzione verso i piedi, e le braccia; l'estremità de quali non si conoscevano distintamente, ma però si vedevano formate le dita delle mani, e piedi. Il minore del corpo era bianco mortificato, eccetto nella piaga del Costato, che era di color livido, e dava nel rosso, dove era una picciola apertura, che dinotava la piaga del Signore. Questa istessa Imagine avea un Pannicello sottile come tela, che li copriva i fianchi, e rappresentava quel panno, che fu messo alli fianchi di Cristo in Croce. (B) Il Flagello, o Frusta era un nervo bianco durissimo della grossezza maggiore d'una penna d'Oca; Dalla parte inferiore di detto nervo vi era una legatura di carne molle, rappresentante quella correggiola, con cui si appendono le Fruste; Dall'altro capo del manico pendevano 5 nervicelli sottili di color livido rosseggiante, & in ciascuno di essi apparivano alcuni piccoli globi simili a nodi nella positura, che fono quei effigiati. (C) La Colonna era rappresentata da un nervo rotondo, e bianco, e per la sua durezza fomigliava pietra, intorno alla quale era un nervicolo sottile, che dinotava la Fune con cui fu legato il Signore. (D) La Corona di Spine veniva dimostrata da un mezzo circolo di nervicioli negri intrecciati insieme, dalla superficie de quali diramavano altri nervicioli corti somiglianti alle Spine di color rosso, e livido. (E) Li Chiodi erano rappresentati da tre nervicioli negri, uno de quali era più grande, e ciascuno legato al cuore nella punta con un filo di carne. (F) La Lancia veniva rappresentata da un nervo, che aveva di essa perfetta somiglianza. (G) La Spogna veniva dimostrata da un nervo di grossezza simile ad una penna d'Oca, nella cui fommità era un congerie di nervicelli quasi biondi. Or chi non stupirà di tali miracoli? Questi facri Misterj, devoto Lettore, scolpiti nel cuore della B. Chiara, fono l'impronta del Santo Regio del Signore, il quale se Sacri Cantici si sa intendere, che pretende scolpito ancora nel nostro cuore (Pone per se Signaculum super cor tuum). Sforziamoci dunque averti sempre avanti gli occhi della mente, perche conforme Noi gli verremo contemplando, il Signore ce gli verrà imprimendo, e se nell'ora della morte ci andarà segnando con questo Divino Sigillo, ci riconoscerà per suoi, e con l'istessa Beata ci farà partecipi della sua gloria. Amen.

IN FOLIGNO; Per Feliciano, e Filippo Campitelli Sampatori. Con Lic. de' Sup.

1   Interior of Chiara of Montefalco's heart with brief details of her life by Battista Piergili, Foligno, *c.*1730. (By permission of the British Library 85/865 C10)

used to crucify Christ were all identified within the heart.[28] In addition, when the sisters examined Chiara's gall bladder they found three globes of equal size, weight and colour, arranged in a triangle as the symbol of the Trinity.[29]

Evidence presented at the unsuccessful apostolic canonization procedure of 1318–19,[30] gives an indication of why the nuns decided to explore Chiara's heart. Sister Francesca of Montefalco testified that the nuns 'agreed that the body of Saint Chiara herself should be preserved on account of her holiness and because God took such pleasure in her body and her heart'.[31] The canonization process is not fully extant but it is clear from the surviving documentation that the reasons for cutting open the body, removing the entrails and heart, and then cutting into the heart, were of considerable interest to the investigators who were keen to eliminate all possibility of fraud or deception. Of the remaining testimonies, the statements of four witnesses bear directly on this matter. All were nuns in Chiara's convent: Giovanna, daughter of Egidio da

---

28 Faloci-Pulignani, 'La vita di Santa Chiara da Montefalco', 2, pp. 232 ff. See also Enrico Menestò, *Il processo di canonizzazione di Chiara da Montefalco* (Quaderni del 'Centro per il Collegamento degli Studi Medievali e Umanistici nell'Università di Perugia' 14, Agiografia Umbra 4, Florence, 1984), p. 26. Article 159 of the apostolic canonization process stipulates that proof was to be sought in relation to the claim that: 'the aforementioned Saint Chiara had in her heart and after her death were found in her heart the mystery and signs of the Passion, that is to say the cross or the true image of the crucified Christ, the whip or scourge with five slender cords, the column, with the other signs of the passion of Christ' ('Item dicit et probare intendit syndicus et procurator predictus quod sancta Clara predicta habuit in corde suo et post eius opitum in eius corde reperta fuerunt misterium et insignia passionis Christi, scilicet crux seu verius ymago Christi crucifixi, fusta seu flagellum cum V funiculis, columpna, cum aliis insigniis passionis Christi'). 29 Enrico Menestò, 'The apostolic canonization proceedings of Clare of Montefalco, 1318–1319' in Bornstein and Rusconi (eds), *Women and religion in medieval and renaissance Italy* pp. 104–29, at p. 105. 30 Unfortunately, complete documentation from the fourteenth-century apostolic canonization process has not survived. For a brief discussion of the surviving documentation, see Menestò, 'The apostolic canonization proceedings', pp. 106–08. The surviving documents have been published by Menestò in *Il processo di canonizzazione*. Chiara's life was first investigated by Berenger of Saint-Affrique in a process lasting from August 1308 until April 1309, instituted by permission of the local bishop. Further testimonies, relating to miracles experienced after April 1309, were taken up until 1315 and it was only then that Berenger was able to present his investigations to Pope John XXII in Avignon. The pope gave Cardinal Napoleone Orsini the job of investigating the matter further. The apostolic canonization process took place between 1318 and 1319 and its findings were summarised between 1328 and 1331 but no decision on Chiara's canonization was taken. See Nessi, 'I processi per la canonizzazione', pp. 105–8. 31 See Menestò, *Il processo di canonizzazione*, p. 339: '… concordaverunt quod corpus ipsius s. Clare deberet conservari propter sanctitatem suam et quia Deus in corpore et corde suo tantum se delectaverat'. 32 See Menestò, *Il processo di canonizzazione*, pp. 85–8, for Giovanna's testimony regarding the disembowelment and discovery of the signs of the passion.

Montefalco;[32] Marina, daughter of Giacomo da Montefalco;[33] Tomassa, daughter of the late Angelo of Montefalco;[34] and Francesca, daughter of Gualtiero of Montefalco.[35] Of these witnesses, only Marina was present at Chiara's disembowelment. Giovanna, who was by the time of the canonization process the abbess of the monastery, testified that she gave orders for the extraction of the heart, but distress at Chiara's death prevented her from being present to witness it. Tomassa, the 'rotaria' at the time, was not present for the disembowelling, but witnessed the discovery of the signs of the Passion in Chiara's heart. Francesca appears to have arrived on the scene slightly later, having been called by a certain sister Margarita to see what had been found within the heart. All were asked the reasons for which the nuns had decided to cut open the body, and all replied as Francesca had done. In addition, most seem to have expected that in death Chiara's body would bear signs of her physical experience of the Passion of Christ whilst alive. Francesca added later in her testimony that the nuns believed that something miraculous would be found in Chiara's heart and the same reason was given by Giovanna and Tomassa.

In opening Chiara's body, the nuns were following what was, from at least the twelfth century, a common funerary practice.[36] Putative saints were eviscerated and their bodies embalmed. In some cases the body of the saint would be displayed. Alternatively, the heart and entrails could be placed in a container for the veneration of the faithful. However, in these cases it does not appear to have been necessary to cut into the heart, only to remove the heart and entrails from the body. Francesca's testimony is specific as to the mode of disembowelment. Her witness statement presents the following information:

> Sister Francesca of Foligno who is [now] dead, and Illuminata and Marina, and Elena who is [now] dead, went to cut open the body, and the said Francesca cut it open from the back with her own hand, just as they told [the witness] herself. And they took out the entrails and put the heart away in a container, and they buried the entrails in the oratory that evening.[37]

---

33 For Marina's testimony on the disembowelment see Menestò, *Il processo di canonizzazione*, pp. 153–5.   34 For Tomassa's testimony see Menestò, *Il processo di canonizzazione*, pp. 245–8.   35 For Francesca's testimony see Menestò, *Il processo di canonizzazione*, pp. 339–41.   36 André Vauchez, *Sainthood in the later Middle Ages*, trans. Jean Birrell (Cambridge, 1997), p.431.   37 The Latin text is given in Menestò, *Il processo di canonizzazione*, pp. 338–41: 'Francescha filia magistri Gualterii de Montefalco' was replying to number 159 of the questions drawn up for use in the apostolic canonization process. In response, Francesca said that: '… soror Francescha, que mortua est, de Fulgineo, et Illuminata et Marina et Elena, que mortua est, iverunt as scidendum corpus, et dicta Francescha sua manu scidit ex parte posteriori, sicut ipse sibi dixerunt, et extrasserunt intestina et recondiderunt cor in una cassa, et intestina humaverunt in oratorio illo sero'.

Thus far, the information given shows that the nuns – although acting in secret and without the knowledge of all the members of the convent – were following a relatively normal procedure for the embalming of the body.[38] However, Francesca then went on to make it clear that part of the process had nothing to do with embalming. She testified:

> Moreover, on the following day, after vespers or thereabouts, the aforementioned Francesca, Margarita, and Lucia and Caterina went to get the heart, which was in the container, just as the aforementioned nuns later told the other nuns. And the said Francesca of Foligno with her own hand cut open the heart which, having been cut, they found the cross or the image of Christ crucified in the heart itself.[39]

This systematic exploration of Chiara's internal organs in the hope of finding miraculous signs of her sanctity reflected the belief, current around 1300 that, 'what happened in and to the cadaver was an expression of the person'.[40] Equally, what happened to the person – and their body – was an expression of those things, particularly visual, on which they focused their minds.

It is, therefore, useful to consider Chiara's reaction to visual imagery in the days leading up to her death. One of the main reasons for the search for the instruments of the Passion was Chiara's insistence before her death that she had Christ within her heart. During her last illness, as testified to in the canonization process, Chiara turned to Sister Giovanna, who was making the sign of the cross over her in order to drive away the possibility of any diabolical presence, and said,

> Sister, why are you making the sign [of the cross] over me? I do not have need of any exterior cross because I have my Jesus Christ crucified inside my [own] heart.[41]

---

38 However, the fact that Chiara's body appears to have been cut open from the back is very unusual. The normal way of opening a body in preparation for the embalming procedure would have been to make a cut from the sternum to the pubes of a body laid on its back. Andrea Carlino, *Books of the body: anatomical ritual and renaissance learning*, trans. John Tedeschi and Anne C. Tedeschi (Chicago and London, 1999), pp. 10–11. See also Nancy G. Siraisi, *Taddeo Alderotti and his pupils: two generations of Italian medical learning* (Princeton, NJ, 1981), p.111. 39 Menestò, *Il processo di canonizzazione*, pp. 338–41: 'Sequenti autem die, post vesperas vel circha, dicta Francescha. Margarita et Lucia et Caterina iverunt ad accipiendum cor ipsum , quod erat in capssa, sicut dicte domine et asseruerunt postea inter dominas. Et dicta Francescha de Fulgineo scindit cor ipsum sua manu, quo scisso invenerunt cruce in corde ipso, seu ymaginem Christi crucifissi.' 40 Caroline Walker Bynum, *The resurrection of the body in Western Christianity, 200–1336* (New York, 1995), p. 325. 41 Menestò, *Il processo di canonizzazione*, pp. 176–7.

Berenger of Saint'Affrique also makes this point by relating that on her deathbed, Chiara stated that she was not afraid because of Christ's cross inside her heart.[42] Berenger goes on to relate that:

> After some days, a nun placed a cross in front of Chiara who was lying in bed. When Chiara saw it she said: 'Why has that cross been placed there?' One of the nuns replied to her: 'Chiara, we have put that cross [there] because of the life-like image of Christ and because it contains very many beautiful things'. Chiara said, 'Sister, it is not necessary that you should place the cross [there] for me, because I have Christ's cross in my heart'. And she repeated this frequently in a low voice.[43]

Chiara's rejection of images in the days leading up to her death and her claim to have 'Christ crucified' in her heart were the culmination of her lifelong identification with Christ as the Man of Sorrows. It was also intimately related to her internalization of her religious experiences, a tendency that can be traced in saints and holy people from the twelfth century.[44] Affective piety centred on Christ's body and which had a physical and tangible effect on the body of the believer seems, as Caroline Walker Bynum has pointed out, 'to have been more characteristic of women than of men'.[45] She goes on to explain that because 'preachers, confessors and spiritual directors assumed the person to be a psychosomatic unity, they not only read unusual bodily events as expressions of the soul but also expected the body itself to offer a means of access to the divine'.[46] For much of her life the main focus of Clare's thoughts had been Christ's suffering during his Passion.[47] According to Berenger of Saint-Affrique, one of her methods of praying was – like Saint Dominic – to extend her arms in the form of a cross.[48] Through this 'affective piety' Chiara re-lived in some way Christ's torments during the Passion and in doing so 'inscribed' his sufferings onto her body. By reliving the Passion in thought and deed, she eventually had an apparition of Christ implanting his cross into her heart and, from then on, according to Francesco, Chiara's brother, 'she always felt a perceptible cross in her heart'.[49] In his *vita*, Berenger stressed the importance of Christ's Passion to Chiara: 'When she was at table to eat, she mentally equated the solid food to the sponge, the drink to the gall and vinegar,[50] [and]

---

42 Faloci-Pulignani, 'La vita di Santa Chiara da Montefalco', vol. 2, pp. 222–3.   43 Ibid., pp. 224–5.   44 Vauchez, *Sainthood in the later Middle Ages*, p. 439.   45 Caroline Walker Bynum, 'The female body and religious practice in the late Middle Ages', in Caroline Walker Bynum, *Fragmentation and redemption: essays on gender and the human body in medieval religion* (New York, 1991), pp. 181–238, at p. 186.   46 Walker Bynum, 'The female body and religious practice', p. 235.   47 Vauchez, *Sainthood in the later Middle Ages*, p. 353.   48 Faloci-Pulignani, 'La vita di Santa Chiara da Montefalco', vol 1, p. 591: '... brachia in crucis similitudinem extendens'.   49 Menestò, *Il processo di canonizzazione*, pp. 176–7.   50 A reference to Matthew 27:34, where it is related that

the light to the eyes of Christ.'[51] Neither Berenger's *vita* of Chiara nor the remaining records of the 1318–19 canonization process indicate any direct 'interaction' with painted or sculpted images. This contrasts with contemporary or near contemporary information about Francis of Assisi, Margherita of Cortona, Aldobrandesca of Siena and Angela of Foligno. Although Chiara did experience a number of visions – such as that of Christ planting his cross within her heart – which were inherently visual, it seems that by the end of her life she had reached a stage of meditation in which exterior visual stimulation had become unnecessary and obsolete because part of her body had been trans-formed into the objects of her meditations.

The idea of God or Christ writing in or inscribing the hearts of his followers was not a new one. The idea that a mystical state could be 'inscribed on the body', and particularly on the heart, is already apparent in biblical and patristic writings. St Paul's description of the heart as a locus for writing was still influential in the Middle Ages (2 Corinthians 3:6):

> You yourselves are our letter of recommendation, written on your hearts, to be known and read by all men; and you show that you are a letter from Christ delivered by us, written not with ink but with the Spirit of the living God, not on tablets of stone, but on tablets of human hearts.

Eric Jager has recently traced the idea of writing on the heart.[52] He has pointed out the centrality of Augustine's writings for the medieval conception of writing in the heart.[53] According to Jager, 'Writing on the heart is a frequent and often vivid image in medieval literature and art.' Saints' legends describe martyrs receiving divine inscriptions in hearts that are later opened and read by others.[54] In the life of St Ignatius of Antioch, as related in the thirteenth century by Jacopo da Voragine in the *Golden Legend*, Christ's name is written in golden letters on the heart of the saint:

> In the midst of all sorts of tortures blessed Ignatius never ceased calling upon the name of Jesus Christ. When the executioners asked him why he repeated this name so often, he replied: 'I have this name written on my heart and therefore cannot stop invoking it!' After his death those who had heard him say this were driven by curiosity to find out if it was true, so they took the heart out of his body, split it down the middle, and found there the name of Jesus Christ inscribed in gold letters. This brought many of them to accept the faith.[55]

before being crucified Jesus 'was offered a draught of wine mixed with gall; but when he had tasted it he would not drink'.   **51** Faloci-Pulignani, 'La vita di Santa Chiara da Montefalco', vol. 1, pp. 599–600.   **52** Eric Jager, *The book of the heart* (Chicago and London, 2000), p. 1. **53** Jager, *The book of the heart*, p. 43.   **54** Jager, *The book of the heart*, p. 1.   **55** Quoted by

The addition of the inscribed heart to the legend of St Ignatius appears for the first time in the *Speculum Historiale* of Vincent of Beauvais of around 1245.[56] This new addition to St Ignatius' life forms part of an increased incidence of miracles relating to the heart than can be traced from the beginning of the thirteenth century. A gathering of Cistercian *exempla* composed in Beaupré in around 1200 includes the legend of a martyr, St Ninias, whose heart was opened after his death and was found to contain the image of the cross of Christ. Such an *exemplum* seems to have been relatively common as a number of authors from this period mention an anonymous martyr whose heart was marked with the image of the cross.[57]

The instruments of the Passion found in Chiara's body went further than the inscriptions or images purported to have been found in the hearts of earlier saints such as Ignatius or Ninias. They were not merely visible signs of the strength of her faith; they made Chiara's body into a reliquary.[58] Relics of the Passion had become more 'common' in the west in the wake of the crusades and the Latin conquest of Constantinople in 1204,[59] and in 1215 the Fourth Lateran Council ruled that ancient relics should not be displayed except within an appropriate reliquary.[60] During her life Chiara's body formed such a reliquary for the *arma Christi*. The cross at least had been present since her vision of Christ implanting it into her heart.[61] After her death, when these relics were discovered by the nuns of Chiara's convent, they were shown within the reliquary of her heart. Chiara's was a body-shaped or so-called 'speaking reliquary'. As Cynthia Hahn has pointed out, body-shaped or body-part shaped reliquaries were not necessarily fashioned in order to indicate their contents. The use of precious materials in reliquaries emphasized the importance of the contents within but, at the same time, the 'lack of correspondence of relic(s) to container' seems to have been quite normal.[62] Hahn has further argued for 'a slippage between the status of the contained and the container.[63] This model works particularly well for Chiara, whose *imitatio Christi* linked her body to that of Christ found within her heart and thus also to the instruments of the

Eric Jager in 'The book of the heart: reading and writing the medieval subject', *Speculum* 71 (1996), pp. 4–26, at p. 16.   56 Marie Anne Polo de Beaulieu, 'La Légende du couer inscrit dans la littérature religieuse et didactique' in *Le 'cuer' au moyen age: réalité e Senefiance.* Senefiance 30 (Aix en Provence, 1991), pp. 297–312, at pp. 302–3. 57 Polo de Beaulieu , 'La Légende du couer inscrit', pp. 304–5.   58 For the idea of the saint as a living reliquary, see Cynthia Hahn, 'The voices of the saints: speaking reliquaries', *Gesta* 35 (1997), pp. 20–31 at pp. 27–28.   59 Gertrud Schiller, *The iconography of Christian art.* Volume 2. *The Passion of Jesus Christ*, trans. Janet Seligman (London,1972), p. 190.   60 David Sox, *Relics and shrines* (London, 1985), p. 27. 61 Dillian R. Gordon, 'Painting in Umbria 1250–1350', Unpublished PhD thesis, University of London, 1979, p. 249, comments that the miraculous implantation of the cross of Christ into the heart is unique amongst contemporary saints' lives.   62 Hahn, 'The voices of the saints', pp. 20–1.   63 Ibid., p. 28.

Passion. The Passion 'relics' enhanced Chiara's sanctity, whilst her holy reputation ensured that the discovery of the instruments of the Passion was taken seriously. The items found within Chiara's heart were not relics in the sense that they were fragments of the cross, whip, column and other instruments of Christ's torture. Nor were they *brandea*, that is to say, objects which had come into contact with the instruments of the Passion. Rather, they were relics in the sense that they had been formed in Chiara's heart through her repeated efforts to 'be present' during the Passion. Chiara's constant re-living of the Passion during her life ensured the alteration of her body to reflect and commemorate Christ's sufferings.

Berenger of Saint-Affrique's description of his inspection of Chiara's heart makes clear the importance of the somatic in his understanding of Clare's spirituality. In part wishing to persuade his readership of the truth of his assertions, he is insistent that he verified the presence of the signs of the passion in Chiara's heart, not by sight alone, but by touch. Furthermore, this touch, whilst reverent, does not shrink from exploration of Chiara's anatomy. Berenger's language stresses the thoroughness of his exploration. He states that he looked at and touched the cross a number of times and also that he touched and pressed the whip with his own hands. It is clear that he tested the strength of the items contained within the heart, for example, when he mentions that the three nails were extremely hard, although he believed that they were made of flesh.[64] The fact that the instruments of the Passion were made out of flesh links Chiara's body to that of St Francis. According to Thomas of Celano in his *Vita Prima*, written in 1228, the stigmata on Francis' hands and feet were 'not nail holes, but the nails themselves made of flesh the brown colour of iron'.[65]

Berenger insisted on the tangible physicality of the phenomenon he investigated through means of his vocabulary; 'I felt', 'I pressed'. However, Chiara's opened heart containing a three-dimensional representation of the *arma Christi* is a visual experience analogous to painted representations of the period of the instruments of Christ's Passion.[66] It is now almost impossible to reconstruct the visual references that were available to those who first looked on Chiara's opened heart but it seems reasonable to assume that at least some of the ecclesiastics who viewed the heart had a fairly high degree of visual literacy. These were people who were exceptionally well travelled, likely to own small private pieces of devotional art and were probably patrons of larger works as

---

64 Faloci-Puligani, 'La vita di Santa Chiara da Montefalco', vol. 2, pp. 235–236.
65 Thomas of Celano, *The Life of Saint Francis of Assisi and the Treatise of Miracles*, trans. Catherine Bolton (Assisi, 1997), p. 107. For a discussion of this understanding of the stigmata, see Chiara Frugoni, 'Saint Francis, a saint in progress', in *Saints: studies in hagiography*, ed. Sandro Sticca (Medieval and Renaissance Texts and Studies, Binghamton, NY, 1996), pp. 161–90, at p. 164.   66 Frugoni, '"Domine, in conspectu tuo omne desiderium meum"', p. 171.

well. The heart was, for example, taken to Rome in order that Cardinal Giacomo Colonna could see for himself the instruments of the Passion.[67] Whilst there it was also inspected by Cardinal Napoleone Orsini, himself an important patron.[68] We have seen that, during the thirteenth and fourteenth centuries, many saints focused on visual images of Christ crucified in order to allow them to meditate more effectively. The same was true of those who were not revered as saints, but who used images in order to facilitate their devotions. Yet, at the end of her life Chiara of Montefalco refused to meditate on the images presented to her. Ironically, by providing her followers with a three dimensional image of the *arma Christi*, Chiara's legacy to those who supported her cult was to provide the visual stimulus that she herself had rejected. Through a lifetime of imitation, Chiara may have risen above the need for exterior painted or sculpted representations, but those who supported her cult had not.

67 Faloci-Puligani, 'La vita di Santa Chiara da Montefalco', vol. 2, pp. 251–3.   68 For Napoleone Orsini as a patron of art, see Andrew Martindale, *Simone Martini* (Oxford, 1988), pp. 170–3.

Women's prospects in early sixteenth-century Germany. Did Martin Luther's teaching make a difference?

Helga Robinson-Hammerstein

In pre-reformation times the prospect before a young woman[1] appears to have been the life of a nun in an all-female community or settling for the less exclusive existence in marriage with defined labours in a household of men, women, children, servants, young and old. The social reality of the later Middle Ages handed the task of determining which of the two it was to be to male members of her family: to stay a virgin and become a nun or get married was never the question of choice for any young woman; in most cases her father or elder brother played the decisive role. For these male blood relations the decision depended on the availability of a suitor of compatible social rank and a satisfactorily negotiated dowry to ensure a marriage that would benefit the families of both spouses. That said, living the celibate contemplative life of a virgin, praying for others, pure and unpolluted by the temptations in a secular society was the higher ideal, for male and female, to which some of the children were being designated to work for the spiritual benefit of relatives past and present. This ideal plan had been outlined by the church Fathers and was advocated by the church throughout the Middle Ages. One should not forget, however, that the cloistered existence was always for a minority; more men and women were integrated into secular society, married and with their own households contributing to the general welfare of the urban and rural communities.

Nevertheless, using works of art and literature as a yardstick, one can discover in the later Middle Ages an unresolved tension between the cloistered and worldly conditions. Before the Lutheran reformation of religion there

---

1 Rather than speaking of 'options' or 'choices' this article follows the lead and adapts the title of Olwen Hufton's book *The prospect before her: a history of women in western Europe, vol. I: 1500–1800* (London, 1995). In a bibliographical essay Hufton reveals trends in women's history. For a bibliographical overview of trends in women's history see Anne Conrad (ed.), *'In Christo ist weder man noch weyb': Frauen in der Zeit der Reformation und der katholischen Reform* (Münster, 1999), p. 8, note 4.

manifested itself an artistic upgrading of marriage, which conceded to the wife an honoured place beside her husband.[2] Even men of the church made their – occasionally idiosyncratic – contribution to such a reassessment: Cardinal Albrecht of Brandenburg had himself and his concubine Ursula Redinger represented as St Martin and St Ursula.[3] Albrecht von Eyb, abbot of Würzburg, doctor of both laws, canon of Bamberg, Eichstedt and Nuremberg, wrote a pamphlet as a New Year gift to the citizens of Nuremberg in which he sang the praises of married life. It is significantly entitled *Whether a Man should take a Wife* (1472). The booklet was obviously written from the perspective of the man and still advocated the cloistered existence as the more sanctified one. This widely read tract was based on classical literary models with additional biblical examples linking the two themes together. Another compilation by Eyb called *Mirror of Social Mores* delineates what was considered the typical female interest of a prospective bride; her aunt seeks to find out whether the intended male will be fit for marital intercourse; she uses a conventional figure of speech, asking whether it was true that the young man might not be prepared 'to eat apples' – a curious adaptation of the original Adam and Eve story where the apple is the symbol of female temptation leading to the Fall of Man. The aunt receives a reassuring answer. The traditional symbol of sinfulness – Eve offering Adam the fruit from the forbidden tree – is turned into a reference to the main imputed interest of the woman and therefore the actual purpose of marriage, the production of children after sexual intercourse, which the woman can demand, interpreting Genesis 3:16b all too literally.[4] Around 1500 the imperial

2 Double portraits of women as the counterpart to their betrothed or husband came into fashion in the late fifteenth century. There is a great number of engagement portraits showing the young couple, starting with the Gotha couple around 1484 and others; see Katharina Flügel, 'Die Entdeckung der Welt und des Menschen', in Staatliche Museen zu Berlin (eds), *Kunst der Reformationszeit* (Berlin/Ost, 1983), pp. 233–92; also Albrecht Dürer's famous portraits of Hans and Felicitas Tucher, 1499, ibid, pp. 218–19 and Israel Meckenem, the most famous printmaker before Dürer, projecting his self-portrait as an image of companionship with his wife, reproduced in *Albrecht Dürer and his legacy*, British Museum catalogue (London, 2002), pp. 24, 228.   3 Albrecht of Brandenburg was the most insistent opponent of Luther at the time. The double portrait of around 1520 flanking an altar in Halle is by Simon Franck (1500–1546/7), reproduced in Cécile Dupeux, Peter Jezler and Jean Wirth (eds), *Bildersturm. Wahnsinn oder Gottes Wille* (Bern, 2000), pp. 180–1.   4 Interpreting Genesis 3:16b, Albrecht von Eyb, *Whether a man should take a wife* (1472 ff.) Trinity College Dublin Library possesses among its early printed books a copy of an Augsburg reprint of 1517 (= DD.nn.51/15). For Eyb's *Mirror of Social Mores*, printed in many editions before 1500 see: Will-Erich Peuckert, *Die Grosse Wende. Geistesgeschichte und Volkskunde* (Darmstadt, 1966), p. 319. Eyb shares the conviction, held throughout the Middle Ages and the early sixteenth century, that women had a stronger sex drive than men, making unattached women especially suspect as people who were – mostly unsuccessfully – fighting their natural disposition; see Merry Wiesner, 'Nuns, wives, and mothers: women and the Reformation in Germany'

literature, initiating a debate on social and political reform plans, made the woman a crucial prop in marriage with the duty to exercise a civilising influence on husband and family.[5]

At the same time also the *Book of the One Hundred Chapters and Forty Statutes* by the Upper Rhenish Revolutionary (not printed, but variously copied and adapted in other pamphlets) maintained categorically in its first chapter that, since God created Adam and Eve as man and wife, he had made marital love the basis of human society. Further on in the same text its anonymous author observed that convents were only for the few who could truly live the lives of virgins.[6] It would be a misconception, however, to think that these writings or the portraits were features of an actively tackled, comprehensive programme for systematic social reform that might include an adjustment of the role of women. In so far as there was any scheme, it was concerned with the higher social ranks only, notably with the patrician and upper bourgeois families. The 'common man' was depicted in a generalized, idyllic picture with peasant couples going to market, attending weddings, dancing and eating their fill.[7]

The purpose of this paper – as already indicated in the title – is to reflect on the impact of Martin Luther's reformation preaching and publishing on the dynamics of life in cloistered and secular communities. In his early years the theologian and Augustinian canon who took his *lectura in Biblia* at the university of Wittenberg very seriously, was faced with social responses he had not anticipated. Many monks and nuns left their cloistered life and sought to be reintegrated into secular communities. This will be contrasted with the somewhat different picture of determined resistance, especially on the part of nuns, a defence that emerged predominantly in the cities of Southern Germany in the course of magistrates, determined re-modelling of the previously well-functioning communal interaction of cloistered and secular family traditions.

By the end of the fifteenth century the majority of rural and many urban female cloisters had the same bad reputation as the male institutions that were the butt of satire and sarcasm. A number of scholars have examined the nature

in Sherrin Marshall (ed.), *Women in Reformation and Counter-Reformation Europe: public and private worlds* (Bloomington, Ind, 1989), pp. 8–28, at p.13.   **5** Johannes Schwitalla, *Deutsche Flugschriften, 1460–1525* (Tübingen, 1983), pp. 228–50.   **6** Upper Rhenish Revolutionary exercised considerable influence on the contemporary discourse through distribution of excerpts in other printed pamphlets. There was a distinct eschatological flavour to his demands for reform; see Peuckert, *Grosse Wende*, pp. 223 ff.; see also Gerald Strauss (ed.), *Manifestations of discontent in Germany on the eve of the Reformation* (Bloomington, Ind.,1971), pp. 208 ff.   **7** Erasmus was one of the few among his contemporaries who did not start from the premise of natural inferiority of women in social and marital relations. See J. K. Sowards, 'Erasmus and the education of women', *Sixteenth-Century Journal* 13 (1982), pp. 77–89. Albrecht Dürer comes closest to capturing social reality in his copperplates and woodcuts of peasants in their social environment, see André Deguer and Monika Heffels (eds), *Albrecht Dürer. Sämtliche*

of anticlericalism that can be assumed to have fed into the Lutheran reformation. They have persuasively argued that intense attacks of the clergy (known as *Paffensturm*) were a recurrent feature in late-medieval life and that the same manifestations could easily be aroused by 'evangelical' preachers.[8] What emerges most forcefully is the display of violence that expressed a disillusionment with the old church and signalled a loss of its moral authority; 'lay standards' of behaviour, intolerant of misconduct, were developed out of the experience of urban and rural communal living and applied to the clergy on whom they exercised immense moral pressure. Thomas Brady speaks of scandals 'colouring the mood' at Strasbourg and forming part of the psychological background to the reformation changes.[9] One can indeed diagnose a natural disintegration of monastic life that was recognized by the laity and led to a demand to reassess the cloistered communal existence.

Luther was aware of the force of lay anticlericalism, but his critique of monasticism started from the premise of general theological reflection. What he called 'the false faith' practised by nuns and monks runs like a red thread through his early writings that are concerned with the *sola fide – sola scriptura* principle. He implies the unsuitability of such an existence for either men or women, never treating the question as a gender issue. Early in 1521, however, priests began to draw what they considered the right conclusion from Luther's teaching and got married. It was on this issue of clerical marriage that he sought to intervene during his enforced absence from Wittenberg. He endeavoured to contain what rapidly developed into a largely anticlerical tumultuous agitation for change in the autumn of 1521. What he heard about the Wittenberg Movement persuaded Luther to work out a more definitive appraisal of vows.[10] It is worth stressing that his tract *The Judgment of Martin Luther on Monastic Vows*, was not published until February 1522, because the elector's secretary, George Spalatin, sought to calm the agitation in Wittenberg by censoring all Luther's messages from the Wartburg. Spalatin had considered the publication of such a critique 'far too explosive', stimulating further religious and social changes in the university town and the territory.[11]

Holzschnitte (Ramerding, 1981). **8** R.W. Scribner, 'Anticlericalism and the cities' in Peter A. Dykema and Heiko A. Oberman (eds), *Anticlericalism in late medieval and early modern Europe* (Leiden, 1994), 147–66, at p. 150. **9** R.W. Scribner, 'Anticlericalism and the cities', p. 159 and Thomas A. Brady, '"You hate us priests": anticlericalism, communalism, and the control of women at Strasbourg in the age of the Reformation' in Dykema and Oberman, *Anticlericalism*, pp. 167–207, at pp. 206, 193. **10** Martin Brecht, *Martin Luther: shaping and defining the Reformation, 1521–1532* (Minneapolis, 1994), pp. 21–24. Luther's bewildered reaction to the marriage of priests is recorded in his letters, see Jaroslav Pelikan and Helmut T. Lehmann (eds), *Luther's Works (American edition)* (St Louis, 1955–86) vol. 48, pp. 231, 235. On the Wittenberg Movement which his overlord, Frederick the Wise, had attempted to head off by forcing Luther to stay away from Wittenberg, see H. Robinson-Hammerstein, *Faith, force and freedom* (Dublin, 2001). **11** see *D. Martin Luthers Werke: Kritische Gesamtausgabe*, 61 vols (Weimar, 1883–1983),

Characteristically, in the dedication of the pamphlet Luther apologized to his father for having become a monk against his will. The text that follows develops the relevant application of the *sola fide – sola scriptura* principle. It is constructed as an exegesis of the First Commandment in which God establishes his connection with mankind; it argues that monastic vows are not anchored in the Word of God and are therefore 'against Christian freedom', because 'everything not necessary for salvation must be free'. It identifies a fundamental contradiction between vows and the gospel. Many church historians have called the *Judgment of Martin Luther on Monastic Vows* a great document of the Reformation, which had the effect of emptying out monastic institutions.[12] Martin Luther's theological dismantling of vows confronted him with the actual disintegration of monasteries and convents. Monks like secular clergy entered relatively effortlessly into marriages and appointments as pastor and preacher in Saxony, often in their former hometowns 'assisted by their social connections'.[13] Luther's enthusiastic approval of the marriage of former monks is demonstrated in his joyous acceptance of invitations to weddings. A typical piece of evidence among many similar ones is his quick note, written on 8 April 1523, to Wenzeslas Link, a friend and former Augustinian, in Altenburg. He announces his own arrival with a group of close friends, Philip Melanchthon, Justus Jonas, Hieronymus Schurf, Johannes Bugenhagen and others, all connected with Wittenberg University; in addition Link should also expect Hieronymus Krappe and Lucas Cranach, the painter, although he could not say whether the wives of Jonas and Schurf would be able to join them. In some cases Luther even helped to arrange wedding feasts, as for Johannes Bugenhagen.[14] Friendship networks that reflected the solidarity of former monks and essential propagandists (like Lucas Cranach with his illustrations of the Luther's reformation message) provided the support structure that assisted the transition from clerical celibacy to a pastoral household.

It is true that Luther received an extraordinary number of requests for help and guidance from men and women wishing to break their vows, but the requests from nuns posed the more difficult problem. In the note to Link he added that he had accepted nine nuns liberated – *ex captivitate* – from Nimbschen (a convent of Cistercian nuns near Grimma). Twelve nuns altogether had left

vol. 44, pp. 251–400 [henceforth cited as *WA*]. On Spalatin's controlling influence on political and religious developments after Worms see Irmgard Höss, *Georg Spalatin. 1484–1545. Ein Leben in der Zeit des Humanismus und der Reformation* (Weimar, 1989), pp. 203–220. 12 Brecht, *Martin Luther*, p. 24. 13 R.W. Scribner, 'Anticlericalism and the cities', p. 152. He points out that about 40% of 'evangelical' preachers had been members of religious orders and he reinforces the point with the following interesting conjecture: 'Part of Luther's popularity stemmed from his public persona as a friar bringing the Bible to the people, and it seems likely that mendicant preaching styles could account for the effectiveness of many popular evangelical preachers'. 14 *WA, Briefe*, III, Nr. 599, Wittenberg, 8 April 1523 and *WA, Briefe*, III, Nr. 566, 2 January 1523.

the convent, significantly on Easter Saturday, 4 April 1523, to celebrate the resurrection of their risen Saviour in freedom. Three of these nuns had been reintegrated immediately into their aristocratic family households, because they lived in the territory under the control of Luther's patron, Elector Frederick the Wise.[15] The presence of the other nine put Luther in the awkward position of having to protect 'masterless' women, who at his instigation had escaped from a convent in the territory of his archenemy, Duke George of Saxony. He wrote a public letter accepting responsibility for his action and defending it as an encouragement to noble parents to free their children from immoral and irreligious bondage.[16] The nuns were mostly members of noble families from his own rural region, including the sister of Johann von Staupitz, the head of the Augustinian Order and Luther's mentor, and Catharina von Bora, whom he eventually married in 1525. Some of the others, in so far as they were young enough, also married Wittenberg professors. The professorial status of these previously celibate men was considered as on a par with the lesser nobility and therefore made them acceptable suitors of noble ladies. It also meant that with the marriage of professors the university was changed from a monastic into a truly secular institution serving the 'common good' of the whole territory. The nuns received compensation from the Elector's brother and successor in the later 1520s and 1530: between twenty and forty guilders in 'compensation' for leaving the convent.[17]

The fate of Magdalene von Staupitz and the experience of Hanna von Spiegel are of particular interest here. One of Luther's colleagues, Nikolaus Amsdorf, who seems to have been assigned to look after the needs of the ex-nuns, first intended her to marry Spalatin, who declined the offer for reasons of his time-consuming employment in the service of the Elector. Magdalene – and later also another refugee nun, Elizabeth von Canitz – was placed to teach reading, writing and household skills at a newly established school for girls. Magdalene found it very difficult to make ends meet, as is evident from letters she wrote to Spalatin, begging for firewood to heat the schoolroom. The girls, being of slight stature, needed to be kept warm more than boys; she also indicated that she felt somewhat inappropriately employed since she had been organist and singer in the convent.[18] The ex-nun Hanna von Spiegel, a member of a noble dynasty, had on her own initiative agreed to marry a non-noble. Sebastian von Kötteritzsch, most likely her brother-in-law, and other relatives, sought to prevent the marriage. Luther wrote to her that it was unnecessary for him to write on her behalf to the Elector, since she had so ably and intelligently defended herself. He assured her that 'one human being was worth the other, if they had only sexual interest in and love for each other'. He emphasized that,

---

15 See note *WA, Briefe*, III, 599, p. 54.   16 See the extensive commentary in *WA, Briefe*, III, Nr.600, pp. 56–7; also for what follows.   17 For these financial arrangements see editor's notes in *WA, Briefe*, III, 600.   18 *WA, Briefe*, III, Nr. 600 (notes).

although he was quite sure of her strong inclination towards this man, she must not forget to seek God's grace and blessing, so as not to rely merely on fleshly passion (*eitel Liebesbrunst*).[19]

In his letter of 6 August 1524 to three cloistered ladies Luther elaborated the theme of vows, matrimony and sexual desires.[20] He seems to have been fascinated by the story of a nun who, in addition to her natural sexual desires escaped from an 'irreligious' convent. Luther dedicated the account of Florentina von Oberweimar's 'liberation' from Neu Helfta at Eisleben to Count Albrecht von Mansfeld who had at that time five of the sixteen nuns from Widerstet under his protection (June 1523). The reformer represented Florentina's as the typical fate of nuns, for whom religious life was far from a matter of choice. He argued that the 'world can see what a devilish thing this "monkery" and nunnery is, in which they think to drive and compel people to God with harshness of blows.' Florentina von Oberweimar had been placed in the convent by her parents when she was six; at the age of eleven she had been committed to a life in virginity without her consent and due understanding; at fourteen she had realized that she was unfit for this vocation and had asked the abbess to be given her freedom. Despite her urgent plea, however, she had been formally received into the order as a professed nun by the command of the abbess and against her will. When she had tried to escape she was betrayed by some other nuns and was subjected to a lengthy process of harsh treatment by the abbess and had to undergo severe and humiliating penance, beating and putting into irons and imprisonment in a cold cell. Eventually she had escaped through the negligence of an attendant, who had left her cell door open.[21]

Luther also wrote several tracts – always written in response to requests from individuals – praising the married estate in general as the foundation of a good society and denouncing the celibate life. There he stressed that parents must not force their sons and daughters to marry where there is no love. He and the leading Zurich reformer, Ulrich Zwingli, made sure that such advice need not be merely wishful thinking. The common chests, which received the property of the dissolved monasteries, must set aside substantial sums to assist loving couples when the parents were unable or refused to support their children; in some cases they ignored the conventions of preserving the social hierarchy, especially of a noble daughter marrying a man of lesser social status. Although the advice and help focused on the couple, it was clear that for women marriage and motherhood was their 'vocation' (*Beruf*). When Margaretha Blarer, the

19 *WA, Briefe*, III, Nr. 695, 14 December 1523.   20 S.C. Karant-Nunn, 'The transmission of Luther's teaching on women and matrimony: the case of Zwickau', *Archive for Reformation History* 77 (1983), pp. 1–46, mentions this letter and points out that it conveys a very pessimistic view of unmarried women's chastity. In the Appendix, I have translated the letter from WA, Briefe, III, Nr. 766, pp. 326–8.   21 Luther gave constant advice to Albrecht von Mansfeld, see *WA Briefe*, III, Nr. 619 & Nr. 814 : *A story how God*

unmarried sister of Ambrosius Blarer, reformer of Constance, who lived with her brother and looked after his children, was accused of being 'masterless', she replied 'those who have Christ for a master are not masterless'.[22] Her response is a telling re-interpretation of the nun in her cloister as 'the bride of Christ'.

The biographies of Catharina von Bora, Catharina Zell and Ursula Weida show how the marriage of a cleric could exercise a significant influence on marriage of 'the laity', an effective extension of Luther's project of the 'priesthood of all believers'. The pastor's wife acting out a totally new 'semi-spiritual' function – an appealing substitute for loss of the 'sacral' role of the cloistered celibate woman – did indeed become a role model for other women in the wider community An anonymous Augsburg pamphlet of 1522, called *A Little Book for Women*, inspired the active women at home and in church by adapting the Old Testament examples of Esther, Sarah, Deborah and Judith for this purpose.[23] The influence of Catherina von Bora is well summarized by R.H. Bainton who highlights her domestic skills.[24] Catherina Zell, the wife of the Strasbourg pastor Matthias Zell, wrote a pamphlet in defence of her marriage rejecting 'the lies' against her husband:

> Paul says that women should be silent in the church [1 Timothy 2:12; 1 Corinthians 14:34]. I reply to this that he also says in Galatians III [verse 28] 'In Christ there is neither man nor woman' and also that God says in the book of the Prophet Joel II [3:1]: 'I shall pour my spirit over all flesh and your sons and daughter shall prophesy'.[25]

For Ursula Weida the representation of marriage as release from false faith and the necessary reintegration of the cloistered folk into communal life of the city was occasioned by the anti-Lutheran tract by Simon Plick, the abbot of Pegau,

helped a nun to get her freedom, March 1524. **22** On arrangements for a common chest in Leisnig see *WA, Briefe*, III, 576 and Nr. 577 and for Zurich on the common chest and marriage ordinance, M.E. Wiesner, 'Nuns, wives, and mothers', pp. 8–20. **23** P. Russell, *Lay theology in the Reformation: popular pamphleteers in southwest Germany* (Cambridge, 1986), p. 189. **24** R.H. Bainton, *Women in the Reformation in Germany and Italy* (Boston, 1971), pp. 23–44; see also *WA, Briefe*, III, Nr. 800 & Nr.883 as well as *WA, Briefe*, IV, Nr.999. *Luther's last will and testament*, edited by T. Fabiny (Dublin and Budapest, 1982) is perhaps the most impressive acknowledgement of the equality of the active wife. Luther put Catharina in charge of all their children, much against contemporary legal prescription of making the eldest son the head of household. **25** *Entschuldigung Katharina Schützinn / für M. Matthes Zellen / iren Eegemahel / der ein Pfarrher vnd dyener ist im wort Gottes zu Straßburg 1524*, cii verso; see also A. Conrad, 'Aufbruch der Laien – Aufbruch der Frauen. Überlegungen zu einer Geschlechtergeschichte der Reformation und katholischen Reform' in Conrad (ed.), '*In Christo ist weder man noch weyb*', pp. 7–22, at p. 10. See also Silke Halbach, 'Publizistisches Engagement von Frauen in der Frühzeit der Reformation' in idem, pp. 49–68 and Bainton, *Women in the Reformation*, pp. 55–76.

in which he described Luther's followers as 'run-away monks and nuns'. Her central point is the glorification of marriage as a liberation from the 'false chastity of monks and nuns'; she also inveighs against the nobility who subject their children to insufferable mental hardship by putting them into cloisters against their will.[26]

The question why monks and nuns responded so readily to the call to become reintegrated into their larger urban or rural communities through their own marriages has been treated by R.W. Scribner. He links it with the discussion of the nature of anticlericalism and observes that reformation preachers never attacked devotional practices directly, because people would have resisted such an approach. What did assist the rejection of Catholic practices – and lifestyles – were the sermons and publications that depicted devotional practices 'as devices invented by the clergy to line their own pockets'. The Lutheran media represented the universal church as made up of cheats.[27] There are indeed many instances in which Luther defends traditional customs as long as they are not practised as means of salvation.[28] Merry E. Wiesner, however, points out that marriage ordinances curtailed women's public ceremonial functions considerably, for example in funerals: 'for Protestant reformers wanted neither professional mourners nor relatives to take part in extravagant wailing and crying'. She observes that female networks, providing emotional and economic assistance to their members, were not tolerated, except perhaps for the lying in period of seven weeks after the birth of a child.[29]

Lutheran preachers offered to liberate from the shackles of the Church; they changed women's lives so that they might play a more active role in the community. Such a prospect seemed to have a general appeal; and yet, it was precisely with nuns and their cloistered communities that the most determined resistance to the Lutheran idea and practice of liberation started. The effect of these protests and their impact on the life of the community can best be traced in the community adjustments of the free imperial city of Nuremberg. This first city that worked out a stable reformation on the basis of Luther's teaching was forced to confront the necessary reassessment of the role of women in a different way.[30] In 1525 the majority of the Council supported Luther's view that the conditions of the life of monks and nuns were unnatural and that they

---

26 Silke Halbach, 'Publizistisches Engagement', pp. 62–6 and Russell, *Lay theology*, pp. 201–3. 27 R.W. Scribner, 'Anticlericalism in the cities', p. 155. 28 H. Robinson-Hammerstein (ed.), Martin Luther, *On prayer and procession in rogation week* (1519) (revised edition, Dublin, 1997). 29 Merry E. Wiesner, 'Nuns, wives, and mothers', p. 14. 30 Gerald Strauss, *Nuremberg in the sixteenth century: city politics and life between Middle Ages and modern times* (Bloomington, Ind., rev. ed.,1976); Beate Lesting-Buermann, *Reformation und literarisches Leben in Nürnberg. Ein Beitrag zur Kommunikationsgeschichte der frühen Neuzeit unter besonderer Berücksichtigung der Predigten A. Osianders, V. Dietrichs und der Schriften Lazarus Spenglers*, Freiburg, 1982.

2 [The monkcalf] Illustration of a polemic by Martin Luther [1522]

failed to lead the life for which they had been destined. The convents had better be closed and the real model of social existence of mutual benefit for families and the whole community was to be married life within the household. Of the six male houses four closed down voluntarily; the two female houses refused.

The leader of the opposition was the abbess of the convent of St Clare, Caritas Pirckheimer.[31] She was one of nine sisters of the internationally renowned Christian humanist, Willibald Pirckheimer, patrician and a leading member of the Inner Council – the actual governing body of the city – who framed the policies. One sister was very advantageously married; the other eight remained in convents to which they had been sent as young girls. They died as abbesses of various convents of Southern Germany, demonstrating that excellent family connections had traditionally not just produced appropriate suitors but also opened access to leading positions in cloisters. Both male and female members of the distinguished patrician family had enjoyed a sound classical education either, as in the case of the brother Willibald, at universities and through travels and visits to learned men in Italy, or, as in the case of at least his sister Caritas, through book learning and exchange of letters with humanist scholars such as Conrad Celtis in Vienna; he dedicated his edition of the poems of Roswitha von Gandersheim to her. She demonstrated her ability to communicate in Latin in many of her letters and her requests to her brother for certain books reveal her deep commitment to learning.

In 1523 the nuns Catharina and Veronica Rem of Augsburg had already refused to leave their convent. They had argued, like Caritas was to do more emphatically a little later, that they had never seen their cloistered existence as 'good works' contributing to their salvation; rather their good works were a direct response to God's prompting.[32] Caritas Pirckheimer's letters and her autobiography bear witness to her fear of chaos as a result of nuns' 'liberation' in the Lutheran fashion; she fully expected that any change in the existing communal institutions would upset the balance within the 'good society'.[33] In her eyes this balance was the guarantor of true freedom. Her nuns' resistance to dissolution laid bare the real rifts within the elite of Nuremberg society. The dominant majority of the Inner Council followed traditional lines in introducing

---

31 What follows is taken from Caritas's edited letters and her autobiography. *Briefe des Äbtissin Caritas Pirckheimer des St Klara-Klosters zu Nürnberg*, ed. G. Deichstetter [in accordance with the original edition by J. Pfanner translated by Sr. B. Schrott], St Ottilien, 1984; *Die Denkürdigkeiten der Äbtissin Caritas Pirckheimer*, ed. F. Renner, St Ottilien, 1982; *'Die Denkwürdigkeiten' der Äbtissin Caritas Pirckheimer des St Klara-Klosters zu Nürnberg*, ed. G. Deichstetter [translation by Sr. B. Schrott], St Ottilien, 1983; *Caritas Pirckheimer, 1467–1532. Eine Ausstellung der katholischen Stadtkirche Nürnberg*, Munich, 1982.   32 Conrad,'Aufbruch der Laien', p. 7.   33 See Irene Leicht, 'Gebildet und geistreich: Humanistinnen zwischen Renaissance und Reformation' in Conrad, *'In Christo is weder man noch weyb'*, pp. 23–48, and p. 46, footnote 68 with references to her most important reflections.

3 A broadsheet woodcut, hand-coloured, used by Hieronymus Emser in an attack on Luther, but also used by Lutherans to denounce monks. [1522 ff.]

change: in the first instance persuasion was to achieve the desired goal of voluntary dissolution of monasteries and convents. When that did not achieve the desired response, the tactics changed to intimidation. Nuns were questioned individually by town officials in the hope that one might 'accuse others of practising but concealing great wickedness'. Frequent Lutheran sermons by Andreas Osiander, Nuremberg's popular preacher, were supposed to open up the women's minds. Then restrictions and isolation were tried. More cut off than ever before, it proved difficult to get food supplies into the convent; their farms were confiscated. Caritas seems to have been most deeply affected by the attacks by Nuremberg lay women; they, rather than men, threw stones over the wall and generally disrupted the traditional services. Mass and confessions were prohibited; families attempted to drag unwilling daughters out into the urban community. None of these devices met with much success, so that the city government eventually decided to leave the convent alone while forbidding the reception of any novices.[34]

In Nuremberg as elsewhere the Lutheran and the Catholic parties sought to undermine the positions of 'the others' by polemics, slander and invective. The Lutherans employed all available media to turn secular priests, monks and nuns into citizens. Everywhere carnevalesque scenes like those uncovered by R.W. Scribner were enacted for this purpose. There is the story of the layman parading in papal garb, who made the Franciscans dress up as devils before they were driven out of the monastery.[35] The Lutherans lost no opportunity to interpret the birth of a deformed child or animal as a warning sign sent by God who had suspended his good creation to demonstrate displeasure with the wicked world. The *monkcalf of Freiberg* did the rounds as the most notorious monster. Luther himself wrote about its significance as a divine indicator that the monastic system had been condemned. In retaliation the birth of this monster was also used by Hieronymus Emser, one of Luther's earliest opponents, to interpret as God's displeasure with Luther for breaking his monastic vows and encouraging others to do the same. Both opponents did not just write slanderous tracts but authorized the publication of hard-hitting cartoons.[36] The detractors of nuns had no such monstrous signal from heaven to hand, but in some ways cloistered ladies were depicted as even more sinister creatures in illustrations. While the housewife was usually assisted in all her actions by the Holy Spirit in the form of a dove, representations of nuns showed them invariably keeping the company of hideous devils either sitting on their backs or lurking by their side writing down their prayers or their conversations.[37]

---

34 M.A. Wiesner, 'Nuns, wives, and mothers', p. 10; for a more detailed account of events see *Caritas Pirckheimer, 1467–1532. Eine Ausstellung*, p. 1.   35 Scribner, 'Anticlericalism and the cities', p. 165.   36 *WA, Briefe*, III, Nr. 568 and notes; see also the contrasting illustrations of the 'monkcalf' and Luther as the devil's bagpipes (figs. 2 and 3).   37 See figs. 4 and 5.

4 Hans Weiditz, *The devil records the prayer of two nuns*, around 1520, woodcut

Lutheran pamphleteers tried their best (or worst) to achieve the aim of reintegration of nuns into the wider community. One such pamphlet of 1524 adopts the form of a letter by a housewife to her cloistered sister.[38] It had been issued anonymously with the approval of Lazarus Spengler, the city scribe and secretary of Nuremberg. As city censor he always studied to remain inconspicuous in his furtherance of Lutheran teaching and sent pamphlets to Augsburg to be published there.[39] The text considers a display of moral superiority an ineffective means of persuasion. The housewife, therefore, humbly appeals to her well-educated sister, a nun, to rely on her education that must teach her that the Lutheran faith of the married couple is not heretical or sectarian, but Christian. She ventures to stress, however, that the nun's education, which she praises as a great adornment of the female (one she herself is lacking) has been misapplied, because it has persuaded her to indulge in 'religious fantasies' (the devil on her shoulder is the symbolic indicator of this state of affairs). Such fantasies deem the female's life in the convent superior to married life. Paraphrasing Luther, the married sister in her studied simplicity recommends to her learned cloistered sibling the true Word of God which she

38 *Ayn bezwungene antwort* (1524). See title page reproduced as fig. 5. 39 Lesting-Buerman, *Reformation und literarisches Leben*, pp. 177 ff.

Ayn bezzvungene ant=
zvozt vber eynen Sendtbzieff/eyner
Closter nunnen/an jr schwester inī Eelichē
standt zūgeschickt/darinī sy jr vil ver
geßner vnnützer sozg fürhelt/vñ
jre gaistliche weißhait vñ
gemalte hayligkait
zū menschli=
chem ge
sicht auff mutzet.

5 Titlepage of the pamphlet, *Ayn be zwungene antwort vber eynen Sendtbrieff eyner Closternunnen an jr schwester im Eelichen standt zugeschickt …* , author and illustrator unknown, printed [Nuremberg, H. Höltzel], 1524. TCD; E. s. 46/6

can read in the good book and hear in Lutheran sermons. She encourages her to accept the Word as the only source of salvation and to discard her 'cloisterly religion' that seeks to 'work for the salvation that is freely given' by God through Christ's death and resurrection. The pamphlet contains all the arguments used in the early years of the reformation to persuade nuns to find their liberation in the life of a humble housewife for the benefit of the integrated community of men and women.

Catholic responses, of which there are quite a number, review the arguments in an attempt to demonstrate that the convent as a community of spiritual women offers the true liberation.[40] In one typical pamphlet the nun points out that Christ is her only saviour and that she knows about him through the Word of God. She weighs the advantages of the celibate and the married estate as means of access to God's grace and denies that her sisters in the convent believe that the religious orders, habits, prayers and fasting confer special graces. The nun describes herself as a woman guided by the principle that Christ enjoined upon Christians: 'not to judge so that they are not judged themselves'. She assures the housewife that 'we certainly believe that you are a good Christian in your married state as are also the citizens of Nuremberg as long as you leave us alone.' The housewife is asked to consider that no one would say 'the whole married estate is bad' because there might be ten wicked married women in a city. Therefore, the nun continues, 'you must not believe the monastic estate to be bad, because Luther has seen some bad nuns.' She takes up a defensive rather than an aggressive position. What she holds principally against the Lutherans is that they derogate everything. Her reply appears to represent the urban reality much more accurately than the sanctimonious wishful thinking of the married sister. She explains,

> … the preachers who come to us do not preach the Word of God, they spend their time running down the pope, bishops, clergy, monks and nuns. If that is what Luther teaches them, I appeal to your intelligence to consider whether this is honey or poison.

She sees – probably with some justification – the preachers of the Word as polemicists who neglect their primary duty of labouring honestly in God's vineyard.

These were precisely the points made in self-defence by the Nuremberg nuns under the leadership of Caritas Pirckheimer. Such a defence was, however, a direct challenge of the majority in the Nuremberg Council that had denounced the cloistered existence as a negation of the urban *bonum commune*. When claiming that the Lutheran preachers taught the wrong kind of freedom,

---

40 See for instance *Anntwurt auf den sendbrieff* (1524), from which the following quotations are derived.

Caritas could point to her own blameless religious life and the exemplary services of her convent to the communal life of the city.

APPENDIX: MARTIN LUTHER TO THREE CLOISTERED LADIES*

Wittenberg, 6 August 1524

Grace and peace in Jesus Christ, Our Saviour !
Dear sisters !
I did receive your letter of some time ago and also the one more recently and I have read [I understand] your concerns.

I would have replied sooner, if I had had an opportunity and if there had been messengers available, for I am extremely busy with other matters at the moment. First, you have understood very well that there are two reasons why one might abandon a cloistered existence and the vows. One is, when human laws and duties in the convent are imposed by force and they are not left free, rather the [abbess and the superiors] burden and constrain consciences. Then it is time to turn away and leave the convent and everything [associated with it] behind. If this is so in your case, namely that the cloistered existence is not a matter of choice, but your consciences were forced, summon your friends and ask them to assist you to leave and that they should take you into their [homes], (if the authorities permit it),[1] or to place you somewhere else to be provided for. If your friends and parents are not willing, seek help from other good people to this end, regardless of whether the parents should not agree – die or get well – for the salvation of the soul and the will of God must always be regarded as above all other considerations, as Christ says: 'He who loves father or mother more than me is not worthy of me.'[2] If the sisters will let you go, however, or if at least you are allowed to read and hear the Word of God, you may [safely] remain there and perform all the work of the convent together with them [in their company], such as spinning and cooking and the like, but do not place your trust in it.[3]

The other reason is the fleshly desire,[4] although women are ashamed to admit it; nevertheless, Scripture and experience teaches that among many

---

* translated from the German in *WA, Briefe*, III, Nr. 766   1 Luther was always very anxious not to offend the secular authorities; he was keenly aware that he might be accused of stirring up unrest by going against the law in civil matters. This became more and more important as the reformation progressed. Rulers like Duke George of Saxony, who was his most determined opponent, should not be given any reason to blame Luther's overlord, Elector Frederick the Wise, for protecting him.   2 Matthew 10:37. 3 Do not expect this as performance of good works by which you might contribute to your salvation. Luther describes the duties of the convent rather mundanely as household chores.   4 Luther calls it simply 'Das Fleisch' – the flesh, which he always

thousands there is not one, who has received God's grace [God's gift] to keep herself in pure chastity. Rather, a woman has no control over herself, God has created her body in such a way that she should be with the man, to bear children and to nurture them, as the Word in Genesis 1 clearly states;[5] and the structure of her body is destined by God Himself for this purpose. It is as natural a part of God's plan as eating, sleeping, cooking, namely that man and woman should be together.[6] This alone is [reason] enough, and no one should be ashamed of that for which God has created and made them, when it is felt that the high, rare gift[7] is not given, then one must leave and do that for which one finds oneself created.

About such things you will read and hear amply and sufficiently when you leave and hear the true gospel preached. For I have given sufficient evidence of it and proved it in the book on monastic vows, also in [advice] how to avoid human doctrine, also in the sermon of married life and in the postilla.[8] If you read those you will find enough instruction on all important questions, be it confession or other matters. It would be far too long and also unnecessary to write more about this now, since I am sure that you will leave the convent, if both reasons apply or even just the first one. You complained about the first one in particular.

Should it, however, happen that the cloister should [in future] come to understand the right freedom, you can go back if you so desire and enjoy God's grace; just as the Council of Bern in Switzerland has now opened up the most famous cloister of Königsfelden.[9] [If a nun decides to leave] they give her what she brought with her when she entered.[10]

God be with you; and please pray for me.

Given at Wittenberg, on the Day of Sixtus, the Martyr, 1524.[11]

To the three cloistered ladies, my dear sisters in Christ, written in friendship.

---

contrasts with the Spirit.   **5** verse 28.   **6** This is the conventional reference to sexual intercourse.   **7** to live a celibate life.   **8** Luther's most frequently read and consulted collection of sermons.   **9** The City Council took the decision on 3 June 1524. It was left to the nuns to decide whether they wished to leave or stay. Luther also mentions this in a letter to Spalatin of 27[?] June 1524: *WA Briefe*, III, Nr. 755.   **10** A nun's dowry was usually less than what she needed to get engaged to an acceptable suitor, but it was the sort of money she needed to begin her re-integration in the world.   **11** One of the early popes who was acceptable to Luther because he lost his life in the persecution at the time of the Roman Emperor Diocletian.

'The weaker vessel'?: the impact of warfare on women in seventeenth-century Ireland

Bernadette Whelan

For most of the seventeenth century the island of Ireland was a battlefield and a site of contention between Protestant and Catholic European monarchs. The lives of people of all religious, political and economic-social backgrounds were affected by warfare. Yet, the title of this essay might be considered a misnomer by those who believe that by definition women could not have been involved in seventeenth-century warfare. How could they when war, as Murtagh points out, involved 'combat, weaponry, strategy, tactics, logistics, command or the organization of armies', activities from which women were excluded by custom, practice and regulation?[1] However, wars neither broke out nor were conducted in isolation from communities or nations. On the contrary, the origin, conduct and conclusion of war involved all society. Viewed from those perspectives, an examination of Irish women's involvement in the warfare of the seventeenth century may go some way towards a revision of the prevailing concepts of war.

In an important pioneering essay, O'Dowd outlined the extensive activities of women in the warfare of the 1640s, thereby showing that the traditional concepts of warfare as an exclusively male activity can no longer prevail.[2]

---

1 Harman Murtagh, Review of T.G. Fraser and K. Jeffrey (eds), *Men, women and war*, Historical Studies XVIII, *History Ireland*, 1 (1993), p. 61. An earlier version of the ideas which are extended in this essay appeared as chapter 11 'Women and warfare, 1641–1691' in Pádraig Lenihan (ed.), *Conquest and resistance: war in seventeenth–century Ireland* (Leiden, 2001), pp. 317–43. The role of royal women and Religious Society of Friends (Quaker) women during the period will be examined in a forthcoming study.
2 Mary O'Dowd, 'Women and war in Ireland in the 1640s' in Margaret MacCurtain and Mary O'Dowd (eds) *Women in early modern Ireland* (Dublin, 1991), pp. 91–112. There is no full-length study of women's involvement in warfare in Ireland; O'Dowd's work was a pioneering study. References to Ireland also appear in Charles Carlton, 'Civilians' in John Kenyon and Jane Ohlmeyer (eds), *The Civil Wars: a military history of England, Scotland and Ireland, 1638–1660* (Oxford, 1998) and in Antonia Fraser, *The weaker vessel: women's lot in seventeenth-century England* (London, 1993).

Moreover, Wiesner redefined the concept of power and made a crucial distinction between power, which she defines as the 'ability to shape political events' and authority which is formally recognized and legitimated.[3] This essay is concerned with investigating the impact of warfare on women during two wars, 1641–53 and 1689–91. Secondly, it examines the ways in which non-royal women exercised 'power' and 'authority' in seventeenth-century Ireland.

While the origins of these wars are not of concern to this paper, the background to these events is the general crisis of mid seventeenth-century Europe when subjects revolted against absolutist ruler, royalism faced parliamentarianism, Protestant opposed Catholic, while in Ireland, conflict between colony and crown added a further feature. The Tudor conquest, in progress since 1534, resulted in complete control of Gaelic, Catholic Ireland in 1603 following victory in the Nine Years War (1593–1603). But Catholics in Ireland revived and by 1641 once again threatened English Protestant authority. Thus, each of the two conflicts to be examined here, the war in 1641–53 and that in 1689–91, were essentially wars of religion, where Irish Catholics fought to establish or maintain a standing within a Protestant three kingdom monarchy.[4]

THE LAUNCH OF WARFARE IN IRELAND

In the case of the Confederate War (1641–53), the fighting began in Ireland with a rebellion in 1641, sparked by Catholic fears of persecution. It had spanned the country within the year, lasted twelve years and was an exceptionally brutal conflict. According to Carlton, the civil wars in Ireland, Scotland and England 'remain the bloodiest man–made event in the history of the three kingdoms'.[5] While the later war, sparked by the birth of a Catholic heir to Mary Beatrice d'Este and James II in June 1688 and the possibility of an Irish Catholic revival,[6] took longer to unfold, it lasted only three years and did not see the same level of barbarity. George Storey, the Williamite officer, calculated that the

---

3 Merry E. Wiesner, *Women and gender in early modern Europe* (Cambridge, 1993), pp. 239–40.   4 By 1641 the terms 'Irish Catholic' or 'Catholics in Ireland' referred to an alliance between 1) the Gaelic Irish, 2) the Old English who were descendants of the Anglo-Norman conquerors mostly living in the Pale, an area stretching around Dublin, the centre of English authority, and 3) some New English, the more recently-arrived Elizabethan and Jacobean settlers. Hiram Morgan, 'Old English and New English' in Seán Connolly (ed.), *The Oxford companion to Irish history* (Oxford, 1998), pp. 408–9. During the Confederate wars 1641–53, Irish Catholics formed themselves into a confederation on 7 June 1642 and in the ensuing English Civil War 1642–51 sided with the royalists against parliament. During the revolution of 1688, Irish Catholics supported James II against William III, prince of Orange, leader of the Protestant elements in England.   5 Carlton, 'Civilians', p. 278.   6 The role of royal women in the diplomacy and high politics of the wars will be examined in a forthcoming article.

earlier war cost the crown approximately three times as much as the Williamite war and twenty to thirty times as much as the Nine Years War.[7]

In terms of personnel, the landing of the Catholic King James II at Kinsale on 12 March 1689, signalled the arrival of the Jacobite army of Irish, French and Scottish which numbered 36,000 in 1689, 45,000 in 1690 and 30,500 in 1691.[8] There were also raparees, or guerrillas who harassed Williamite quarters and the 9–10,000 Ulster and Connacht Gaels led by Hugh Balldearg O'Donnell.[9] Protestant William of Orange's army of Dutch, Danish, German and French along with Irish Protestants would number 37,000 at the Boyne.[10] Until then, these soldiers represented the largest-ever number of combatants in Ireland. Oliver Cromwell's army which campaigned in Ireland between 15 August 1649 and 26 May 1650 amounted to approximately 20,000 soldiers and by 1652 the occupying forces amounted to 30,000 men including English, Danish and Huguenots.

In this context, the demographic and economic impact of the two wars was profoundly different. The cumulative impact of a decade of warfare, October 1641 to June 1652, fell heaviest on Ireland with wartime population loss in the 15–20 per cent range. Most of this can be attributed to the final phase of the war, characterized by a bitter counter-insurgency campaign, man-made famine, refugee movement, and epidemic disease. In Ulster, replenished somewhat by post-war British immigration, a comparison of 1630 muster rolls with hearth-money rolls of the 1660s suggests that less than 50 per cent of 1630s surnames survived in their neighbourhoods, indicating 'a huge turnover in population'.[11] Thus, while the scale of the military operations in the later war was undoubtedly larger, it caused less social dislocation overall because it was shorter.

The moral context was radically different. The Lords Justices in June 1642 could excuse the killing of women on the dubious basis of collective Irish blood guilt for the Catholic insurgent killings of Protestant settlers:

> We have hitherto where we came against the rebels, their adherents, relievers and abettors, proceeded with fire and sword, the soldiers sometimes not sparing the women, and sometimes not children, many women being manifestly very deep in the guilt of their rebellion, and as

7 Quoted in Raymond Gillespie, 'The end of an era: Ulster and the outbreak of the 1641 rising' in Ciaran Brady and Raymond Gillespie (eds), *Natives and newcomers: essays on the making of Irish colonial society, 1534–1641* (Dublin, 1986), p. 191.   8 Diarmuid and Harman Murtagh, 'The Irish Jacobite army 1688–91', *Irish Sword*, 18 (1990–1), p. 33. 9 Ibid., p. 34.   10 Kenneth Ferguson, 'The organisation of King William's army in Ireland 1689–92,' *Irish Sword*, 18 (1990–1), p. 62. Pádraig Lenihan, 'War and population, 1649–52', *Irish Economic and Social History* 24 (1997), p. 1; Raymond, Gillespie, *The transformation of the Irish economy, 1550–1700* (Dundalk, 1991), p. 16.   11 James Scott Wheeler, 'The logistics of conquest' in Pádraig Lenihan (ed.), *Conquest and resistance: war in seventeenth–century Ireland* (Leiden, 2001), pp. 189–91.

we are informed, very forward to stir up their husbands, friends and kindred to side therein, and exciting them to cruelty against the English acting therein and in their soils even with the rage and fury with their own hands.[12]

The indiscriminate brutality implied by these remarks did not, it must be said, characterize the entire war, as government and later Royalist and Parliamentary forces came to see the practical benefits of offering protection to neighbouring civilians in order to secure regular contributions. However, the opening eighteen months of the war were marked by several massacres of civilians by insurgents and government troops; the account by James Turner, a Scottish officer in Ulster, of the capture of Newry from the Irish in 1642 illustrates a typical incident of the period:

> Our sojors (who sometimes are cruell, for not other reason bot because man's wicked nature leads him to be so, as I have shoune in my Discourse on Crueltie) ... runne uppon a hundred and fiftie women or thereby, who had got together in a place before the bridge, whom they resolved to massacre by killing and drowing ... bot before I got at them they had dispatched about a dozen; the rest I saved.[13]

In contrast, from the outset there was no question of the contending forces in the Jacobite wars habitually massacring women and children; the tone of the Williamite reconquest was set by the Williamite commander, Friedrich Schomberg, in August 1689 after accepting the surrender of the Irish soldiers and camp-followers at Carrickfergus:

> ... the country people were so incensed with them that they stripd most part of the women and forced a great many arms from the men and took it very ill that the Duke did not order them all to be put to death.[14]

Thus, the difference in the moral context of the two wars is to be explained by the greater willingness of commanders to restrain their soldiers and civilian

12 O'Dowd, 'Women and war in Ireland in the 1640s', p. 100. 13 J.T. Gilbert (ed.), *The history of the Irish confederation and the war in Ireland, 1641–9*, 7 vols (Dublin, 1882–9), vol. 2, pp. 574–5. 14 George Story, 'A true and impartial history', *Old Limerick Journal* 28 (1990), p. 10. Among the letters of protection he issued to cover enemy estates was one to Lady Antrim on 19 August 1689. Her husband was Alexander McDonnell, third earl of Antrim, who was one of James II's leading supporters in Ulster. However, the withdrawal of the Jacobite army from the northern part of the island following the unsuccessful siege of Derry, left Antrim's estates at the mercy of the local Williamites until his wife obtained official protection. Eileen Black (ed.), *Kings in conflict: Ireland in the 1690s* (Antrim, 1990), p. 156.

followers. The commanders in 1641–2 took their cue from a political leadership which encouraged (explicitly so, in the case of the government) war against the entire enemy population rather than soldiers in arms. Finally, the treatment of a town taken by storm was a special case where the normal conventions, such as they were, did not apply. A protracted siege was so potentially destructive to the besiegers that the threat of massacre for unduly prolonged resistance was justifiable. Consequently, Cromwell could claim that the massacre of women in Drogheda in 1649 was within the brutal letter, if not the spirit, of seventeenth-century conventions of warfare. It would, he hoped, 'save much effusion of blood in the future'.[15] Nevertheless, similar massacres were not a feature of the later war.

THE DAILY EXPERIENCE OF TRAVELLING ARMIES: PROTECTION AND POLITICS

In a pioneering essay of the activities of Irish women in the warfare of the 1640s, Mary O'Dowd challenged the traditional concept of warfare as an exclusively male activity. According to O'Dowd, 'women's direct involvement in the military conflict of the 1640s took a variety of forms, depending on their class and economic background'.[16] From the beginning of the conflicts when the armies began to arrive, women's role as home-makers placed them at the centre of the conflict. In both periods the campaigning armies of all sides marched through the countryside, wreaking havoc. Plunder and pillage was commonplace, necessitated by the lack of regular pay and other problems. Crops were destroyed, houses were burned, animals and inhabitants taken or killed.

The homes of wealthier women were obvious targets for the armies in both periods due to convenient location, comfort and political sympathy. In the absence of male heads of households women became protectors of home, lands and family. Shortly after the outbreak of the 1641 rising, Lady Elizabeth Dowdall defended her own castle and estate at Kilfinny in Co. Limerick along with other royalist-owned property against the Catholic rebels. Her account of her military actions provided details of her army, her strategy, the seizing of enemy prisoners and horses and the hanging of their men. When her surrender was demanded by Richard Stephenson and his 3,000 men, Lady Dowdall 'sent him a shot in the head that made him bid the world good night, and routed the whole army'. She fought for forty weeks with the enemy until the 'great army beseiged me' and Lord Inchiquin sent a convoy to redeem her. She left just 'wearing linen'.[17] Her political motivation shines through in her account of her

---

15 Tom Reilly, *Cromwell: an honourable enemy: the untold story of the Cromwellian invasion of Ireland* (Dingle, 1999), p. 102.   **16** O'Dowd, 'Women and war in Ireland in the 1640s', p. 92.   **17** Quoted in 'Lady Elizabeth Dowdall' in *Field Day anthology of Irish writing*, vol. 5 (Cork, 2002), pp. 22–4.

achievements. Similarly Lady Forbes in Castle Forbes gathered arms, ammunition and food and offered shelter to two hundred Protestants for a nine month period.[18]

During the later conflict, a Williamite supporter, Lady Newcomen defended her castle at Kenagh, Co. Longford, along with a number of Protestants who had taken refuge there.[19] It was taken eventually. The *chatelaine* of Moret castle in Laois responded to the threat to hang her husband, if she did not surrender; 'I won't render my keep, and I'll tell you why–Elizabeth Fitzgerald may get another husband, but Elizabeth Fitzgerald may never get another castle.' The besiegers carried out their threat and the unfortunate husband 'was seen dangling and performing various evolutions in the air' but the lady kept her castle, for a time at any rate.[20] Whether motivated by political commitment, friendship or the basic desire to protect hearth and home, the women of these castles and estates were placed at the heart of the military activity.

But more typical of the daily experience of warfare was the experience of settler and Religious Society of Friends' (Quaker) women. These were women born into the Reformation tradition who had settled in Ireland during the mid-seventeenth century. Frances Curtis was a member of the Covenant of the Church in Dublin and its minister, John Rogers recorded forty-five spiritual testimonies in 1650. During the wars she 'was stripped by the rebels ... and came home so, through sad tempests, and since have [been] through great troubles, and very many'. A while later her husband was killed by the rebels, her home was attacked 'cannon–bullets flew over my head; and in a few days I was turned out of doors, with my child in my arms'.[21] Mary Turrant, also a member of Rogers' church, was widowed after her children were 'murdered by the rebels'.[22] The experiences these women underwent seem to have led to some form of conversion experience.

It was the outward appearance of other women settlers that attracted rebel attention also. The outbreak of violence in 1641 provided native Irish settlers with the opportunity to seize the clothes of Scottish and English settlers, particularly women's dresses, which were interpreted as a political symbol. Elizabeth Pierce of Newry recalled that she 'saw neighbours clothes' worn after they died at Irish rebel hands. The latter 'resolved that after the Irish had gotten the victory, all the women in Ireland should as formerly go only in smocks, mantles and broughs as well as ladies as others and the English fashions to be quite abolished'.[23] Indeed within two years of the outbreak of the earlier

18 Carlton, 'Civilians', p. 284; O'Dowd, 'Women and war in Ireland in the 1640s', p. 92. 19 J.T. Gilbert, *A Jacobite narrative of the war in Ireland, 1688–9* (reprint, Shannon, 1971), pp. 91–2.   20 Jonah Barrington, *Personal sketches and recollections of his own times* (Glasgow 1887), p. 9.   21 'Experience of Frances Curtis' quoted in *Field Day anthology of Irish writing*, vol. 4 (Cork, 2002), p. 481.   22 'Experience of Mary Turrant' quoted in *Field Day anthology of Irish Writing*, vol. 4, pp. 481–2.   23 Quoted in O'Dowd,

rebellion, among the many homeless and destitute women who sought refuge and help from the government in Dublin in 1642 were a group of 'distressed ladies and gentlewomen' from Protestant backgrounds who had to flee the countryside, leaving behind all their material possessions. They petitioned the government for help as a separate group, as they felt that their higher social standing meant that the usual charity offered did not befit their status.[24]

The plain and simple apparel of members of the Friends' Society, along with their opposition to war and the bearing of arms, also differentiated them from others in Irish society.[25] The Quakers came to Ireland in 1655 and were a new group within the Protestant tradition. During the Williamite wars, Quaker families were attacked and robbed on a daily basis by soldiers of both sides. Friends' homes in rural areas were liable to have soldiers of both sides quartered on them, which involved providing shelter, food and drink. Women, therefore, bore the brunt of the soldiers' presence. As early as 1687, Sir Maurice Eustace's Jacobite troop wrought havoc on the Friends' community in Queen's county. For example, when Mary Edmundson of Rosenallis brought the usual Friends' meal of oat bread, milk, cheese, new butter and boiled veal to the table, the soldiers 'slighted and scorned' her and the fare.[26] On Tuesday, 1 January 1688, Elizabeth Sheercroft of Mulinanard told one soldier that

> he was welcome to such quarters as they had but was afraid she had had
> bread such as he would like in the house … and when he had tasted the
> ale he threw the tankard and ale into her face – then came two more
> strangers … and called for ale and a glass then they broke the glass and
> gave her many threatening words – calling of her whore and shot several
> times … and swore they would set fire on the house …[27]

In addition to the immediate economic suffering to women and their families caused by quartering, Friends' widows had cereals, animals, bedding and clothes

'Property, work and home: women and the economy, c.1170–1850' in *Field Day anthology of Irish writing*, vol. 5, pp. 467–8.   24 Quoted in O'Dowd, 'Women and war in Ireland in the 1640s', p. 100.   25 Grubb relates that only four Quaker men took up arms and were 'disowned' by their community. Isabel Grubb, *Friends in Ireland, 1654–1900* (London, 1927), p. 36. By the late seventeenth century, the community numbered between 5,000 and 6,000; most lived in Dublin and in Queen's County (Laois) with isolated groups in Ulster and Connacht. Grubb, *Friends*, p. 36 and Maurice J Wingham, *The Irish Friends: a short history of the Religious Society of Friends in Ireland* (Dublin, 1992), p. 25.   26 Historical Library of the Religious Society of Friends in Ireland, Dublin [hereafter H.L.D.], Sharp Manuscript [hereafter Sharp Ms], SH 30D, A letter from William Edmundson to Anthony Sharp and John Burnyeat, 3 March 1687, section vi, letter no. 28.   27 H.L.D., 'The examination of Daniel Conraghey servant to William Sheercroft of Mulinanard, Queen's County taken before me Robert Warneford, Esq.', 2 January 1688, section vi, letter no. 40.

taken from them by soldiers. The war period was made even more difficult for the Friends, because the community had to continue paying fines as they refused to pay tithes for the upkeep of the Church of Ireland. The 'Book of Sufferings' reveals, that between 1689 and 1691, ten women had crops and animals taken from them *in lieu* of tithes, in addition to experiencing the upheaval and disruption of the war.[28]

The Friends' religious beliefs had long been a source of persecution for them which clearly increased during the war. The quartering, plundering, imprisonments and physical and verbal abuse brought the frightening experience of war into the homes of Friends women, perhaps more than others, because of their non-alignment with either side. But they were determined not to allow the 'trying times' to disrupt their lives.[29]

Clearly the marauding armies brought soldiers and enemy women into close contact but references to rape in both conflicts are rare although there were many stories about its occurrence during the civil wars in England.[30] For example, during the 1641–52 war, an exceptionally brutal conflict, there are many authenticated examples of massacres of women and children by the Irish and English troops but few examples of rape. The 1641 depositions for Co. Armagh offer two references and none came from the thirty women who gave evidence. However one petition to the English House of Commons noted the 'savage and unheard of rapes exercised upon our sex in Ireland'.[31]

During the later period, there appears to be only two accounts of rape, both recorded by Richard Baldwin, a dedicated Williamite. His propaganda pamphlet, published before 1690, offers an exaggerated account of the Jacobite persecutions of Protestants in Ireland and sought to discredit James in the eyes of his supporters. However, both rapes are detailed; one was linked to Lord Galmoy's troops as they moved into Ulster in March 1689, and the other in Co. Tipperary by Jacobite dragoons.[32] The explanation for the Irish context remains a matter of controversy. Some suggest that instances of rape during war is always underreported because it is the 'mother's milk of militarism' even though it was included in the list of crimes punishable under military law in the 1640s and 1690s.[33] Furthermore, Brownmiller and Porter both associate rape with the context of warfare.[34] Nevertheless, it is difficult to prove either argument.

28 H.L.D., Book of Sufferings.   **29** H.L.D.,'An epistle from the Women's Meeting at Limerick to the Women's Meeting at Cork', 21 February 1689, section vi, letter no. 51. **30** O'Dowd, 'Women and war in Ireland in the 1640s', p. 101; Carlton, 'Civilians', p. 292.   **31** Hilary Simms, 'Violence in county Armagh, 1641' in Brian MacCuarta (ed.), *Ulster 1641: aspects of the rising* (Belfast, 1993), p. 136; O'Dowd, 'Women and war in Ireland in the 1640s', p. 101.   **32** Richard Baldwin, *A true narrative of the murders, cruelties and oppressions, perpetrated on the Protestants in Ireland by the late King James's agents, since his arrival there* (London, 1690), pp. 25, 28.   **33** Carlton, 'Civilians', pp. 294–5.   **34** S. Brownmiller, *Against our will: men, women and rape* (London, 1976), chapter 3; R. Porter, 'Rape: does it have a historical meaning?' in S. Tomaselli and R.

ESCAPE AND CONSEQUENCES

Other women's response to the warfare was to flee Ireland. During the 1640s, settler women such as Alice Stonier, whose husbands were killed and had no means of surviving, fled back to their homes in England and Scotland.[35] Elizabeth Chambers along with Frances Curtis and Mary Turrant of the Christ Church congregation in Dublin all escaped to England and returned in the late 1640s which suggests that they were financially secure.[36] Landed women also had the resources to leave. Although Lady Offaly successfully defended her home, Geashill castle in Co. Offaly in 1642, she eventually left it for England.[37] Among the Williamite women who fled before the fighting began was Margaret, dowager countess of Orrery, a one-time supporter of Cromwell, who went to London in 1688. Her son, Captain Henry Boyle, saw the wisdom of her departure and hoped his wife and family would join her. He explained to his mother that 'it is high time they were gone for all the towns and villages are filled with soldiers'.[38] Lady Powerscourt also fled, causing her mother, Elizabeth Lady Ponsonby, to write to Margaret Orrery that it would be a 'great ease' to her if she knew that her daughter was out of that 'miserable kingdom'.[39] Although flight from Ireland may have brought security and comfort to these wealthy women, it was also a disloyal and treasonous act against James II.

At the Dublin 'patriot' parliament of May 1689, James II reluctantly agreed to the act of attainder. Simms points out that failure to acknowledge James II, rather than religion, was the criterion for being branded a traitor.[40] Katherine, dowager countess of Ranelagh, is the only woman to appear in the first category of individuals who joined in the rebellion. Unless she surrendered and was acquitted following a trial her traitorous activities left her liable (in the event of a Jacobite victory) to the penalties of confiscation and execution. Another category consisted of ninety names of those who 'by reason of sickness and nonage' had left the country. Sixty-six were women, including Margaret Orrery and Elizabeth Ponsonby, who were not attainted but the crown took control of their lands and rents, which would be returned to them only if they returned and behaved as loyal citizens of James II.[41] When it came to matters of loyalty,

Porter (eds), *Rape* (Oxford, 1986), pp. 216–36. Further on this topic see Shani D'Cruze, 'Approaching the history of rape and sexual violence: notes towards research', *Women's History Review*, 1 (1992), pp. 377–97. **35** O'Dowd, 'Property, work and home', p. 467. **36** Phil Kilroy (ed.), 'Memoirs and testimonies of Nonconformist women in seventeenth-century Ireland' in *Field Day anthology of Irish writing*, vol. 4, p. 480. **37** Martyn Bennett, *The civil wars in Britain and Ireland, 1638–51* (Oxford, 1997), p. 7. **38** Edward MacLysaght (ed.), *Calendar of the Orrery papers* [hereafter *Cal. Orrery*], (Dublin, 1941), pp. 368–71. **39** Ibid., p. 268. **40** J.G. Simms, *War and politics in Ireland, 1649–1730: Studies in Irish history, vii* (London, 1986), p. 74. **41** National Library of Ireland, 'A list of such names of the nobility, gentry and commonalty of England and Ireland who are all by an act of the pretended parliament 7 May 1689

men and women were usually treated with equal severity. There were, of course, those who escaped penalties due to their political influence and high connections, such as Frances Tyrconnell, wife of the duke of Tyrconnell, the Jacobite governor of Ireland, cases which will be examined later.

ENGAGEMENT IN MILITARY ACTIVITY

Other women availed of the opportunity of war to show 'courage above one's sex'. The circumstances of the outbreak of rebellion in 1641 revealed another avenue through which women of all classes could influence and participate in politics. While the rising was intended as a quick *coup d'état*, the insurgent leadership lost control of what quickly became a popular revolt. Women participated as members and, indeed, leaders of the mob. In Athlone, Galway, Mullingar and Kilkenny women appear in these roles.[42] The wife of Brian Kelly, a rebel captain, appears in accounts of a massacre near Loughgall, county Armagh. Witnesses' depositions in 1642 recorded that she drowned at least twelve and at most forty-five people.[43]

In addition to political motives, among the local factors which prompted women's fighting was shortages of food. In Belfast in May 1641 this was a probable source of disorder involving women. Women were also involved in Protestant mob violence. Wentworth's attempt to force Scottish settlers in Ireland to swear an oath of loyalty to the king, in an attempt to undermine support for Scottish Presbyterians at war against England in 1639 and 1640, provoked a crowd of women 'with their laps full of stones and men armed with swords' to invade a burial service in Killinchy, Co. Down.[44] These women were motivated by the same factors which motivated men; political belief, economic need and an instinct for survival.

It was not surprising therefore, that George Story recounted on 27 August 1690 when a Williamite assault on Limerick city was repelled by the Jacobite forces:

> The Irish then ventured upon the breach again, and from the walls and every place so pestered us upon the counterscarp, that after nigh three hours' resisting bullets, stones (broken bottles from the very women, who boldly stood upon the breach, and were nearer our men than their own), and whatever ways could be thought on to destroy us, our communications being spent, it was judged safest to return to our trenches.[45]

attainted of high treason', (London, 1690), p. 11, pp 37–8.   42 O'Dowd, 'Women and war in Ireland in the 1640s', pp. 95–6; Nicholas Canny, 'Religion, politics and the Irish rising of 1641' in Judith Devlin and Ronan Fanning (eds), *Religion and rebellion: papers read before the 22nd Irish Conference of historians* (Dublin, 1997), p. 52.   43 Hilary Simms, 'Violence in county Armagh, 1641', p. 131.   44 Raymond Gillespie, 'Destabilizing Ulster, 1641–2' in Mac Cuarta, *Ulster 1641*, p. 111.   45 George Story, 'A true and impartial

While there are no figures for the number of women killed in the fighting in the Limerick sieges or in the 1640s conflict, they were sometimes active participants. Along with other instances of women fighting such as the siege of Estagel in 1639, in tax riots in seventeenth century Holland and in eighteenth-century France, women were present at some of the Irish sites of fighting either as participants or supporters and also alongside men.

Nonetheless, the one aspect of warfare which was in theory an exclusively male activity was soldiering. William of Orange's view that it would not 'be agreeable for a lady to be where the battlefield is' was echoed in the universal exclusion of women as soldiers.[46] However, during both conflicts in Ireland and England a small number of women dressed as men and participated directly. Accounts of women fighting in England during the civil war led Charles I to forbid the practice of women cross-dressing as soldiers as 'a thing which nature and Religion forbid and our Soul abhors'. Indeed a ballad written in 1655 called the 'gallant she-soldier' celebrates the prowess of a Mrs Clarke who served in the same regiment as her husband.[47] One of the very few known Irish examples occurred at the Battle of Ballintober, Co. Roscommon, in 1642, when the Irish dead were being stripped 'one pulling the Mountero from the head of one, there fell down long tresses of flaxen hair, who being further searched was found a woman.'[48]

A better documented example was that of Catherine, or Kit, Kavanagh, also known as Mother Ross or Kit Davies or Mrs Christian Ross or Mrs Jones, because she had four husbands. Celebrated by Daniel Defoe, who also embellished her adventures, it is accepted that she was born in Dublin in 1667. She inherited a drinking house from her aunt, married a servant, Richard Welch, and bore him three children. She disguised herself as a man and enlisted in the Williamite army in 1693 to look for her husband who had been conscripted: 'I cut off my hair and dressed me in suit of my husband's having had the precaution to quilt the waistcoat to preserve my breasts from hurt which were not large enough to betray my sex and putting on the wig and hat I had prepared I went out and bought me a silver hilted sword and some Holland shirts.' This simple change of appearance deceived the army authorities. She subsequently served under Marlborough against the French in Holland, but soon transferred to her husband's regiment, the Scots Greys, remaining with them during the campaigns of 1702–3:

history', *Old Limerick Journal*, 28 (1990), p. 97. The exclusion of the reference to the women from Story's abridged edition should not be over-emphasised as other details were also excluded. See Larry Walsh, 'Eye-witness and contemporary accounts,' *Old Limerick Journal*, 28 (1990), p. 57. A further reference to the Limerick women fighting is made in 'Letters of Jean Payen de la Fouleresse to the king of Denmark,' *Old Limerick Journal*, 28 (1990), p. 127.   **46** John Miller, *The life and times of William and Mary* (London, 1974), p. 49.   **47** Carlton, 'Civilians', pp. 282–3.   **48** Edmund Borlase 'The history of the execrable Irish rebellion trac'd from many preceding acts (London, 1682)'

We spared nothing, killing, burning or otherwise destroying whatever we could not carry off. The bells of the churches we broke to pieces, that we might bring them away with us. I filled two bed-ticks, after having thrown out the feathers, with bell-metal, men's and women's clothes, some velvets and about a hundred Dutch caps, which I had plundered from a shop; all of which I sold by the lump to a Jew, who followed the army to purchase our pillage, for four pistoles.[49]

Though she was reunited with her husband, she remained in the army and fought at the siege of Lille in 1708. Her sex was discovered when she was wounded at Ramillies but she was allowed to stay with the dragoons as a 'sutler', providing the soldiers with food and drink and foraging. When she retired from the army, Queen Anne rewarded her with a pension of one shilling per day for life and she lived as an out-pensioner at the Royal Hospital in Chelsea. When she died in 1739, she was buried with military honours, in recognition of her fifteen-years service as an active soldier.[50]

Kavanagh's original motive was a desire to find her husband, but once she did that, she stayed with the army and joined in the fighting. The official exclusion of women from army service meant that very few women could have been 'she-soldiers', but women were present within the institution of the army. From the fourteenth until well into the nineteenth century, the lines between army and society were not so sharply drawn. Armies were likened by Redlich to 'a vast moving city with its own community life' complete with 'shops, services and families, all defended by walls of iron-the weapons of its soldiers'.[51]

A number of persons – authorized and unauthorized – followed the army to provide services. The term 'camp follower' has often been used pejoratively, but the women who followed the armies were not all prostitutes and troublemakers; many were soldiers' wives who more than earned their keep by foraging, cooking, laundry, needlework and nursing. From the officers' wife or mistress to the local girl, women were necessary for maintaining both comfort and morale, while at the same time an army on the move might have been an exciting attraction for many women. In the Irish context, women appear at the two major conflicts under review. During the earlier war, English army authorities encouraged wives of soldiers to follow their husbands to Ireland, because they were regarded as the best nurses for the sick and wounded. But if widowed, they caused problems for the authorities along with Protestant settler women

in Gilbert, *History of Irish confederation*, p. 81.   **49** Cited in Kate Adie, *Corsets to camouflage: women and war* (London, 2003), p. 4; Jennifer Sillglow (ed.), *Macmillan dictionary of women's biography* (London, 1982), p. 102.   **50** Adie, *Corsets to camouflage*, p. 5. Diarmuid Murtagh, 'The Irish associations of "Mother Ross",' *Irish Sword 1* (1949–53), pp. 146–7.   **51** Quoted in Barton C. Hacker, 'Women and military institutions in early modern Europe: a reconnaissance,' *Signs: Journal of Women in Culture and*

whose husbands volunteered or were pressed into the war. Destitute soldiers' widows and wives figured prominently among the large numbers of women who were in Dublin in 1642 seeking material help and refuge.[52]

Many of the Jacobite soldiers in the later period were accompanied by women and children, 'they having an aversion to stay at home under the arbitrary comportment of an heretical or infidel army'.[53] The proliferation of women with the Irish Protestant militia led Richard Cox, a Williamite officer, to complain to George Clarke, the special secretary-at-war for Ireland; 'if you did know how I am teased by the starving wives and children of our militia, that are at Killaloe, you would hasten them home'.[54] As early as January 1690, petitions were submitted from the impecunious widows and children of Williamite soldiers who died at Enniskillen and Derry. Ferguson relates that in 1689 local forces were paid at a lower rate than regulars and, even though this inequality was resolved in January 1690, the surviving men and the 'real sufferers' – two thousand widows and orphans – unsuccessfully petitioned parliament for the following thirty years to recover arrears.[55]

Also numbered among camp followers in this early modern period were prostitutes. Prostitution was certainly prevalent in Dublin during the winter of 1689–90 when it swarmed with Jacobite soldiers. Contemporary reports reveal that it caused a problem for the Jacobite authorities. John Stevens reported:

> The women were so suitable to times that they rather enticed men to lewdness than carried the least face of modesty, in so much that in every corner of the town might be said to be a public stew. In fine, Dublin seemed to be a seminary of vice, an academy of luxury or rather a sink of corruption, and living emblem of Sodom.[56]

In 1689, soldiers of all ranks were involved 'in all manner of debauchery, luxury and riot', resulting in James issuing 'repeated orders for all officers to repair to their commands'.[57]

Prostitution was evident also in Limerick in the 1640s, if the remarks of the acerbic French traveller, Sieur de La Boullaye-Le-Gouz, can be believed. In 1644 he remarked that 'in this city there are great numbers of profligate women, which I could not have believed, on account of the climate'.[58] Leaving Le-Gouz's speculations about climatic influences on prostitution to one side, perhaps one indication of its prevalence was the introduction in 1702 by the

Society 6 (1981), p. 647.   52 O'Dowd, 'Women and war in Ireland in the 1640s', p. 98. 53 J.T. Gibson (ed.) *Manuscripts of the earl of Fingall* [hereafter *Fingall Mss*], (London) p. 136.   54 Ferguson, 'Organisation of King William's army in Ireland', p. 74. 55 Ibid., pp. 65–6.   56 Robert H. Murray (ed.), *The journal of John Stevens, containing a brief account of the war in Ireland, 1689–1691* (Oxford, 1912), p. 93.   57 Ibid., pp. 92, 93 n.2.   58 Ibid., pp. 92–3.

lord justices of a bill 'For the encouraging of piety and virtue, and for the preventing and punishing of vice, profaneness, and immorality.' All 'bawdy' and 'disorderly' houses were suppressed and persons running such establishments punished. Soldiers in her majesty's armies were also warned to avoid 'all profaneness, debauchery, and other immoralities, and that by their own good and virtuous lives and conversations, they do set good examples to all such are under their care and authority'.[59]

While the presence of women may have been good for the army's morale, it was bad for its supply, movement and discipline but ultimately commanders could not prevent them from travelling. Life for the women who followed the army could not have been easy. Even though Cromwell tried to ensure that his soldiers were paid on a regular basis, in both conflicts on both sides, there were shortages of food, shelter and clothing for the soldiers not to mind their wives and families. Although limits were imposed on the number of wives who might accompany an army unit, conditions had not improved by the beginning of the nineteenth century. Storer notes that during the Napoleonic wars army women would face hunger, disease, violence and bad weather and they often lived in the open air, under home-made bivouacs or in cramped tents with other soldiers. He cites the descriptions of the awful conditions for both men and women as the British army retreated to Vigo and Corunna in the winter of 1808–9.[60]

Life was somewhat easier for the officers' wives and families and some semblance of normal life continued for them. A determination to maintain the rituals of social life, even in the midst of the fighting, enabled the daughters of the Williamite officer, Colonel George Hamilton, stationed at Bandon, and the daughters of the Jacobite, Colonel O'Donovan, stationed at Castelhaven, to meet at Clough Castle for an evening's entertainment.[61] While courtship and marriage also continued, in the earlier conflict Major-General Robert Munro (the perpetrator of the Newry massacre) met and married the Protestant widow of Lord Montgomery of the Ards. The couple settled eventually in Co. Down. A number of his officers made similar marriages, although after 1651, soldiers could be dismissed and flogged for marrying Catholic Irish women.[62]

Other soldiers' female relatives took up more active roles as go-betweens and messengers within armies and between courts during both wars. Rosa O'Doherty, the wife of Owen Roe O'Neill, who returned to Ireland in 1642 with a Continental army, acted as a messenger between the Irish troops in Ireland and their

59 *Calendar of the manuscript of the marquess of Ormonde* [hereafter *Ormonde Mss*], 8 vols, (London, 1902–20), ii, pp. 463, 464.   **60** Ian Storer, '"Johnny I hardly knew you". Women, wives and camp followers of the Napoleonic era,' *The Age of Napoleon* 27 (1998), pp. 17–23. Hacker, 'Women and military institutions', p. 659.   **61** John D'Alton (ed.), *Illustrations of King James' Irish army list* (1689), (second edition, Dublin,1869, first published in one volume 1855), ii, p. 718.   **62** Carlton, 'Civilians', p. 286; Peter Berresford Ellis, *Hell or Connaught! The Cromwellian colonisation of Ireland 1652–1660*

European supporters. The sole surviving letter of her correspondence was written from Louvain to an anonymous priest on 16 September 1642.[63] In March 1690, Gerhardt Neve, chief secretary of the Danish force in Ireland, wrote from Chester that communications with Ireland were difficult and carefully watched – 'a week ago two ladies, one of them the wife of a Jacobite colonel, were placed under arrest on suspicion of communicating with the Jacobites'.[64] When the wife of the Williamite captain, Henry Boyle, joined her mother-in-law, Margaret, dowager countess of Orrery, in London, she carried papers belonging to her husband and his nephew, Lord Burlington. Boyle acknowledged the danger involved, if she were searched by Jacobite soldiers, as not a 'messenger goes from house to house but he is searched and stripped for letters'.[65] When Mrs Gautier, a Jacobite agent was arrested in Dublin by the Williamites after the first siege of Limerick in 1690 'considerable papers were found in her house and about her'.[66]

Women could also assist in keeping troops supplied with the resources of war. In July 1689, Frances Kilmallock was asked by her husband to meet Lord Melfort, James' secretary of state, and request him to forward money for the purchase of arms and order cloth for his soldier's uniforms.[67] Supplying himself and his troops was a constant concern of Kilmallock's, and as late as May 1691 his wife forwarded him 'a tent, six chairs and stool, five pewter dishes, a dozen plates, a frying pan and a pot with a cover'. She also sent him the luxuries of oil, vinegar, sugar, paper and cloves and 'such small necessaries'. The conduct of warfare depended on the necessities of life as much as on arms and horses.[68] Fortunately Lady Kilmallock was not caught, unlike Sir John Burke's wife during the 1640s war, when she attempted to transport guns and ammunition in her carriage from Dublin to the midlands.[69] Women on both sides were willing and able to arrange for the purchasing and transportation of goods.

THE AFTERMATH

Women on both sides became the subject of much government legislation in the 1650s. The land accumulated as a result of confiscation was intended, in the first instance, to satisfy 'adventurers' (those who had financed the abortive reconquest of 1642) and arrears of soldiers' pay. Older widows of royalist soldiers who were owed arrears were eventually given cash payments in place of

(London, 1975), p. 110.   63 Mary O'Dowd (ed.), 'Rosa O'Doherty,' in *Field Day anthology of Irish writing*, vol. 5, p. 30.   64 K. Danaher and J.G. Simms, *The Danish force in Ireland* (Dublin, 1962), p. 30.   65 *Cal. Orrery*, p. 370.   66 F.J. Routledge (ed.), *Calendar of the Clarendon state papers* [hereafter *Cal. Clar.*], 5 vols (Oxford, 1970), v, p. 690.   67 J.G. Simms (ed.) 'Lord Kilmallock's letters to his wife,' *Journal of the Royal Society of Antiquaries of Ireland*, 87:1 (1957), p. 136.   68 Ibid., p. 137.   69 O'Dowd,

land, while younger widows were allowed to claim the arrears in the form of land debentures. In practice, if women did not have some financial support or influence, long delays were encountered in the processing of such claims. These problems were experienced also by wealthier royalist women whose husbands were exiled. Such difficulties were, in part, the result of the Cromwellian land settlement.

Under the settlement, landlords who had failed to display their 'constant good affection' to parliament during the war forfeited their lands, while those deemed to be enemies were to be removed to the counties of Galway, Roscommon, Mayo or Clare where they would receive either two-thirds, one-third or one-fifth of their former lands. Cromwell's aim was to free up most of the land for English and Scottish settlers. The degree of guilt of Catholic landowners was decided by a commission which met at Athlone and land was allocated by another at Loughrea.[70]

O'Dowd details the importance of women in the transplantation process. Firstly, as wives of transplanted landowners, women often had to manage forfeited land while their husbands attended the commissions, and secondly as landowners in their own right. This latter group was created despite the legal conventions which dictated that all property was owned by a husband or his family. However, for the purposes of the land settlement widows and wives of exiled royalists were treated as landowners and therefore became eligible for transplantation. In other words, these Catholic women became landowners to enable the government to remove them from their forfeited lands, which could then be settled by Cromwellians. Although the settlement was applicable to all Catholics whether they were Gaelic or English in origin, it does appear that women in the latter category who had influence could have transplantation delayed. Viscountess Thurles resisted transplantation throughout the 1650s and was restored to her estate in 1660. The same applied to women who married an English Protestant and converted to that religion.[71] In total Catholic ownership of land was about 60% in 1641, between 8% and 9% in 1660 when the Commonwealth ended and 20% in 1685.[72]

What happened to many poorer and less fortunate women, when the estimated 30–40,000 Irish soldiers departed for Spain and France, is suggested by an order of July 1653 from the parliamentary commissioners:

> Upon consideration had of the multitude of persons, especially women and children wandering up and down the country, that daily perish in ditches, and are starved for want of relief: it is thought fit that such

'Women and war in Ireland in the 1640s', p. 94. **70** Ibid., pp. 104–5. See also 'Transplantation (to Connacht)' in S.J. Connolly (ed.), *The Oxford companion to Irish history* (Oxford, 1998), p. 549. **71** O'Dowd, 'Women and war in Ireland in the 1640s', pp. 104–5. **72** J.G. Simms, *Jacobite Ireland, 1685–91* (London, 1969), p. 4. According

women as have able bodies to work, and such children of about twelve
years, whose husbands and parents are dead or gone beyond the seas ...
may be taken up by the overseer of the poor and that to prevent the said
persons from starving, the overseers are hereby authorised to treat with
merchants for the transplanting the said persons into some English
plantation in America.[73]

The Irish did not share the Cromwellians' view that transportation was a
charitable and beneficent act 'for their own good and, and likely to be of so great
an advantage to the public'.[74] In many respects the condition of captive
indentured labour in the tobacco and sugar plantations of Barbados, Jamaica or
St Kitts was worse than that of slaves; the master, at least, had an interest in
keeping his slaves alive because they were a form of property. Petty's estimate
of 6,000 women and children transported to the West Indies must be regarded
as a minimum because a priest's visitation in 1666 found double that number.[75]
John Lynch, writing in 1666, lamented that 'the women were sold cheaply in
the public markets in these English [West] Indian colonies to gratify their
master's passions, or to be their slaves'.[76]

   Little is known about the lives and circumstances of the women who left
Ireland voluntarily in the earlier period. One exception is Leonora O'Moore,
the daughter of Rory O'Moore, one of the leaders of the 1641 rising. She left
Ireland in 1652, the year before her father took refuge on Inishbofin, off county
Galway and subsequently disappeared. She married Arturo O'Neill in Madrid.
Her husband was born in Glasdrummond, Co. Armagh, around 1620 and was
the son of Catalina O'Neill, a niece of Eoghan Roe. Arturo had also left Ireland
in 1652 with recruits for the Spanish army and was appointed colonel of the
Regiment of Tyrone in 1660. Although Leonora was widowed within ten years,
her connections and influence ensured that her family was well maintained. Indeed
in 1666 her eldest son, Daniel O'Neill, was awarded the rank of Knight of the
Military Order of Calatrava, a title his father had previously held. Of further
interest in Leonora's case, was the information she provided of the circumstances
of her departure from Ireland. Leonora was asked to produce family papers on the
occasion of the elevation of her son and she replied under oath:

   The truth is this that at the time of leaving Ireland fleeing from the
   tyranny of the heretics, I spent eight days hidden underground and both
   myself and my husband and the others only thought of saving our lives

to Bennett, during the 1640s, women became liable for war taxation in their own right
in Dublin and Youghal in Ireland and in Worcestershire, England. Bennett, *Civil wars in
Britain and Ireland*, pp. 199, 200.   73 Beresford Ellis, *Hell or Connaught*, p. 83.   74 P.F.
Moran, *Historical sketch of the persecutions suffered by the Catholics of Ireland* (Dublin,
1884), p. 325.   75 Ibid., p. 323.   76 Cited ibid., p. 324.

without looking after any possessions or papers whatever, nor could we have done so, and so I neither have them nor can say anything more than what I have said already, which is true and I say and swear'.[77]

The surrender at Limerick in 1691 signalled the end of the Williamite wars in Ireland. Jacobite widows and wives had to ascertain whether their spouses had been in the territories included under the articles of the Treaty of Limerick and then petition the Court of Claims at Chichester House, if they were to escape attainder and loss of land. In 1700, the court began to hear claims from women who were widows, wives and guardians and had an interest in an estate forfeited due to either outlawry, the treaties of Limerick and Galway or royal grants.[78] Not all claims were successful – Clara Roche, widow of Philip, who did not come under the articles of Limerick, claimed her jointure of his forfeited Cork estates but this was rejected by the court.[79]

The maintenance of Irish families in exile was also dependent on land settlements in Ireland. Following the Jacobite defeats, the earl of Clancarty forfeited his lands to the earl of Portland when he left for France. Had he stayed in Ireland, he would have been included as a serving Jacobite officer within the terms of the Treaty of Limerick. His wife, who followed him into exile, claimed 'a competent maintenance' from Portland. This was rejected by the Court of Claims and she died in June 1704, in Germany.[80]

Even though they were on the winning side, Irish Williamite widows could also face difficult circumstances; Margaret Hamilton, a widow, petitioned the Irish House of Commons for assistance in 1697, because her husband, Gustavus Hamilton, had been one of the first to take up arms and had used borrowings and savings to fortify Enniskillen, where he was governor in 1689. His debts were still owing and she appealed that his service and 'the miserable conditions of herself and her five children' be considered. She was given assistance.[81]

In 1693 the Irish lord justices outlawed Frances, duchess of Tyrconnell, thereby preventing her from inheriting the deceased Tyrconnell's estate, because she 'has been so very remarkable here in her actions against their majesties and the Protestant interest'.[82] However, Frances was influential; Queen Anne intervened on her behalf and a private act was passed restoring her lands. The bishop of Clogher wrote to the bishop of Ossory on 2 April 1702, of the Irish bishops' inability to oppose the act:

77 Micheline Walsh, 'Some notes towards a history of the womenfolk of the wild geese,' *Irish Sword* 5 (1961/2), pp. 135–7. The author provides further evidence to suggest that Rory O'Moore was alive and in Ireland in 1666. Ibid., p. 137.   78 J.G. Simms, *The Williamite confiscation in Ireland, 1690–1703: Studies in Irish history, vol. vii* (London, 1956), p. 20.   79 D'Alton, *Illustrations*, p. 56.   80 Ibid., pp. 118–19.   81 Ibid., p. 193.

> My lady Tyrconnell's bill was hurried with such unusual expedition
> through both houses, both whigs and tories striving who could favour it
> most, that we could not overtake it with our saving in either house; this is
> to be the sister of a favourite; indeed I do not know of any bill this session
> that has passed so very quietly and unanimously.[83]

One woman for whom the war provided an opportunity to prosper was
Elizabeth Villiers, William's mistress from 1679 to 1695. Jonathan Swift noted
that 'her advice hath many years been asked and followed in the most important
affairs of state.'[84] She received from William the most valuable of all the granted
estates – James' 'private estate' of 95,649 acres spread over sixteen counties.
According to Simms, the gross income was £26,000 per annum, which included
£3,000 per annum for Arabella Churchill and Susannah Bellasis, James' mistresses.[85] Although it was a controversial decision, which was cancelled in 1700
along with William's other grants, Villiers did not concede her claim without a
fight and endowed Middleton College with land in Co. Cork in order to
strengthen it. She did not succeed in her claim, though the school survived.
Cancellation was a personal affront to William's authority and he was furious at
having his grants challenged. Villiers, by now countess of Orkney, did, however,
come out of the whole affair with an endowment of £1,500 per year. The
forfeited land was added to that already in the hands of the commissioners.[86]

The majority of women in the 1690s were not, however, landowners or
related to landowners; thus, their fate remains unknown. In return for
surrendering Limerick city, their last stronghold, the Jacobites were given free
passage to France in addition to other concessions from those who stayed
behind. Consequently, the first and second of the military articles in the Treaty
of Limerick included provision for Jacobite women and children either to
return to their original homes or to go to the continent.[87] Thirty ships arrived
at the mouth of the Shannon on 30 October 1691, not to transport the defeated
Jacobites, but to continue the fighting. However, the fleet sailed from Limerick
on 16 November with 6,659 Irish including men, women, children and servants.
Further ships left on 28 November with 3,022 Irish on board, and English
vessels left Cork carrying 3,400 Irish troops but there is no reference to women
or children.[88] However, Würtemberg, in a letter to Christian V on 6 November
1691, stated that 4,000 Irish women and children would be transported to
France. The last group left from Cork with Sarsfield in January 1692 with 2,804

---

82 *Calendar of the State Papers, domestic series*, [hereafter *Cal. S.P. dom.*], iv, 1693,
(London, 1903), pp. 357–8.   83 Simms, *Williamite confiscation*, p. 92.   84 F. Elrington
Ball (ed.), *The correspondence of Jonathan Swift*, 6 vols (London, 1910–14), ii, appendix
iii, p. 409.   85 Simms, *Williamite confiscation*, p. 92.   86 Black, *Kings in conflict*, pp.
286–7, 291.   87 Gilbert, *A Jacobite narrative*, p. 302.   88 Sheila Mulloy, 'The French
navy and the Jacobite war in Ireland 1689–91,' *Irish Sword* 18 (1990–1), p. 30.

Irish troops. In total between 15,000 to 16,000 men went to France after the Treaty, adding to the 5,000 who went during the war, and approximately 10,000 Irish women left also.[89]

However, it does appear that not all of the women who wanted to accompany their husbands were able to do so, as the treaty did not detail the transportation arrangements for the women and children. Prior to the arrival of the ships in the Shannon the situation forced Sarsfield to write to Ginkel on 17 October 1691. He outlined the difficulties he faced during the embarkation of the 'wives and children belonging to our troops'. He hoped that 'sincerity and candour' would prevail but if this was not so, he threatened to halt the embarkation, as the troops would not leave without their families. Ginkel provided more ships, but many women and children were still left behind.[90] Charles O'Kelly describes embarkation day in Cork:

> when the ablest men were once got on shipboard, the women and babes were left on shore, exposed to hunger and cold without any manner of provision, and without any shelter in that rigorous season but the canopy of heaven and in such a miserable condition that it moved pity in some of their enemies.[91]

Most of the women who fled after Limerick in 1691 sought refuge in France, and not in Spain or its European possessions, as had been the case after the battle of Kinsale in 1601. Life in a foreign country was not easy for any exile, but there were degrees of hardship as is clear from the petitions made to the French authorities.

Queen Mary Beatrice wrote to a friend about the thousands of Irish wives and children who came to St Germain-en-Laye 'who are poverty itself' and when the men moved on with the French armies they 'remain on our hands'.[92] According to Oman, she spent hours trying to find places in convents, schools and lodgings for the dependants of Irish soldiers.[93]

The wives, daughters and mothers of the members of the five Irish regiments who opposed the Austrians in the War of the Spanish Succession in 1701, remained at the army post in Grenoble. The commanding officer wrote to Chamillart, the minister for war:

> There are at Grenoble more than 60 wives of Irish officers who have remained there in the hope that their husbands' regiments would return

89 Danaher and Simms, *The Danish force*, p. 137.   90 Gilbert, *A Jacobite narrative*, pp. 309–12.   91 Charles O'Kelly, 'Macariae Excidium' in T.C. Croker (ed.), *Narratives illustrative of the contests in Ireland in 1641 and 1690* (London, 1841), p. 106.   92 Quoted in Grace Cantillon, 'Honora Bourke – a wife's story' in B. Dewar (ed.), *Living at the time of the siege: essays in social history* (Limerick, 1991), p. 18.   93 Carola Oman, *Mary of*

to this province for winter quarters. All of them are burdened with children and are in great want and, seeing that those regiments are not returning, they are persecuting me for permits to enable them to go and join their husbands.[94]

The permits would enable them to get shelter and food at army posts along their route. Chamillart did not wish to issue permits, as he and the governor of the province wanted the women to move on and at the least expense. The governor was cautious about giving money for 'having received this money, they may not go or may use the money to move to another town of the province; this happens frequently with women of that nation for, in the majority of cases, the salaries of their husbands is not sufficient for their maintenance'.[95] It is not clear what happened to these women who were at the mercy of the French authorities, but other women with connections fared relatively better.

Some Jacobite supporters were fortunate to be assigned a foreigner's pension from Louis XIV. The wife of William Coppinger, high sheriff of Cork, who had followed James to France was one such example. After Coppinger's death Louis assigned her a 'foreigner's pension' and conferred on her a *don d'aubaine* or exemption from the *droit d'aubaine*. The latter allowed the French monarchy to inherit the property of foreigners.[96] Anastasie Dillon, widow of Alexander Barnewell, who had been killed in Italy in 1703, petitioned Chamillart the following year for an increase in her pension. She had come to France with her brother and father who also died in the war. Bochu commented on this request, also revealing the varying attitudes towards Irish women of different classes. Bochu wrote that Anastasie was 'a lady of great virtue who always went into a convent during her husband's absences and campaigns and, since his death, she has not left the convent where she is bringing up her two daughters'.[97] Her disposition and status as the widow of a lieutenant-colonel made Bochu seek a doubling of her pension to six hundred *livres*. While she was not successful in securing the increase, despite the support of the duc de la Feuillade who was married to Chamillart's daughter, Anastasie did prosper. Her daughter's education was paid for by marquise de Maintenon, wife of Louis XIV, and she became governess of the duc de Chartres, grandson of the duc d'Orleans, the regent during Louis XV's minority. She had also managed to have her pension increased to one thousand *livres* and to have an investment of twenty thousand *livres*. When she died in 1736 she was living in the royal palace in Paris with servants to whom she left sums of money.[98]

Modena (London, 1962), p. 207.   **94** Micheline Kerney Walsh, 'Irish women in exile, 1600–1800,' *The O'Mahony Journal* 11 (1981), p. 43.   **95** Kerney Walsh, 'Irish women', p. 43.   **96** Richard Hayes, 'Biographical dictionary of Irishmen in France,' *Studies* (September 1942), p. 337.   **97** Kerney Walsh, 'Irish women', p. 43.   **98** Ibid., p. 43.

For other widows remarriage was the only way to avoid 'the bondage of poverty'.[99] Hanora Bourke, Sarsfield's wife, who had been 'outlawed' along with Sarsfield and set up home at St Germain-en-Laye and with her daughters, Lady Kilmallock and Lady Mount Leinster, received small pensions from Louis XIV. She continued entertaining there and one visitor was 'received … with great generosity, and treated … with much good nature'.[100] When Sarsfield was killed in 1693, she married the duke of Berwick, James' natural son by Arabella Churchill, on 23 March 1695. She had met him at her home, Portumna Castle, during the Irish wars.

There were, of course, Irish women who had relationships with Williamite soldiers, who remained with their regiments and went into exile also. After Limerick, William's regiments went into winter quarters and then carried on fighting against James in Flanders, Savoy and Silesia. Between 1692 and 1697 passes to leave Ireland were issued by the lord justices in Dublin as well as army authorities to such women. Mary Neale, Mary Wilson and Theresa Mullon were allowed by the army 'to go to Silesia for their husbands being Irishmen'.[101]

CONCLUSION

It is clear that warfare presented women with the opportunity to partake in fighting, to exercise independent action and to act on their political beliefs and it was also the case that in the 1650s women enhanced their status as landholders in the land settlement. However, during the 1640s women (and children) experienced extreme levels of physical attack, after the war the level of destitution women encountered created a 'woman' problem for the authorities and women faced transportation for the first time. Furthermore, in both periods of warfare, while women availed of the opportunities presented by warfare, it was always on male-defined terms. In other words, mainly within the context of male networks of power or in the absence of male heads of households or male leadership of popular discontent. Thus, it may be concluded that neither the war of the 1640s nor that of 1688–91 altered attitudes and assumptions about women in the seventeenth century, who remained the 'weaker vessel'.

99 Jerold Casway, 'Irish women overseas' in MacCurtain and O'Dowd, *Women in early modern Ireland*, p. 123.   100 D'Alton, *Illustrations*, pp. 153, 155.   101 Author unknown, 'Passes to Irish soldiers, 1692–7,' *Irish Sword*, 15 (1982), p. 115.

The mistress and matrimony: attitudes to marriage at the court of Louis XIV (1660–1715)

Linda Kiernan

Where in the world does one find a husband
who loves only his spouse and does not have
someone, be it mistresses or boys, on the side?
Charlotte Elizabeth, duchess d'Orléans.[1]

Il y a de bons mariages, mais il y n'y en a point de délicieux.
La Rochefoucauld.[2]

The figure of the royal mistress has traditionally been examined in the biographical genre. This approach has, in its customary attention to the more glamorous aspects of the position, led to the stereotyping of this prominent role at the court in terms of either sexual predator and/or political manipulatrix.[3] In this light recent scholarship has questioned the significance of the mistress due to the perceived insecurity of her position. It is undeniable that her proximity to the king was reliant on their continued relationship; however, it is arguable that she did not differ so much from the rest of the court. Every other courtier relied upon the king's favour to maintain status, though in shorter measure. Examination of the role through the social and ideological constructs surrounding her may offer a clearer picture of her actual court position.[4] Examination of

---

1 Charlotte Elizabeth, duchesse d'Orléans, *A woman's life in the court of the sun king: letters of Liselotte von der Pfalz*, translated and introduced by Elborg Forster (Baltimore, Md. and London, 1984), p. 87.   2 'There are good marriages, but there are none that are delightful': François VI de La Rochefoucauld, *Maximes, mémoires, œuvres diverses* (Paris, 1992), Maxim 113, p. 138.   3 Olwen Hufton, 'Reflections on the role of women at the early modern court', *Court Historian* 5 (2000), pp. 1–14. Hufton briefly mentions the problems of looking at women's history in a constructive and analytical way. In particular she refers to the proliferation of *vies intimes*, works with regard to prominent female positions at the court; queens, regents, queens consorts and mistresses.   4 This article constitutes part of a PhD thesis in progress, 'Perceptions of power: the role of the *maîtresse royale* at the court of Louis XIV'. Other facets of the role to be explored

marriage as the mistresses' foil and facilitator and the similarity of the two institutions with regards to their ability to negotiate and broker within the court may help to place the position of mistress on firmer ground than previously thought and also query the independence which seventeenth-century court society allowed women.[5]

This piece will examine the attitudes and perceptions of marriage during the reign of Louis XIV. How did views of marriage and of the husband-wife relationship allow for infidelity of the husband, and did these attitudes in turn facilitate a mistress in gaining influence? It will look at the common procedure of marriage and in particular the steps taken to arrange and execute a royal marriage at the highest level. The status of the mistress rested upon the co-operation of the court hierarchy as well as the continuing attentions of the king.[6] An examination of marriage in this respect may present a more lucid idea of how this hierarchy was prepared to collaborate. It will firstly give a brief over-view of the ecclesiastical views on marriage and how it should be conducted, and will then show how the French monarchy reacted to church intervention, before examining several marriages to gauge the effect of this legislation on the state of matrimony. By then looking at the king's own marriage it is possible to explore the specific circumstances from which a royal mistress emerges. Finally we will turn to the marriages of both Mme de Montespan and Mme de Maintenon, before considering the relationship of marriage and motherhood, the latter state being extremely significant in the position of both queen and mistress.

The court of Louis XIV was a court based on status. The construction and maintenance of a hierarchy depended upon the careful preservation of family lines and in turn the wealth and influence associated with a family name. One key factor to this conservation of dynastic power was the marriage choices made by the scions of each respective house. Without wise decisions at the altar a family's fortune or favours, royal or otherwise, might find themselves dissipated. Therefore a fully informed decision upon which wife or husband to take was usually based, not upon the whims or fancies of the prospective spouses, but upon the cold dictates of business and the advice of the court. Of course this is not to deny that the court witnessed happy marriages, but it was highly unusual for the court to observe the blossoming of a romance into a marriage which served both parties and their families equally well. In this atmosphere adultery was readily accepted. In fact for a man to take a mistress was considered a wise decision, not only as compensation for the sacrifice he had made in marriage, but also as an indicator of social standing. However, while a husband may have

include her involvement with court etiquette and ceremonial, her effect on the king's divine right to rule and the significance of the legitimated children which arise from these relationships.   5 On brokerage and patronage see Sharon Kettering, 'Brokerage at the court of Louis XIV', *Historical Journal* 36 (1993), pp. 69–87: 'The patronage power of early modern French noblewomen', *Historical Journal* 32 (1989), pp. 817–41.

taken a mistress and thinly veiled his infidelities, the wife was not at liberty to take the same measures as a comfort in a possibly loveless marriage. Nevertheless, popular culture extolled romantic visions of love, and allowed women greater sexual freedom, so long as this did not contravene family interest.[7]

FRENCH FAMILY VALUES: THE RELIGIOUS AND SECULAR APPROACH TO THE ALTAR, 1448–1697

Marriage at the French court was an essential component of a strong and stable aristocracy. Marriage provided a conduit for the exchange or consolidation of title, wealth, land, and status. Mutually beneficial unions were of the utmost importance for the preservation and, if lucky, the elevation of a family lineage. If love blossomed it was truly blessed; if not it was of the majority. This is not to say, however, that love matches did not occur; these were applauded so long as they were in accordance with the wishes of the respective families. The importance of parental consent is evident throughout the history of the French court. Its legislation increasingly weighed in favour of family interest. A marriage without parental consent was almost always viewed as worthless, either in terms of prestige or of finance. The church traditionally held that marriage relied on the consent of both parties concerned, thus opposing the idea of parental control and the idea of misalliances.[8] Church legislation on marriage was traditionally superseded by that of the French monarchy. One particularly disputed matter was that of 'clandestine marriages'. At the council of Tours in 1448 secret marriages were deemed punishable by excommunication, and it was stated that marriages should only take place in church. Again in 1485 at the council of Sens the fear of clandestine and supposed disadvantageous unions was addressed by declaring that marriages could no longer take place in domestic chapels. 'Ce sont le respect dû à la dignité du sacrement qui confère la grâce comme les autres sacrements, & la nécessité de prévenir tout soupçon de concubinage.'[9] This opinion of secret marriages is repeated right up until the

6 For detailed studies of the structure of the French court see firstly Norbert Elias, *The court society* (Oxford, 1983), and Jean-François Solnon, *La cour de France* (Paris, 1987). Daniel Gordon, *Citizens without sovereignty: equality and sociability in French thought, 1670–1789* (Princeton, 1994), provides some healthy opposition to the long established theories of Elias, while John Adamson, *The princely courts of Europe, 1500–1750* (London, 1999), presents an interesting comparative study.   7 J. Dewald, *Aristocratic experience and the origins of modern culture: France 1570–1715* (Berkeley, CA, 1993), p. 126.   8 For an excellent introduction to the medieval idea of marriage see Georges Duby, *Medieval marriage: two models from the twelfth century* (Baltimore, 1978).   9 'These are the respect due to the dignity of the sacrament which confers grace like the other sacraments, and the need to avoid any suspicion of concubinage': Jean Pierre Gilbert, *Tradition: ou histoire de l'église sur le sacrement de mariage* (Paris, 1725), vol. 1, p. 79.

reign of Louis XIV. In February 1556 Henri II allowed parents to disinherit their offspring if they married without permission, which was necessary for men up to the age of thirty and women until the age of twenty-five.[10]

The council of Trent provoked reaction rather than co-operation from the French monarchy. The decree *Tametsi*, while abhorring clandestine marriage, recognized the legitimacy of all marriages that had taken place in church. Henri III answered with the Ordonnance of Blois in May 1579 which outlined punishment not only for those who obtained illegal marriages, but also those who performed them. In 1629 and again ten years later Louis XIII reiterated this legislation. In 1697 Louis XIV granted parents the rights to oversee the remarriage of their widowed daughters, stating that widows required the written consent of their relatives.[11] Louis XIV also decreed that priests could marry only those who had at least six years residence within the parish.[12] This legislation reinforced marriage as a family contract and meant that its sanctity was subject to its secular suitability.[13] The effect of this progress of legislation is seen by Joan Davis as a politicization of marriage; however, it would appear that disobedient and rebellious children were a persistent problem, giving rise to the repeated enactment of very similar legislation. It also displays the fact that familial control of marriage was of the utmost importance. Marriage was much more of a union of families than of individuals.

The effect of familial consent in unsuitable matches is superbly displayed by the case of Mlle de Montpensier and the comte de Lauzun.[14] The disparity in status and wealth of the two protagonists was pronounced. The legacies of her father, Gaston d'Orléans, and mother, Marie de Montpensier, made Mademoiselle the wealthiest heiress in France. Over a period of ten years it appears that she developed a fondness for the young comte de Lauzun. Lauzun, or Puygeilhem as he was known before his father's death, though a minor member of the aristocracy, was a holder of the king's jacket, the *justaucorps à brevet*. Lauzun's membership of this elite singled him out as a confidante of the king, who had also made him captain of his dragoons. This honour was advantageous but did

---

10 Henri II had ulterior motives for this statute. Although it echoed legislation already in place, it allowed him to proclaim the marriage of a young Montmorency null, which allowed him to marry one of his illegitimate daughters into a prestigious family. For a detailed account of marriage within this family see Joan Davis, 'The politics of the marriage bed: matrimony and the Montmorency family, 1527–1612', *French History* 6 (1992), pp. 63–95.   11 Gilbert, *Tradition*, vol. 1 p. 347.   12 Olwen Hufton, *The prospect before her: a history of women in western Europe, 1500–1800* (New York, 1996), p. 103. 13 For informative introductions to marriage in seventeenth-century France see Jean-Claude Bologne, *Histoire du mariage en occident* (Paris, 1997), François Lebrun, *La vie conjugale sous l'ancien régime* (Paris, 1975) and Francis Ronsin, *Le contrat sentimental: débats sur le mariage, l'amour, le divorce de l'Ancien Régime à la Restauration* (Paris, 1990). 14 Anne-Louise d'Orléans, duchesse de Montpensier (1627–1693) known at the court as La Grande Mademoiselle; Antoine Nompar de Caumont, duc de Lauzun (1633–1723).

not propel him into the grade of his admirer. The match was so ill-conceived in terms of status that it led Mme de Sévigné to relay the news thus: 'it is the most marvellous, the most miraculous ... the most incredible ... something which can hardly be believed in Paris.'[15] La Grand Mademoiselle, the duchesse de Montpensier, was a princess of the blood, a *fille de France*, a fact she was eminently proud of and always took into consideration when viewing prospective husbands. She was born several years before the king, but was seen as a potential wife for Louis before the treaty of the Pyrenees. In their childhood, her pet name for the young king was *mon petit mari*; my little husband. On two occasions she was expected to become Holy Roman Empress, but on both occasions her hand was rejected in favour of other political alliances. She considered herself worthy only of an archduke, king, or emperor, as these were the only three equivalent titles she did not hold herself by birth. Her income of 500,000 livres a year made her extremely wealthy but her involvement in the Fronde cost her many years at court. Yet her infatuation with Lauzun was intense and the relationship was born of love, unlike those marriages previously considered for her. She described him fondly as ' the most honest man in the world, the nicest, and nothing would make me happier than marrying a man like him, whom I will love and who will love me too.'[16]

Despite Lauzun's good record with the king, he was in the habit of displeasing the king, leading to several stays in the Bastille. After finding that Lauzun was attempting to blackmail his own cousin, the Princess of Monaco, a *passade* of the king, the king quietly advised the would-be extortionist to betake himself to the Bastille.[17] Six months in the Bastille did not dissuade him from seeking further advancement at the court. His campaign to gain the post of 'Grand-mastership of artillery' brought him once again en route for the gates of the Bastille, following a particularly daring eavesdropping episode in the private chamber of the king and Mme de Montespan. His latest venture, that is making a highly unsuitable marriage was a no-win situation; either he wished to secure his own elevation, however improbable, or as La Bruyère put it 'to play the fool and marry for love.'[18] Despite this, when Mlle de Montpensier had overcome such obstacles as persuading the king that her marriage to Monsieur, Phillipe, duc d'Orléans, the king's recently widowed brother, was not a good idea, she secured the king's (temporary) approval for the marriage of her choice.[19] The decision was unsurprisingly opposed due to the importance of

15 Mme de Sévigné, *Lettres* (3 vols., Paris, 1953), vol. 1, p. 181. 16 Mlle de Montpensier, *Mémoires* (Paris, 1728), vol. 4, pp. 92–94, reproduced in Alain Niderst (ed.), *Les Français vus par lui-mêmes: le siècle de Louis XIV* (Paris, 1997), p. 61. 17 Ibid., p. 156. It should be noted that those whom the king sent to the Bastille were usually accompanied by a guard. Lauzun was afforded the dignity of making his own way to the château. 18 Jean de La Bruyère, *Characters: or, the manners of the age: with the moral characters of Theophrastus* (Dublin, 1776), p. 247. 19 Since 1635 princes of the blood were required to secure the consent of the king to marry. Not only did this apply to

Mlle de Montpensier's wealth and her enduring potential as a means of diplomatic reconciliation. Indeed Lauzun's own petulant behaviour may have influenced the king's final decision. He had foolishly expected greater recognition of his impending nuptials than was suitable to his rank; for example he expected the king and queen to attend on the ceremony.[20]

Her meeting with the king confirmed what she had expected; the marriage was banned. The king told her that everyone was convinced that he was ready to sacrifice her to benefit Monsieur de Lauzun. To Lauzun Louis promised his standing at court would be unaffected and that his decision had been forced by the general opinion at court.[21] In Louis's position it is reasonable to suggest his thoughts on the matter were that if she refused to make a marriage for the good of the country, then she would certainly not make one to its detriment. The queen and Monsieur had more practical considerations. They were determined not to see their cousin's great fortune pass outside the royal family, and they were seconded in their opposition by Condé – who had listened in to the king's refusal of marriage and resented the slight to their blood implicit in the bestowal of a royal princess on a mere gentleman. His presence in this matter suggests that Mademoiselle's hearty involvement in the Fronde had no bearing on the matter, as the king had sided with the greatest participant in the rebellion.

Saint-Simon's memoirs pay great attention to the concept of alliances and misalliances and to the etiquette of marriage arrangements and it is unions of persons from dissimilar status that irritate him the most. In Louis XIV's France it was considered normal for the status of the wife's family to be slightly inferior to that of the husband, and this had no bearing on the status of their children.[22] As Le Roy Ladurie comments, using Saint-Simon as a direct source, women who married did not always maintain their station or rise to a higher one, but an 'invisible hand' seems to have prevented the daughters of the highest aristocracy from descending below the line separating sword from gown.[23] Since the Paulette of 1604, which allowed the transmission of hereditary offices from spouse to spouse, misalliances had become more common. Unfortunately for Mademoiselle de Montpensier her love for Lauzun was deemed irrelevant in the face of court interests. She remained a potential bargaining chip for the French state, however; despite her eventual secret marriage with Lauzun in 1681, the foresight of Mme de Montespan had secured her wealth for her own children in the event of her death.

Mademoiselle, as a woman she also needed permission from her relatives. For an example of the king's written permission to marry, see Marie d'Orléans, duchesse de Nemours, *Mémoires suivis de letters inédites de Marguerite de Lorraine, duchesse d'Orléans* (Paris, 1990), pp. 320–7. 20 La Rochefoucauld, *Maximes*, p. 749. 21 Ibid. 22 Emmanuel Le Roy Ladurie, *Saint-Simon and the court of Louis XIV*, translated by Arthur Goldhammer (Chicago, 2001), p. 188. 23 Ibid., p. 192.

Marriages for monetary gain and status were derided somewhat in contrast to dutiful political marriages. Writers took low views of the more 'mercenary' alliances, especially of the lower aristocracy. One example shows a highly cynical view of marriage. The comte de Guiche on being asked by Richelieu to marry Mlle du Plessis-Chivray instead of Mlle de Pontchateau, replied that 'c'était son Eminence qu'il épousait, et non ses parentes, et qu'il prendrait celle qu'on lui donnerait.'[24] Saint-Simon was also guilty of hunting out favourable families, while not having special preference for individual members. His own marriage to Gabrielle des Lorges, the granddaughter of a financier, resulted in love although it had been considered a mismatch, albeit a slight one; her father had been Saint-Simon's superior during the Rhineland campaign, which offset the imbalance.[25] His earlier attempts to secure a wife belie a shrewd business sense. He petitioned M. de Beauvilliers, comte de Saint-Aignan[26] repeatedly for one of his eight daughters, the eldest of whom was then aged fourteen. Saint-Simon was rejected as a suitor for each of the girls, although he would have been a financially viable candidate for the duke's twelve-year-old.[27] The girls, however, were either too young or determined to enter the convent rather than marry.[28]

Le Roy Ladurie's research on the marriages mentioned in Saint-Simon's memoirs, shows that 54.2% of marriages were endogamous, that is that both bride and groom came from the same social rank and we assume did not give rise to the tense diplomacy displayed above.[29] Saint-Simon favoured these matches as they maintained the 'social order'. For Saint-Simon, Ladurie opines, the most important thing about any marriage was whether or not it tended to preserve or destroy the differences of degree that he believed were necessary to the stability of aristocratic society, indeed of society in general.[30] In saying this Saint-Simon did not merely promote marriage for the superficial gains it promised; he applauded a good love match as long as no misalliance or other catastrophe was involved.

Another episode concerning Saint-Simon shows a rather ruthless approach to securing a suitable and beneficial marriage. The family of Saint-Simon had a long-standing quarrel with the Noailles family, who following the death of the regent (Philippe d'Orléans) occupied a much stronger position than that of

24 Wendy Gibson, *Women in seventeenth-century France* (Basingstoke, 1989), p. 46 ('it was his eminence whom he was marrying, not his female relatives, and that he would take the one given to him'.) 25 Ibid., p. 4. 26 M. de Beauvilliers, comte de Saint-Aignan (1648–1714), then in high favour, a minister of state and more importantly a gentleman of the bedchamber. 27 Olwen Hufton, *The prospect before her*, p. 113. 28 Louis de Rouvroy, duc de Saint-Simon, *Memoirs*, edited and translated by Lucy Norton (London, 1960) pp. 36 et seq. 29 This suggests that almost half the marriages mentioned by Saint-Simon were technically 'mismatches'. This can be explained by the Paulette of 1604, allowing the transmission of hereditary offices, thus leading titled families to ally with lesser families who held lucrative offices. 30 Le Roy Ladurie, *Saint-Simon and the court of Louis XIV*, p. 179.

Saint-Simon. The duke's memoirs attest to this family's insistence on healing the rift, despite the fact that Saint-Simon had much more to gain in the event.[31] They proposed to marry their younger daughter, Catherine Charlotte to Saint-Simon's elder son, Jacques-Louis.[32] Unfortunately the only obstacle in the way was Catherine's ailing husband, Philippe Alexandre, prince de Bournonville. The swiftness of events upon the obligingly premature death of the young prince (he was 28) reveals a heartless and methodical strategy even in the event of untimely death, especially when it appears contingency plans were already in place awaiting the demise of first husband:

> We had already agreed that when the event occurred we would go immediately and make the offer to the cardinal ... Mme de Saint-Simon found [the cardinal] having his supper ... He left the table and came to meet her with arms outspread and a beaming smile ... he said 'I can see what brings you. God's will be done! We are free! I shall go at once to the Maréchale de Gramont, and you shall hear from me very soon.[33]

The widow had two months to mourn her husband before her marriage into the Saint-Simon family was finalized; personal grief (if indeed she mourned at all) was overridden by family considerations. What is also interesting to note is that a reconciliation between the two families was deemed possible only through the marriage of their offspring. Simply to shake hands was wholly insufficient; the merging of family and more importantly of assets clearly signified commitment to a reconciliation.

One example which contradicts this tenet of parental consent and was deemed to upset the social rankings was the marriage of M. le duc de Chartres, the king's nephew, and Mlle de Blois, second daughter of the king and Madame de Montespan.[34] The only daughter of the king and Mlle de La Vallière had married a prince de Conti, but as Saint-Simon observed mercifully died childless (Saint-Simon hated to see the perpetuation of a bastard line).[35] The eldest daughter of Louis and Mme de Montespan had married Louis, duc de Bourbon, heir to the house of Condé.[36] These marriages were seen as a way to ease the king's illegitimate children into the legitimate royal line. However, marriage of a royal bastard to the king's only nephew was seen as crossing the

31 Saint-Simon, *Memoirs*, vol. 2 (London, 1968), pp. 483–6. The Noailles family held governorships, while many members of the family held different offices. The head of the family was senior captain of the king's bodyguard.   32 Catherine Charlotte Thérèse de Gramont (1707–55); Jacques-Louis, duc de Ruffec (1698–1746).   33 Saint-Simon, *Memoirs*, vol. 2, p. 484.   34 Philippe II, duc de Chartres, then d'Orléans, regent 1715–23 (1674–1723) married Françoise-Marie de Bourbon (1677–1749).   35 Marie-Anne (1666–1739) married Louis-Armand de Bourbon, prince de Conti (1661–85).   36 Louise-Françoise de Bourbon, Mlle de Nantes (1673–1743), legitimized 1680, married in 1685 to Louis III de Bourbon-Condé (1668–1710).

line, literally. As a grandson of France, the duc de Chartres far outranked the princes of the blood. In addition his father, Monsieur, kept his own court, a pleasure only afforded to the king and himself.

The most vociferous opposition to the match came from Monsieur's wife, the Princess Palatine. It seems that Monsieur and M. le duc de Chartres quite easily gave in to the king's suggestions, and in turn expected Madame to do likewise. She was shrewd enough not to oppose the marriage so openly as to draw unwanted attention or the king's displeasure; however, the accounts left by Saint-Simon and the Princess Palatine betray an extremely disgruntled reaction. Louis cleverly offered the marriage in the guise of a favour for his nephew. He explained 'that the encircling war had put many eligible princesses out of reach, that no princess of the blood was of suitable age, and that he could show his love no better than by offering him his own daughter, both of whose sisters were already married to princes of the blood'. (So it would seem they had themselves been elevated along with their sister.) 'Such an alliance would make him more than a nephew, [it would make him] a son-in-law; but nonetheless, eager though he might be for the match, he had no desire to force him but would leave him free to choose for himself.'[37] This of course was no choice and the conduct of the Princess Palatine clearly shows her frustration with the situation. On hearing of the news from the king she dropped the briefest of curtseys and had her back turned before the king looked up. The following day M. le duc de Chartres approached her, as he did every day, in order to kiss her hand; at that moment Madame slapped his face so hard that the sound was heard several paces away and caused him great embarrassment at the court.[38]

It appears this marriage was not Madame's worst fear realized. She excused the marriage somewhat for the fact that it was her son who gave rank to Mlle de Blois. This is the point that Le Roy Ladurie makes, that for the husband to give rank is acceptable, but the bride's power to bestow her wealth and status was somewhat diminished in comparison. In 1692 Madame celebrated on the news that the marriage of the Duc du Maine and Anne-Louise-Bénédicte de Bourbon had been arranged. She gleefully wrote: 'I believe that the old trollop [Mme. de Maintenon, who had campaigned for the best marriages possible for her former wards] must have been told what the populace of Paris are saying, and that must have frightened her. They say very loudly that it would be shameful for the king to give his bastard daughter to a legitimate prince of the house. However, since my son gives his rank to his spouse, they would let it pass albeit it regretfully.'[39] It is uncertain whether the Parisian populace would be so concerned with the intricacies of rank and marriage. It is certain that the court was finely attuned to the intrigues surrounding the negotiations for marriages, but to examine whether Madame's assertion that 'if the old woman should have

37 Saint-Simon, *Memoirs* vol. 1 (London, 1967), p. 14.   38 Charlotte Elizabeth, duchesse d'Orléans, *A woman's life*, p. 75.   39 Ibid.

the gall to give my daughter to M. du Maine they would throttle him before the marriage was concluded'[40] would actually come to pass would be interesting. This sounds like a comforting delusion on the part of Madame. Nevertheless the middle classes were subject to the same principle of parental consent and among the professional groups it was common for children of the same profession to marry and consolidate businesses. In agriculture a marriage could unite two considerable farms.[41] Despite teething problems the marriage of Mlle de Blois and the duc de Chartres was a happy one by all accounts. It is also of note that during these objections and scenes of stamping feet and slapping faces the young bride was not consulted, nor was her attitude to the marriage recorded as important.

THE POLITICAL MARRIAGE: LOUIS XIV AND MARIE-THÉRÈSE

While the marriages contracted by members of court were sensitive to familial requirements, the marriage of the sovereign was obliged to meet the needs of the state. It is reasonable to suppose that Louis XIV never considered anything other than a marriage that would stabilize the monarchy and contribute to the *gloire* of the state. While many marriages at court came about purely as the result of dynastic considerations and for financial gain, the marriage of the Infanta was elevated above these not merely by rank but by nature. The 'political marriage' was respected for its air of duty and perhaps of sacrifice. Wendy Gibson views such a marriage in the context of state security and notes that there were few protests against the custom.[42] Marie Thérèse was brought up in expectation of marriage abroad. Louis never doubted that his own marriage could only be one of advantage to the kingdom, perhaps the only time of uncertainty being during his teenage affair with Marie Mancini, niece of Mazarin.[43] Mancini recalled that the king approached marriage as he was expected to, with duty. She wrote: 'When the persuasions of the queen, his mother, and those of Mazarin, coupled with reasons of state, would not let grow what he desired.'[44]

The political marriage was viewed in an elevated state only for what it meant outside the union. If the reason for this was the sacrificial element involved from the two parties, it raised questions of the marriage as a functioning relationship. The emphasis was very much upon the negotiations and the resulting treaty. This marriage was valued for its immediate honours, wealth

40 Charlotte Elizabeth, duchesse d'Orléans, *A woman's life*, p. 76.   41 For more detail on the intermarriage of the middle and lower classes, see Hufton, *The prospect before her*, pp. 102–36.   42 Gibson, *Women in seventeenth-century France*, p. 45.   43 Mazarin married Marie to the Connétable Colonna and she was given a generous allowance. For a detailed biography see Claude Dulong, *Marie Mancini* (Paris, 1993).   44 Marie Mancini, *Mémoires* (Paris, 1965), p. 110.

and political significance. There was very little said of life beyond the vows, save perhaps Louis's ambitions upon non-payment of his wife's dowry and, of course, the matter of producing heirs. Indeed the issue of the dowry was of extreme importance: not only did it signify the surrender of the new queen's political power in her country; it was only payable upon her physical 'surrender' to the king. The physical and the political become one in this respect; the first payment of the dowry was only payable upon proof that the marriage has been consummated. While Louis was able to fulfil his conjugal obligations, the non-payment of the dowry allowed him to claim his wife's political inheritance also. It is interesting to note that, while the birth of an heir was essential to the success of the union, the very consummation of the marriage was of high symbolic value also, which raises questions about the king's own physical relationship with his mistresses.

Abby Zanger has concentrated on the wedding ceremony itself and how symbols and adornment reinforced and consolidated the image of a controlled queen. The wedding ceremony in general was extremely important, not only for the advantages it would bring for its participants, but also as an opportunity for display of finery, wealth and above all status. One incident illustrates the lengths to which courtiers went to insure they would not face embarrassment at such an event. Saint-Simon retells particularly farcical goings-on in the approach of the marriage of the duc de Bourgogne. The need for finery had resulted in a shortage of tailors and dressmakers. The memoirist recounted 'Mme la Duchesse took it into her head to send archers (yeomen, who wore smocks like workmen and so looked innocent) to kidnap those [dressmakers] working for the duc du Rohan, but the king learned of it and was not pleased, he made her return them at once.'[45]

Zanger has also commented on the nature of the political marriage and concentrates solely on that of Louis and Marie Thérèse.[46] Zanger sees the marriage as a 'depowerment' of the queen. This idea is not a new concept in light of seventeenth-century marriage. It was a common trait of marriages that the wife was the subservient figure; coupled with this, Marie Thérèse became subject to French Salic law, which restricted the independent rule of royal females.[47] In saying this, it should be noted that this position had produced extremely powerful women in the past, for example Catherine de Medici, Marie de Medici and to a certain extent Louis's mother, Anne of Austria.

---

45 Saint-Simon, *Memoirs*, vol. 1, p. 97. For a further account of the expense of marriage see Mme de la Tour du Pin, *Memoirs* (London, 1969), pp. 66–70.   46 Abby Zanger, *Scenes from the marriage of Louis XIV* (Stanford, 1997).   47 For an examination of the role of the queen see Fanny Cosandey, *La reine de France: symbole et pouvoir*, (Paris, 2000).

THE MARRIED MISTRESS: MME DE MONTESPAN

In contrast to the marriage of the king are the marriages of both his *maîtresse royale* and of his *passades*. The princesse de Soubise conducted her affair with the king incredibly discreetly and, unlike the marquis de Montespan, her husband profited unashamedly from his wife's dalliances at court.[48] His immense income of 400,000 livres a year was due in great part to the appreciation of Louis, as Saint-Simon recorded: 'It was the fruit of discretion such as few would care to imitate ... of heeding the lesson learned from the example of M. de Montespan.'[49] Indeed the subservience of the queen is striking when compared to the case of Mme de Montepan's own husband. The marriage of Mme de Montespan, Louis's ambitious and charismatic *sultane-reine*, provided Louis with troublesome opposition. The relationship between Louis and Mme de Montespan initially astonished the courtiers. Previously the king's affairs with married women had been discreet and thoroughly screened. The public liaison with Mlle de La Vallière involved one adultery only – the king's own, which was nothing new. This, however, was double adultery, in a time when the dalliances of the husband were forgiven but the flirtations of a wife judged insufferable. Madame, the king's sister-in-law, also wrote once of another young lady at the court: 'Does the young duchesse not know that a woman's honour consists of having commerce with no-one but her husband, and that it is not shameful to have mistresses but shameful indeed to be a cuckold?'[50] In a society which used marriage as a tool of social stratification, adultery was virtually taken for granted. This cavalier attitude remained in the male domain; women's emotional and sexual activities were confined to marriage, while men's were free to roam.[51] Barbara Woshinsky has commented that society did not expect a husband and wife to love one another. In fact the couple who remained tediously faithful to one another may have lost out on certain political advantages,[52] and certainly in this case the political gain was impossible to resist. This public 'double-adultery', as Saint-Simon called it, was a novelty, but an insulting one to the court and above all to the discarded marquis de Montespan.

More revealing in this episode than the outrage of a woman leaving her husband is the scorn with which the marquis was treated as the cuckolded husband. His behaviour in trying to retrieve his wife was treated with the utmost frivolity and his antics became well known at the court. His conduct was ridiculed not only by the courtiers but also by Mme de Montespan herself. Primi Visconti recorded that the persistent cuckold, who had refused monetary

48 Anne Chabot de Rohan, princesse de Soubise (1648–1709), daughter of duc Henri de Rohan-Chabot, married her cousin François de Rohan-Soubise in 1663.   49 Saint-Simon, *Memoirs*, vol. 2, p. 264.   50 Charlotte-Elizabeth, duchesse d Orléans, *A woman's life*, p. 87.   51 Ibid., p. 25.   52 Barbara Woshinsky, *La princesse de Clèves: the tension of elegance* (The Hague, 1973), p. 69.

compensation from the king, acted as though his wife was dead.[53] His 'bereavement' for his wife led him to stage full mourning for her.[54] He draped his coach in black, decorated it with antlers (acknowledging the cuckold accusations) and paraded under the very eyes of the king.[55] Mlle de Montpensier approached Mme de Montespan one day with reports of her estranged husband's latest activities. The report began: 'He came to me one evening and repeated a speech which he claims to have delivered to the king, during which he quoted countless passages from the Scriptures and made many arguments to oblige him [that is, the king] to return his wife to him and to fear the judgement of God.' Mlle de Montpensier told him: 'you are mad. No-one will ever believe you actually delivered this speech.'[56] At Saint-Germain Mlle de Montpensier informed Mme de Montespan that her estranged husband was 'madder than ever' and that she had told him, if he did not hold his tongue he deserved to be locked up. Mme de Montespan wryly replied to the news: 'He is the laughing stock in the court. I am ashamed that not only my parrot but my husband too serve to amuse the riff-raff.'[57]

Louis dealt with the situation thus, by having the rightful husband arrested and packed off to his estates in Guyenne, and then arranging a speedy dissolution of the marriage. One legitimate criticism the court made of the marquis de Montespan is that he did not come looking for his wife immediately upon her infidelity with the king. The affair seems to have been some years old before the marquis took extreme offence, and it was not until after the birth of Mme de Montespan's fifth child by the king that the marriage was dissolved. The king forced M de Montespan to accept 100,000 écus as a royal gift which led to whispers that M de Montespan had sold his wife, albeit in a forced sale.

This episode is extremely interesting in that not only did the mistress succeed in establishing herself at court in spite of the king's marriage, but did so also in spite of her own. Those who sought favour through Mme de Montespan ignored the fact that she not only defied the king's marriage but also denied her own. Her significance lay in that she held the king's attention for the foreseeable future, and while she held the king's attention she held that of the court. The expulsion of M. de Montespan is symbolic also of Mme de Montespan's position; she became the dominant figure of the marriage. The marquis's humiliation was not only a personal failure; it signalled to the court that a woman capable of securing a wealthy and powerful protector could control the fate of her traditionally domineering partner. In contrast, the queen had fulfilled her role in becoming queen and providing heirs, thus perpetuating the

53 Primi Visconti, *Mémoires sur la cour de Louis XIV, 1673–1681* (Paris, 1988), p. 16.
54 P. René Rapin, *Mémoires de la compagnie de Jésus sur l'église et la société, la cour, la ville, et le jansénism.* (Farnborough, 1972; reprint of Lyons edition, 1865), vol. 3, pp. 490–1.
55 Francis Steegmuller, *La Grande Mademoiselle* (London, 1955), p.158.   56 Gillette Ziegler, *The court at Versailles* (London, 1960), p. 62.   57 Ibid., p. 63.

royal line and maintaining a clear stratification in contrast to the birth of Mme de Montespan's illegitimate children. It is reasonable to assume that there were those who clung to the queen, who realized that on the untimely death of the king power would be obliged to pass to her. However, the situation never arose.

The expulsion of this husband also led to an interesting symmetry of relationships around the king. The close proximity of the queen and the mistress, one on either side, reflects a pervading theme in the structure of Louis's court. The founding of parallel lines of royal blood physically embodied this symmetry. The death of the queen and the marriage of the king to Mme de Maintenon does not conform to this symmetry; however, it is possible that after the 'affair of the poisons' Louis regarded the safety of the body politic as greater than a need for passionate diversions and thus disrupted this dynamic.

THE MISTRESS MARRIES: MME DE MAINTENON AS ROYAL WIFE

With the death of Marie Thérèse in 1683, the establishment of a female regency, save the possible official remarriage of the king, seemed unlikely. Power would not be left to the queen but would pass on only after the death of Louis himself. The precise date of the marriage of Mme de Maintenon and the king is disputed; however, it appears to have quickly followed the death of the queen. His mourning for the queen was apparently a chore. Mme de Maintenon wrote to Mme de Brinon: 'do not be tired of getting the king prayed for; he stands now more than ever in need of Graces to persevere in a State contrary to his Inclinations and Habits.[58] It is clear that Mme de Maintenon certainly pushed for the marriage, although she denied her desire for it.[59] Her insistence has been attributed to her devout religious convictions, and it is possible that her years in the service of Mme de Montespan had ingrained a revulsion in her for the position of *maîtresse royale*, but it is very likely she had clearly recognized how fragile that position was in the hands of the king. Granted, Mme de Montespan was mistress to a husband and not to a widower, but Louis could still have used his second marriage as a tool of diplomacy, rather than establishing a cosy private relationship in his twilight years. According to La Beaumelle, Mme de Maintenon's early biographer, it was the king's Jesuit confessor, Père de la Chaise, who proposed a secret union.[60] Nevertheless this marriage ceremony was kept extremely secret, to such an extent that the exact date of the marriage is placed anytime between 1683, as soon as four days after the death of the queen, and four years later. However, it is likely that the marriage took place between March and June of 1684. In a letter to her brother dated 18 June 1684,

---

58 Mme de Maintenon, *Letters*, translated by G. Faulkner (Dublin, 1758), vol. 1, p. 32.
59 Ibid., p. 34.   60 Laurent Angliviel de La Beaumelle, *Memoires pour servir à l'histoire de Mme de Maintenon* (Amsterdam, 1755), vol. 3, p. 55.

she made reference to the diversity of their lives, which would suggest that the marriage and her official and legal rise in status had already taken place. Previous letters do not allude to this, but do make reference to the king in a most affectionate tone. In explaining to her brother their respective positions, 'mine is turbulent and splendid, yours calm and obscure', she asserts that 'It is God that has raised me and he knows that I did not seek after it, nay that I did not even forsee it. I shall never rise higher.'[61] In July she writes somewhat wearily: 'Except those who fill the highest stations, I know none so unhappy as those who envy them. Did you but know what it is! If I live long enough to effect it, my niece shall be well married. The thoughts of it comfort me for the loss of my liberty.'[62] In 1687 Madame wrote 'because of what I know of marriage in this country, I do not believe that if they were married they would be so much in love as they are. But then, perhaps secrecy adds a special spice that other publicly married people do not have.'[63] So if this description is accurate perhaps the king allowed himself what he had been denied in his youth and had refused others.

Mme de Maintenon's view on the duties of a wife in marriage is almost identical to Molière's tongue-in-cheek approach. While Molière used the 'Maxims of marriage' of *L'École des Femmes* to their comic limit, Mme de Maintenon presented them as social tenets.[64] Mme de Maintenon's brother seems to have experienced some marital dysfunction, and turned to his sister for advice on how his naïve young wife was expected to conduct herself.[65] While Mme de Maintenon was extremely modest on her talents as a marriage counsellor, this did not stop her from writing a long letter detailing the ideal attributes of a respectable and virtuous wife :

> She had Piety; endeavour to promote it. Your interest is connected with Religion; for though plain in her person, she would find Lovers. Let her never go abroad alone. Yet let her not assume the airs of a great Lady; she will make herself ridiculous. Do not keep her under too much restraint; for that would make you look so.[66]

Mme de Maintenon, writing in 1678, four to five years before her second marriage, is clear that the wife's duty is to represent her husband well in society. There appears to be a lack of trust on the part of the husband. Mme de Maintenon thinks the girl, given any sort of encouragement, would prove

61 Mme de Maintenon, *Letters*, p. 37.   62 Ibid., p. 40 (letter dated 11 July 1684, at Versailles).   63 Charlotte Elizabeth, duchesse d'Orlèans, *A woman's life*, p. 53.   64 For a specific study on Molière see Robert McBride, 'The sceptical view of marriage and the comic vision in Molière', *Forum for Modern Language Studies* 5 (1969), pp. 26–46. 65 Monsieur d'Aubigné married Mlle Genieve Pietre, daughter of Simeon Pietre, Counsellor to the king, Attorney to His Majesty, and to the city of Paris.   66 Mme de Maintenon, *Letters*, p. 1.

unfaithful. Mme de Maintenon continues stating that the girl should watch her vanity, and for her to keep only the gentlewomen she needed.[67] Although Mme de Maintenon had some reservations about the girl improving herself cosmetically, she had no objections as to her intellectual advancement. She advised her brother, 'Let her habituate herself to read good books,' but this was to be tempered with a certain degree of social abstention. She continued that her new sister-in-law should 'keep herself indoors.'[68]

What is extremely interesting about this letter is Mme de Maintenon's view of her own first marriage. She comments to her brother that she is not qualified to give ample advice. 'You will think it odd perhaps that a woman who never was married should give you so much advice concerning the married state.'[69] This comment is intriguing. It reflects the view of many contemporaries, including that of Madame de Sévigné, who saw the young Françoise as Scarron's nurse rather than his wife; indeed one court anecdote records that he was in a state of decrepitude and 'her exemplary conduct as his nurse rather than his wife.'[70] Also it is unlikely that the marriage was ever consummated. She was fifteen when the marriage took place, Scarron in his forties. Mme de Maintenon claimed that she was qualified to give guidance as 'the great confidence which people have always placed in me has taught me more in this respect, than my own Experience could have done.'[71]

It is clear that Mme de Maintenon recognized legitimacy as the only form of survival within the royal family. Mistresses, despite giving birth to children of the king, remained outside the legitimate house, while their offspring were legitimized and in effect became more associated with their father. Mme de Montespan's children, notably the duc du Maine and the duc de Toulouse, became powerful figures under the tutelage of Mme de Maintenon. Nevertheless it would appear that in bringing his illegitimate children into the fold he reduced the likelihood of their rebellion. By legitimising them he sated their appetites somewhat, but not so much as to give them rights of succession. Mme de Maintenon obtained the greatest security of all, her marriage to the king. Although the marriage remained secret, it was made known to the people who mattered and in following years became very much an open secret. In the last years of Louis' reign, when it became clear that preparations were needed in anticipation of the succession of a five-year-old great grandson, Mme de Maintenon allied with the duc du Maine and duc de Toulouse in attempt to wrest power from the proposed regency council. This alliance of the legitimized bastards and, in effect a legitimized mistress, is a puzzle. The close relationship of the three is explained by Mme de Maintenon's previous occupation as their governess; however, it might be expected that she would side with her husband

67 Ibid., p. 2. 68 Ibid. 69 Ibid., p. 3. 70 Daniel Lizars (publisher, author not specified), *Court anecdotes* (London, 1825), p. 152. (J399042, The Joly Collection, National Library of Ireland.) 71 Mme de Maintenon, *Letters*, p. 2.

rather than with the children of her predecessor. Perhaps faced with the prospect of losing her point of contact with power, Mme de Maintenon sought an alternative.

MATRIMONY, MATERNITY AND THE MISTRESS

While legislation was strict in its regulation of the upper age limit for approved marriages it also provided for the cases of pre-pubescent marriages. The aforementioned legislation invariably prescribed the ages of twelve and fourteen for girls and boys respectively.[72] These ages reflect the natural capacity for reproduction, and indeed matrimony and maternity were inextricably linked. The marriage of Henri IV and Marguerite of Navarre was dissolved after twentyseven years of childless marriage in favour of Marie de Medici, who would give birth to Louis XIII. The betrothal of Louis XV to the very young Spanish Infanta was abandoned in favour of the more mature and, more importantly, fertile Maria Lesczcyński of Poland. The capacity of the queen to bear the legitimate children of the king was essential and upon its occasion it was made as public as possible. The queen was commonly shown with her children in portraiture; indeed royal births were public events. The mistress, however, was usually shown alone without the trappings of motherhood. It would seem that the children of this illegitimate union were not the problem as they gained recognition in their own portraits. The sight of the pregnant mistress also appears to have been extremely distasteful to the queen especially. She would pay the king's natural children attention, but 'never stooped so low as to countenance the mothers while they were in a state of pregnancy.'[73]

A legal precedent led to the legal dissociation of the mistress and her illegitimate children. The duc de Longueville, Charles-Paris d'Orléans, who died in 1672, stipulated in his will that he wished his illegitimate son by a married woman (Mme la maréchale de la Ferté) to be legitimized. On 7 September of the same year Louis XIV gladly signed letters patent declaring the legitimacy of the Chevalier d'Orléans, but significantly the papers did not formally identify the mother. It was not difficult then to legitimize the children of Mme de Montespan without mentioning her name. Their association with the mistress is the problem as is reflected in their legitimization by Louis. Their birth certificates denoted the father's name; however, they neglected to acknowledge the mother, hoping (unsuccessfully) to provide some thin disguise for the union.

72 For a detailed study of teenage marriage in seventeenth-and eighteenth-century France see Jean Pierre Bardet, 'Early marriage in pre-modern France', *History of the Family* 6 (2001), pp. 345–63.   73 Jean-Pierre Anquetil, *Mémoires of the court of France during the reign of Louis XIV and the regency of the duke of Orleans* (Edinburgh, 1791), vol. 1, pp. 229–30; François Bluche, *Louis XIV* (Paris, 1986), p. 395.

CONCLUSION

The prominence of the mistress at court was an accepted consequence of purposeful royal and aristocratic marriages. The position was an influential one; symbolically the mistress was an escape from the staid duties of marriage. But the physical element of the relationship, the birth of a parallel royal (albeit illegitimate) line signified an irreversible entrance into the royal household. While marriage was essential to respectability and within the family interest, there were few protests to bending vows a little. Indeed the king's example afforded the 'office' of mistress a higher degree of status in general. The fashion for a mistress, and if possible a French mistress, crossed Europe, especially within the small German courts and the English court. It is clear that while in theory the mistress (as a position) wholly opposed the sanctity of marriage, in reality she could co-exist quite peacefully and profitably with it.

Spanish queens and aristocratic women at the court of Madrid, 1598–1665

Alistair Malcolm

In January 1658, the seventh duke of Montalto, a long-time holder of provincial governorships and perpetual supplicant for advancement within the Spanish political hierarchy, was about to come to the end of a tour of duty as viceroy of Valencia. Ever mindful of his future prospects, he instructed his agent in Madrid to begin lobbying for a senior office within the central government to which he believed he was now entitled. The person most likely to satisfy the duke's ambitions was Don Luis de Haro, the king's favourite (or *valido*), who at that time was the pre-eminent figure in the court and government of Philip IV. But, in order to be certain that Haro would heed his entreaties, Montalto also instructed that approaches be made to Haro's daughter-in-law, the marchioness of Heliche, who in turn happened to be the duke's own cousin. As he informed his agent:

> Don Luis de Haro has nobody who is as obliged to him as me, and who in consequence may hold so high a place in his trust. The grandchildren of Don Luis will be of the House of Montalto [...] and for our relationship to work properly, it will always be necessary for His Excellency to consider me as one of his own. No valido has ever neglected this policy because it is reason of state as well as common sense.[1]

ABBREVIATIONS

ADA   Archivo de los Duques de Alba, Madrid.
ADR   Archivo de las Descalzas Reales, Madrid.
AGP   Archivo General del Palacio, Madrid.
AGS   Archivo General de Simancas.
AHN   Archivo Histórico Nacional, Madrid.
ASMa Archivio di Stato di Mantova.
ASMo Archivio di Stato di Modena.
BBMS Biblioteca de Bartolomé March Servera.
BL   British Library.
CSMA *Cartas de Sor María de Jesús de Ágreda y de Felipe IV*, ed. Carlos Seco Serrano, 2 vols.,

Biblioteca de Autores Españoles, cviii-cix (Madrid, 1958).
FLE   *Felipe IV y Luisa Enríquez Manrique de Lara, condesa de Paredes de Nava: un epistolario inédito*, ed. Joaquín Pérez Villanueva (Salamanca, 1986).
RAH   Real Academia de la Historia, Madrid.
RAV   *Relazioni degli stati europei lette al senato dagli ambasciatori veneti nel secolo decimosettimo*, ed. Nicolò Barozzi and Guglielmo Berchet, 6 vols. (Venice, 1860). All references are taken from Series I, vol. II (Spagna).

1 Montalto's instructions to Padre Fray Francisco de la Santísima Trinidad, 15 January

This appeal to kinship in order to secure preferment is a typical example of how high politics in seventeenth-century Madrid are often understood to have worked. Spanish government, like that of other early modern states, depended on an awkward combination of public and private communication, where the formal bureaucratic channels of the councils and secretariats could often be undermined by the informal ascendancy of those who were personally and physically close to the king and his ministers. Within this situation the influence of Spanish queens and aristocratic women was potentially crucial, because they not only enjoyed informal domestic access to their powerful male relatives, but also possessed considerable social and economic importance in their own right. They could inherit titles and property; they were able to engage in all kinds of legal transactions; and they enjoyed a measure of control over the increasingly disproportionate sums of money granted to them as dowries. Although they could not go to university like the younger sons of noble families who were destined for posts in the church or judiciary, many women were educated to a high level, some of them attending the literary academies that formed a central part of Spanish noble society and others taking the bolder step of publishing works in prose and verse.[2] So, in principle at least, there were wide opportunities for Spanish women, as members of the queen's household, as the wives and daughters of ministers, or as important members of the female religious orders, where the chance to acquire authority over

1658, BBMS MS 26/6/4, ff. 36r–40v. Don Luis Guillén de Moncada y Aragón, seventh duke Montalto (*c*.1613–72), was grandson of Don Juan de la Cerda, sixth duke of Medinaceli (1569–1607), by the latter's first marriage to Doña Ana de la Cueva; Doña Antonia María de la Cerda, first marchioness of Heliche (1635–70), daughter-in-law of Don Luis de Haro and Montalto's cousin, was granddaughter of the sixth duke of Medinaceli by his second marriage to Doña Antonia de Toledo y Dávila: Francisco Fernández de Bethencourt, *Historia genealógica y heráldica de la Monarquía Española, Casa Real y Grandes de España*, 10 vols (Madrid, 1897–1920), vol. 5, pp. 255–6, 264–9 and 276–7.   2 James Casey, *The history of the family* (Oxford, 1989), pp. 74–9 and 84–5; idem, *Early modern Spain: a social history* (London and New York, 1999), pp. 28–9, 145–7 and 199–201. Jeremy Robbins has emphasized that women who participated in the literary academies rarely published their poems, *Love poetry of the literary academies in the reigns of Philip IV and Charles II* (London, 1997), pp. 16–17; idem, *The challenges of uncertainty: an introduction to seventeenth-century Spanish literature* (London, 1998), pp. 32–4 and 35–7. Yet instances of female authorship (albeit outside the academy framework) are numerous. They include celebrated writers like the countess of Aranda, María de Zayas and Sor Juana Inés de la Cruz, as well as less well-known figures, such as the countess of Paredes who took the veil as Sor Luisa de Jesús in 1648 (see below) and ten years later published her *Año Santo: Meditaciones para todo el día del año sacadas especialmente de Fray Luis de León y de otros libros españoles, latinos e italianos* (Madrid, Domingo García Morrás, 1658). Doña Ana Francisca Abarca de Bolea, a Cistercian nun and the daughter of the Aragonese marquis of Las Torres, also published extensively. I am grateful to Professor Terence O'Reilly for having drawn my attention to the doctoral thesis by María de los Ángeles Campo Guiral, 'Edición y estudio de la vigilia y octavario de San Juan Bautista de doña Ana Francisca Abarca de Bolea' (University of Zaragoza, 1990).

convents could extend even to those of very humble background who were able
to demonstrate unusual levels of personal sanctity.[3] The present discussion is
intended to approach the issue of female participation in Spanish political society
from the point of view of the queens, their households and a few individual women
of social significance in seventeenth-century Madrid. It will be argued that
although their direct involvement in shaping events at the court of Spain is in
fact more conjectural than their privileged social and economic situation might
lead us to expect, study of their lives, careers and correspondence is nonetheless
essential in allowing us to appreciate the bigger picture of how Spanish political
society functioned during the early modern period, and of how the rulers and
ministers dealt with the broader requirements of patronage and government.

The most important venue for aristocratic women was the royal palace. For
most of the time the Spanish Habsburgs resided in the Alcázar in Madrid. This
was a medieval structure that underwent extensive renovations in the late
sixteenth and early seventeenth centuries before being destroyed by fire in 1734.
The Alcázar housed the meeting chambers of the councils and the offices of the
secretariats, but well over half of the building was devoted to the queen's
household, which – unlike the king's retinue whose members withdrew to their
homes at night – lived permanently on site.[4] After the closure of official
government business for the night, the queen, her ladies-in-waiting and their
servants were literally locked into their apartments until the palace doors were
reopened the following morning.[5] While administrative control of the queen's
household was in the hands of male officials, practical authority was entrusted
to elderly female, and usually widowed, titled aristocrats who held the senior
offices of *camarera mayor, guarda mayor de damas* and *dueña de honor*.[6] Under
their direction was a staff that numbered about three hundred and which

---

3 Ronald Cueto, *Quimeras y sueños: los profetas y la Monarquía Católica de Felipe IV*
(Valladolid, 1994).   4 José Manuel Barbeito, *Alcázar de Madrid* (Madrid, 1992), pp.
14–17, 20, 52 and 136–40.   5 Dalmiro de la Válgoma y Díaz-Varela, *Norma y ceremonia
de las reinas de la Casa de Austria* (Madrid, 1958), pp. 42–3, 46 and 90–2.   6 The most
important office of *camarera mayor* would have been equivalent to that of Mistress of
the Robes or Chief Gentlewoman of the Privy Chamber in the household of the English
queen. During the first half of the seventeenth century it was held in succession by the
countess of Lemos (1603–21), the duchess of Gandía (1621–27), the countess of
Olivares (1627–43), the countess of Medellín (1649–53) and the marchioness of
Villanueva de Valdueza (1654–still alive in 1679), AGP Sección Administrativa, legajo
627. The *guarda mayor de damas* was a widowed aristocrat who had responsibility for the
discipline and upbringing of the ladies-in-waiting. During the 1640s and 1650s the post
was held in succession by the countesses of Paredes and Salvatierra, who both also
performed the office of governess (*aya*) of the royal children: AGP Registro 182, ff. 50r
and 79v (first foliation) and f. 149v (second foliation). The *dueñas de honor* were widowed
titled noblewomen who played a supplementary role in the management of the
household, often standing in for the other two offices. There was usually more than a
single *dueña de honor* at any one time: La Válgoma, *Norma*, pp. 33–4, 41–2, 50 and 99.

included between fifteen and twenty *damas*, or ladies-in-waiting who lived as members of the queen's household in preparation for their subsequent marriage to prospective spouses of the titled aristocracy. In theory, the *damas* were subjected to a tight regime in which their lives were carefully controlled to ensure the preservation of decorum. The only way in which they were officially allowed to meet and talk to people outside the immediate confines of the household was in the awkward setting of one of the semi-public chambers of the queen's apartments, where the lady in question would be allowed to converse with her relations whilst seated on a special bench and chaperoned by an older female courtier.[7] In practice, however, such strict regulation was rarely enforced, not least because the written stipulations concerning the seclusion of the queen's ladies conflicted with an unwritten custom that allowed them to be accompanied by a single male admirer when the queen ate in public or went on excursions outside the palace.[8]

Perhaps the best visual snapshot that we have of this rarefied existence is Velázquez's celebrated painting, *Las Meninas* [fig. 6]. The picture was given its title in the nineteenth century in reference to the *damas meninas*, who were young girls of noble birth, brought up and educated in the company of the *infantas* (princesses) until such time as they were old enough to be regarded as proper ladies-in-waiting. The setting of Velázquez's painting is a room on the first floor of the Alcázar, where the artist appears to be depicting himself painting a large canvas in the presence of the younger daughter of Philip IV, the Infanta Margarita, together with her small retinue of dwarfs, officials and court ladies. This charming domestic scene has just been interrupted by an occurrence taking place outside the picture and in the viewer's space, which would seem, by the reflection in a mirror on the back wall of the chamber, to be the entrance of the king and queen. The *meninas* of the picture are the two girls on either side of the Infanta. To the right of the princess is Doña Isabel de

---

7 La Válgoma, *Norma*, pp. 44–5; royal decree to the duke of Nájera, 24 September 1650; *consulta* of the duke of Montalto, 16 March 1664, AGP Sección Histórica, caja 55/7. This was the procedure followed when the future Charles I of Great Britain was allowed to meet his intended bride, the Infanta Maria, on Easter Day 1623; Glyn Redworth, *The prince and the infanta: the cultural politics of the Spanish match* (New Haven and London), 2003, pp. 97–8.   8 La Válgoma, *Norma*, pp. 107–111. This convention was known as *galanteo* and was intended to allow a limited and controlled amount of mixed company as a preliminary to marriage. Usually, however, and despite all official efforts to regulate the practice, the queen's ladies could be found conversing with their admirers at all hours and in all places and regardless of whether or not the suitor might already be married to someone else: La Válgoma, *Norma*, pp. 112–15; François Bertaut, 'Journal du voyage d'Espagne fait en l'année mil six cens cinquante neuf, à l'occasion du traité de la paix', ed. by F. Cassan, *Revue Hispanique* 47 (1919), pp. 1–317 at pp. 206–7; Antoine Brunel, 'Voyage d'Espagne', ed. by Charles Claverie, *Revue Hispanique* 30 (1914), pp. 119–375 at p. 186. For Charles I's adoption of the practice when he visited Madrid as Prince of Wales in 1623, see Jonathan Brown and John Elliott (eds), *The sale of the century: artistic relations between Spain and Great Britain, 1604–1655* (New Haven and London, 2002), p. 176.

6 Velázquez, *Las Meninas*. Museo del Prado, Madrid.

Velasco, who would probably not have been much more than ten years old when she was first admitted to the palace in June 1649 in preparation for the imminent arrival of the new queen, Mariana of Austria. In Velázquez's painting of 1656 we see her in full bloom of youth and she would come to be regarded as the most beautiful of the queen's ladies, only for her life to be tragically cut short in the autumn of 1659.[9] The other *menina*, shown kneeling to the left of the princess, was Doña María Agustina de Isasi Sarmiento, daughter of the councillor of war Don Diego de Sarmiento. She had entered the queen's household at the same time as her companion, but enjoyed better fortune, departing the palace to marry the count of Aguilar in a wedding that took place in February 1659 and which I will allude to at the end of this paper. After Aguilar's death in 1668, she went on to get married a second time, to the count of Barajas.[10]

Young women such as Doña Isabel de Velasco and Doña María Agustina de Isasi Sarmiento were therefore in daily attendance on the royal family and could in theory use this privilege for the benefit of their own families, or to the detriment of rival interests within the nobility. The potential importance of informal personal influence operating alongside the formal machinery of government has led to a great deal of recent historiographical emphasis on the study of courts.[11] By the seventeenth century it had become a matter both of honour and necessity for the titled aristocracy to attend on the royal family on a daily basis and thus receive visual recognition of their status, as well as the chance to influence public appointments, manipulate the judicial procedure in favour of family lawsuits, acquire wealth through gifts and pensions and even perhaps sway executive decision-making. As courts became more exclusive in their composition, many monarchs are understood to have been overwhelmed by their new surroundings, no longer in command of their own lives and trapped in a gilded cage of etiquette that was defined by precedent and held in place by the demands of the aristocracy. Spanish kings in particular tended

9 Francisco Javier Sánchez Cantón, *Velázquez, Las Meninas y sus personajes* (Barcelona, 1943), p. 17; Jonathan Brown, *Velázquez: painter and courtier* (New Haven and London, 1986), pp. 257 and 261; Steven N. Orso, *Philip IV and the decoration of the Alcázar of Madrid* (Princeton, NJ, 1986), pp. 165–73; AGP Registro 182, f. 60r (first foliation) and f. 139r (second foliation). Doña Isabel was described by Montalto as 'dama de las que más lucían en palacio', Montalto to marquis of Castel Rodrigo, 18 November 1659, AHN Estado libro 104. Bertaut was probably referring to her when he wrote: 'celle-là estoit fort jolie, mais elle mourut le jour que nous prismes congé du Roy & de la Reyne' Bertaut, 'Voyage d'Espagne', p. 204.   10 Sánchez Cantón, *Velázquez*, p. 16; AGP Registro 182, f. 59r (first foliation) and f. 149r (second foliation); Montalto to Castel Rodrigo, 25 February 1659, AHN Estado libro 104.   11 David Starkey (ed.), *The English court from the Wars of the Roses to the Civil War*, 4th ed. (London and New York, 1996); Ronald G. Asch and Adolf M. Birke (eds), *Princes, patronage and the nobility: the court at the beginning of the modern age, c. 1450–1650* (Oxford, 1991); John Adamson (ed.), *The princely courts of Europe, 1500–1700*, 2nd ed. (London, 2000).

during the seventeenth century to delegate their authority to a succession of favoured noblemen, or *validos*, such as the duke of Lerma, the count-duke of Olivares and Don Luis de Haro,[12] and it has often been argued that these latter used their personal influence with the king in order to pack the royal households with their friends, relations and political supporters, thereby limiting any contact that the king might have with rival sources of influence, who might strengthen his resolve to take the reins of government into his own hands.[13]

One of the problems with such an interpretation is that our understanding of the nature of seventeenth-century Spanish political society has been hamstrung by a lack of sources. The bulk of our knowledge has been derived from notarial and palace records which provide us with information on appointments to offices, duties within the palace, property ownership and personal affiliations, but otherwise are unhelpful in giving more general information about how Spanish noblemen and noblewomen thought, behaved and interacted with each other. New evidence from journals and private correspondence, on the other hand, suggests that our understanding of the role of the Spanish court is in need of greater clarification, partly because the number of people enjoying daily access to an adult monarch could at times be much greater than is usually appreciated, and partly because the willingness of royal figures to lend ear to their warnings and entreaties has often been exaggerated.[14] While the *validos* certainly did their best to control access within the court, in the final analysis the actual composition of the royal entourage mattered much less than the Spanish kings' almost unshakeable loyalty towards their favourites and the Spanish queens' occasional ability to turn to their advantage the expectations placed upon them within this constrained and artificial world.

12 J.H. Elliott, *The count-duke of Olivares: the statesman in an age of decline* (New Haven and London, 1986); Patrick Williams, 'Lerma, Old Castile and the travels of Philip III of Spain', *History*, 73 (1988), pp. 379–97; Alistair Malcolm, 'Don Luis de Haro and the political elite of the Spanish monarchy in the mid-seventeenth century' (unpublished D. Phil thesis, University of Oxford, 1999); Antonio Feros, *Kingship and favoritism in the Spain of Philip III, 1598–1621* (Cambridge, 2000).   13 J.H. Elliott, 'Philip IV of Spain: a prisoner of ceremony' in A.G. Dickens (ed.), *The courts of Europe: politics, patronage and royalty, 1400–1800* (London, 1977), pp. 168–89 at pp. 169 and 175; idem, 'The court of the Spanish Habsburgs: a peculiar institution?' in idem, *Spain and its world, 1500–1700* (New Haven and London, 1989), pp. 142–61 at pp. 148–9 and 156; Antonio Feros, 'Lerma y Olivares: la práctica del valimiento en la primera mitad del seiscientos' in John Elliott and Ángel García Sanz (eds), *La España del conde duque de Olivares: encuentro internacional sobre la España del conde duque de Olivares celebrado en Toro los días 15–18 de septiembre de 1987* (Valladolid, 1990), pp. 195–224 (pp. 206–7); idem, *Kingship and favoritism*, pp. 81–6 and 91–9; Magdalena S. Sánchez, *The empress, the queen, and the nun: women and power at the court of Philip III of Spain* (London and Baltimore, 1998), pp. 39–41.   14 See my other contribution on this subject, 'La práctica informal del poder. La política de la Corte y el acceso a la Familia Real durante la segunda mitad del reinado de Felipe IV', *Reales Sitios* xxxviii / 147 (2001), pp. 38–48.

To illustrate how complicated the operation of personal alliances could be, we may return to the particular instance of the duke of Montalto and his overtures to Haro's daughter-in-law. Six weeks after sending his instructions to his agent in Madrid Montalto was writing again to say that Haro had been in touch with him, and, in typical courtly manner, had expressed high esteem for their joint relationship to the marchioness of Heliche. So far so good, but Haro nonetheless refused to be drawn on the question of the duke's desire for appointment to the council of State.[15] Two months later, and still no further on, Montalto was growing exasperated at what he considered to be his cousin's lack of interest in his affairs, declaring to his agent, in a colourful phrase that loses something in translation: 'Tell me, Your Reverence, whether my lady the marchioness of Heliche regards me as her relation or as her sputum'.[16] It was not until over a year afterwards that the duke's efforts were finally rewarded by appointment to the Mastership of the Queen's Horse, a senior court office which he regarded as a poor consolation prize for Haro's refusal to allow him a formal position in the government.[17] Montalto's experience therefore suggests two conclusions: (1) that important female connections did not necessarily produce results, especially when (as the duke seems to have believed), the woman in question had no interest in providing the desired intercession and (2) that household intimacy with the monarchs did not always translate into real political influence, a fact that seems to have been appreciated both by Haro (who was happy for Montalto to be chosen as Master of the Queen's Horse) and by Montalto (who accepted the nomination with resignation rather than enthusiasm).

In more general terms, it seems to have been the case that for women to play a major political role at the Spanish court there needed to be some kind of factional situation, such as might arise if the king were a child and affairs of state were placed in the nominal control of his mother (for example, during the regency of Carlos II), or if he were particularly indecisive (as was often the case with Habsburg rulers) or if he were unusually sexually or emotionally dependent on women (like the Bourbon kings in the early eighteenth century). Philip III and Philip IV, to a greater or lesser extent and on different occasions during their reigns, showed most of these characteristics, but their rigid adherence to those ministers upon whom they first chose to bestow their favour tended to discourage the development of factionalism. Despite current attempts to rehabilitate the personality of Philip III,[18] little real evidence has come to light that contradicts the traditional view that he was hopelessly dependent on

15 Montalto to Fray Francisco, 5 February, 4 and 18 March 1658, BBMS MS 26/6/4, ff. 50r–51v, 71r–72r and 93r–94v.   16 'Dígame Vuestra Paternidad si mi Señora la Marquesa de Eliche me tiene por su pariente o por su gargajo', Montalto to Fray Francisco, 20 May 1658, BBMS MS 26/6/4, ff. 192r–193v.   17 Montalto to Castel Rodrigo, 19 June 1659, AHN Estado libro 104.   18 Feros, *Kingship and favoritism*, pp. 7–8, 124–6, 235 and 266–7; Paul C. Allen, *Philip III and the Pax Hispanica, 1598–1621: the failure of grand strategy* (New Haven and London, 2000), p. 9.

the duke of Lerma; even when he eventually chose to dismiss him, he did so only after the duke himself had already abdicated most of his responsibilities to his son, the duke of Uceda, who would continue as *valido* until the king's death in 1621.[19] Philip IV was an altogether more complicated character. In his maturity he seems to have been very uneasy about accepting advice from, or even so much as engaging in informal conversation with, people that he did not know extremely well; and he would latterly take great care to avoid becoming surrounded by the placemen (and placewomen) of his ministers.[20] So at least from the 1640s – and possibly from before then as well – household officials tended not to be selected by the *valido*, but instead were drawn from a relatively small group of families, each of which had a long tradition of service in the palace. Again the two Velázquez *meninas* provide good examples: Doña Isabel de Velasco was from the family of the counts of Fuensalida who repeatedly married members of the royal household and swelled its ranks with their own relations;[21] Doña María Agustina de Isasi Sarmiento was the granddaughter of the countess of Salvatierra, who was herself *aya* (governess) of the Infanta Margarita, and Doña María Agustina's two husbands were also from prominent courtier families.[22] And with the members of the royal households selected for reasons of family tradition and loyalty in service, rather than high politics, the Spanish court inevitably became less factional and more apolitical as a result.[23] Neither Don Luis de Haro's daughter in law, the marchioness of Heliche, nor any of his own three daughters were admitted into the retinue of Mariana of Austria and (unlike previous *validos*) he does not appear to have made any attempt to install them there.

19 Patrick Williams, 'Lerma, 1618: dismissal or retirement?', *European History Quarterly* 19 (1989), pp. 307–32. **20** Malcolm, 'La práctica informal del poder', p. 45. **21** Velasco is one of the most frequently recurring surnames within the households of seventeenth-century Spanish queens. Doña Isabel de Velasco's mother had served as *dama menina* to Elizabeth of Bourbon between 1621 and 1633: AGP Reinados (Felipe IV) legajo 8. Two other *damas*, Doña Andrea de Velasco and Doña Ana María de Velasco, left the palace in 1651 and 1654 in order to marry the count of Alba de Liste and the count of Fuensalida respectively: AGP Registro 182, ff. 136v and 141r (second foliation). **22** Counts of Aguilar were appointed as acting gentlemen of the king's bedchamber in 1632 and 1675: AGP Sección Administrativa legajo 633; AGP Reinados (Carlos II) caja 92 expediente 1. Successive counts of Barajas were *mayordomos* (stewards) to Philip IV throughout his reign. **23** Historians of the English court under the late Tudors and early Stuarts have pointed to a similar absence of faction within the royal households, where favourites like the earl of Leicester, the duke of Buckingham, or the earl of Holland were unable to use their court offices for overtly political ends. See Pam Wright, 'A change in direction: the ramifications of a female household, 1558–1603' in Starkey (ed.), *The English court*, pp. 147–72 at pp. 148, 157–61 and 172; Kevin Sharpe, 'The image of virtue: the court and household of Charles I, 1625–1642', in idem, pp. 226–60 at pp. 252–7; and Caroline M. Hibbard, 'The role of a queen consort: the household and court of Henrietta Maria, 1625–1642' in Asch and Birke (eds), *Princes,*

If the political role of the women of the queen's household was restricted to exceptional circumstances, the same could be said for the situation of the royal consorts of Philip III and Philip IV. The influence accorded to Spanish queens was usually limited to domestic and religious spheres: they had to provide their husbands with children, and dedicate their lives to prayer and the dispensation of charity. Their diplomatic role extended no further than courteous exchanges with other rulers from their immediate family, to whom they would pass on greetings at Christmas and Easter and send congratulations on the occurrence of royal births and marriages, as well as condolences at times of mourning. Occasionally Spanish queens would hold diplomatic audiences, but these encounters were inevitably conducted in such a way as to make informal conversation all but impossible: the visitor would make some vague declaration regarding the nature of his or her business and the queen would respond with some expression of polite interest, whereupon the meeting would be over.[24] In all other respects, she was specifically forbidden from interfering in state affairs.[25]

Procedure governing the daily existence of Spanish queens was defined by the *etiquetas* (books of orders). These were rules of ceremony that stipulated the duties, salaries and rights of access permitted to each official within the royal households, and laid down the protocols to be observed at the public events at which members of the royal family were expected to be present. The first set of *etiquetas* for the queen's retinue was drawn up by Philip II in 1575 on behalf of his fourth wife, Anna of Austria. The king's intentions had been twofold: to recreate the style of household that was understood to have prevailed within the Portuguese entourage of his mother, the Empress Isabel, and to exert a closer control over the queen's personal expenditure in the aftermath of the huge debts that had been run up by Philip II's previous consort, Elizabeth of Valois.[26] Henceforward the identity of those noblemen who were to have rights of access to the various antechambers of the queen's apartments were very precisely restricted, and the queen was not allowed to make any payment unless it were counter-signed by her *mayordomo mayor* and formally recorded in the household accounts. Neither, for that matter, could she so much as write a letter without it being endorsed by her secretary.[27] The result was to condition a way

---

patronage and the nobility, pp. 393–414 at pp. 401 and 407–8. Hibbard nonetheless emphasizes how Henrietta Maria's servants became politicized during the crisis of the Bishops' Wars of 1638–1641: ibid., pp. 412 and 413–14.   **24** Descriptions of audiences with Mariana of Austria can be found in Edward, earl of Clarendon, *The history of the Rebellion and Civil Wars in England*, ed. W. Dunn Macray, 6 vols (Oxford, 1888), vol. 5, p. 90; *The memoirs of Anne, Lady Halkett and Ann, Lady Fanshawe*, ed. John Loftis (Oxford, 1979), pp. 165–6; Bertaut, 'Voyage d'Espagne', pp. 29–31 and 35–6.   **25** La Válgoma, *Norma*, pp. 144–5; Sánchez, *Empress*, pp. 99 and 105.   **26** La Válgoma, *Norma*, pp. 26–7; Henry Kamen, *Philip of Spain*, 2nd ed. (New Haven and London, 1998), pp. 102, 194–5 and 205–6.   **27** La Válgoma, *Norma*, pp. 66–9 and 72. Examples of Mariana of Austria's laconic missives to the duke of Mantua and Empress Leonora

of life in which for most of the time Spanish queens were kept indoors, surrounded by women and priests, with their powers of patronage severely
curtailed by, and in the interests of, their immediate entourage.

Of course, these restrictions could still be circumvented by an astute queen
who was prepared to exploit the particular qualities that were most expected
from Spanish female rulers. Recent research has argued that Philip III's
consort, Margaret of Austria (reigned 1599–1611), played a significant role in
undermining the influence of her husband's chief minister and *valido*, the duke
of Lerma. Thanks to her manipulative nature and personal charm the queen
proved very adept at winning over the women that Lerma attempted to install
in her household, and it became necessary in 1603 to implement a new set of
etiquetas that further enhanced the authority of the queen's *mayordomo mayor* at
the expense of her female servants.[28] Undeterred, Margaret continued to enjoy
the indulgence of her husband for whom she produced a large brood of children.
She also made a very favourable impression on her subjects because of her deep
personal piety, which threw into stark relief the corruption of Lerma's government.[29] The queen may even have been involved in the disgrace of a number of
the duke's close associates in a court scandal that took place during the winter
of 1606–1607.[30] Yet there is a danger in exaggerating her involvement in the
downfall of Don Alonso Ramírez de Prado and Don Pedro Franqueza because
their malpractices had become so blatant that even Lerma realized that he
needed to wash his hands of them.[31] Neither, for that matter, can the influence
of Margaret of Austria really be said to have been very important in foreign
policy; despite securing pensions for her relatives in Central Europe, all her

Gonzaga can be found in ASMa Archivio Gonzaga, busta 584. They are endorsed by
her secretary, Don Juan de Avilés, who would refer her letters to the council of State if
there were the slightest uncertainty about how she should respond: *consulta de Estado*,
23 March 1660, AGS Estado legajo 2677. Her letters to the nuncio, Camillo de Massimi,
were similarly short and courteous, although she did promise to intercede with her
husband in the recipient's favour: BL MS Additional 26,850, ff. 266r, 289r, 296r, 317r,
321r, 325r, 340r and 363r. To Anne of Austria, Mariana was slightly more expansive in
the reservations that she expressed about the Spanish custom of allowing children to be
breast-fed until they were three years old: BL MS Additional 21,526, f. 51r. In the mid-
seventeenth century the *mayordomos mayores de la reina* were the duke of Gandía
(1630–32), the marquis of Santa Cruz (1632–46), the duke of Nájera (1646–52), the
count of Altamira (1652–63) and the duke of Montalto (1663–67): AGP Sección
Administrativa legajo 641. The English equivalent of this post would have been Lord
Chamberlain. **28** La Válgoma, *Norma*, pp. 28 and 105–6; Sánchez, *Empress*, pp. 37, 43,
51–2 and 102. **29** Sánchez, *Empress*, pp. 72, 117, 137–8 and 150–1. **30** Sánchez, *Empress*,
pp. 33, 96 and 169–70; Bernardo José García García, 'Pedro Franqueza, secretario de sí
mismo. Proceso a una privanza y primera crisis del valimiento de Lerma (1607–1609)',
Annali di storia moderna e contemporanea 5 (1999), pp. 21–42. **31** Bernardo José García
García, *La* Pax Hispanica: *política exterior del duque de Lerma* (Leuven, 1996), pp.
217–19; Feros, *Kingship and favoritism*, pp. 173–4 and 176–7.

efforts to divert more substantial military and financial assistance to the Austrian Habsburgs were thwarted by Lerma's insistence that precious resources be confined to the more important and manageable requirements of defending Spain's interests in the Mediterranean.[32] It was not until a good seven years after Margaret's death that Lerma was eventually dismissed, just as the outbreak of revolt in Bohemia finally created the need for the dynastic rapprochement that the queen had failed to obtain in her lifetime.

But even if the political influence of Spanish queens could be more apparent than real, the potential threat that they posed remained genuine enough in the minds of those who were jealous of the intimacy that they might hold with their husbands and the popularity that they could command from their subjects. So, the first half of Philip IV's reign witnessed a similar situation to that which had prevailed under Philip III. Elizabeth of Bourbon (reigned 1621–44) had come to Spain in an exchange of princesses that had taken place in 1615. At that time she had been only twelve-and-a-half years old and her husband little more than ten, which meant that she was initially brought up with the other royal children and the couple did not begin to live as man and wife until 1620.[33] Although the young queen was regarded as somewhat frivolous during her early years in Madrid, she would later grow into a woman who was intelligent, respected and very popular, especially after she gave birth to a son in 1629. Like Margaret of Austria, Elizabeth was careful to cultivate a reputation for piety which enabled her to conform to and flourish within the Spanish expectations of what a queen should be.[34] Yet, for most of her life, Elizabeth was prevented from exercising any independent influence because of the political ascendancy of the count-duke of Olivares, and the concomitant supremacy exerted within the queen's household by his overbearing wife.[35]

Philip IV's reliance on Olivares was mainly due to the young king's personal lack of resolution which made him depend on the greater experience, energy and assertiveness of an older man who had ambitious plans to reinvigorate the Spanish Monarchy, as well as an exalted vision for the future of its ruling

32 Peter Brightwell, 'The Spanish origins of the Thirty Years' War', *European Studies Review* 9 (1979), pp. 409–31 at pp. 423–4; Jonathan I. Israel, *The Dutch Republic and the Hispanic world, 1606–1661*, 2nd ed. (Oxford, 1986), pp. 3–14; García García, *La Pax Hispanica*, pp. 83–8; Sánchez, *Empress*, pp. 37, 53, 90, 95, 104, 115–16 and 121–2; Feros, *Kingship and favoritism*, pp. 139, 146, 193–7, 202 and 243–5.   33 Elliott, 'Philip IV of Spain: prisoner of ceremony', p. 178.   34 Gregorio Marañón, *El conde-duque de Olivares: la pasión de mandar*, 26th ed. (Madrid, 1998), pp. 309–11; La Válgoma, *Norma*, p. 129.   35 Marañón, *El conde-duque de Olivares*, p. 340; Elliott, *Olivares*, pp. 373 and 640. The countess of Olivares held the post of *camarera mayor* between 1627 and her dismissal in the autumn of 1643. Before that she had been governess of the (short-lived) royal children: AGP Expedientes Personales caja 754/30. Her only daughter, Doña María de Guzmán, had been appointed *dama menina* to the queen in January 1622 before being transferred to the household of Philip IV's sister, the queen of Hungary, in

dynasty.[36] Yet there was also something rather unseemly about a relationship which brought enormous riches to Olivares and his adherents, and which in its initial stages appears to have been based on the count-duke's supervision of Philip's sexual education through nightly escapades to the red-light districts of seventeenth-century Madrid.[37] These adventures led to the arrival of a succession of illegitimate children who were subsequently found places in the military and ecclesiastical hierarchy or in the royal convents.[38] None of Philip's mistresses was of any significance and they were almost without exception of lowly birth, which meant that the presence of a French-style *maîtresse en titre* was out of the question in the more austere atmosphere of the Spanish court. For Olivares Philip's nocturnal excursions also had the effect of distracting any passion that the young man might have had for the queen and which could have undermined his own pre-eminence within the Spanish court. But Elizabeth's very public distress at her husband's infidelity gained her sympathy with her Spanish subjects, which increased during the final years of her life when the Monarchy was beset by a series of revolts, financial crises and military defeats that brought Olivares' government into disrepute and obliged Philip to leave Madrid in order to combat a French invasion of Catalonia and Aragon.[39] In his absence Elizabeth was appointed governor of Castile, and the vigour with which she fulfilled her duties – to the point of allegedly pawning her jewels in order to provide money for the military campaigns – gained her a reputation as an effective ruler in her own right, which increased still further when Olivares and his family were sent into forced retirement during the course of 1643.[40]

There is no real evidence to suggest that Elizabeth was in any way responsible for the fall of Olivares and, even if she had been, her triumph was soon cut short by her own death in October 1644.[41] Yet she was unlikely to have been distressed by a turn of events which for two or three short years made her the figurehead for all those wanting a change in government. Ministers and

December 1624: AGP Reinados (Felipe IV) legajo 8.   **36** J.H. Elliott, *Richelieu and Olivares* (Cambridge, 1984), ch. 2; idem, *Olivares*, pp. 82, 169–202 and 295.   **37** José Deleito y Piñuela, *El rey se divierte* (Madrid, 1988), pp. 13–15; Marañón, *El conde-duque de Olivares*, pp. 63–7 and 376; Elliott, *Olivares*, pp. 104, 108, 112, 138–40 and 274–7. **38** The Venetian ambassador, Domenico Zane, estimated in 1658 that Philip had sired thirty-two bastards: *RAV*, p. 261. Some of their names are provided by Deleito y Piñuela, *El rey se divierte*, pp. 16 and 82–5; and in *Testamentos de los Reyes de la Casa de Austria*, ed. by Antonio Domínguez Ortiz, 5 vols (Madrid, 1982), vol. 4 (introduction), p. xlvii. The only one of Philip's bastards to be officially recognised was Don Juan José de Austria.   **39** J.H. Elliott, *Imperial Spain, 1469–1716*, ninth ed. (London, 1985), pp. 341–9; R.A. Stradling, *Philip IV and the government of Spain, 1621–1665* (Cambridge, 1988), pp. 179–85 and 212–21.   **40** Marañón, *El conde-duque de Olivares*, pp. 312–14 and 438–40; La Válgoma, *Norma*, p. 137; Elliott, *Olivares*, pp. 628 and 640; Stradling, *Philip IV*, pp. 240–1.   **41** Marañón, *El conde-duque de Olivares*, pp. 315, 375, 429, 435–8 and 440–3.

grandees who were associated with Elizabeth included the Inquisitor General, the president of the council of Castile and the young duke of Montalto, who was married to one of her ladies-in-waiting in a palace ceremony that took place in the spring of 1644.[42] In addition to these mainstream figures were a variety of charismatic religious visionaries, who associated themselves with the queen's party and formulated a godly agenda not dissimilar to that which had previously been advocated by religious supporters of Margaret of Austria.[43] They demanded closure of the theatres and the introduction of regulations to restrict expenditure on luxuries, whilst preaching hell and damnation against the king for his reliance on unpopular ministers. The person most closely associated with the atmosphere of intense religiosity pervading the Spanish court during the difficult years of the early and mid-1640s was the mystic Franciscan nun, Sor María de Ágreda, who also seems to have been in communication with Elizabeth at the time of her first introduction to Philip IV in July 1643.[44] Space does not permit a detailed examination of the king's relations with Sor María, and it will have to suffice to say that her political influence, like that of Elizabeth, was restricted to a comparatively short period of time. Although Philip corresponded with the nun for twenty-two years, evidence from her letters to other members of the Spanish nobility indicates that he ceased to pay much attention to her recommendations from about the time of the conclusion of his second marriage, to the Archduchess Mariana of Austria (reigned 1649–65).[45]

The new queen arrived in Spain in the autumn of 1649, and Philip was immediately smitten. As his niece she was nearly thirty years younger than him, and only four years older than the Infanta María Teresa, for whom Mariana

42 Juan Manuel Giraldo, *Vida, y heroycos hechos del excelentissimo y venerable Señor Don Diego de Arze Reynoso* (Madrid, Juan García Infançón, 1695), pp. 26, 43–4, 131–2 and 134; Carlos Puyol Buil, *Inquisición y política en el reinado de Felipe IV: los procesos de Jerónimo de Villanueva y las monjas de San Plácido, 1628–1660* (Madrid, 1993), p. 340; Cueto, *Quimeras y sueños*, pp. 86, 110–11 and 134; Malcolm, 'Public morality and the closure of the theatres in the mid-seventeenth century: Philip IV, the Council of Castile and the arrival of Mariana of Austria' in Richard Pym (ed.), *Rhetoric and reality in early modern Spain* (forthcoming); Padre Hippolito Camillo Guidi to the duke of Modena, 27 January 1644, ASMo Cancelleria Ducale, Spagna, busta 54; *Copia del poder que la Reyna de España, Doña Isavel de Borbon, dio a su marido el Rey Don Phelipe Quarto para testar en 5 de octubre de 1644*, AHN Estado libro 872, f. 12r.   43 Williams, 'Lerma, 1618', 320–21; Cueto, *Quimeras y sueños*, chs. 5–7; Sánchez, *Empress*, pp. 23, 57 and 97; Feros, *Kingship and favoritism*, pp. 226–7, 236–8 and 255–6.   44 *CSMA*, vol. 1, p. 4; Sor María to Don Fernando de Borja, 10 July 1643, ADR F/156, no. 19. The nun came to depend on the queen's former confessor, Fray Juan de Palma, as her protector and confidant in Madrid, Sor María to Philip IV, 30 March 1647, 5 July 1647, Philip IV to Sor María, 3 April 1647, *CSMA*, vol. 1, pp. 100, 101 and 112; Sor María to Don Francisco de Borja, 4 May 1647, ADR F/156, no. 67.   45 Sor María to Don Francisco de Borja, 16 August, 13 and 26 December 1647, 6 and 28 March, 8 and 29 May 1648, ADR F/156, nos. 74, 79, 80, 83, 85, 88 and 89. Mariana survived her husband by 31 years until her death in 1696, but for the purposes of this paper discussion will be limited to the period of her marriage to Philip IV.

seems to have played the role of elder sister.[46] In 1651, there arrived another
member of the family with the birth of the Infanta Margarita, and two years
later, Philip had Velázquez paint their portraits as a gift for the countess of
Paredes, who had been a confidante of Elizabeth of Bourbon before taking vows
as a Carmelite nun with the name of Sor Luisa de Jesús.[47] In a letter written to
her in the summer of 1653 the king conveyed an idyllic picture of his family life
which gently gave the lie to persisting and ungrounded rumours of his
infidelity. Referring to his correspondent's description of the nuns' pleasure at
the portraits, he quipped:

> I do not doubt it in the least, for even painted they merit praise indeed,
> but nothing like as much as the originals who are just wonderful and I more
> happy with each day that passes in the company of my little companion [ie.
> Mariana] that I assure you that you would never believe how much I have
> changed, nor that anything else could be as suited to my taste and condition,
> whereby (with God's help) I am free of all the temptations that you refer to
> in your letter and do nothing else than give infinite thanks for His mercy.[48]

Philip's idealistic depiction of his happy family is to some extent corroborated
by foreign ambassadors. For the Venetian, Domenico Zane, writing in 1658,
Mariana was a woman of great virtue and exemplary piety, who was much loved
by her subjects, particularly when she finally provided Philip with an heir in the
autumn of 1657, but:

46 Philip IV to Sor Luisa de Jesús, 18 October, 16 November 1649, 12 April 1650, 21
November 1651, 9 June 1653, 23 June 1654, 29 December 1654, 2 March 1655 and 15
April 1658, *FLE*, pp. 102, 108, 127, 163, 200, 233, 244, 246 and 308.   47 Philip IV to
Sor Luisa de Jesús, 13 August 1652, 9 June 1653, *FLE*, pp. 173 and 200.   48 Philip IV
to Sor Luisa de Jesús, 8 July 1653, *FLE*, p. 204. Sor María de Ágreda's concern about
the persistence of Philip IV's philandering was ungrounded (letters to Don Francisco
de Borja, 8 May, 12 June 1648, 24 July 1655 and 14 January 1656, ADR F/156, nos. 88,
91, 188 and 193). It was probably based on malicious gossip fed to her by sources hostile
to the king's favourite, Don Luis de Haro, and therefore likely to depict an unduly
negative image of the court. Sor Luisa de Jesús, as countess of Paredes, had been close
to Haro, whom Sor María detested, and the latter's feelings seem to have been carried
over in the hint of scorn with which she greeted the news of the countess's decision to
take the veil (letter to Don Francisco de Borja, 14 March 1648, ADR F/156, no. 84).
Philip IV's letters to Sor Luisa, as a former intimate of the royal family and friend of the
valido, convey much greater freshness and sincerity than his correspondence with Sor
María. For this reason we should take seriously Philip's description of his happy family
life; he made no bones about his former indiscretions, but assured Sor Luisa that he was
now a changed man and even expressed some concern about his declining ability to
perform his duties as husband (letters to Sor Luisa de Jesús, 9 May 1649, 7 March, 24
May, 16 August 1650, 11 April 1651 and 26 October 1653, *FLE*, pp. 92, 121, 130, 132,
148 and 211). Philip IV's celebrated liaison with the duchess of Veraguas (Deleito y Piñuela,
El rey se divierte, pp. 18–19; Marañón, *El conde-duque de Olivares*, p. 65 and n. 18; Giacomo

not for all that has Her Majesty attempted to increase the authority of her station now that she is mother of a future king. Rather, she limits herself to the confines of her exemplary modesty, preferring to be loved by her husband as a woman than as a queen, and knowing full well that she will rule with greater security in the former capacity, because Don Luis [de Haro] will love her all the more if he does not fear her. She therefore shuns all matters of business, and is devoid of curiosity for anything that might distract her from the devotions in which she passes most of her time, without even so much as wanting to present the king with a memorial in order not to disrupt her quiet life.[49]

Here then was a perfect consort for the king of Spain – her confessor even went so far as to tell Philip that she had never required absolution for anything serious in all her life.[50] But Mariana's sweet submissiveness was complemented by an assertiveness in the pursuit of her own pleasures. Evidence from court correspondence and accounts of her journey from Vienna to Spain reveal her as a fun-loving young girl, who was oppressed by the restrictions of life in the Alcázar, who found the court dwarfs hilarious and lived for the family trips to the royal estates in the country, which she would use all manner of childish deviousness to prolong. Indeed, her unwillingness to abide by palace etiquette had the effect of reducing her household to chaos, as her public meals gave way to a general mêlée of servants, dwarfs and onlookers, intermingling in an atmosphere of general abandon, and as young noblemen climbed over the walls of the palace gardens, and broke down doors and windows in order to court her ladies, and hurl abuse at the duke of Montalto and other palace officials whenever they tried to impose order.[51]

The queen also loved the theatre, and her arrival in Spain had been preceded by a grand series of festivities held in honour of the forthcoming marriage. The first announcement of the engagement in August 1647 had been followed in December by the celebration of a masque in honour of the new queen's birthday, which was performed in the Alcázar by none other than the Infanta María Teresa with the ladies of her household.[52] Exactly a year later, and again in honour of Mariana's birthday, the same performers staged a much more elaborately conceived production, and again with the ten-year-old princess in the starring role.[53] Although there was nothing new in the participation of

Quirini, April 1656, *RAV*, pp. 236–7), which supposedly took place in the early 1650s, is therefore almost certainly apocryphal.　**49** Domenico Zane, April 1658, *RAV*, p. 265. See also, Giacomo Quirini's reports of April 1656 and May 1661, *RAV*, pp. 238 and 305. **50** Philip IV to Sor Luisa de Jesús, 24 December 1657, *FLE*, p. 299.　**51** La Válgoma, *Norma*, pp. 114–115; Malcolm, 'La práctica informal del poder', p. 44; anonymous court *aviso*, 10 February 1664, RAH MS 9/7159 (unfoliated).　**52** This was recounted in Gabriel de Bocángel's poem *La piedra candida*, which specified the participation of each of the Infanta's seventeen *meninas* and ladies-in-waiting; N.D. Shergold, *A history of the Spanish stage from medieval times until the end of the seventeenth century* (Oxford, 1967), p. 302.　**53** *El nuevo Olimpo*, again written by Bocángel; Shergold, *History of the Spanish stage*, pp. 302–3;

members of the royal family in theatrical productions,[54] the involvement of the then heiress to the Spanish Monarchy must have been intended as a clear message that the past four or five years of mourning, recriminations and sanctimonious restrictions on public entertainment were now at an end. Many of the figures who had been close to Elizabeth of Bourbon and associated with the implementation of godly agendas in the mid-1640s had now either died or been dismissed, whilst Sor María de Ágreda was left to confide her disgust at the turn of events to the coded letters that she wrote to her other confidants.[55]

Mariana, of course, had no direct involvement in these plays which were staged before her arrival and conformed to precedents that had been established by Olivares in the 1630s in order to cater for Philip's own fascination for the theatre.[56] Neither was she responsible for the splendid display of horseback masquerades, bullfights, fireworks and still more plays, which greeted her formal entrance to Madrid in the autumn of 1649.[57] However, the personality of the new queen was vital in ensuring that the public events organized in 1647–49 would continue to mark the tone of the Spanish court for the rest of the reign. This was the great age of the machine plays that were written by Gabriel de Bocángel, Pedro Calderón de la Barca and Antonio de Solís, and performed to music by Juan Hidalgo, with scenery and sophisticated mechanical props designed by the Italian engineers, Baccio del Bianco and Antonio Maria Antonozi. Yet in addition to these elaborate music dramas that were performed

journal of Don Pedro de Villacampa, AHN Consejos libro 2029, ff. 24r–24v.   **54** La Válgoma, *Norma*, p. 83. For a recent discussion of Lope de Vega's *El premio de la hermosura*, in which roles were taken by the future Philip IV, Anne of Austria and her household, see Elizabeth R. Wright, *Pilgrimage to patronage: Lope de Vega and the court of Philip III, 1598–1621* (London, 2001), pp. 117–19.   **55** Sor María de Ágreda to Don Francisco de Borja, 6 and 28 March 1648, ADR F/156 nos. 83 and 85. A number of the grandees who opposed the growing influence of Don Luis de Haro were disgraced after a failed conspiracy in the spring of 1644; the king's confessor Fray Juan de Santo Tomás died in the summer of 1644, a few months before Elizabeth of Bourbon's death in October; Fray Juan de Palma, confessor of Elizabeth of Bourbon and the Infanta María Teresa, as well as intermediary with Sor María de Ágreda, died in May 1648; the President of the Council of Castile, Don Juan Chumacero, was dismissed in June 1648. By this time the only important former associates of Elizabeth of Bourbon to remain in office were the count of Castrillo, who was president of the council of the Indies, and Don Diego de Arce Reinoso, the Inquisitor General, neither of whom were particularly involved in the policies of moral reform that had been attempted in the mid-1640s. See Malcolm, 'Public morality and the closure of the theatres'.   **56** Deleito y Piñuela, *El rey se divierte*, pp. 191–6 and 212–32. Jonathan Brown and J.H. Elliott, *A palace for a king: the Buen Retiro and the court of Philip IV* (New Haven and London, 1980), pp. 199–207.   **57** Clarendon, *The history of the Rebellion*, vol. 5, pp. 79 and 80–83; Deleito y Piñuela, *El rey se divierte*, pp. 232–6; J.E. Varey and N.D. Shergold, 'Datos históricos sobre los primeros teatros de Madrid: prohibiciones de autos y comedias y sus consecuencias (1644–1651)', *Bulletin Hispanique* 162 (1960), pp. 286–325 at pp. 295–7, 301–3 and 305; Orso, *Philip IV and the decoration of the Alcázar*, pp. 123 and 133–4.

before the king and all his councillors and courtiers, more modest productions were staged in the queen's private apartments, sometimes on a twice-weekly basis. Indeed, such was Mariana's appetite for theatre that substantial compensation had to be paid to the administrators of the public theatres for the time during which actors were prevented from fulfilling their principal function of providing entertainment for the citizens of Madrid.[58]

So this ideal situation of a queen who was submissive, devout, fecund and passionately interested in theatre not only entailed domestic bliss for Philip, but had important and largely unstudied ramifications for literary patronage during the mid-seventeenth century. It also considerably reduced the potential for factional unrest which was greatly to the benefit of Don Luis de Haro, whose son, the marquis of Heliche, was responsible for organizing the court entertainments of the late 1650s. But the queen's personality could only continue to be an asset for as long as there was no necessity for her to take the reins of power into her own hands. When Philip IV died in 1665, she was left in command of the Spanish monarchy during the disastrous eleven-year minority of her son, Carlos II. During these years Mariana's chronic lack of experience became all too evident in the excessive confidence that she placed in her Austrian confessor, in her failure to discipline the unruliness of her household and in her mismanagement of a whole string of political crises at home and foreign mishaps abroad. None of this was Mariana's fault, for she had been placed in a situation for which her limited expectations as consort to the king of Spain had left her hopelessly unqualified. Where she did fall short, however, was in the fulfilment of her requirements as a royal widow, most important of which was the provision of a proper upbringing for the heir to the throne. And it was Carlos II's lack of any formal preparation for government – rather than the celebrated Habsburg endogamy – that was the main reason for the political chaos into which Spanish government descended in the later seventeenth century.[59]

A great deal more research needs to be done before we can really begin to understand properly the role of Spanish women within the higher echelons of seventeenth-century Madrid. But for the moment some of the preceding observations may be brought together with reference to another particular

58 N.D. Shergold and J.E. Varey, *Fuentes para la historia del teatro en España, I. Representaciones palaciegas: 1603–1699. Estudio y documentos* (London, 1982), pp. 236–7; Shergold, *History* pp. 314–15, 527.   59 Gabriel Maura Gamazo, *Carlos II y su corte*, 2 vols (Madrid, 1911 and 1915), vol.1, pp. 300–2; Henry Kamen, *Spain in the later seventeenth century, 1665–1700*, 2nd ed. (London and New York, 1983), pp. 21–2. It is interesting to compare the regency of Mariana of Austria in Spain with that of Marie Christine of Savoy. The expectations placed on female regents were broadly similar, but while Charles Emmanuel II of Savoy was given every possible preparation for kingship, Carlos II could still barely read and sign his own name by the time he reached adulthood. See Martha D. Pollak, *Turin, 1564–1680: urban design, military culture, and the creation of the absolutist capital* (Chicago and London, 1991), pp. 108–11, 144–5 and 153–5.

instance of the play of social and political relationships during this period. Perhaps the most important surviving source for our understanding of the Spanish court at this time is the journal of the marquis of Osera, an Aragonese nobleman who was in Madrid for just under two years between the autumn of 1657 and the summer of 1659. Osera's brother, the commander of a regiment in the Army of Catalonia, had been accused of rape, and was being held prisoner in Barcelona at the behest of the girl's family in an attempt to make him agree to a marriage.[60] It was in the hope of securing his brother's release that Osera came to court; he was a gentleman of the king's bedchamber and initially believed that his right of access to the king would give him special influence. No such luck: Philip simply ignored his entreaties, preferring instead to defer to the opinion of his councils.

So, Osera's next course of action was to resort to two of his aunts, who willingly agreed to deploy their connections with the wives and daughters of the king's councillors and secretaries. One of these aunts was the countess of Osorno, an important figure within Madrid society during the 1650s. She had the honour of escorting Velázquez's *menina*, Doña María Agustina de Isasi Sarmiento, from the palace just before her marriage in February 1659,[61] which formed the background to the marquis's negotiations and which he described in effusive terms:

> Today the lady Doña María Agustina got married at noon. She looked enchanting, and there was also a banquet which I attended, and a little after the wedding there came news that the Army of Galicia had entered Salvatierra, which made the wedding all the merrier, because the countess of Salvatierra [...] is grandmother of the bride.[62]

Doña María Agustina was also the daughter of Don Diego de Sarmiento, one of the councillors of War, and this proximity was of potential use to Osera, as was his aunt's acquaintance with José González, a senior minister within the council of Castile.[63] The latter had already been approached by another of Osera's

60 For the broader social context in which these events took place, see Casey, *History of the family*, pp. 96–7. I would like to thank Fernando Bouza for drawing my attention to the Osera journal, and José Manuel Calderón for assistance in consulting it. 61 'La de Osorno es cierto está aquí con estimación [...] y el otro día fue la que sacó de palacio a la hija de Sarmiento que está ya casada con el conde de Aguilar, grande de España, y esta función tocaba a una señora grande, o que fuese parienta de los novios con parentesco conocido y grande': Osera to Don Josef de Villalpando, 1 March 1659, ADA Montijo caja 17. The eighth countess of Osorno was Doña Ana Polonia Manrique de Luna (c.1605–63), who was married to the third marquis of Malpica, one of the most important officials in the palace of Philip IV, Luis de Salazar y Castro, *Historia genealógica de la Casa de Lara*, 4 vols (Madrid, 1694–97), vol. 1, pp. 666–8. 62 Osera journal, 24 February 1659, ADA Montijo caja 17. 63 Osera journal, 7 February 1659, ADA Montijo caja 17.

aunts, the dowager marchioness of Mancera, who was trying to influence González through his favourite niece, whilst at the same time engaging in an intensive letter-writing campaign with the wives of the ministers of the council of Aragon.[64] But once again, it was all to no avail; when we look beyond the interplay of friendships and social alliances, there is little to indicate that they bore any more direct fruit in Osera's negotiations than the duke of Montalto's abortive attempts to secure appointment to the council of State through the mediation of Haro's daughter-in-law. In fact, king, *valido* and councillors all seem to have been impervious to such personal approaches, male or female, as they spent literally years debating the jurisdictional subtleties of the case, while Osera's brother was left to fester in a Barcelona dungeon and the marquis frittered away his diminishing resources on expensive living in Madrid.

So, clearly the social and political world of seventeenth-century Madrid depended much less on rights of access to the royal family than is often imagined. Attendance at court meant different things to different people. For Haro, it was the basis of his hold over the king, but only because his relationship with Philip IV had already been built up over the course of a lifetime. For Osera, daily admission to the royal presence was ultimately of much less importance than the right to approach the king's secretaries in order to pump them for new information concerning his brother's case. The duke of Montalto, after his initial expression of disappointment at being chosen for the queen's household, soon established a niche for himself as a marriage broker for his friends overseas. And, while Spanish queens and aristocratic women seem only to have been of marginal political significance, their privileged position nonetheless brought them more subtle influence in other important areas. Margaret of Austria and Elizabeth of Bourbon contributed to an atmosphere of public criticism against the *validos* that was orchestrated by confessors, preachers and religious mystics who looked to the queens for protection. Mariana of Austria, though apparently withdrawn and diffident, still indirectly (and unwittingly) contributed to the cultural vibrancy that characterized the later years of Philip IV's reign. The high social reputations of the marchionesses of Heliche and Mancera and of the countess of Osorno acted indirectly to the benefit of the duke of Montalto and the marquis of Osera, because it was necessary for these men to flatter the honour of the king's ministers by making approaches to their female relations.[65] Most important of all, the very difficulty of securing influence through access to the royal family in itself speaks volumes about the enigmatic personalities of the Spanish kings. Philip III was certainly

---

64 Osera journal, 9, 10, 19 and 20 February 1659, ADA Montijo caja 17. Doña María de Salazar Enríquez de Navarra had been married to Don Pedro de Toledo, first marquis of Mancera, until the latter's death in 1654, Salazar y Castro, *Lara*, vol. 1, 265–6. The favourite niece of José González was probably Doña Josefa Jiménez de Arellano.
65 Osera journal, 20 February 1659, ADA Montijo caja 17.

irresolute, and the same could be said to a lesser extent for Philip IV, but neither king was in any way capricious in their relations with their courtiers. Even if they only occasionally paid heed to the women in their lives, the same could be said for most of the men, with the obvious exception of their *validos*, to whom they adhered through thick and thin. Philip IV also shared informal relations of friendship with half a dozen or so close personal acquaintances, most of whom he had known since childhood. It was from this background that Don Luis de Haro rose to the fore during the 1640s, and it was always his fear that the king might lend ear to the hostile calumny of one of his other companions. Yet Philip's high sense of propriety, his deep attachment to the routines of court and administration and his very clearly defined personal likes and dislikes rendered the kind of political instability, that was so often associated with other courts, unlikely though by no means entirely impossible. Everything would change after 1665, when the transfer of government to a devout, submissive woman, who was totally ill-equipped to wield power and seemingly unaware of her responsibilities to prepare her young son for the duties that he would eventually have to assume as monarch, finally brought an end to the political stability that for so long had been the principal asset of the Spanish monarchy.

John Millar's peculiar footnote: the 'Science of Man' and the 'Condition of Women'

Michael Brown

This story begins with a footnote. It appears in the first section of the first chapter of John Millar's *The Origin of the Distinction of Ranks*, and reads as follows:

> It seems unnecessary to observe, that what is here said with regard to marriage, together with many other Remarks which follow concerning the manners of early nations, can only be applied to those who had lost all knowledge of the original institutions, which as the sacred texts inform us, were communicated to mankind by an extraordinary revelation from heaven.[1]

The footnote was there from the beginning, outlasting even the original title for the work, *Observations concerning the Distinction of Ranks in Society*, which Millar altered for the third 'corrected and enlarged' edition.[2] Yet, its omnipresence across the three editions the author prepared in his life does not undermine, rather it underlines, its importance. It indicates that in many ways the literature on John Millar has been conceptually limited.

John Millar has been little studied and less understood. Born in 1735, to the east of Edinburgh, he was to gain fame in his day as the Professor of Civil Law at the University of Glasgow, where he had studied. He was appointed in 1761 and soon became a celebrated teacher.[3] He published the first edition of the *Origin* a decade later, with a second, 'greatly enlarged edition' emerging in 1773.[4] He revised it again under the new title in 1779. He also penned *An*

---

1 John Millar, *Origin of the distinction of ranks* (4th edition, Edinburgh and London, 1806, reprinted, Bristol, 1990), p. 19. 2 Ibid., p. vi. 3 For an assessment of the content of Millar's teaching load, see John Cairns, '"Famous as a School for Law as Edinburgh ... for Medicine": legal education in Glasgow, 1761–1801' in Andrew Hook and Richard B. Sher (eds.), *The Glasgow Enlightenment* (East Linton, 1995), pp. 133–59. 4 Millar, *Origin of ranks*, p. vi.

Historical View of the English Government (1787; 2nd edition 1790) and at least
one anonymous work, *The Letters of Crito*, which appeared in the *Scots Chronicle*
from May to September 1796. He died in 1801, still teaching. Despite these
achievements, and his regular appearance in lists of Scottish luminaries of the
period, scholars have relatively neglected Millar.[5] Only one major study, the
1960 work of William Lehmann, has been published and there is only a thin
body of articles yet devoted to illuminating his thought.[6]

Ironically, Millar's neglect is due in large part to the unusual nature of his
views.[7] His notorious Jacobin sympathies found expression in the *Letters of Crito*,
which criticized the government's prosecution of the war with Revolutionary
France, and in his teaching of a number of leading Scottish reformers, most
notably Thomas Muir, who was sentenced to fourteen years' transportation to
Australia for sedition in 1793, a legal action prompted by his leading part in the
Friends of the People in Scotland.[8] These sympathies have resulted, however, in
his exclusion from the recent renaissance in the academic study of the Scottish
Enlightenment. He was an uncomfortable companion for many of the men who
made up the Moderate party of the Church of Scotland, which modern scholarship has tended to associate with the Enlightenment.[9] For instance, their contemporary group biographer and attractive social memoirist, the Reverend Alexander
Carlyle of Inveresk wrote, recalling his first encounter with Millar in 1768:

> This last had even then begun to distinguish himself by his democratical
> principles, and that sceptical philosophy which young noblemen and

5 For example, Christopher Berry offered Kames, Hume, Robertson, Ferguson, Smith,
Dunbar and Stuart: Christopher Berry, *Social theory of the Scottish Enlightenment*
(Edinburgh, 1997), pp. 19–20.   6 William C. Lehmann, *John Millar of Glasgow*
(Cambridge, 1960). The articles of particular importance here are Paul Bowles, 'John
Millar, the four-stages theory and women's position in society', *History of Political
Economy* 16 (1984), pp. 619–38; Michael Ignatieff, 'John Millar and individualism' in
Istvan Hont and Michael Ignatieff (eds), *Wealth and virtue: the shaping of political
economy in the Scottish Enlightenment* (Cambridge, 1983), pp. 253–70 and Knud
Haakonssen, *Natural law and moral philosophy: from Grotius to the Scottish Enlightenment*
(Cambridge, 1996), pp. 154–81.   7 For the general context in which Millar's work on
the history of women appeared see Jane Rendall, 'Clio, Mars and Minerva: the Scottish
Enlightenment and the writing of women's history' in T.M. Devine and J.R. Young,
(eds), *Eighteenth-century Scotland: new perspectives* (East Linton, 1999), pp. 134–51,
especially pp. 139–42 for comments on Millar.   8 On Muir see Ken Logue, 'Thomas
Muir' in *History is my witness* (ed) Gordon Menzies (London, 1976), pp. 14–37 and
Marjorie Masson and J.F. Jameson, 'The Odyssey of Thomas Muir', *American Historical
Review* 29 (1923), pp. 49–72. On Scottish reform politics in the 1790s see Henry W.
Meikle, *Scotland and the French Revolution* (Glasgow, 1912, reprinted in facsimile,
London, 1969) and Elaine W. McFarland, *Ireland and Scotland in the age of revolution*
(Edinburgh, 1994).   9 See, authoritatively, Richard B. Sher, *The church and university in
the Scottish Enlightenment: the moderate literati in Edinburgh* (Edinburgh, 1985).

gentlemen of legislative rank carried into the world with them from his law course, and, many years afterwards, particularly at the period of the French Revolution, displayed with popular zeal, to the no small perversion to all those under their influence.[10]

In as much as the study of the Scottish Enlightenment has followed Carlyle's lead and associated the movement with the 'Whig Presbyterian ideology' he favoured, Millar has simply fallen from view.[11]

I

Where Millar has found his celebrants has been among the now unfashionable Marxist school of sociology. For example, Ronald Meek sees Millar as a formidable precursor to Karl Marx himself.[12] Meek emphasizes how Millar offered a theory of economic development which centralized the role of the means of production in determining such epiphenomena as manner, morals and the mechanics of power. Meek contends that 'the four stages theory' of social development represents 'a guiding principle' of historical writing in the eighteenth century and, 'by 1780, this guiding principle had become so important an element in the intellectual scheme of things, so much an integral part of the social thought of the Enlightenment, that there were very few historians and social thinkers who remained unaffected by it.'[13] Of this principle, Millar's formulation was both the clearest and most sophisticated. Meek argues that 'In Millar's books and lectures, it is hardly too much to say, the new social science of the Enlightenment comes of age.'[14]

This new social science is, for Meek, built upon two assumptions. First, a materialist reading of social development built upon what Marx would later term 'the means of production' and which Meek believed Millar had worked towards if not fully adumbrated. That he had 'recognised the need for such a methodology, and himself moved as far as he did along the road towards it,' however, for Meek identified Millar as 'one of the boldest spirits of the Enlightenment.'[15]

Second, Millar offered a master narrative of human history, which perceived social development as occurring across a number of stages, best defined, if not

10 Alexander Carlyle, *Autobiography* (Edinburgh, 1910), p. 516.   11 The phrase is Richard Sher's. See Richard B. Sher, 'Professors of virtue: the social history of the Edinburgh Moral Philosophy chair in the eighteenth century' in M.A. Stewart (ed), *Studies in the philosophy of the Scottish Enlightenment* (Oxford, 1990), pp. 87–126. 12 Ronald L. Meek, 'The Scottish contribution to Marxist sociology' in his *Economics and ideology and other essays* (London, 1967), pp. 34–50.   13 Ronald L. Meek, *Social science and the ignoble savage* (Cambridge, 1976), p. 174.   14 Meek, *Social science*, p. 161. 15 Ibid., p. 173.

in fact determined, by the means of production. This placed him within an historical genre known as 'stadialism'. Formulations of stadial history can, as Meek notes, be found in many 'Scottish pioneers of the 1750s' – notably Lord Kames and Sir John Dalrymple – and in their followers such as Adam Ferguson and William Robertson.[16] Yet, Meek argues that it was 'Millar's great achievement … to transform the four stages theory and the more general ideas associated with it into a true *philosophy of history*.'[17]

Millar's central and clearest formulation of stadialism is in the introduction to the *Origin*. There, in one sweeping passage, he narrated the rise of society from its barbarous past to its commercial present. Beginning by noting 'in man a disposition and capacity for improving his condition', Millar argued that 'the similarity of his wants as well as of the faculties by which those wants are supplied, has everywhere produced a remarkable uniformity in the several steps of his progression.'[18] This shared developmental trajectory Millar then described, in a remarkable, if lengthy passage, how:

> A nation of savages, who feel the want of almost everything requisite for the support of life, must have their attention directed to a small number of objects, to the acquisition of food and clothing, or the procuring shelter from the inclemencies of the weather; and their ideas and feelings in conformity to their situation, must, of course, be narrow and contracted. Their first efforts are naturally calculated to increase the means of subsistence, by catching or ensnaring wild animals, or by gathering the spontaneous fruits of the earth; and the experience acquired in the exercise of these employments, is apt, successively, to point out the methods of taming and rearing cattle, and of cultivating the ground. According as men have been successful in these great improvements, and find less difficulty in the attainment of their bare necessities, their prospects are greatly enlarged, their appetites and desires are more and more awakened and called forth in pursuit of the several conveniences of life; and the various branches of manufacture and commerce, its inseparable attendant, and with science and literature, the natural offspring of ease and affluence, are introduced, and brought to maturity. By such gradual advances in rendering their situation more comfortable, the most important alterations are produced in the state and condition of a people: their numbers are increased; the connections of society are extended; and men, being less oppressed with their own wants, are more at liberty to cultivate the feelings of humanity: property, the great source of distinction among individuals is established; and the various rights of mankind, arising from their multiplied connections, are recognised and protected: the laws of a country are thereby rendered numerous; and a more complex form of government becomes

16 Ibid., pp. 99–130.   17 Ibid., p. 161.   18 Millar, *Origin of ranks*, p. 3.

necessary, for distributing justice, and for preventing the disorders which proceed from the jarring interests and passions of a large and opulent community.[19]

In speaking to students, Millar put his construction in even balder terms: 'by tracing the progress of wealth we may thus expect to discover the progress of government. I shall take notice of 4 *great stages* in the acquisition of property: 1. Hunters and Fishers, or mere Savages ... 2. Shepherds ... 3. Husbandmen ... 4. Commercial people.'[20] Here we find both aspects of Meek's concern: the stadial master narrative of human development, and its materialist basis upon the means of production or, in Millar's terms, the source and nature of property.

II

Yet, the Marxist story tells only half the tale. In concentrating attention on the stadialism and on the economic aspect of his ideas, it places Millar in relation with his teacher and great inspiration, Adam Smith.[21] In doing so, it fails to link Millar's work with the thought of his other great contemporary, David Hume. John Craig, Millar's earliest biographer, understood that Millar appreciated Hume's genius just as much as that of Smith. Indeed, he insightfully wrote of how Millar considered that in the matter of ethics: 'little appeared to be wanting, but to combine their systems.'[22] Millar was 'a zealous admirer of Hume's philosophical opinions, which he had early adopted and the truth of which, after inquiries increased his conviction, he was necessarily engaged in frequent debate with Dr Reid.'[23] We can illustrate Hume's appreciation in turn through the progress of his nephew, also David Hume, who attended Millar's law lectures, and with whom Millar was evidently pleased. The philosopher was in contact with the lecturer, telling his nephew that 'I must give y[ou the] satisfaction of telling you that Mr Millar is very pleased with you.'[24]

The debt of inspiration Millar owed to the philosopher was evident in three ways within the *Origin*. First, his method of constructing his narrative was akin to that Hume expanded upon in his *Treatise of Human Nature* (1739–41).

19 Ibid., pp. 3–4.   20 John Millar, lecture notes of the duke of Hamilton quoted in Meek, *Social science*, p. 166.   21 For an interesting analysis of Millar's theory of manners in the light of Smith's own remarks, see John Dwyer, 'Smith, Millar and the natural history of love' in his *The age of the passions: an interpretation of Adam Smith and Scottish Enlightenment culture* (East Linton, 1998), pp. 81–100.   22 John Craig, 'Account of the life and writings of the author' in Millar, *Origin of ranks*, p. xxvi.   23 Craig, 'Life', p. lxi. Thomas Reid (1710–96) was successively regent at King's College Aberdeen and the Professor of Moral Philosophy at the University of Glasgow. His 'common sense' philosophy was developed in opposition to David Hume's ideas. 24 Millar, *Origin of ranks*, p. vi.

Therein, Hume had argued that knowledge was founded on experience of particular events. General theories of how the world operated were the result of speculative induction. The test of knowledge was its correspondence with evidence and not with pre-established principles. The aim of the philosopher was not to deduce practical conclusions from divine scripture or previously established truths, but to examine assumptions empirically and to develop theoretical conclusions from practical observations. When this method was applied to human activity, Hume argued we were practising a 'science of man' akin to the kind of natural philosophy that had led to Newton's discovery of gravity.[25]

This method required that the evidential base for conclusions be drawn from as broad an array of sources as possible. This Millar certainly did, not only using the evidence of social organization found in recent travelogues and in the narratives of ancient historians, but even drawing on biblical text (itself a radical treatment of the Scriptures) and creative writing.[26] So heavy was the pressure that the methodological demand to offer compelling circumstantial evidence placed on his narrative, Millar felt obliged to offer the following to plea to the reader for tolerance:

> This observation, it is hoped will serve as an apology for the multiplicity of facts that are sometimes stated in confirmation of the following remarks. At the same time, from an apprehension of being tedious, the author has on other occasions, selected only a few, from the greater number to the same purpose, that might easily have been procured.[27]

Millar's approval of Humean empiricism led him to an acceptance of a second, and crucial, aspect of Hume's philosophical vision, namely, the thesis that man's knowledge of the universe was radically limited. As information about the world was drawn from experience – either personal or related by trusted testimony – it was by no means complete or wholly reliable. However extensive our life experience and however well read we became, we could not begin to achieve a complete, holistic comprehension of the workings of the world. That remained the preserve of the deity. Thus, human knowledge had to remain within the realm of the probable. Conclusions were either more or less accurate, but were not provable to the point of certainty. This differed from the

25 David Hume, *A treatise of human nature*, edited by David Fate Norton and Mary J. Norton (Oxford, 2000), p. 4.   26 For the use of travelogues, see the reference to Father Tachard 'superior of the French Missionary Jesuits in the East Indies' in the notes on Millar, *Origin of ranks*, pp. 54–5. For the use of classical history, see the quotation from Caesar, p. 43. For the use of the Bible, see the lengthy insertion of a passage from Proverbs, pp. 91–2. For creative writing, see the use made of the Ossianic sequence, pp. 62–5.   27 Millar, *Origin of ranks*, p. 13.

position of the religiously orthodox, who drew their understanding of the universe from the precepts inscribed in divine revelation and in the conclusions that could be deduced from it. One import of Millar's footnote is that he was aware of that difference in approach and of its consequences.

Finally, Millar was drawn to a third component in Hume's theory. If human beings gain knowledge through experience, they tend to act in a predictable nature. If a method of responding to external circumstances was successful in the past, humans tended to repeat the response, if confronted with similar circumstances. Thus, human beings were creatures of habit. These habits, if regularly recurring, became customs and these politicians inscribed into the organization of the community by articulating laws. By bringing to bear a further assumption, that humans were constant in time and space – similar faculties producing broadly similar responses – Millar had the grounds for a speculative, or philosophical, history of humanity. As John Craig explained:

> Mr Millar is frequently obliged to rest the truth of his opinions on this internal proof. Ascending to a period of which the records are scanty and disfigured with fable, he often, without reference to uncertain authority, produces a conviction, stronger perhaps than can ever be derived from the testimony of an individual, always liable to be deceived. His argument, founded on unconnected circumstances all tending to one effect; his successive positions, derived from the acknowledged condition of the several ranks of inhabitants, flowing naturally from the state of manners and property, and leading, by an easy transition, to what we know was afterwards established; his frequent illustrations, by reference to similar institutions existing in other countries, and by a distinct enumeration of circumstances in some nations leading to opposite results: His disquisitions, so conducted, produce a confidence in his conclusions, to which the authority of rude and careless annalists can have no pretension.[28]

Human behaviour in the here and now, as well as narratives of past behaviour, could illuminate the broad structures underpinning social development.[29] In an extended illustration, the development of habits into social custom and hence legal theory was used by Millar to explain the emergence of the social institution of marriage.

28 Craig, 'Life', pp. lxxxi–lxxxii.   29 This method of reconstructing past societies was termed 'conjectural or theoretical history' by Dugald Stewart. See Dugald Stewart, 'An account of the life and writings of Adam Smith' in *The collected works of Dugald Stewart*, ed. William Hamilton (Edinburgh and London, 1854–60, reprinted, Bristol, 1994), vol. 10, p. 34.

III

Millar's discussion of marriage is to be found in the opening chapter of the *Origin*. Covering some 108 pages in the third edition, and divided into six sections, it offered a narrative and analysis 'Of the Ranks and Condition of Women in Different Ages'. In this study, he recognized that marriage was a frequent settlement, even within the most underdeveloped of social organizations. Yet, he explained that:

> When a child has been produced by the accidental correspondence of his parents, it is to be expected that, from the influence of natural affection, they will be excited to assist one another in making some provision for his maintenance. For this purpose, they are led to take up their residence together, that they may act in concert with each other and unite their efforts in the preservation and care of their offspring.[30]

It should be noted in passing here that what Millar was partially implying, and made explicit elsewhere, was that the sexual behaviour of savages was predominately promiscuous, only settling on sole partners when children had resulted from congress. He asserted: 'The members of different families, being all nearly upon a level, maintain the most familiar intercourse with one another, and, when impelled by natural instinct, give way to their mutual desires without hesitation or reluctance.'[31] It was a natural, and not a religious explanation for marriage – making it a secular and not a divine institution.[32]

These origins would only produce marriages of limited duration, however, unless habit and custom intervened to stabilize these relations. Thus, Millar contended that:

> the long culture which is necessary in rearing the human species, will generally afford to the parents a second pledge of their commerce, before their assistance can be withdrawn from the former. Their attention, therefore, is extended from one object to another, as long as the mother is capable of child-bearing; and their union is thus continued by the same causes which first gave rise to it. Even after this period, they will naturally be disposed to remain in a society to which they have long been accustomed: more especially, as by living at the head of a numerous family, they enjoy a degree of ease, respect and security, of which they would otherwise be deprived, and have reason, in their old age, to expect the assistance and protection of their posterity, under all those diseases and infirmities by which they are rendered incapable of providing for themselves.[33]

---

30 Millar, *Origin of ranks*, p. 18.   **31** Ibid., p. 15.   **32** Millar elsewhere writes without disapproval of divorce, see Millar, *Origin of ranks*, pp. 103–5.   **33** Ibid., p. 19.

2222111

This analysis, importantly, drew on materialistic, naturalistic and customary explanations for the continuance of marriage beyond the period of procreative power. And it is here, at the end of this passage, that the footnote appears. Millar was evidently aware that his treatment of marriage had obviated any need to resort to scriptural authority, and was conscious that this might well be controversial. In this light, the footnote is both protective of Millar's reputation – an assertion of his intrinsic public religious orthodoxy – and revealing of his private heterodox opinions concerning the natural state of humankind. Far from being the 'customary bow to the ecclesiastics of his day', as Meek describes the note, it was a necessary defence of his work, and himself, from potential declamation by the Church of Scotland – whose treatment of Hume may have been in Millar's mind.[34]

Millar further accentuated the subversive nature of his text by explicitly comparing man to creatures of the animal kingdom who share characteristics of nurturing offspring and remaining partners for life. Far from flattering humans by asserting their supposed superiority to the creatures of the animal kingdom, he drew a parallel between our social formation and that of certain animals. He wrote of how:

> among inferior animals, we may discern the influence of the same principle in forming an association between individuals of different sexes … in some species of birds, however, the young which are hatched at one time, are frequently incapable of procuring their own food before the mother begins to lay eggs anew; and the male and the female are, there-fore, apt to contract a more permanent attachment. To this circumstance, we may ascribe the imagined fidelity of the turtle, as well as the poetical honours that have been paid to the gentleness of the dove.[35]

This naturalistic approach to human history might however overshadow one central tenet of Millar's conceptual history, which needs to be emphasized. The formation of society was indeed natural to humankind, built as it was upon principles of social affection that Millar assumed to be intrinsic to human nature. The specific outcomes of that natural instinct, however, were customary in their nature, and were not pre-determined in any way. Importantly, while the *Origin* narrated human sexual relations as the outcome of natural affections, the actual form and content of the treatment of women was understood to be the consequence of custom and habit. Thus, as society developed across the four great stages of human activity, the treatment of women also altered. Yet, while the shift in social norms surrounding women changed in each stage, they

34 Meek, *Social science*, p. 167 n.147. On Hume's difficulties with the Presbyterian Church see M.A. Stewart, *The kirk and the infidel* (Lancaster, 1994). 35 Millar, *Origin of ranks*, p. 18.

remained customary in their origin. Customs emerged and transformed as the means of production and the political organization of the community modified, and no one aspect held causative supremacy for Millar. As Jane Rendall notes, Millar's work was 'broadly a history of progress, conceived not only in material terms but also in terms of manners.'[36] Thus, the narrative of economic development was capable of narration through the prism of the treatment of women. This is what Millar proceeded to offer.

In the second stage of society, Millar identified a shift away from the promiscuous practice of sexual congress found among the savages and towards the recognition of chastity as a central female virtue. This was further accentuated when the society moved into the third stage. Among the great communities of ancient Greece and medieval Europe, female virtue held such importance that men honoured women more at a distance than pursued them in physical proximity. As Millar wrote of the system of chivalry, the social structure, with many equally powerful lordships competing for political dominance, precluded social interaction among the sexes:

> It was not to be expected that those opulent chiefs, who maintained a constant opposition to each other, would allow any sort of familiarity to take place between members of their respective families ... The young knight, as he marched to the tournament, saw at a distance the daughter of a chieftain by whom the show was exhibited; and it was even with difficulty that he could obtain access to her, in order to declare the sentiments with which she had inspired him ... the lady herself was taught to assume the pride of her family, and to think that no person was worthy of her affection who did not possess an exalted rank and character. To have given way to a sudden inclination would have disgraced her for ever in the opinion of all her kindred; and it was only by a long course of attention, and of the most respectful service, that the lover could hope for any favour from his mistress.[37]

IV

Despite the general application Millar assumed for his historical theory, there was, however, nothing preordained about the progressive trajectory of human society. While society was prone to develop from barbarism to commercial society, its teleological inclination might fall at any stage from its course, halt or even reverse. The problem for Millar was that by accepting the probabilism at the heart of Hume's epistemology, nothing could be determined with complete accuracy. His narrative remained plausible but depended just as much on

36 Rendall, 'Clio, Mars and Minerva', pp. 139–40.   37 Millar, *Origin of ranks*, pp. 76–7.

customary practice as it did on the natural instincts he perceived operating within human nature.

In this light, economics and morals emerge as potentially unstable and prone to deterioration. As Millar noted in the introduction to the *Origin*, while 'there is, thus in human society, a natural progress from ignorance to knowledge, and from rude to civilized manners ... various accidental causes, indeed, have contributed to accelerate, or to retard this advancement in different counties.'[38] Note here the emphasis on 'accident' – highlighting just how insecure was the developmental plan Millar had described. In this Millar was at least partially in line with the general characteristics of the Scottish school of history writing. As Jane Rendall has remarked:

> the most significant features of eighteenth-century 'philosophical' history ... include the adoption of a stadial theory of development, through three or four stages, mainly understood as stages defined by material development, from what were regarded as savage states to contemporary western European civilisation. The 'conjectural' use of comparative material to fill in gaps was also common, though not especially original ... In spite of the progressive nature of their history they retained a sense of the significance of the accidental and unpredictable variety of human history. And finally they shared a common politics which was broadly whiggish if socially conservative, though within that definition there was ample room for disagreement.[39]

With this last point, Millar certainly disagreed. While, as we have seen, he shared in the first three elements Rendall identifies as distinctive in Scottish historical thought of the period, it was his failure to subscribe to the 'socially conservative' Whiggery, which contemporaries and historians have identified as axiomatic in the Scottish Enlightenment, that accounts for Millar's neglect. But what were the grounds of this rejection?

V

Crucially, the threat of decline was not just from the accidents of fate. Millar proceeded in the main text to identify a structural deficiency in commercial society itself. Commercial society, with its emphasis upon trade, served to liberate women from the constraints chivalry had imposed. Rather than being distant objects of adoration, they were encouraged to quit their isolation and become subjects in their own right. As Millar explained:

38 Ibid., pp. 4–5.   39 Rendall, 'Clio, Mars and Minerva', p. 138.

Women of condition come to be more universally admired and courted upon account of the agreeable qualities which they possess, and upon account of the amusement which their conversation affords. They are encouraged to quit that retirement which was formerly esteemed so suitable to their character, to enlarge the sphere of their acquaintance, and to appear in mixed company, and in public meetings of pleasure. They lay aside the spindle and the distaff, and engage in other employments more agreeable to the fashion.[40]

Yet, this apparent benefit, this improvement, carried within it the seeds of its own destruction. He warned:

It should seem, however, that there are certain limits beyond which it is impossible to push the real improvements arising from wealth and opulence. In a simple age, the free intercourse of the sexes is attended with no bad consequences; but in opulent and luxurious nations, it gives rise to licentious and dissolute manners, inconsistent with good order, and with the general interest of society. The love of pleasure, when carried to excess, is apt to weaken and destroy those passions which it endeavours to gratify, and to pervert those appetites which nature has bestowed upon mankind for the most beneficial purposes. The natural tendency, therefore, of great luxury and dissipation is to diminish the rank and dignity of the women, by preventing all refinement in their connection with the other sex, and rendering them only to the purposes of animal enjoyment.[41]

In identifying this structural flaw and its concomitant potential for retarding or even reversing social development, Millar was shifting register from natural law to commonwealth thought, from a concern with rights and justice to privilege and ethics.[42] This second rhetorical tradition was concerned with identifying flaws in the body politic that required amending. Notably, it associated commerce with luxury, and hence vice and moral turpitude. In this, Millar can be situated within the long indigenous tradition of social critique dating back to the 1650s and associated with the names of James Harrington, John Milton and, later, Algernon Sidney. Mapped by Caroline Robbins in her study *The eighteenth-century Commonwealthman*, commonwealth thought

---

40 Millar, *Origin of ranks*, p. 100.   41 Ibid., pp. 101–2.   42 This shift in register has been the cause of a significant debate within the literature on Millar. See J.G.A. Pocock, *The Machiavellian moment: Florentine political thought and the Atlantic republican tradition* (Princeton, 1975), pp. 502–3; Ignatieff, 'John Millar and individualism', pp. 253–270; and Haakonssen, *Natural law and moral philosophy*, pp. 154–81. What is of concern here is the fact of the shift, not its mechanics or its broader interpretative consequences for Millar's thought.

transferred down the years through Irish thinkers like William Molyneux and Robert Molesworth to the Scots.[43] Millar's contemporary, Adam Ferguson was a formidable adherent to some of the ideas but Millar really reinvested the language with its critical political edge.[44] As Robbins characterized his political thought:

> He supported various reforming movements of the day. He urged a change in representation. So long as prerogative was balanced by nobility he felt the faults of the old system were not serious. He was not a proponent of universal suffrage as such, but of a wider and fairer franchise. He was much concerned to remove patronage from ministerial hands. He felt that a swollen bureaucracy had immensely increased royal power since the Revolution [of 1688] ... He would have liked to see offices filled by some sort of freehold vote. He opposed slavery. He welcomed the French Revolution. He was in short a fairly typical Commonwealthman of the late eighteenth century.[45]

While this summation is broadly accurate, Robbins typically underestimates the corrosive nature of Commonwealth thought in the context of the period. Notably, Millar was partially rejecting the formulations of commercial humanism offered by Smith and Hume, which had softened the language from one of critique to a justification of the status quo. He reasserted the critique of luxury, emphasising its capacity to assail modern society, and proposed alternate modes of social interaction, even while moving from the agrarian economic base favoured by Harrington and Smith towards a more fully commercialized economy.[46]

   Crucially, these ideas informed his description of sexual relations. For Millar, the significance of the domestic world resided in his understanding that virtue begins in the home. As John Dwyer notes this is not because men and women

---

43 Caroline Robbins, *The eighteenth-century Commonwealthman: studies in the transmission, development and circumstances of English liberal thought from the Restoration of Charles II to the war with the Thirteen Colonies* (Cambridge, Mass., 1959).   44 Adam Ferguson (1723–1816) was Professor of Moral Philosophy at the University of Edinburgh and the author of *An essay on the history of civil society* (1767), ed. Fania Oz-Salsburger (Cambridge, 1995). On his debt to commonwealth thought see the comments in Pocock, *The Machiavellian moment*, pp. 499–501.   45 Robbins, *Eighteenth-century Commonwealthman*, p. 215.   46 On this tension between Millar and Smith see Dwyer, 'Natural history of love', p. 90: 'Whereas Smith's commercial society was still one dominated by agriculture, Millar's model was more in tune with Britain's overseas expansion and her developing role as the pre-eminent trader in the western world.' On Harringtonian agrarianism see J.G.A. Pocock, 'Machiavelli, Harrington and English political ideologies in the eighteenth century' in his *Politics, language and time: essays on political thought and history* (Chicago, 1971), pp. 104–47.

are to be considered equal. Rather 'Millar fascinates precisely because he so fully describes the new "rank and station" which women are now to occupy and which "appears most agreeable to reason", namely the traditional concerns of domestic management and child rearing.'[47] However, the treatment of women by their spouses generates habits of behaviour of consequence to relations forged beyond the domestic sphere. His history of the 'condition of women', through the interaction of his stadial theory of history and his history manners, linked the family, the economy and the state inextricably together, contending that the one was a measure and consequence of the other.

This is the very heart of Millar's argument. Hume's insight into the insecure foundations of habit and custom, and hence of morality and civilization, led him to fear the collapse of social order. This brought him in turn to a position we now term sceptical or scientific Whiggism, but commonly understood in the eighteenth century as Tory.[48] In contrast, Millar's sharing of this insight drove him in the opposite direction – and towards a political analysis similar to true or real Whigs, and, although the foundations of his thought were different, ultimately made him sympathetic to the Jacobin revolutionaries in the 1790s.[49] He believed that society was malleable, open to alteration – both negative and, importantly, positive. This belief in improvement prepared him to move towards revolutionary politics precisely because he saw that if society were to stagnate it would regress. The need was to struggle towards finer ways and means of organising political society, managing economic resources and of treating our fellow human beings, an important gauge of which was the proper treatment of your spouse.

What Millar was offering in the first section of the *Origin of the Distinction of Ranks* was, in a vein similar to Hume's analysis of the spiritual impulse in his *Natural History of Religion*, a natural history of sexual relations.[50] His study assessed the impact of the changes in mores between the sexes in a series of historically delineated social structures. At the heart of this analysis was an understanding of how the power relations that existed between men and women accorded with, affected and amended social relations writ large. Maltreatment in the home was thereby fused with slavery in the polis, and despotism at the hearth was intimately connected with oppression in the fields.[51]

47 Dwyer, 'Natural history of love', p. 91. As Dwyer notes, 'this is not necessarily a role that today's women would relish.'   48 For a treatment of Millar as a sceptical Whig, see Haakonssen, *Natural law and moral philosophy*, pp. 154–81. For the classic formulation of scientific Whiggery, see Duncan Forbes, *Hume's philosophical politics* (Cambridge, 1975). For his reading of Millar, see Duncan Forbes, 'Scientific Whiggism: Adam Smith and John Millar', *Cambridge Journal* 7 (1954), pp. 643–70.   49 The absence of an active citizenry is noted in Bowles, 'John Millar, the four-stages', p. 637. Millar's rejection of a theory of political rights is argued by Craig, 'Life', p. cxiv.   50 David Hume, *Natural history of religion* in David Hume, *Dialogues and natural history of religion*, edited by J.C.A. Gaskin (Oxford, 1993), pp. 134–85.   51 For Millar's treatment of slavery as an extant institution, see Millar, *Origin of ranks*, pp. 282–96.

Women and divorce legislation: a quest for liberty during the French Revolution

Colm Ó Conaill

Without question, women never enjoyed equal political participation in the French Revolution with their fellow men. The Declaration of the Rights of Man and the Citizen (1789) and the constitution of 1791 excluded women and other sectors of society from formal participation in the articulation of the laws of the new regime. However, our understanding of civil, social and political action should not be reduced to the formal procedure of voting for national representatives, debating and passing law in the National Assemblies, and although the Rousseauist-Montagnard discourse on women's participation in public life was exclusionary, the practice and experience of revolutionary life was often different.

I will concentrate on one aspect of revolutionary legislation that was important to men and women alike: revolutionary divorce legislation. We shall see that women played a part in the promulgation of the liberal divorce law of September 1792 and attempted to influence amendments to the law through petitions to the Convention and Council of Five Hundred.[1]

THE INTRODUCTION OF DIVORCE AND THE PHILOSOPHY BEHIND THE LEGISLATION

When the discussion on divorce legislation opened on 30 August 1792, Aubert-Dubayet (1759–1797) informed by the arguments of the pro-divorce pamphleteers and by Albert Hennet in particular, appealed for the introduction of divorce on both idealistic and practical grounds.[2] He was supported in his arguments by

1 See appendix 1. 2 Arguments for divorce in the Legislative Assembly drew heavily from a body of secular, pro-divorce pamphlets, published between 1789 and 1792. The most important of these, was Albert Hennet's *Du Divorce* (Paris, Desenne, 1789). The divorce discussions are found in *Archives Parlementaires de 1787 à 1860; Receuil complet*

Cambon (1754–1820), Leonard Robin (1745–1802), Guadet (1758–94) and
Sédillez (1745–1820).[3] They argued for divorce in an optimistic language,
suggesting that an enlightened divorce law would guarantee liberty in the home
and society, happiness for all and equality in the domestic home. They saw the
law as an instrument that would strengthen and purify society of the evils of
unhappy marriages. The deputies treated the idea of marriage and the family
very seriously. They did not want to weaken marriages, they said, but believed
in the possibility of improving marriages. They thought that a society could not
be founded on families where strife and conflict existed, and they believed that,
if women gained equality in the home through divorce, men would not mistreat
their spouses for fear of divorce. This was a crucial aspect of the legislation and
was recognized as such. Even if women were denied the ability to act publicly
without fear of censure, advocates of divorce stressed that society could not
function fully, if women were denied equality in the home. Aubert-Dubayet
concluded his speech by saying that divorce would encourage individuals to
work harder at their marriages, thus strengthening them. This argument was
also borrowed from Hennet, who thought that the existence of divorce would
encourage spouses to care for one another:

> Divorce ... est moins l'art de détruire les mauvais mariages, que l'art de
> rendre tous les mariages heureux.[4]

The members of the Legislative Assembly did not believe that divorce was
merely a mechanism for terminating marriages. They thought it was a crucial
component to the revolutionary project, embodying the ideals of liberty for all
in society and equality for women in the domestic sphere. They also recognized
that such a law would have to be practical and accessible to the majority of the
population, if it was to fulfil these ideals. They rendered divorce procedure
straightforward and affordable. Individuals could divorce by mutual consent or
unilaterally by claiming incompatibility of character. A list of other grounds for
unilateral divorce was also put forward. Therefore, any man or woman could
divorce their spouse, even if the other party opposed them.[5]

The importance of divorce legislation for women can be seen by the extent
to which they availed of it. It is estimated that women initiated 70% of divorce

des débats législatifs et politiques des Chambres français. Première série, 1787–1799, sous la
direction de M.J. Mavidal et de E. Laurent, avec la collaboration de MM Louis Claveau
et Constant Pionnier (Paris, 1909; Kraus reprint, 1969), vol. 48, p. 400; vol. 49, pp. 117,
432, 609, 643.   **3** For further information on the deputies, see Marcel Garaud, Romauld
Szramkiewicz, *La Révolution Française et la famille* (Paris, 1978).   **4** 'divorce ... is less
the art of destroying bad marriages. Rather, it is the art of making all marriages happy',
Albert Hennet, *Divorce*, p. 115.   **5** The specific reasons for divorce were insanity,
criminal conviction of one's spouse, crimes or violence towards the other party,
dissolution of morals, abandonment of one spouse by the other for at least two years,

cases.[6] In Toulouse, there were 347 divorces from September 1792 to September 1802. Of these, 155 were for abandonment, absence and separation. Women took ninety-six of these cases which suggests that men were more likely to abandon their spouses than women.

Divorce legislation served as a means of regulating family breakdown, but there was also a philosophical and political aspect to the legal instrument. The advocates of divorce, *philosophes*, pamphleteers, deputies and even ordinary petitioners never lost sight of the conceptual basis of the law. They believed the divorce law to be more than a regulatory mechanism for marital breakdown. It also expressed the transition from the dark into the light, from indissoluble Catholic marriage of duty to secular marriage of happiness. Divorce was not only allowed for domestic violence and adultery, but individuals could also seek divorce due to incompatibility, without forwarding a specific reason. This became the most contentious aspect of the divorce law.

Critique of marital legislation was neither unique to the revolutionary situation nor to the eighteenth century. Ever since the Reformation the concept of marital indissolubility had been called into question. Throughout the eighteenth century the *philosophes* attacked Catholic teaching on marriage. Some pointed to historical precedent for divorce, while others cited marriage custom in other lands.[7] In the *Lettres Persanes*, Montesquieu claimed that marital indissolubility denuded marriage of pleasure and discouraged the young from marrying for fear that they would be forever bound together in a potentially disastrous union. He insisted that marriage entailed freedom of choice and emotional attachment and therefore, one had to accept the possibility of a change of heart. He understood marriage as a private contract entered into by two individuals who were equally free to break their ties:

> No account was taken of distaste, personal whims, and temperamental incompatibility; an effort was made to control the human heart, the most variable and inconsistent thing in nature; people were coupled together irrevocably and hopelessly, a mutual burden, almost always ill-assorted.'[8]

absence without news of one spouse for a minimum of five years and political emigration. See Département de Seine et Marne, *Loi qui détermine les causes, les modes et les effets du Divorce. Du 20 septembre 1792, l'an 4 de la liberté* (Melun, 1792). The text of the law is also in Francis Ronsin, *Le contrat sentimental. Débats sur le mariage, l'amour, le divorce, de l'Ancien Régime à la Restauration* (Paris, 1990), pp.109–21.   6 Roderick Phillips, *Putting asunder: a history of divorce in western society* (Cambridge, 1988), p. 275.   7 Montesquieu (trans. C.J. Betts), *Persian letters* (1721), (London, 1973); Montesquieu, *De l'esprit des lois* (Paris, 1748); Voltaire, 'Divorce' in the *Dictionnaire Philosophique* (1765), in Voltaire, *Œuvres Complètes*, ed. Louis Molard (Paris, 1870–1880); Diderot, *Supplément au voyage de Bougainville* (1796); Boucher d'Argis, 'Divorce' in Diderot and D'Alembert (eds), *Encyclopédie Raisonnée des Sciences, des Arts et des Métiers. Nouvelle impression en facsimile de la première édition de 1751 à 1780* (Stuttgart, 1988).   8 Montesquieu, *Persian letters*,

Voltaire was also a critic of marital indissolubility. He gave the example of an unhappy marriage to highlight the injustice and hypocrisy of Catholic teaching. Voltaire's article on adultery in the *Dictionnaire Philosophique* (1764) describes an honest magistrate who married a woman previously debauched by a priest. As a result of this debauchery, she engaged in public scandals while married and the unfortunate magistrate obtained a legal separation. Voltaire believed that this course of action punished the innocent magistrate as he still desired the company of a woman, but did not wish to take a concubine or frequent prostitutes. According to Voltaire, matrimonial law punished this man by leaving him with no option apart from celibacy or fornication. He argued that unhappiness and immorality were natural consequences of marital indissolubility:

> Mon épouse est criminelle et c'est moi qu'on punit ... Les lois civiles d'aujourd'hui, malheureusement fondés sur le droit canon, me privent des droits de l'humanité. L'église me réduit à chercher ou des plaisirs qu'elle réprouve, ou des dédommagements honteux qu'elle condamne; elle veut me forcer d'être criminel.[9]

The themes of individual happiness, freedom and the injustice of marital indissolubility were central to the liberal arguments for divorce in the early years of the French Revolution. Hennet and Bouchotte both stressed the importance of happiness for individuals and the injustice of indissolubility. They asked the deputies to implement a divorce law that would not only regulate marital breakdown, but would also spread happiness and Enlightenment throughout revolutionary France.[10] For these reasons, the divorce law of 1792 was not only a social measure, but one also bound up in the political culture of the time. The law reflected the deputies' desire to improve society and spread happiness throughout all levels of society. They understood that women and the popular classes should have equal recourse to divorce alongside the wealthy and men, even if the law threatened man's pre-eminence in the domestic sphere.

(London, 1973), letter 116, p. 209.   **9** 'My wife is a criminal and I am punished ... current civil law, unfortunately founded upon canon law, deprives me of human rights. The church reduces me to seeking either pleasures that it disapproves of, or shameful compensations that it condemns. It forces me to be a criminal': Voltaire, 'Adultère' in *Dictionnaire Philosophique*. Cited in 'Extrait du *Dictionnaire Philosophique*,' Albert Hennet, *Pétition à l'Assemblée Nationale par Montagne, Charron, Montesquieu, et Voltaire, suivi d'une Consultation en Pologne et en Suisse* (Paris, Desenne, 1791), p. 17.   **10** Hennet wrote that he was inspired to advocate divorce by Enlightenment figures such as Voltaire and Montesquieu. See Hennet, *Divorce*, pp. 1–19.

ETTA PALM D'ÆLDERS AND DIVORCE LEGISLATION

Etta Palm d'Ælders was an important advocate of divorce before the legislation was introduced. Her actions prefigure the petitioners who tried to change the divorce law once enacted, and perhaps inspired some of them. She was involved in the Cercle Social in 1791. This group was an important debating arena and the most prolific printing house in Paris at the time. Among its members were Nicolas Bonneville, the marquis de Condorcet, Thomas Paine and Jacques-Pierre Brissot.[11] Her thoughts on divorce and the general predicament of women in revolutionary society illustrate the point that many participants in the revolution, from '*hommes politiques* to *femmes ordinaires*', believed that the reform of marriage law was an important part of the legislative change enacted between 1789 and 1792. If the revolutionary family was stable and imbued with the spirit of liberty, then the possibility of achieving an equal society was that much closer.

In the *Appel aux Français sur la Régénération des Mœurs, et Nécessité de l'Influence des Femmes dans un Gouvernement Libre* (1791) Etta Palm d'Ælders outlined her general thoughts on the need for equality between men and women in all aspects of life, not simply in the home, although she thought equality in the home and a divorce law were essential and urgent.[12] In a passionate plea to the National Assembly and more generally, to all Frenchmen, Etta Palm d'Ælders pleaded that French women be allowed play a full role in the French Revolution. She insisted that justice, equality and liberty be applied to women as they were to men. To achieve this she believed that women should be allowed to participate in public life; they should receive an adequate education; they should enjoy equality in marriage. Divorce would encourage equality in the home.

She appealed to men to show justice to women and to accord them liberty. Only then, could women respect the constitution and become part of the new regime. She believed that through education and the full protection of the law women could become good citizens and serve the state. The freedom to choose one's partner was an essential component of liberty for women. Otherwise, they would languish in slavery, as they had done under the *Ancien Régime*:

11 For a comprehensive treatment and of the Cercle Social, its aims and membership, see Gary Kates, *The Cercle Social, the Girondins, and the French Revolution* (Princeton, 1983). Etta Palm d'Ælders was born in Holland and probably died there. From 1790, she appeared in Parisian clubs that admitted women and was close to Fauchet and other members of the Cercle Social. She was sent to the United Provinces to spread republican ideas during the Revolution, returned to Paris and again went to the United Provinces in 1793. See Claude Manceron, *La Révolution Français: dictionnaire biographique* (Paris, 1989), pp. 462–3. 12 Etta Palm d'Ælders, *Appel aux Français sur la Régénération des Mœurs, et Nécessité de l'Influence des Femmes dans un Gouvernement Libre* (Paris; Imprimerie du Cercle Social, 1791). The author claims that she published this text to refute claims in the *Gazette Universelle* (19 and 25 July 1791) that she was an agent of the Prussian court and a 'démocrate outrée'. The work is made up of several

Hé! quoi de plus injuste! notre vie, notre liberté, notre fortune, n'est point à nous; sortant de l'enfance, livrée à un despote, que souvent le cœur repousse … tandis que notre fortune devient la proie de la fraude et de la débauche.[13]

Furthermore, she criticized those men who believed that women would always be subordinate to men, and said that such statements were as absurd as saying that Frenchmen were born to slavery and should not have demanded their rights in 1789.[14]

In the same vein as the marquis de Condorcet, Etta Palm d'Ælders insisted that, while men may be physically stronger, women were created to be the equal companions of men possessed of equal moral strength and superior imagination, sentiment and patience. She believed that women might even surpass men, if they received the benefit of an enlightened education. Etta Palm d'Ælders was convinced that women could serve the Revolution, if given the opportunity and education: then they could raise their children and give comfort to their husbands.[15] They could also serve the Revolution by other acts. Women could establish '*cercles des femmes*' to supervise wet nurses. They could protect girls from the dangers of city life, teach them the rights of man, instil respect for the law and impart the duties of the citizen in '*écoles de charité*'.[16] Etta Palm d'Ælders did not expect women to desert their traditional role of mother and wife, but she did believe that women deserved the right to education and the full benefit of the law, so that they might enjoy the rights and duties of citizenship. All these forms of public participation would give women a legitimate role in public life, while not undermining the rights of men. In fact, while Etta Palm d'Ælders argued for the public participation of women in French society, she accepted that women would probably not fulfil the same functions as men, and instead asked that they might be allowed control over areas traditionally regulated by women, such as childbirth and the protection of women. In doing this, they could act publicly and fulfil their civic duties, while not threatening male authority.

speeches: 'Discours sur l'Injustice des Lois en Faveur des Hommes, au dépend des Femmes, lu à l'Assemblée Fédérative des Amis de la Vérité' (30 December 1790); 'Extrait du registre des délibérations de la municipalité de Creil-sur-Oise' (8 February 1791); 'Discours d'une Amie de la Vérité. Palm d'Ælders, Hollandaise, en recevant la cocarde et la médaille nationales envoyées pour elle à l'assemblée fédérative par la municipalité de Creil' (14 February 1791); 'Discours … et justification sur la dénonciation de Louise Robert (12 June 1791)'; 'Adresse des citoyennes françaises à l'assemblée nationale.'   13 'Hey! What could be more unjust! Our life, our freedom, our fortune never belong to us; upon leaving childhood, we are delivered unto a despot, whom our hearts find repellent … while our fortune becomes the prey of fraud and debauchery', Ibid., pp. 4–5.   14 Ibid., p. 6. Here she cites L.S. Mercier's *Tableau de Paris* (1782–3).   15 Ibid., p. 13.   16 Ibid., pp. 26–7.

She believed that women and men must enjoy liberty and freedom in the home so that they could enjoy such values in society. She concluded by insisting that the Revolution could only succeed if women were granted a decent education, equality in marriage, and the right to divorce. She insisted that if a woman were trapped in a loveless and oppressive marriage, like a slave, she would break her chains, and the correct way to allow women to exercise liberty in marriage was to give them the opportunity to break from an unloving or tyrannical husband legitimately. Then they would not destroy the natural order (by cuckolding their spouses or fleeing their authority), but would help maintain it by dissolving the marriage before exposing their partner to public ridicule.[17]

PETITIONS FROM WOMEN FOR THE LIBERALIZATION OF DIVORCE LEGISLATION

While the strident arguments of an educated and wealthy foreign woman may be put down to exceptional behaviour on the part of one individual, it is striking that 'ordinary' women participated as best they could in the debate surrounding the reform of divorce legislation. It might be argued that they fulfilled a Rousseauist vision of citizenship through the participation in the formation of the laws. Many female citizens who petitioned the National Convention on the subject of divorce law phrased their petitions in the revolutionary language of rights, duties and liberty. They did not simply ask for the reform of an inefficient law; they asked that the law might be changed in order to fulfil its mission of liberation and transformation of a society. Yes, they expressed their desire for a practical method of regulating their marital problems, but they also couched their demands in a language of rights and liberty familiar to the *philosophes* and revolutionary deputies. Petitions to the National Convention and the Council of Five Hundred engaged in a dialogue with the deputies as to the philosophical, political and social merits of the divorce law, and it is instructive to see how the deputies reacted.

Three petitions to the National Convention, all written by women, illustrate the importance of the revolutionary foundations of the divorce law. These women argued for changes in the legislation because they believed the law was incomplete. They argued for practical changes to the law on principled grounds, stating that such alterations would bring about the flourishing of justice, liberty and equality in revolutionary society. They were careful not to demand reform for particular interest, instead they argued on the ground of general revolutionary principles. None of the petitioners criticized the intentions of the 1792 divorce law. They believed the legislation to be incomplete and hoped that the legislators would develop the existing law in order to bring about the liberty and

17 Ibid., p. 40.

equality promised by the initial divorce legislation. The deputy Oudot, for the committee on legislation, agreed with the petitioners when presenting his report and *projet de loi on 27 germinal* II. He stated that the revolutionary government would have to reform certain laws in order to make them more just; included in these was the 'incomplete' divorce law.[18] It is important to note that the women petitioners were not excluded from the political dialogue and discourse of the time. It helped, no doubt, that the deputies agreed with the general thrust of the petitions, but the point remains that the National Convention was willing to enter into some form of dialogue with female petitioners at the height of the radical revolution.

The petition of the *citoyenne* Girod relied heavily on the language of rights and equality. She implored the deputies to change some of the procedural measures of the 1792 legislation.[19] Girod believed the principles of the law to be sound, but argued that it nevertheless favoured the interests of the powerful and wealthy over the poor. She cited the particular difficulties women experienced in obtaining divorce as an example of the practical problems that hampered the direct flow of justice and equality to all members of society. Girod's technique is common to those who petitioned the assembly for changes in the divorce legislation. They began with praise of the pillars of the Revolution, lauding the advances the deputies had made in legislating for justice, equality and liberty. Then they outlined the problems with the divorce legislation, explaining that it did not live up to all the promises it made to instil liberty and equality in the heart of revolutionary society. While praising the conceptual basis of the law, they observed that further refinement was necessary if the 1792 divorce law was to fulfil its lofty aspirations.

Girod argued for a particular change to divorce legislation on the grounds of general revolutionary principle while praising the deputies for implementing laws that facilitated greater equality between citizens. She claimed that the deputies had re-established:

> ... l'égalité qui exige que le citoyen pauvre obtienne justice aussi facilement que l'homme riche auquel les sacrifices ne coûtent point.[20]

18 'Le membre Oudot, au nom du comité de la législation, fait un rapport sur plusieurs pétitions tendante à faire entreprêter différentes dispositions de la loi du 10 septembre 1792 sur le divorce et à y ajouter plusieurs articles.' ('Deputy Oudot presents a report to the committee on legislation on a number of petitions tending to make interpretations of various dispositions of the law of 10 September 1792 and to add several articles to it.') In Mavidal and Laurent, *Archives Parlementaires*, vol. 88, pp. 652–4. The title refers to the law of 10 September 1792, but should read 20 September 1792.   19 'Séance du 9 *pluviôse* an II. La citoyenne Girod à la Convention, s.d.' In Mavidal and Laurent, *Archives Parlementaires*, vol. 85, pp. 741–2.   20 '... the equality that demands that the poor citizen obtains justice as easily as the rich man for whom the sacrifices cost him nothing', Mavidal and Laurent, *Archives Parlementaires*, vol. 85, p. 741.

Girod lamented the fact that the 1792 divorce law allowed inequality to subsist between the rich and the poor and between men and women. Specifically, she claimed that the practice of petitioning for divorce in the commune of domicile of the husband discriminated against all women, but especially against poor women. She gave the example of women who were forced to leave their husbands in difficult circumstances, often in search of work. Other women were forsaken by their husbands for the army, for commercial reasons or for emigration. Girod claimed that these women were often unaware of the last place of domicile of their spouses, thus rendering it impossible to petition for divorce there. Others might not have sufficient resources to undertake such a journey. Girod accepted that public notification of a divorce action was necessary, but found it unacceptable that it had to take place in the commune of the husband as this rendered the divorce law inequitable. She asked the legislators to reflect upon her comments and proposed the following changes to the divorce law:

> La loi nouvelle pourrait autoriser les femmes qui auront acquis un domicile d'un an dans un lieu autre que le domicile de leur mari, ou celles dont leurs maris auraient depuis six mois abandonné de fait de leur domicile, et l'auraient elles-mêmes fixés ailleurs en y prenant un état, à poursuivre leur divorce dans le lieu de leur domicile actuel.'[21]

Girod asked that women be allowed to formulate divorce petitions in their own commune of domicile if they had been living apart from their husbands for over a year or if they had been abandoned for over six months. Deputy Oudot, speaking for the committee on legislation, responded to this petition and others regarding divorce. He agreed with the general opinions expressed by the petitioners on the subject of divorce and agreed that the law required reform. Oudot stated that the goal of marriage was happiness, reproduction and care of children. If these functions were not fulfilled, then the marriage was not a real union. Furthermore, he stated that the institution of marriage was superior to all others, when it had not been corrupted and that the existence of a divorce law was necessary to purify marriage.[22]

Articles I to IV of the decree of 4 *floréal* year II dealt with the demands of the *citoyenne* Girod. The legislator acceded to the demands of the petitioner and

21 'The new law could authorise women who have acquired a domicile for one year in a place other than that of their husband's home, or for those women whose husbands have abandoned the family home for over six months and have themselves [the wives] established their domicile elsewhere, to pursue their divorce cases in the place of their current residence', Mavidal and Laurent, *Archives Parlementaires*, vol. 85, p. 742.
22 C.F. Oudot, *Essai sur les principes de la législation des mariages privés et solennels, du divorce et de l'adoption qui peuvent être déclarés à la suite de l'acte constitutionnel* (Paris; Imprimerie Nationale, 1793), p. 7.

made the law easier to obtain. Not only could the petitioner (male or female) pursue divorce in their new commune of residence, if the couple were separated and the petitioner was living there for over six months, but they could also obtain divorce on grounds of separation for more than six months on production of an *acte de notoriété* to this effect. The other party would be informed by an *agent national*, who would post the divorce notification at the town hall of the former joint commune of residence.[23] Article II of the decree stated that, if it were proven that separation for over six months had taken place by the abandonment of one spouse by the other, then no notification would be necessary. Wives of soldiers or public functionaries serving far from their domestic home were exempt from this last stipulation. Wives of these men could petition for divorce in the commune of the last domestic home or in the current place of residence of their husbands.[24] Thus, on entering a dialogue with the female petitioners the deputies assessed the effectiveness of their legislation, analyzed it in accordance with revolutionary principles and found the law imperfect. They assented to the changes requested by Girod, but also made divorce easier to avail of for all by reducing the statutory period of separation or abandonment to six months before divorce could be obtained.

PETITIONS FROM WOMEN AND THE REFORM OF DIVORCE LEGISLATION

The worries of those concerned with divorce in 1796 were different from those of their counterparts of 1794. They continued to demand reform of the divorce law, but the idealism of 1792 to 1794 had disappeared. The experience of divorce had made private individuals and the political class realize that the advent of the French Revolution and the introduction of a liberal divorce did not solve all marital problems. Couples continued to divorce at a stable rate, and many of these divorces were based on grounds of incompatibility or mutual consent.[25] A number of petitions were sent to the Council of Five Hundred criticizing this aspect of divorce legislation, all opposing the exercise of divorce

23 Article I of the decree of 4 *floréal* year II. In Département de Seine et Marne, *Décret (no.2329) de la Convention Nationale, des 4ième et 5ième jours de Floréal, an II de la République Française, une et indivisible* (Melun, 1794), pp. 1–2.   24 Articles II and IV, *Décret (no.2329) de la Convention Nationale*, p. 2. The deputies feared that women might avail of this provision to divorce husbands serving the state far from home. The property, alimony, and childcare settlements of divorces under article IV of this decree (as settled by the *tribunaux de famille*) would remain provisional until the return of the husband from duty. This was to prevent the wife from gaining an unfair settlement without the knowledge of the husband.   25 In the years IV, V, VI, VII, VIII, IX and X, there were 22, 21, 13, 21, 22, 20 and 21 divorces in Toulouse. *Archives Départementales de la Haute Garonne, Etat Civil*, 5 Mi. The figures for Troyes for the same period are as follows: 27, 22, 19, 21, 16, 15 and 12. *Archives Départementales de l'Aube, Etat Civil*, 5 Mi. For the conversion of the revolutionary calendar to the Gregorian, see appendix 2.

on grounds of incompatibility of character.[26] Marie-Anne Campion wrote to the Council of Five Hundred complaining about incompatibility of character. Like most other petitioners, she did not criticize the divorce law, but claimed that it needed much reform. Campion wrote that she was happily married until her husband suddenly decided to leave her:

> C'est sans motif et sans prétexte quelconque que mon mari abuse de la loi du 20 septembre 1792.[27]

A *citoyenne* Bresse, for the department of the Yonne sent a similar petition to the Council of Five Hundred on 17 November 1796. She accepted the necessity of a divorce law, but condemned the 'frivolous' clause of incompatibility of character, which her husband was using to divorce her. She demanded that the deputies suspend this provision of the divorce law. The Council decided to charge the commission on the classification of laws with presenting a report on the possibility of suspending divorce by incompatibility of character.[28]

Deputy Favard presented the commission's report regarding the matter on 20 *nivôse* year V. He insisted that the role of the committee was only to examine the question of divorce by incompatibility of character. They would not pass judgement on the appropriateness of divorce *per se*, as this would be dealt with in the discussions on the *Code Civil*.[29] Favard favoured the suspension of divorce by incompatibility and relied on arguments typical of other republican opponents of divorce, such as Toussaint Guiraudet.[30] They argued that the stability of the family was essential for the maintenance of society, as the family acted as the safeguard of morals in the community. Favard believed that wise laws should protect marriage for these reasons:

26 Between *pluviôse* year IV and *germinal* year V, petitions protesting against divorce by incompatibility of character were sent on eight occasions (30 *pluviôse* year IV, 9 *messidor* year IV, 29 *messidor* year IV, 27 *brumaire* year V, 5 *nivôse* year V, 12 *germinal* year V, and on two other undated occasions. See Bibliothèque Nationale, *Catalogue de l'Histoire de France* (Paris, 1968), vol. 3.   27 'My husband abuses the law of 20 September 1792 without the slightest motive or excuse', Marie-Anne Campion, *Pétition présentée au Conseil des Cinq Cents le 29 messidor, l'an quatrième de la République française. Pour réclamer contre les Abus du Divorce sur la simple allégation d'incompatibilité d'humeur et de caractère*, (Paris, an IV).   28 'La citoyenne Bresse ... au Conseil des Cinq Cents, 27 brumaire an V.' In Bibliothèque Nationale, *Catalogue de l'Histoire de France*, vol. 3. Also in *Table de la Seconde Législature* (Paris; Baudouin, *nivôse* an VII), p. 560.   29 Corps Législatif, Conseil des Cinq Cents, *Rapport par Favard sur le Divorce au nom d'une commission spéciale composée des représentans Cambacérès, Boissy, Méaulle, Blutel & Favard* (Paris; Imprimerie Nationale, 20 *nivôse* an V).   30 Charles-Philippe-Toussaint Guiraudet, *De la famille, considérée comme l'élément des sociétés* (Paris; Imprimerie de A.-C. Forget, an V). In this work, Guiraudet argued that the fundamental element of republican society was the patriarchal family and not the individual. Without stable

... le mariage corrige les vices, active la population, et règle les mœurs qui doivent faire le pivot d'une république.[31]

Those in favour of the suspension of divorce for incompatibility insisted on the primacy of social stability and the integrity of the family over the liberty advocated by apologists for the 1792 divorce law. Favard concurred with the petitions opposing incompatibility. He said that such dissolutions were motivated by fickle and often transitory reasons. Favard believed that the individuals divorced by this means were victims of the stupidity of their partners:

> ... il est bien reconnu que ce mode de divorce, souvent plus imaginaire que réel exige de grandes modifications, puisque'il n'a produit jusqu'ici que de très mauvais effets.'[32]

The arguments in favour of the suspension or abolition of divorce by incompatibility of character displayed a marked change from the idealistic dialogue of the deputies in the Legislative Assembly and Convention.[33] Previously deputies had argued that the introduction of a liberal divorce law would produce happy marriages, stable society and few divorces. The deputies of the Council of Five Hundred had lived with the experience of divorce and had lost their idealism. Many agreed with the petitioners that divorce for incompatibility of character was too easy to obtain, but accepted that divorce, even if it was destructive to the family, had become a social reality and could not simply be abolished. They acknowledged that divorce did not have a purifying effect on republican marriages, but were unwilling to abolish it completely. Favard, for the commission, stated that divorce by incompatibility was too easy to obtain and that, if couples wished to divorce, they would have to base divorce applications on the grounds of mutual consent or tangible fault as laid out by the 1792 legislation.

family units the family could not survive, therefore men should rule in the domestic and public sphere. Divorce was therefore a threat to the stable patriarchal family that served as the foundation of the republican state.   31 'Marriage corrects vices, stimulates population growth and regulates the morals which must form the pivot of the republic', *Rapport par Favard sur le divorce*, p. 2.   32 '... it is well known that this form of divorce, often more imaginary than real, requires great modification. Up to this moment it has produced nothing but very negative effects.' Ibid., p. 4.   33 The deputy Siméon also favoured the suspension of the incompatibility provision, while Duprat thought that it should be abolished outright. Corps Législatif, Conseil des Cinq Cents, *Opinion de Siméon sur la Suspension du Divorce par Incompatibilité* (Paris; Imprimerie Nationale, 5 *pluviôse* an V). Corps Législatif, Conseil des Cinq Cents, *Opinion de Duprat sur la Suspension du Divorce pour Cause d'Incompatibilité d'Humeur et de Caractère* (Paris; Imprimerie Nationale, 13 *pluviôse* an V). While these deputies reluctantly accepted the need for some form of divorce law, at least until the completion of the *Code Civil*, the deputy Bancal des Issarts argued that divorce, as a threat to the family and therefore society, should be abolished outright. Corps Législatif, Conseil des Cinq Cents, *Opinion*

Two deputies defended the article on incompatibility of character during this debate. Lecointe-Puyraveau repeated the liberal pro-divorce arguments of 1792, but Félix Faulcon was a more sophisticated defender of divorce.[34] He acknowledged the imperfections of the divorce law and the undesirability of a high divorce rate, but maintained an ultimately successful practical and principled defence of divorce in general and divorce by incompatibility.[35] Faulcon accepted criticism of the divorce law of 1792 but he insisted that it was necessary to ensure liberty in society. He also believed that the provision on incompatibility was necessary to safeguard public decency:

> ... le motif d'incompatibilité est comme un voile heureux qu'il faut bien se garder de lever, parce qu'il dérobe au grand jour une foule de détails hideux qui sont l'opprobre des mœurs ...[36]

Faulcon argued strongly that divorce was necessary for the protection of the individual and the maintenance of happy marriages. The incompatibility clause was important in that it maintained the privacy of the intimate private sphere and protected society from witnessing the terrible events that could occur within a family. Faulcon had acted as a judge prior to the introduction of divorce and experienced legal separations. He believed that these separations were detrimental to the moral well being of society, as they exposed the public to terrible private scandals. Without the provision for incompatibility, divorce would be reduced:

> ... au niveau de ces scandaleuses demandes en séparation de corps, qui, en dévoilant publiquement les turpitudes cachées des ménages, furent le long fléau des mœurs, ainsi que de la dignité du lien conjugal.'[37]

Faulcon acknowledged the need to reform divorce legislation but he success- fully maintained the provision for divorce by incompatibility. He achieved this

sur le Divorce par Jean-Henri Bancal (Paris; Imprimerie Nationale, 12 *pluviôse* an V). 34 Corps Législatif, Conseil des Cinq Cents, *Opinion de Lecointe-Puyraveau sur le projet de suspension de l'article III de la loi de 20 septembre 1792 qui permet le divorce pour incompatibilité d'humeur ou de caractère* (Paris; Imprimerie Nationale, 5 *pluviôse* an V). 35 Félix Faulcon, *Opinion relative à la Suspension du Divorce pour Cause d'Incompatibilité d'Humeur* (Paris; Imprimerie Nationale, an V); Félix Faulcon, *Opinion sur le Divorce et les Ministres des Cultes* (Paris; Baudouin, an V); Félix Faulcon, *Rapport de Félix Faulcon. Au nom de la Commission Chargée de Présenter des Vues sur la Législation du Divorce* (Paris; Imprimerie Nationale, an V). 36 '... the motive of incompatibility resembles a felicitous veil which must be kept drawn, as to open it would reveal a mass of hideous details which are the opprobium of morals', Faulcon, *Opinion ... relative à la Suspension du Divorce*, p. 2. 37 '... to the level of these scandalous requests for legal separation, which, by publicly revealing the hidden depravity of relationships, were the scourge of

by proposing the formation of yet another commission to discuss divorce and that all other discussion of divorce be suspended until this commission presented its report. The Council of Five Hundred accepted Faulcon's proposal and the commission presented its report eight days later.[38] The report accepted that the divorce legislation should be reformed but despite opposition to divorce by incompatibility of character, this mechanism was retained. Faulcon had successfully defended this part of the divorce law by insisting on its importance in providing a veil to protect society from the atrocities that occur in some marriages and also by stating that the motives for divorce were not always easy to prove. At the same time, he agreed with opponents of divorce by incompatibility that the divorce law had not succeeded in purifying marriages.

CONCLUSION

The fascinating aspect of the two attempts to modify divorce in the years II and V is that both were prompted to some extent by calls from women in the greater revolutionary society and not from within the restricted and restrictive political class. In the first case, the female petitioners used a political language of rights reminiscent of earlier pro-divorce pamphleteers to argue for more liberty and equality in the divorce law. Remarkably, the deputies accepted their demands and modified the divorce law to make it more liberal. In the second instance, petitioners and deputies criticized the excesses allowed by the liberal divorce law. They focussed their attacks on divorce by incompatibility of character, claiming that this method of divorce led to the dissolution of otherwise stable marriages and threatened social stability and morality. While some deputies accepted this argument and proposed the suspension of divorce by incompatibility of character, Félix Faulcon defended this section of the law on grounds of public decency. He also reasoned that, despite the fact that divorce had not purified the institution of marriage, as some claimed it would, it was still necessary in order to regulate marital breakdown.

The impact of social pressure, and especially that of women, on the modification the 1792 divorce law is undeniable, but one must also observe the integral part political ideas and culture played in the modification of the law. Arguments on the issue were framed in a political language of rights, liberty and equality. The deputies accepted these arguments and implemented the changes to the divorce law demanded by the petitioners. In the year V, despite the social experience of divorce and considerable opposition to the divorce law as it stood,

morals and of the dignity of the conjugal bond.' Faulcon, *Opinion … relative à la Suspension du Divorce*, p. 5.   **38** The commission presented its report on 28 *prairial* year V. The members of the commission were Vauvilliers, Grégoire de Rumare, Charles, Dumolard, Favart, Pison, Galand and Faulcon.

the Council of Five Hundred decided to maintain the provision of divorce by incompatibility of character, based on Faulcon's defence of the article. Divorce was not only a social demand translated into legislative reality by the political actors of the French Revolution. In the legislation of 1792, it was also a highly political law imbued with the aspirations of secular Enlightenment thought. The issue of revolutionary divorce shows how revolutionary politics and society interacted in a way that sought to advance political justice and civil society through an ongoing dialogue between actors in the social and political spheres. Political actors acknowledged the need to communicate with civil society, while private individuals still believed in their ability to mould the world they lived in through politics and civil influence on legislation.

APPENDIX I: SUMMARY OF DIVORCE LEGISLATION AND SIGNIFICANT AMENDMENTS

Law on divorce, 20 September 1792

1. Marriage is dissolved by divorce.
2. Divorce may take place by mutual consent of the couple
3. One spouse may proceed with divorce on the simple allegation of an incompatibility of humour or character (*incompatibilité d'humeur ou de caractère*).
4. One spouse may also have divorce declared for the following motives:

   i. Insanity (*la démence, la folie ou la fureur de l'un des époux*).
   ii. Criminal conviction (*la condamnation de l'un d'eux à des peines afflictives ou infamantes*).
   iii. Crime or severe maltreatment of one spouse by the other (*les crimes, sévices, ou injures graves de l'un envers l'autre*).
   iv. Dissolution of morals (*le dérèglement de mœurs notoire*).
   v. Abandonment of one spouse by the other for at least two years (*l'abandon de la femme par le mari ou du mari par la femme, pendant deux ans au moins*).
   vi. Absence without news for at least five years (*l'absence de l'un d'eux, sans nouvelles, au moins pendant cinq ans*).
   vii. Political emigration (*l'émigration dans les cas prévus par les lois, notamment par le décret du 8 avril 1792*).

5. Couples who have legally separated may also divorce.
6. All incomplete legal separations are null and void. Legal separations under appeal are also null and void.
7. Legal separations are abolished. Couples who wish to terminate their marriages must use the divorce legislation.

Decree on divorce, 8 nivôse year II (28 December 1793)

1. Article one confirms the competence of the *tribunaux de famille* to adjudicate in disputes regarding divorce and subsequent financial settlements. The *tribunaux* must come to their decision no more than one month after their formation. Either or both spouses may bring the decision of the *tribunal de famille* before the local *tribunal de district* if a decision is not made within the specified time limits.
2. The divorced husband may marry immediately after a divorce is pronounced. The divorced wife must wait for at least ten months.
3. If it can be shown that the husband has abandoned his domicile and wife for at least ten months, then she may remarry immediately after the divorce.

Decree of 4 floréal year II (23 April 1794)

The main provision of this decree was to allow for divorce after six months of separation.

Decree of 15 thermidor year III (2 August 1795)

The provisions in the decrees of 8 *nivôse* year II and 4 *floréal* year II on divorce are suspended and a committee is formed to examine the divorce legislation.

Decree of 1st supplementary day year V (17 September 1797)

The waiting period before a divorce by incompatibility of humour or character can be pronounced is extended by six months (after the date of the final act of non-reconciliation).

APPENDIX 2: THE REVOLUTIONARY CALENDAR[39]

Each revolutionary month has thirty days.

Vendémiare	22 September to 21 October.
Brumaire	22 October to 20 November.
Frimaire	21 November to 20 December.
Nivôse	21 December to 19 January.
Pluviôse	20 January to 18 February.
Ventôse	19 February to 20 March.
Germinal	21 March to 19 April.
Floréal	20 April to 19 May.

39 Roderick Phillips, *Family breakdown in eighteenth-century France: divorces in Rouen, 1792–1803* (Oxford, 1980); appendix B, p. 207.

Prairial	20 May to 18 June.
Messidor	19 June to 18 July.
Thermidor	19 July to 17 August.
Fructidor	18 August to 16 September.
Jours complémentaires	17 to 21 September.

Revolutionary years coincided with Gregorian years as follows:

Year I	1792–3	Year VIII	1799–1800
Year II	1793–4	Year IX	1800–1
Year III	1794–5	Year X	1801–2
Year IV	1795–6	Year XI	1802–3
Year V	1796–7	Year XII	1803–4
Year VI	1797–8	Year XIII	1804–5
Year VII	1798–9	Year XIV	1805–31 Dec. 1805.

Bibliography

PRINTED PRIMARY MATERIAL

Note: Individual items contained in large-well known collections, such as the *Monumenta Germaniae Historica* or *Patrologia Latina* have not been listed separately in the Bibliography.

Ambrosius Autpertus, *Expositionis in Apocalypsin Libri i–v*, ed. R. Weber. Corpus Christianorum Series Latina, 27, Turnhout, 1975.

Andrew of St Victor, *Andreae de Sancto Victore opera: I, Expositionem in Heptateuchum*, ed. C. Lohr and R. Berndt. Corpus Christianorum Continuatio Mediaevalis, 53. Turnhout, 1986.

Anna Commena, *The Alexiad*, trans. E.R.A. Sewter. London, 1979.

Anonymous, *Court anecdotes*. Daniel Lizars, publisher, London, 1825.

Anonymous, *Gesta Francorum*, trans. and ed. R. Hill. London, 1962.

Anonymous, *The Anglo-Saxon Chronicles*, trans. and ed. Michael Swanton. London, 2000.

Anquetil, Jean-Pierre, *Mémoires of the Court of France during the reign of Louis XIV and the regency of the duke of Orleans*. Edinburgh, 1791.

Augustine, Saint, *De Genesi contra Manicheos*, ed. D. Weber. Corpus Scriptorum Ecclesiasticorum Latinorum, 91, Vienna, 1998.

—— *De vera religione*, ed. K.-D. Daur. Corpus Christianorum Series Latina, 32, Turnhout, 1962, pp. 171–274.

Baldwin, R. , *A true narrative of the murders, cruelties and oppressions, perpetrated on the Protestants in Ireland by the late King James's agents, since his arrival there*. London, 1690.

Barozzi, N. and Berchet G. (eds) *Relazioni degli stati europei lette al senato dagli ambasiatori veneti nel secolo decimosettimo*. 6 vols. Venice, 1860.

Barrington, J. *Personal sketches and recollections of his own times*. Glasgow, 1887.

Benton, John F. (trans.), *Self and society in medieval France: the memoirs of Abbot Guibert of Nogent (1064?–c.1125)*. New York, 1970.

Bertaut, F., 'Journal du voyage d'Espagne fait en l'année mil six cens cinquante neuf, à l'occasion du traité de la paix', ed. F. Cassan, *Revue Hispanique* 47 (1919), pp. 1–317.

Bolland, W.C., Maitland, F.W. and Harcourt, L.W. Vernon (eds), *The eyre of Kent of 6 and 7 Edward II (1313–14)*, Selden Society, 24, London, 1909.

Bonaventure, Saint, *The life of Saint Francis of Assisi*, ed. Cardinal Manning. Rockford, IL., 1988 (first published, 1867).

Brunel, A., 'Voyage d'Espagne', ed. Charles Claverie, *Revue Hispanique* 30 (1914), pp. 119–375.

Calendar of the manuscripts of the marquess of Ormonde. 8 vols. London, 1902–20.

Calendar of the Orrery papers, ed. E. MacLysaght Dublin, 1941.

Calendar of the State Papers, domestic series, iv, 1693. London date 1903.

Carlino, Andrea, *Books of the body: anatomical ritual and renaissance learning*, trans. J. Tedeschi and A.C. Tedeschi. Chicago and London, 1999.

Carlyle, A., *Autobiography*. Edinburgh, 1910.

Cartulaire de Marmoutier pour le Dunois, ed. E. Mabille. Châteaudun, 1874.

Chanson d'Antioche, ed. P. Paris. Slatline Reprints of the edition of 1832–48. Geneva, 1969.

Charlotte Elizabeth, duchesse d'Orléans, *A woman's life in the court of the Sun King: letters of Liselotte von der Pfalz*, trans. Elborg Forster. Baltimore, Md. and London, 1984.

Clanchy, M. (ed.), *Roll and writ file of the Berkshire eyre of 1248*. Selden Society 90, London, 1973.

Corps Législatif, Conseil des Cinq Cents, *Opinion de Duprat sur la Suspension du Divorce par Incompatibilité d'Humeur et de Caractère*. Paris, Imprimerie Nationale, 13 *pluviôse* an V.

Corps Législatif, Conseil des Cinq Cents, *Opinion de Lecointe-Puyraveau sur le projet de suspension de l'article III de la loi de 20 septembre 1792 qui permet le divorce pour incompatibilité d'humeur ou de caractère*. Paris, Imprimerie Nationale, 5 *pluviôse* an V.

Corps Législatif, Conseil des Cinq Cents, *Opinion de Siméon sur la Suspension du Divorce par Incompatibilité*. Paris, Imprimerie Nationale, 5 *pluviôse* an V.

Corps Législatif, Conseil des Cinq Cents, *Opinion sur le Divorce par Jean-Henri Bancal*. Paris, Imprimerie Nationale, 12 *pluviôse* an V.

Corps Législatif, Conseil des Cinq Cents, *Rapport par Favard sur le Divorce au nom d'une commission spéciale composée des représentans Cambacérès, Boissy, Méaulle, Blutel & Favard*. Paris. Imprimerie Nationale, 20 *nivôse* an V.

Croker, T.C. (ed.), *Narratives illustrative of the contests in Ireland in 1641 and 1690*. Camden Society 14, London, 1841.

Cusimano, R.C. and Moorhead, J. (trans.), *The deeds of Louis the Fat*. Washington D.C., 1992.

D'Ælders, Etta Palm, *Appel aux Français sur la Régénération des Mœurs, et Nécessité de l'Influence des Femmes dans une Gouvernement Libre*. Paris, Imprimerie du Cercle Social, 1791.

Départment de Seine et Marne, *Loi qui determine les causes, les modes et les effets du Divorce. Du 20 septembre 1792, l'an 4 de la liberté*. Melun, 1792.

    Décret (no. 2329) de la Convention Nationale, des 4ième et 5ième jours de Floréal, an II de la République Française, une et indivisible. Melun, 1794.

Diderot, D., *Supplément au Voyage de Bougainville*. 1796.

Diderot D. and D'Alembert, J. le Rond (eds), *Encyclopédie Raisonnée des Sciences, des Arts et des Métiers. Nouvelle impression en facsimile de la première édition de 1751 à 1780*. Stuttgart, 1988.

Duchesne, A. (ed.), *Histoire généologique de la maison royale de Dreux et quelques autres familles illustres*. Paris, 1631.

Dufour, J. (ed.), *Recueil des actes de Louis VI, roi de France 1108–37*. 4 vols., Paris, 1992–4.

Edward, earl of Clarendon, *The history of the rebellion and civil wars in England*, ed. W. Dunn Macray. 6 vols., Oxford, 1888.

Ekkehard of Aura, *Chronica*, ed. F.-J. Schmale and I. Schmale-Ott. Darmstadt, 1972.

Encomium Emmae Reginae, ed. A. Campbell. Camden Third Series 72, London, 1949.

Entschuldigung Katharina Schützinn/ für M. Matthez Zellen/ iren Eegemahel/ der ein Pfarrher vund dyener ist im wort Gottes zu Straßburg 1524. Strasbourg, 1524.

Faloci-Pulignani, M., 'La vita di Santa Chiara da Montefalco scritta da Berengario di Sant'Africano', *Archivio storico per le Marche e per l'Umbria* 1 (1884), pp. 557–625 and 2 (1885), pp. 193–266.

Faulcon, Félix, *Opinion relative à la Suspension du Divorce pour Cause d'Incompabilité d'Humeur*. Paris, Imprimerie Nationale. 5 pluviôse an V.

    Opinion sur le Divorce et les Ministres des Cultes. Paris, Bauduoin, an V.

    Rapport de Félix Faulcon. Au nom de la Commission Chargée de Présenter des Vues sur la Législation du Divorce. Paris, Imprimerie Nationale, an V.

Ferguson, A., *An essay on the history of civil society*, ed. Fania Oz-Salsburger. Cambridge, 1995.

Foulcois of Beauvais, 'Epitaphes métriques en l'honneur de différents personnages du XIe siècle composées par Foulcoie de Beauvais, Archdiacre de Meaux', no. 9, in H. Omont (ed.), *Mélanges Julien Havet* (Paris, 1895), pp. 211–36.

Fouleresse, Jean Payen de la, 'Letters of Jean Payen de la Fouleresse to the king of Denmark', *Old Limerick Journal* 28 (1990), pp. 125–7.

Gaimar, Geffrei, *L'Estoire des Engleis*, (ed.) A. Bell. Anglo-Norman Text Society, vols.14–16, Oxford, 1960.

Gibson, J.T. (ed), *Manuscripts of the earl of Fingall*. London, n.d.

Gilbert, J.P., *Tradition: ou histoire de l'église sur le sacrement de mariage*. Paris, 1725.

Gilbert, J.T. *A Jacobite narrative of the war in Ireland, 1688–91*. Dublin, 1892.

Gilo of Paris et al., *Historia Vie Hierosolimitane*, ed. C.W. Grocock and J.E. Siberry. Oxford, 1997.

Giraldo, J.M., *Vida, y heroycos hechos del excelentissimo, y venerable Señor Don Diego de Arze Reynoso*. Juan García Infançón, Madrid, 1695.

Guibert of Gembloux, *Guiberti Gemblacensis Epistolae*, (ed.) A. Derolez. Corpus Christianorum Continuatio Mediaevalis, 66A, Turnhout, 1989.

Guibert of Nogent, *Gesta Dei per Francos*, ed. R.B.C. Huygens. Turnhout, 1996.

Guibert of Nogent, *The deeds of God through the Franks*, trans. by Robert Levine. Woodbridge, 1997.

Guibert of Nogent, *De vita sua*, ed. E.-R. Labande. Paris, 1981.

Guiraudet, Charles-Philippe-Toussaint, *De la famille, considerée comme l'élément des societés*. Paris, Imprimerie A.-C. Forget, an V.

H. Hagenmeyer (ed.), *Epistulae et Chartae ad Historiam Primi Belli Sacri spectantes quae supersunt aevo aequales ac genuinae*. Reprint, Hildesheim, 1973.

Halphen, L. and Poupardin, R. (eds), *Gesta Ambaziensium dominorum in Chroniques des comtes d'Anjou et des seigneurs d'Amboise*. Paris, 1913.

Hanawalt, B.A. (ed.), *Crime in East Anglia in the fourteenth century: Norfolk gaol delivery rolls, 1307–16*. Norfolk Record Society, 44, Norwich,1976.

Healey, C.E.H. Chadwyck (ed.), *Somerset pleas Richard 1 – 41 Henry III*. Somerset Record Society 11, Frome, 1897.

Hennet, A., *Du divorce*. Paris, Desenne,1789.

Hennet, A., *Pétition à l'Assemblée Nationale par Montagne, Charron, Montesquieu, et Voltaire, suivi d'une consultation en Pologne et en Suisse*. Paris, Desenne,1791.

Henry of Huntingdon, *Historia Anglorum*, ed. D. Greenway. Oxford, 1966.

Hugh the Chanter, *The history of the church of York, 1066–1127*, ed. C. Johnson, rvsd. by M. Brett, C.N.L. Brooke and M. Winterbottom. Oxford, 1990.

Hume, D., *A treatise of human nature*, ed. D. Fate Norton and M.J. Norton. Oxford, 2000.

—— *Dialogues and natural history of religion*, ed. J.G.A. Gaskin. Oxford, 1993.

Hunnisett, R.F. (ed.), *Wiltshire coroner's bills, 1752–1796*. Wiltshire Record Society, 36, Devizes, 1981.

Isidore, *Etymologiarum sive originum libri xx, 11.2 Isidori Hispalensis episcopi*, ed. W.M. Lindsay, 2 vols., Oxford, 1911.

Iunctae Bevegnatis. Legenda de Vita et Miraculis Beatae Margaritae de Cortona, ed. F. Iozelli. Biblioteca Franciscana Ascetica Medii Aevi 13, Grottaferrata, 1997.

Johan of Mantua, *Iohannis Mantuani in Cantica Canticorum et de Sancta Maria Tractatus ad Comitissam Matildam*, ed. B. Bischoff and Taeger. Spicilegium Friburgense, 19, Freiburg, 1973.

John of Salisbury, *Ioannes Saresberiensis episcopi Carnotensis Policratici sive De nugis curialium et vertigiis philosophorum libri VIII*, ed. C.C.J. Webb 2 vols., Oxford, 1909.

John Scottus Eriugena, *Annotationes in Marcianum*, ed. Cora E. Lutz Cambridge, Mass., 1939.

La Beaumelle, Laurent Angliviel de, *Mémoires pour servir à l'histoire de Mme de Maintenon*. Amsterdam, 1755.

La Bruyère, Jean de, *Characters: or, the manners of the age: with the moral characters of Theophrastus*. Dublin, 1776.

La Rochefoucauld, François VI de, *Maximes, mémoires, œuvres diverses*. Paris, 1992.

Lactantius, *Divinarum institutionem*, ed. P. Monat. *Institutiones divines*, Sources chrétiennes 326, Paris, 1986.

Liber Eliensis, ed. E.O. Blake. Camden Third Series, 91, London, 1962.

Life of King Edward who rests at Westminster, ed. F. Barlow. 2nd ed., Oxford, 1992.

Loftis, J. (ed.), *The memoirs of Anne, Lady Halkett and Ann, Lady Fanshawe*. Oxford, 1979.

Luther, Martin, *Luther's Works*, ed. J. Pelikan and H.T. Lehmann. 55 vols., St Louis, 1955–86.

—— *D. Martin Luthers Werke: Kritische Gesamtausgabe*. 61 vols., Weimar, 1883–1983.

—— *Luther's last will and testament*, ed. T. Fabiny. Dublin and Budapest, 1982.

—— *On Prayer and Procession in Rogation Week (1519)*, ed. H. Robinson-Hammerstein. Dublin, 1997.

Maintenon, Mme de, *Letters*, trans. G. Faulkner. Dublin, 1758.

Mancini, Marie, *Mémoires*. Paris, 1965.

Marie d'Orléans, duchesse de Nemours, *Mémoires suivis de lettres inédites de Marguerite de Lorraine, duchess d'Orléans*. Paris, 1990.

Martianus Capella, *De nuptiis philologiae et mercurii, libri viiii*, ed. A. Dick and J. Préaux. Stuttgart, 1969.

Maurus Servius Honoratus, *Servii grammatici qui feruntur in Vergilii carmina commentarii, 12.468*, ed. G.Thilo. Leipzig, 1878–87.

Mavidal, M.J. and Laurent, E., *Archives Parlementaires de 1787 à 1860: recueil complet des débats legislatifs et politiques des Chambres francais. Première série (1787–1799)*. Paris, 1909.

Meditations on the life of Christ: an illustrated manuscript of the fourteenth century, Isa Ragusa and Rosalie B. Green (eds). Princeton, NJ, 1961.

Meekings, C.A.F. (ed.), *Crown pleas of the Wiltshire eyre of 1249*. Wiltshire Archaeological and Natural History Society, 16, Devizes, 1961.

Millar, John, *Origin of the distinction of ranks*. 4th ed., Edinburgh and London, 1806, reprinted Bristol, 1990.

Montesquieu, Charles de Secondat, baron de, *Persian Letters (1721)*, trans. C.J. Betts. London, 1973.

—— *De l'esprit des lois*. Paris, 1748.

Montpensier, Mlle de, *Mémoires*. Paris, 1728.

O'Kelly, C., 'Macariae Excidium' in T.C. Croker (ed.), *Narratives illustrative of the contests in Ireland in 1641 and 1690* (London, 1841), pp. 25–149.

Orderic Vitalis, *The Ecclesiastical History of Orderic Vitalis*, ed. Marjorie Chibnall. 6 vols., Oxford, 1969–80.

Ortiz, Antonio Domínguez (ed.), *Testamentos de los Reyes de la Casa de Austria*, 5 vols, Madrid, 1982.

Osbert of Clare, *The letters of Osbert of Clare*, ed. E.W. Williamson, Oxford, 1929.

Oudot, C.F., *Essai sur les principes de la législation des marriages privés et solonnels, du divorce et de l'adoption qui peuvent être declares à la suite de l'acte constitutionnel*. Paris, Imprimerie National, 1793.

Paul of Bernried, *Vita Gregorii VII*, ed. J.M. Watterich. Vitae Pontificum Romanorum 1, Leipzig, 1862.

Pétition présentée au Conseil des Cinq Cents le 29 messidor, l'an quatrième de la République française. Pour réclamer contre les Abus du Divorce sur la simple allegation d'incompatabilité d'humeur et de caractère. Paris, an IV.

Pirckheimer, Caritas, *Briefe des Äbtissin Caritas Pirckheimer des St Klara-Klosters zu Nürnberg* [*in accordance with the original edition by J. Pfanner trans. by Sr.B. Schrott*], ed. G. Deichstetter, St Ottilien, 1982.

—— *'Die Denkwürdigkeiten' der Äbtissin Caritas Pirckheimer des St Klara-Klosters zu Nürnberg*, trans. Sr. B. Schrott, St Ottilien, 1983.

Prou, M. (ed.), *Recueil des acts de Philippe Ier, roi de France (1059–1103).* Paris, 1908.

Pseudo-Bede, *'De mundi celestis terrestrisque constitutione': a treatise on the universe and the soul*, 421, ed. and trans. Charles Burnett. London, 1985.

Pugh, R.B. (ed.), *Gaol delivery and Trailbaston trials, 1275–130.* Wiltshire Record Society, 33, Devizes, 1978.

Rapin, P. René, *Mémoires de la compagnie de Jésus sur l'église et la société, la cour, la ville, et le jansénisme.* Lyons 1865, reprinted, Farnborough, 1972.

Rather of Verona, *Ratherii Veronensis Praeloquiorum Libri VI*, ed. P.D.L. Reid. Corpus Christianorum Continuatio Mediaevalis, 46A, Turnhout, 1984, pp. 3–196.

Remigius of Auxerre, *Commentum in Martianum Capellam, libri i–ix*, ed. Cora E. Lutz, 2 vols. Leiden, 1965.

Routledge, F.J. (ed.), *Calendar of the Clarendon state papers.* 5 vols. Oxford, 1970.

Saint-Simon, Louis de Rouvroy, duc de, *Memoirs*, ed. and trans. Lucy Norton. London, 1960.

Salazar y Castro, Luis de, *Historia genealógica de la Casa de Lara*, 4 vols., Madrid, 1694–1697.

Saxo Grammaticus, *Danorum Regum Heroumque Historia, books x–xvi*, trans. by E. Christiansen. 3 vols., British Archaeological Reports, International Series, 118, Oxford, 1981.

Schmale, F.-J. and I. Schmale-Ott (eds), *Quellen zur Geschichte Kaiser Heinrichs IV (Ausgewählte Quellen zur deutschen Geschichte des Mittelalters 12).* Darmstadt, 1963.

Serrano, Carlos Seco (ed.), *Cartas de Sor María de Jesús de ´Agreda y de Felipe IV*, 2 vols., Biblioteca de Autores Españoles, 108–9. Madrid, 1958.

Sévigné, Mme de, *Lettres.* 3 vols., Paris, 1953.

Sextus Pompeius Festus, *De verborum significatu*, ed. W.M. Lindsay. Leipzig, 1913.

Simms, J.G. (ed.), 'Lord Kilmallock's letters to his wife', *Journal of the Royal Society of Antiquaries of Ireland* 87 (1957), pp. 135–40.

Sor Luisa de Jésus, *Año Santo: meditaciones para todo el día del año sacadas especialmente de Fray Luis de León y de otros libros españoles, latinos e italianos* Madrid, 1658.

Stevens, John, *The journal of John Stevens, containing a brief account of the war in Ireland, 1689–1691*, ed. R.H. Murray. Oxford, 1912.

Stewart, Dugald, *The collected works of Dugald Stewart*, ed. William Hamilton. Edinburgh and London, 1854–60, reprinted, Bristol, 1994.

Sturlason, Snorri, *Heimskringla, or Lives of the Norse Kings*, trans. A.H. Smith, ed. E. Monsen. Cambridge, 1932.

Suger, *Vita Ludovici Grossi regis*, ed. and trans. Henri Waquet. Paris, 1929.

Summerson, H. (ed.), *Crown pleas of the Devon eyre of 1238.* Devon and Cornwall Record Society, n.s., 28, Torquay, 1985.

Swift, Jonathan, *The correspondence of Jonathan Swift*, ed. F. Elrington Ball, 6 vols. London, 1910–14.

Table de la Seconde Législature. Paris, Baudouin, *nivôse* an VII.

Thomas of Celano, *The Life of Saint Francis of Assisi and the Treatise of Miracles*, trans. Catherine Bolton. Assisi, 1997.

Tour du Pin, Mme. de la, *Memoirs.* London, 1969.

Tugwell, Simon, O.P. (ed.), *Early Dominicans: selected writings*. London, 1982.

Villanueva, Joaquín Pérez (ed.) *Felipe IV y Luisa Enríquez Manrique de Lara, condesa de Paredes de Nava: un epistolario inédito*. Salamanca, 1986.

Visconti, Primi, *Mémoires sur la cour de Louis XIV, 1673–1681*. Paris, 1988.

Voltaire, *Oeuvres Complètes*, ed. Louis Molard. Paris, 1870–80.

William of Malmesbury, *Chronicle of the kings of England before the Norman Conquest*, trans. J. Stephenson. Lampeter, 1989.

—— *Gesta regum Anglorum*, ed. and trans. R.A.B. Mynors, R.M. Thomson, and M. Winterbottom, 2 vols. Oxford, 1998–9.

—— *Historia novella*, ed. E. King. Oxford, 1998.

William of Tyre, *Historia rerum in partibus transmarinis gestarum*, ed. R.B.C. Huygens. Corpus Christianorum Continuatio Mediaevalis, 63 and 63A, Turnhout, 1986.

—— *A history of deeds done beyond the sea*, trans. E.A. Babcock and A.C. Krey. 2 vols., New York, 1943.

Woodbine, G. (ed.), *Bracton de Legibus et Consuetudinibus Angliae*, trans. S.E. Thorne, 4 vols. New Haven, 1968.

SECONDARY SOURCES

Adamson, J., *The princely courts of Europe, 1500–1750*. Second edition, London, 2000.

Allen, P.C., *Philip III and the Pax Hispanica, 1598–1621: the failure of grand strategy*. New Haven and London, 2000.

Adie, K., *Corsets to camouflage. Women and war*. London, 2003.

Ariès, P. and Duby, G. (eds), *A history of private life*. 5 vols., Cambridge, Mass. and London, 1987–91,

Asch, R.G. and Birke, A.M. (eds), *Princes, patronage and the nobility: the court at the beginning of the modern age, c.1450–1650*. Oxford, 1991.

Backhouse, J., Turner, D.H. and Webster, L. (eds), *The Golden Age of Anglo-Saxon art*. London, 1984.

Bainton, R.H., *Women in the Reformation in Germany and Italy*. Boston, 1971.

Baker, D. (ed.)., *Medieval women: essays presented to R.M.T. Hill*, Studies in Church History, subsidia 1. Oxford, 1978.

Baker, J.H., *An introduction to English legal history*. London, 1979.

Baldwin, W., *The language of sex: five voices from northern France around 1200*. Chicago, 1994.

Barbeito, J.M., *Alcázar de Madrid*. Madrid, 1992.

Bardet, J.P., 'Early marriage in pre-modern France', *History of the Family* 6 (2001), pp. 345–63.

Beattie, J.M., *Crime and the courts, 1600–1800*. Oxford, 1986.

Bellamy, J.G., 'The Coterel gang: an anatomy of a band of fourteenth-century criminals', *English Historical Review* 79 (1974), pp. 698–714.

—— *Crime and public order in the later Middle Ages*. London and Toronto, 1972.

Bennett, M., *The civil wars in Britain and Ireland, 1638–51*. Oxford, 1997

Berry, C., *Social theory of the Scottish Enlightenment*. Edinburgh, 1997.

Bibliothèque Nationale, *Catalogue de l'histoire de France*. Paris, 1968.

Biddick, K., 'Genders, bodies, borders: technologies of the visible', *Speculum* 68 (1993), pp. 389–418.

Bisson, T.N. (ed.), *Cultures of power: lordship, status, and process in twelfth-century Europe*. Philadelphia, 1995.

Black, E. (ed.), *Kings in conflict: Ireland in the 1690s*. Antrim, 1990.

Blake, E.O. and Morris, C., 'A hermit goes to war: Peter and the origins of the First Crusade', *Studies in Church History* 22 (1984), pp. 79–107.

Bloch, M., *Feudal society*, trans. L.A. Manyon. Chicago, 1961.

Bluche, F., *Louis XIV*. Paris, 1986.

Bologne, J.-C, *Histoire du mariage en occident*. Paris, 1997.

Bornstein, D. and Rusconi R. (eds), *Women and religion in medieval and renaissance Italy*, trans. by M.J. Schneider. Chicago and London, 1996.

Bowles, P., 'John Millar, the four-stages theory and women's position in society', *History of Political Economy* 16 (1984), pp. 619–38.

Brady, C. and Gillespie, R. (eds), *Natives and newcomers: essays on the making of Irish colonial society, 1534–1641*. Dublin, 1986.

Brady, T.A., '"You hate us priests": anticlericalism, communalism, and the control of women at Strasbourg in the age of the Reformation' in P.A. Dykema and H.Oberman, (eds), *Anticlericalism in late medieval and early modern Europe* (Leiden, 1994), pp. 167–207.

Brecht, M., *Martin Luther: shaping and defining the Reformation, 1521–1532*. Minneapolis, 1994.

Brightwell, P. 'The Spanish origins of the Thirty Years' War', *European Studies Review* 9 (1979), pp. 409–31.

British Museum, *Albrecht Dürer and his legacy*. Exhibition catalogue, London, 2002.

Brizzi, G., 'Contribuo all'iconografia di Francesca Romana' in G. Picasso (ed.), *Una Santa tutta Romana: saggi e ricerche nel VI centenario della nascità di Francesca Bussa dei Ponziani* (Siena, 1984), pp. 267–362.

Brown, J., *Velázquez: painter and courtier*. New Haven and London, 1986.

Brown, J., and Elliott, J.H., *A palace for a king: the Buen Retiro and the court of Philip IV*. New Haven and London, 1980.

Brown, J. and Elliott, J. (eds), *The sale of the century: artistic relations between Spain and Great Britain, 1604–1655*. New Haven and London, 2002.

Brownmiller, S., *Against our will: men, women and rape*. London, 1976.

Brucker, G., *The society of renaissance Florence*. New York, 1971.

Brundage, J.A., *The Crusades, holy war and canon law*. Variorum, Aldershot, 1991.

—— 'Prostitution, miscegenation and sexual purity in the First Crusade' in his *The Crusades, holy war and canon law*. (Variorum, Aldershot, 1991) Item XIX, pp. 57–65 first published in P. Edbury (ed.), *Crusade and settlement*. Cardiff, 1985.

—— *Sex, law and marriage in the Middle Ages*. Aldershot, 1993.

Bullough, D.A., 'The continental background of the reform' in D. Parsons (ed.), *Tenth-century studies*. London, 1975, pp. 2–36.

Bullough, V.L. and Bullough, B., *Cross dressing, sex and gender*. Philadelphia, 1993.

Butler, A., *Butler's lives of the saints*. London, 1999. (first published, 2 vols., London, 1887)

Bynum, C. Walker, *The resurrection of the body in Western Christianity, 200–1336*. New York, 1995.

—— 'The female body and religious practice in the late Middle Ages' in *Fragmentation and redemption: essays on gender and the human body in medieval religion* (New York, 1991), pp. 181–238.

—— *Metamorphosis and identity*. Cambridge, Mass., 2001.

Cadden, J., *Meanings of sex difference in the Middle Ages*. Cambridge, 1993.

—— 'It takes all kinds: sexuality and gender differences in Hildegard of Bingen's "Book of Compound Medicine"', *Traditio* 40 (1984), pp. 149–74,

Cairns, J.W. and McLeod, G. (eds), *The dearest birth right of the people of England: the jury in the history of the common law*. Oxford and Portland, 2002.

Cairns, J., '"Famous as a School for Law as Edinburgh ... for Medicine": legal education in Glasgow, 1761–1801' in A. Hook and R.B. Sher (eds), *The Glasgow Enlightenment* (East Linton, 1995), pp 133–59.

Campbell, M.W., 'Queen Emma and Aelfgifu of Northampton, Cnut the Great's women', *Medieval Scandinavia* 4 (1971), pp. 66–79.

Cannon, J. and Vauchez, A., *Margherita of Cortona and the Lorenzetti: Sienese art and the cult of a holy woman in medieval Tuscany*. University Park, PA, 1999.

Canny, N., 'Religion, politics and the Irish rising of 1641' in J. Devlin and R. Fanning (eds), *Religion and rebellion: papers read before the 22nd Irish Conference of historians* (Dublin, 1997), pp. 40–70.

Cantillon, G., 'Honora Bourke – a wife's story' in B. Dewar (ed.), *Living at the time of the siege: essays in social history* (Limerick, 1991), pp. 15–20

Cantón, F.J. Sánchez, *Velázquez, Las Meninas y sus personajes*. Barcelona, 1943.

Caritas Pirckheimer, 1467–1532. Eine Ausstellung der katholischen Stadtkirche Nürnberg. Munich, 1982.

Carlton, C., 'Civilians' in J. Ohlmeyer and J. Kenyon (eds), *The Civil Wars: a military history of England, Scotland and Ireland, 1638–1660* (Oxford, 1998), pp. 272–305.

Casey, J., *The history of the family*. Oxford, 1989.

—— *Early modern Spain: a social history*. London and New York, 1999.

Casway, J., 'Irish women overseas' in M. MacCurtain and M. O'Dowd (eds), *Women in early modern Ireland* (Dublin, 1991), pp. 112–32.

Chibnall, M., 'Women in Orderic Vitalis', *Haskins Society Journal* 2 (1990), pp. 105–22.

Ciletti, E., 'Patriarchal ideology in the renaissance iconography of Judith' in M. Migiel and J. Schiesari (eds), *Refiguring women: perspectives on gender and the Italian Renaissance* (Ithaca and London, 1991), pp. 35–70.

Connolly, S. (ed.), *The Oxford companion to Irish history*. Oxford, 1998.

Conrad, A., 'Aufbruch der Laien – Aufbruch der Frauen. Überlegungen zu einer Geschlechtergeschichte der Reformation und katholischen Reform' in A. Conrad (ed.), *'in Christo ist weder man noch weyb'. Frauen in der Zeit der Reformation und der katholischen Reform* (Münster, 1999), pp. 7–22.

—— (ed.), *'in Christo ist weder man noch weyb': Frauen in der Zeit der Reformation und der katholischen Reform*. Münster, 1999.

Corbet, P. *Les saints ottoniens: sainteté dynastique, sainteté royale et sainteté féminine autour de l'an Mil*. Sigmaringen, 1986.

Cosandey, F., *La reine de France: symbole et pouvoir*. Paris, 2000.

Coulson, J. (ed.), *The saints : a concise biographical dictionary*. London, 1958.

Cowdrey, H.E.J., *Pope Gregory VII, 1073–1085*. Oxford, 1998.

Cueto, R., *Quimeras y sueños: los profetas y la Monarquía Católica de Felipe IV*. Valladolid, 1994.

Cushing, K.G., *Papacy and law in the Gregorian revolution: the canonistic work of Anselm of Lucca*. Oxford, 1998.

D'Alton, J. (ed.), *Illustrations of King James' Irish army list, 1689*. Dublin, 1855, 2nd ed. 2 vols., 1869.

D'Cruze, S., 'Approaching the history of rape and sexual violence: notes towards research', *Women's History Review* 1 (1992), pp. 377–97.

Danaher, K., and Simms, J.G., *The Danish force in Ireland*, Dublin, 1962.

Davis, J. 'The politics of the marriage bed: matrimony and the Montmorency family, 1527–1612', *French History* 6 (1992), pp. 63–95.

Davis, N. Zemon, *Society and culture in early modern France.* Stanford, CA, 1975.

Dean, T. (ed.), *Crime in medieval Europe.* London, 2001.

Deguer, A. and Heffels, M. (eds), *Albrecht Dürer. Sämtliche Holzschnitte.* Ramerding, 1981.

Deleito y Piñuela, J., *El Rey se divierte.* Madrid, 1988.

Derbes, A., *Picturing the Passion in late medieval Italy: narrative painting, Franciscan ideologies, and the Levant.* Cambridge, 1996.

Desmond, M., *Reading Dido: gender, textuality, and the medieval 'Aeneid'.* Medieval Cultures, no. 8, Minneapolis, 1994.

Devine, T.M. and Young, J.R. (eds), *Eighteenth-century Scotland: new perspectives.* East Linton, 1999.

Devlin, J. and Fanning, R. (eds), *Religion and rebellion: papers read before the 22nd Irish Conference of historians.* Dublin, 1995.

Dewald, J., *Aristocratic experience and the origins of modern culture: France, 1570–1715.* Berkeley, CA, 1993.

Dewar, B.(ed.), *Living at the time of the siege: essays in social history.* Limerick, 1991.

Dhondt, J., 'Sept femmes et un trio de rois', *Contributions à l'histoire économique et sociale* 3 (1964–5), pp. 35–70.

Dickens, A.G. (ed.), *The courts of Europe: politics, patronage and royalty, 1400–1800.* London, 1977.

Dodwell, C.R., *Anglo-Saxon art.* Manchester, 1982.

Dublin, L.I., *Suicide: a sociological and statistical study.* New York, 1963.

Duby, G., *Women of the twelfth century. Vol.1: Eleanor of Aquitaine and six others*, trans. by J. Birrell. Oxford,1997.

—— 'Women and power' in T.N. Bisson (ed.), *Cultures of power: lordship, status, and process in twelfth-century Europe* (Philadelphia, 1995), pp. 69–85.

—— 'The structure of kinship and nobility: northern France in the eleventh and twelfth centuries' in *The chivalrous society*, trans. Cynthia Postan (Berkeley, 1977, 1980), pp. 134–148.

—— *Le chevalier, la femme et le prêtre: le mariage dans la France féodale.* Paris, 1981.

—— *The knight, the lady and the priest: the making of modern marriage in medieval France*, trans. Barbara Bray. New York, 1983.

—— *Medieval marriage: two models from the twelfth century.* Baltimore, 1978.

Dulong, C., *Marie Mancini.* Paris, 1993.

Dupeux, C., Jezler, P., and Wirth, J. (eds), *Bildersturm. Wahnsinn oder Gottes Wille.* Bern, 2000.

Dwyer, J., *The age of the passions: an interpretation of Adam Smith and Scottish Enlightenment culture.* East Linton, 1998.

Dyer, C.C. (ed.), *Everyday life in medieval England.* London and Rio Grande, 1994.

—— with Penn, S.A.C., 'Wages and earnings in late medieval England: evidence from the enforcement of the labour laws' in C.C. Dyer (ed.), *Everyday life in medieval England* (London and Rio Grande, 1994), pp. 167–187.

Dykema, P.A. and H.A. Oberman (eds), *Anticlericalism in late medieval and early modern Europe.* Leiden, 1994.

Edgington, S.B., '"Sont çou ore les fems que jo voi la venir?" Women in the *Chanson d'Antioche*' in S.B. Edgington and S. Lambert (eds), *Gendering the crusades* (Cardiff, 2000), pp. 154–62.

——— 'The First Crusade: reviewing the evidence' in J. Phillips (ed.), *The First Crusade: origins and impact* (Manchester, 1997), pp. 57–77.

Edgington, S.B. and Lambert, S. (eds), *Gendering the crusades*. Cardiff, 2000.

Edwards, V.C., 'The case of the married spinster: an alternative explanation', *American Journal of Legal History* 21 (1977), pp. 260–5.

Elias, N., *The court society*. Oxford, 1983.

Elliott, J.H., *The count-duke of Olivares: the statesman in an age of decline*. New Haven and London, 1986.

——— 'Philip IV of Spain: a prisoner of ceremony' in A.G. Dickens (ed.), *The courts of Europe: politics, patronage and royalty, 1400–1800* (London, 1977), pp. 168–89.

——— 'The court of the Spanish Hapsburgs: a peculiar institution?' in *Spain and its world, 1500–1700* (New Haven and London, 1989), pp. 142–61.

——— *Richelieu and Olivares*. Cambridge, 1984

——— *Imperial Spain, 1469–1716*. 9th ed., London, 1985.

——— and Sanz, Á. García (eds), *La España del conde duque de Olivares. Encuentro internacional sobre la España del conde duque de Olivares celebrado en Toro los días 15–18 de septiembre de 1987*. Valladolid, 1990.

Ellis, P. Berresford, *Hell or Connaught! The Cromwellian colonisation of Ireland, 1652–1660*. London, 1975.

Erdmann, C., *Die Entstehung des Kreuzzugsgedankens*. Stuttgart, 1935.

Erler, M. and Kowaleski, M. (eds), *Women and power in the Middle Ages*. Athens, Ga., 1988.

Esquirol, J.E.D., *Mental maladies: a treatise on insanity*. New York, 1965.

Evergates, T. (ed.), *Aristocratic women in medieval France*. Philadelphia, 1999.

Facinger, M., 'A study of medieval queenship: Capetian France 987–1237', *Studies in Medieval and Renaissance History* 5 (1968), pp. 1–48.

Farmer, D., *Oxford dictionary of saints*. Oxford, 1978.

Feeley, M. and Little, D., 'The vanishing female: the decline of women in criminal proceedings 1687–1912', *Law and Society Review* 25 (1991), pp. 719–57.

Ferguson, K., 'The organisation of King William's army in Ireland 1689–92', *Irish Sword* 18 (1990–1), pp. 62–79.

Fernández de Bethencourt, F., *Historia genealógica y heráldica de la Monarquía Española, Casa Real y Grandes de España*. 10 vols., Madrid, 1897–1920.

Feros, A., *Kingship and favoritism in the Spain of Philip III, 1598–1621*. Cambridge, 2000.

——— 'Lerma y Olivares: la práctica del valimiento en la primera mitad del seiscientos' in J. Elliott and Á. García Sanz (eds), *La España del conde duque de Olivares: encuentro internacional sobre la España del conde duque de Olivares celebrado en Toro los días 15–18 de septiembre de 1987* (Valladolid, 1990), pp. 195–224.

Ferrante, J.F., *To the glory of her sex: women's roles in the composition of medieval texts*. Bloomington, Ind., 1997.

Fliche, A., *Le règne de Philippe 1er, roy de France 1060–1108*. Paris, 1912.

Flügel, K., 'Die Entdeckung der Welt und des Menschen', in Staatliche Museen zu Berlin (ed.), *Kunst der Reformationszeit* (Berlin/Ost, 1983), pp. 233–92.

Forbes, D., *Hume's philosophical politics*. Cambridge, 1975.

——— 'Scientific whiggism: Adam Smith and John Millar', *Cambridge Journal* 7 (1954), pp. 643–70.

Foucault, M., *Discipline and punish: the birth of the prison*. First published as *Surveiller et punir: naissance de la prison*, Paris, 1975. English trans. Alan Sheridan, London, 1977, London, 1979.

Fraser, A., *The weaker vessel: women's lot in seventeenth-century England*. London, 1993.

Freedberg, D., *The power of images: studies in the history and theory of response*. Chicago and London, 1989.

Frugoni, C., 'Female mystics, visions and iconography' in D. Bornstein and R. Rusconi (eds), *Women and religion in medieval and renaissance Italy*, trans. M.J. Schneider (Chicago and London, 1996), pp. 130–164.

—— '"Domine, in conspectu tuo omne desiderium meum": visioni e immagini in Chiara of Montefalco' in C. Leonardi and E. Menestò (eds), *Chiara di Montefalco e il suo tempo* (Florence, 1985), pp. 155–182.

—— 'Saint Francis, a saint in progress' in Sandro Sticca (ed.), *Saints: studies in hagiography*, (Medieval and Renaissance Texts and Studies, Binghamton, NY, 1996), pp. 161–190.

Gamazo, G.M., *Carlos II y su corte*. 2 vols., Madrid, 1911–1915.

Garaud, M. and Szramkiewicz, R., *La révolution française et la famille*. Paris, 1978.

García, B.J., *La Pax Hispanica. Política exterior del duque de Lerma*. Leuven, 1996.

—— 'Pedro Franqueza, secretario de sí mismo. Proceso a una privanza y primera crisis del valimiento de Lerma (1607–1609)', *Annali di storia moderna e contemporanea* 5 (1999), pp. 21–42.

Gauvard, C., *De grace especial: crime, état et société en France à la fin du moyen âge*. Paris, 1991.

Geldsetzer, S., *Frauen auf Kreuzzügen 1096–1291*. Darmstadt, 2003.

Gibson, W., *Women in seventeenth-century France*. Basingstoke, 1989.

Gilbert, J.T. (ed.), *The history of the Irish confederation and the war in Ireland, 1641–9*. 7 vols., Dublin, 1882–9.

Gillespie, R., 'Destabilizing Ulster, 1641–2' in B. MacCuarta (ed.), *Ulster 1641: aspects of the rising* (Belfast, 1993), pp.107–121.

—— 'The end of an era: Ulster and the outbreak of the 1641 rising' in C. Brady and R. Gillespie (eds), *Natives and newcomers: essays on the making of Irish colonial society 1534–1641* (Dublin, 1986), pp. 191–213, 235–7.

—— *The transformation of the Irish economy, 1550–1700*. Dundalk, 1991.

Given, J., *Society and homicide in thirteenth-century England*. Stanford, CA, 1977.

Godman, P. (ed.), *The poetry of the Carolingian Renaissance*. London, 1985.

Goez, E., *Beatrix von Canossa und Tuszien: Eine Untersuchung zur Geschichte des 11. Jahrhunderts*. Sigmaringen, 1995.

Gold, P. Schine, *The lady and the Virgin: image, attitude, and experience in twelfth-century France*. Chicago, 1985.

Goodich, M.E., *Violence and miracle in the fourteenth century: private grief and public salvation*. Chicago and London, 1995.

Goody, J., *The development of the family and marriage in Europe*. Cambridge, 1983.

Gordon, D., *Citizens without sovereignty: equality and sociability in French thought, 1670–1789*. Princeton, 1994.

Gradowicz-Pancer, N., 'De-gendering female violence: Merovingian female honour as "an exchange of violence"', *Early Medieval Europe* 11 (2002), pp. 1–18.

Graham, T.F., *Medieval minds: mental health in the Middle Ages*. London, 1967.

Green, T.A., 'Societal concepts of criminal liability for homicide in medieval England', *Speculum* 47 (1972), pp. 669–94.

—— *Verdict according to conscience: perspectives on the English criminal trial jury 1200–1800*. Chicago, 1985.

Grégoire, R., *Bruno de Segni: exégète médiéval et théologien monastique*. Spoleto, 1965.

Groot, R.D., 'Petit larceny, jury lenity and Parliament' in J.W. Cairns and G. McLeod (eds), *The dearest birth right of the people of England: the jury in the history of the Common Law* (Oxford and Portland, 2002), pp. 47–61.

Grubb, I., *Friends in Ireland, 1654–1900*. London, 1927.

Guillot, O., *Le comte d'Anjou et son entourage au XIᵉ siècle*. 2 vols., Paris, 1972.

Haakonssen, K., *Natural law and moral philosophy: from Grotius to the Scottish Enlightenment*. Cambridge, 1996.

Hacker, B.C., 'Women and military institutions in early modern Europe: a reconnaissance', *Signs: Journal of Women in Culture and Society* 6 (1981), pp. 643–671.

Hahn, C., 'The voices of the saints: speaking reliquaries', *Gesta* 35 (1997), pp. 20–31.

Hajdu, R., 'Family and feudal ties in Poitou, 1100–1300', *Journal of Interdisciplinary History* 8 (1977–8), pp. 117–39.

—— 'The position of noblewomen in the *pays des Coutumes, 1100–1300*', *Journal of Family History* 5 (1980), pp. 122–44.

Halbach, S., 'Publizistisches Engagement von Frauen in der Frühzeit der Reformation', in A. Conrad (ed.), *'in Christo ist weder man noch weyb'. Frauen in der Zeit der Reformation und der katholischen Reform* (Münster, 1999), pp. 49–68.

Hamburger, J., *Nuns as artists: the visual culture of a medieval convent*. Berkeley, Los Angeles and London, 1997.

Hammond, P.W., *Food and feast in medieval England*. Stroud, 1993.

Hanawalt, B.A., *Crime and conflict in English communities 1300–1348*. Cambridge, Mass., 1979.

—— 'The female felon in fourteenth-century England', *Viator* 5 (1974), pp. 253–68.

—— *'Of good and ill repute': gender and social control in medieval England*. New York and Oxford, 1998.

Hayes, R., 'Biographical dictionary of Irishmen in France', *Studies* 31 (September 1942), p. 111.

Helmholz, R., 'Infanticide in the province of Canterbury during the fifteenth century', *History of Childhood Quarterly* 2 (1975), pp. 382–9.

Henry, A., and Short, J., *Suicide and homicide*. Glencoe, 1954.

Herlihy, D., *Medieval households*. Cambridge, Mass., 1985.

Hibbard, C.M., 'The role of a queen consort: the household and court of Henrietta Maria, 1625–1642' in R.G. Asch and A.M. Birke (eds), *Princes, patronage and the nobility: the court at the beginning of the modern age, c.1450–1650* (Oxford, 1991), pp. 393–414.

Hill, D. (ed.), *Aethelred the Unready: papers from the Millennary Conference*. British Archaeological Reports, British Series, 59, Oxford, 1978

Holt, J.C., 'Feudal society and the family in early medieval England, IV: the heiress and the alien', *Transactions of the Royal Historical Society*, 5th ser., 35 (1985), pp. 1–28.

Hont, I. and Ignatieff, M. (eds), *Wealth and virtue: the shaping of political economy in the Scottish Enlightenment*. Cambridge, 1983.

Hood, W., *Fra Angelico at San Marco*. New Haven and London, 1993.

Höss, I., *Georg Spalatin, 1484–1545. Ein Leben in der Zeit des Humanismus und der Reformation*. Weimar, 1989.

Howell, M., *Eleanor of Provence: queenship in thirteenth-century England*. Oxford, 1998.

Hufton, O., *The prospect before her: a history of women in western Europe*. London, 1995, New York, 1996.

—— 'Reflections on the role of women at the early modern court', *the Court Historian* 5 (2000), pp. 1–14.

Huneycutt, L.L., 'Images of high medieval queenship', *Haskins Society Journal* 1 (1989), pp. 61–71.

Hurnard, N.D., *The King's pardon for homicide before A.D. 1307*. Oxford, 1969.

Ignatieff, M., 'John Millar and individualism' in I. Hont and M. Ignatieff (eds), *Wealth and virtue: the shaping of political encomy in the Scottish Enlightenment* (Cambridge, 1983), pp. 253–270.

Israel, J.I., *The Dutch Republic and the Hispanic world, 1606–1661*. 2nd ed., Oxford, 1986.

Jacobs, J.A., Gender equality and Higher Education', *Annual Review of Sociology* 22 (1996), pp. 153–85.

Jaeger, C.S., *The origins of courtliness: civilizing trends and the formation of courtly ideals, 930–1210*. Philadelphia, PA, 1985.

Jager, E., *The book of the heart*. Chicago and London, 2000.

—— 'The book of the heart: reading and writing the medieval subject', *Speculum* 71 (1996), pp. 4–26.

Kamen, H., *Philip of Spain*. 2nd ed., New Haven and London, 1998.

—— *Spain in the later seventeenth century, 1665–1700*. 2nd ed., London and New York, 1983.

Karant-Nunn, S.C., 'The transmission of Luther's teaching on women and matrimony: the case of Zwickau', *Archive for Reformation History* 77 (1983), pp. 1–46.

Kates, G., *The Cercle Social, the Girondins, and the French Revolution*. Princeton, 1983.

Katzenellenbogen, A., *Allegories of the Virtues and Vices in medieval art*. New York, 1964.

Kellum, B.A., 'Infanticide in England in the later Middle Ages', *History of Childhood Quarterly* 1 (1973–4), pp. 367–388.

Kettering, S., 'Brokerage at the court of Louis XIV', *Historical Journal* 36 (1993), pp. 69–87.

—— 'The patronage power of early modern French noblewomen', *Historical Journal* 32 (1989), pp. 817–841.

Keynes, S., 'The Aethlings in Normandy', *Anglo-Norman Studies* 13 (1991), pp. 173–205.

Kilroy, P. (ed.), 'Memories and testimonies of Nonconformist women in seventeenth-century Ireland', in *Field Day anthology of Irish writing*, vol. 4, *Irish women's writing and traditions* edited by. A. Bourke and others (Cork, 2002), pp. 480–9.

King, C., 'Effigies: human and divine' in D. Norman (ed.), *Siena, Florence and Padua: art, society and religion, 1280–1400*. Volume 2. *Case Studies* (New Haven and London, 1995), pp. 105–127.

—— *Renaissance women patrons: wives and widows in Italy, c.1300–1550*. Manchester and New York, 1998.

Kittel, R., 'Rape in thirteenth-century England: a study of the Common Law courts' in D. Kelly Weisberg (ed.), *Women and the law: the social historical perspective* (2 vols., Cambridge, Mass., 1982), vol. 2, pp. 101–115.

Kraus, H., *The living theatre of medieval art*. Philadelphia, 1972.

La Válgoma y Díaz-Varela, D. de, *Norma y ceremonia de las reinas de la casa de Austria*. Madrid, 1958.

Laqueur, T., *Making sex: body and gender from the Greeks to Freud*. Cambridge, Mass., 1990.

Lawson, M., *Cnut: the Danes in England in the early eleventh century*. London, 1993.

Le Jan, R., *Famille et pouvoir dans le monde franc, VIIe–Xe siècle: essai d'anthropologie sociale*. Paris, 1995.

Le Roy Ladurie, E., *Saint-Simon and the court of Louis XIV*, trans. Arthur Goldhammer. Chicago, 2001.

Lebrun, F., *La vie conjugale sous l'ancien régime*. Paris, 1975.

Lehmann, W.C., *John Millar of Glasgow*. Cambridge, 1960.

Leicht, I., 'Gebildet und geistreich: Humanistinnen zwischen Renaissance und Reformation' in A. Conrad (ed.), *'in Christo ist weder man noch weyb'. Frauen in der Zeit der Reformation und der katholischen Reform* (Münster, 1999), pp. 23–48.

Lenihan, P., 'War and population 1649–52', *Irish Economic and Social History*, 24 (1997), pp. 1–21.

—— (ed.), *Conquest and resistance: war in seventeenth-century Ireland*. Leiden, 2001.

Lesting-Buermann, B., *Reformation und literarisches Leben in Nürnberg. Ein Beitrag zur Kommunikationsgeschichte der frühen Neuzeit unter besonderer Berücksichtigung der Predigten A. Osianders, V. Dietrichs und der Schriften Lazarus Spenglers.* Freiburg, 1982.

Leyser, H., *Medieval women: a social history of women in England 450–1500.* London, 1997.

Leyser, K.J., *Rule and conflict in an early medieval society: Ottonian Saxony.* Oxford, 1979.

Logue, K., 'Thomas Muir' in G., Menzies, (ed.), *History is my witness* (London, 1976), pp. 14–37.

LoPrete, K.A., 'The gender of lordly women: the case of Adela of Blois' in C. Meek and C. Lawless (eds), *Studies in medieval and early modern women: pawns or players?* (Dublin, 2003), pp. 90–110.

——— 'Adela of Blois: familial alliances and female lordship' in T. Evergates (ed.), *Aristocratic women in medieval France* (Philadelphia, 1999), pp. 7–43, 180–200.

Lord, M.L., 'Dido as an example of chastity: the influence of example literature', *Harvard Library Bulletin* 17 (1969), pp. 22–44, 216–32.

Luchaire, A., *Louis VI le Gros: annales de sa vie et de son règne 1081–1137.* Paris, 1890.

Lunden, W.A., *Facts on crime and criminals.* Ames, Iowa, 1961.

MacCurtain, M. and O'Dowd, M. (eds), *Women in early modern Ireland.* Dublin, 1991.

McKie, R., 'The Y Chromosome', *The Observer*, supplement, 'Men uncovered: the state they're in,' 24 June 2004.

Malcolm, A., 'La práctica informal del poder. La política de la Corte y el acceso a la Familia Real durante la segunda mitad del reinado de Felipe IV', *Reales Sitios* xxxviii, 147 (2001), pp. 38–48.

——— 'Public morality and the closure of the theatres in the mid-seventeenth century: Philip IV, the Council of Castile and the arrival of Mariana of Austria' in Richard Pym (ed.), *Rhetoric and reality in early modern Spain* (forthcoming).

Manceron, C., *La Révolution Française: dictionnaire biographique.* Paris, 1989.

Mannheim, H., *Comparative criminology.* London, 1965.

Marañón, G., *El conde-duque de Olivares: la pasión de mandar.* 26th ed., Madrid, 1998.

Martindale, A., *Simone Martini.* Oxford, 1988.

Masson, M. and Jameson, J.F., 'The Odyssey of Thomas Muir', *American Historical Review* 29 (1923), pp. 49–72.

McBride, R., 'The sceptical view of marriage and the comic vision in Molière', *Forum for Modern Language Studies* 5 (1969), pp. 24–46.

McClintock, F.H. and Gibson, E., *Robbery in London: an enquiry by the Cambridge Institute of Criminology.* London, 1961.

McFarland, E.W., *Ireland and Scotland in the age of revolution.* Edinburgh, 1994.

McNamara, J. and Wemple, S., 'The power of women through the family in medieval Europe, 500–1100', *Feminist Studies* 1 (1973), pp. 126–42.

Meek, C. and Lawless, C. (eds), *Studies in medieval and early modern women: pawns or players?* Dublin, 2003.

Meek, R.L., 'The Scottish contribution to Marxist sociology' in R.L. Meek, *Economics and ideology and other essays* (London, 1967), pp. 34–50.

——— *Social science and the ignoble savage.* Cambridge, 1976.

Meikle, H.W., *Scotland and the French Revolution.* Glasgow, 1912, reprinted in facsimile, London, 1969.

Meiss, M., *Painting in Florence and Siena after the Black Death.* Princeton, NJ, 1951.

Menestò, E., 'The Apostolic canonization proceedings of Clare of Montefalco, 1318–1319' in D. Bornstein and R. Rusconi (eds), *Women and religion in medieval and renaissance Italy*, trans. by M.J. Schneider (Chicago and London, 1996), pp. 104–129.

—— *Il processo di canonizzazione di Chiara da Montefalco*. Quaderni del 'Centro per il collegamento degli studi medievali e umanistici nell'università di Perugia' 14, Agiografia Umbra 4, Florence, 1984.

Menzies, G. (ed.), *History is my witness*. London, 1976.

Migiel, M. and Schiesari, J. (eds), *Refiguring women: perspectives on gender and the Italian Renaissance*. Ithaca and London, 1991.

Miller, J., *The life and times of William and Mary*. London, 1974.

Milsom, S.F.C., *Historical foundations of the common law*. London, 1981.

Moore, E.W., *The fairs of medieval England*. Toronto, 1995.

Moran, P.F., *Historical sketch of the persecutions suffered by the Catholics of Ireland*. Dublin, 1884.

Morgan, H., 'Old English and New English' in S. Connolly (ed.), *The Oxford companion to Irish history* (Oxford, 1998), pp. 408–9.

Moskowitz, A.F., *Nicola Pisano's Arca di San Domenico and its legacy*. University Park, PA, 1994.

Mulloy, S., 'The French navy and the Jacobite war in Ireland 1689–91', *Irish Sword* 18 (1990–1), pp. 17–31.

Murtagh, D., 'The Irish associations of "Mother Ross"', *Irish Sword* 1 (1949–53), pp. 146–7.

Murtagh, D. and Murtagh, H., 'The Irish Jacobite army 1688–91', *Irish Sword* 18 (1990–1), pp. 32–48.

Murtagh, H., Review of T.G. Fraser and K. Jeffrey (eds), Men, women and war. Historical Studies XVIII, *History Ireland* 1 (1993), p. 61.

Nelson, J., 'Inauguration rituals' in P. Sawyer and I. Wood (eds), *Early medieval kingship* (Leeds, 1977), pp. 50–71.

Nessi, S., 'I processi per la canonizzazione di Santa Chiara da Montefalco', *Bollettino della Deputazione di Storia Patria per l'Umbria* 65/2 (1968), pp. 103–160.

Newman, B., *From virile woman to WomanChrist: studies in medieval religion and literature*. Philadelphia, 1995.

Nicholson, R.L., *Tancred: a study of his career and work in their relation to the First Crusade and the establishment of the Latin states in Syria and Palestine*. Chicago, 1940.

Niderst, A. (ed.), *Le Français vus par lui-mêmes: le siècle de Louis XIV*. Paris, 1997.

Norma y ceremonia de las reinas de la casa de Austria. Madrid, 1958.

Norman, D. (ed.), *Siena, Florence and Padua: art, society and religion 1280–1400*. Volume II: *Case studies*. New Haven and London, 1995.

O'Connor, P., 'A bird's eye view ... resistance in academia', *Irish Journal of Sociology* 10 (2001), pp. 86–104.

O'Dowd, M., 'Property, work and home: women and the economy, c.1170–1850' in *Field Day anthology of Irish Writing*. vol. 5, *Irish women's writing and traditions*, edited by Angela Bourke and others (Cork, 2002), pp. 464–529.

—— 'Rosa O'Doherty' in *Field Day anthology of Irish Writing*. vol. 5, *Irish women's writing and traditions*, edited by Angela Bourke and others (Cork, 2002), p.30.

—— 'Women and war in Ireland in the 1640s' in M. MacCurtain and M. O'Dowd (eds), *Women in early modern Ireland* (Dublin, 1991), pp. 91–112.

Ohlmeyer, J. and Kenyon, J. (eds), *The Civil Wars: a military history of England, Scotland and Ireland, 1638–1660*. Oxford, 1998.

Oldham, J., 'Jury research in the English Reports in CD-ROM' in J.W. Cairns and G. McLeod (eds), *The dearest birth right of the people of England: the jury in the history of the Common Law* (Oxford and Portland, 2002), pp. 131–153.

——— 'On pleading the belly: a history of the jury of matrons', *Criminal Justice History* 6 (1985), pp. 1–64.

Oman, C., *Mary of Modena*. London, 1962.

Orso, S.N., *Philip IV and the decoration of the Alcázar of Madrid*. Princeton, NJ, 1986.

Parsons, D. (ed.), *Tenth-century studies*. London, 1975.

Parsons, J.C. (ed.), *Medieval queenship*. New York, 1993.

Pedersen, F., *Marriage disputes in medieval England*. London, 2000.

Penco, G., 'La preghiera a forma di croce', *Vita Monastica* 21 (1967), pp. 131–6.

Peuckert, W.-E., *Die Grosse Wende. Geistesgeschichte und Volkskunde*. Darmstadt, 1966.

Phillips, J. (ed.), *The First Crusade: origins and impact*. Manchester, 1997.

Phillips, R., *Family breakdown in eighteenth-century France: divorces in Rouen 1792–1803*. Oxford, 1980.

——— *Putting asunder: a history of divorce in western society*. Cambridge, 1988.

Picasso, G. (ed.), *Una santa tutta romana: saggi e ricerche nel VI centenario della nascità di Francesca Bussa dei Ponziani*. Siena, 1984.

Platelle, H., 'Le problème du scandale: les nouvelles modes masculines aux XIe et XIIe siècles', *Revue Belge de Philologie et d'Histoire* 53 (1975), pp. 1071–96.

Pocock, J.G.A., *The Machiavellian moment: Florentine political thought and the Atlantic republican tradition*. Princeton, 1975.

——— *Politics, language and time: essays on political thought and history*. Chicago, 1971, London, 1972.

Pollak, M.D., *Turin, 1564–1680: urban design, military culture, and the creation of the absolutist capital*. Chicago and London, 1991.

Pollak, O., *The criminality of women*. Philadelphia, 1950.

Pollock, F. and Maitland, F.W., *The history of English law*. 2 vols., London, 1956.

Polo de Beaulieu, M.A., 'La Légende du couer inscrit dans la littérature religieuse et didactique' in *Le 'cuer' au moyen age, Réalité e Senefiance*. Senefiance 30 (Aix en Provence, 1991), pp. 297–312.

Porter, R., 'Rape: does it have a historical meaning?' in S. Tomaselli and R. Porter (eds), *Rape* (Oxford, 1986), pp. 216–36.

Portmann, M.-L., *Die Darstellung der Frau in der Geschichtschreibung des früheren Mittelalters*. Basel, 1958.

Pugh, R.B., *Imprisonment in medieval England*. Cambridge, 1968.

Puyol Buil, C., *Inquisición y política en el reinado de Felipe IV: los procesos de Jerónimo de Villanueva y las monjas de San Plácido, 1628–1660*. Madrid, 1993.

Quinney, R., 'Suicide, homicide and economic development', *Social Forces* 43 (1965), pp. 401–6.

Radzinowicz, L., and Turner, J.W.C. (eds), *Mental abnormality and crime*. London, 1944.

Redworth, G., *The prince and the infanta: the cultural politics of the Spanish match*. New Haven and London, 2003.

Reilly, T., *Cromwell: an honourable enemy: the untold story of the Cromwellian invasion of Ireland*. Dingle, 1999.

Rendall, J., 'Clio, Mars and Minerva: the Scottish Enlightenment and the writing of women's history' in T.M. Devine and J.R. Young (eds), *Eighteenth-century Scotland: new perspectives* (East Linton, 1999), pp. 134–51.

Ridyard, S., *The royal saints of Anglo-Saxon England*. Cambridge, 1988.

Rigaux, D., 'Women, faith and image in the late Middle Ages' in L. Scaraffia and G. Zarri (eds), *Women and faith: Catholic religious life in Italy from late Antiquity to the present* (Cambridge, Mass., and London, 1999), pp. 72–82.

Riley-Smith, J., *The First Crusaders, 1095–1131*. Cambridge, 1997.

Ringbom, S., *Icon to narrative: the rise of the dramatic close-up in fifteenth-century devotional painting*. 2nd ed., Doornspijk, 1984.

Robbins, C., *The eighteenth-century Commonwealthman: studies in the transmission, development and circumstances of English liberal thought from the restoration of Charles II to the war with the Thirteen Colonies*. Cambridge, Mass., 1959.

Robbins, J., *The challenges of uncertainty: an introduction to seventeenth-century Spanish literature*. London, 1998.

—— *Love poetry of the literary academies in the reigns of Philip IV and Charles II*. London, 1997.

Robinson, D.N., *Wild beasts & idle humans: the insanity defence from antiquity to the present*. Cambridge, Mass., 1998.

Robinson, H. (ed.), *Feminism-art-theory: an anthology, 1968–2000*. Oxford, 2003.

Robinson, I.S., 'Gregory VII and the soldiers of Christ', *History* 58 (1973), pp. 169–192.

—— '"Political allegory" in the biblical exegesis of Bruno of Segni', *Recherches de Théologie Ancienne et Moderne* 50 (1983), pp. 69–98.

Robinson-Hammerstein, H., *Faith, force and freedom*. Dublin, 2001.

Rollason, D., 'Relic-cults as an instrument of royal policy, *c*.900–*c*.1050', *Anglo-Saxon England* 15 (1986), pp. 91–103.

Ronsin, F., *Le contrat sentimental: débats sur le mariage, l'amour, le divorce, de l'Ancien Régime à la Restauration*. Paris, 1990.

Rosener, W., *Peasants in the Middle Ages*. Cambridge, 1992.

Ruane, F. and Sutherland, J.M., *Women in the labour force*. Dublin, 1999.

Russell, P., *Lay theology in the Reformation: popular pamphleteers in southwest Germany*. Cambridge, 1986.

Sánchez, M.S., *The empress, the queen and the nun: women and power at the court of Philip III of Spain*. London and Baltimore, 1998.

Sawyer, P. and Woods, I., (eds), *Early medieval kingship*. Leeds, 1977.

Scaraffia, L. and Zarri, G. (eds), *Women and faith: Catholic religious life in Italy from late antiquity to the present*. Cambridge, Mass., and London, 1999.

Schiller, G., *The iconography of Christian art*. Volume 2. *The Passion of Jesus Christ*, trans. Janet Seligman. London, 1972.

Schwitalla, J., *Deutsche Flugschriften, 1460–1525*. Tübingen, 1983.

Scott, J.W., 'Gender: a useful category of historical analysis', *American Historical Review* 91 (1986), pp. 1053–1075.

Scribner, R.W., 'Anticlericalism and the cities' in P.A. Dykema and H.A. Oberman (eds), *Anticlericalism in late medieval and early modern Europe* (Leiden, 1994), pp. 147–166.

Sergi, G., *Lexikon des Mittelalters*. Munich, 1980–99.

Sharpe, J.A., *Crime in early modern England 1550–1750*. London and New York, 1999.

Sharpe, K., 'The image of virtue: the court and household of Charles I, 1625–1642' in D. Starkey (ed.), *The English court from the Wars of the Roses to the Civil War*. 4th ed. (London and New York, 1996) pp. 226–260.

Sher, R.B., *The church and university in the Scottish Enlightenment: the moderate literati in Edinburgh*. Edinburgh, 1985.

—— 'Professors of virtue: The social history of the Edinburgh Moral Philosophy chair in the eighteenth century' in M.A. Stewart (ed.), *Studies in the philosophy of the Scottish Enlightenment* (Oxford, 1990), pp. 87–126.

Shergold, N.D., *A history of the Spanish stage from medieval times until the end of the seventeenth century*. Oxford, 1967.

—— and Varey, J.E., *Fuentes para la historia del teatro en España*, 1. *Representaciones palaciegas: 1603–1699. Estudio y documentos*. London, 1982.

Sillglow, J. (ed.), *MacMillan dictionary of women's biography*. London, 1982.

Simms, H., 'Violence in county Armagh, 1641' in B. MacCuarta (ed.), *Ulster 1641. aspects of the rising* (Belfast, 1993), pp. 123–138.

Simms, J.G., *Jacobite Ireland, 1685–91*. London, 1969.

—— *War and politics in Ireland, 1649–1730*. London, 1986.

—— *The Williamite confiscation in Ireland, 1690–1703. Studies in Irish history*, vol. vii. London, 1956.

Siraisi, N.G., *Taddeo Alderotti and his pupils: two generations of Italian medical learning*. Princeton, NJ, 1981.

Smith, J.M.H., 'The problem of female sanctity in Carolingian Europe', *Past and Present* 146 (1995), pp. 3–37.

Solnon, J.-F., *La cour de France*. Paris, 1987.

Sowards, J.K., 'Erasmus and the education of women', *Sixteenth-Century Journal* 13 (1982), pp. 77–89.

Sox, D., *Relics and shrines*. London, 1985.

Stafford, P., 'The king's wife in Wessex, 800–1066', *Past and Present* 91 (1981), pp. 3–27.

—— 'The portrayal of royal women in England, mid-tenth to mid-twelfth centuries' in J.C. Parsons (ed.), *Medieval queenship* (New York, 1993), pp. 143–67.

—— *Queens, concubines and dowagers: the king's wife in the early Middle Ages*. Athens, GA, 1983.

—— *Queen Emma and Queen Edith*. London, 1997.

—— 'The reign of Aethelred II: a study in the limitations on royal policy and action' in D. Hill (ed.), *Aethelred the Unready: papers from the Millennary Conference* (British Archaeological Reports, British Series, 59, Oxford, 1978), pp. 15–46.

—— 'Sons and mothers: family politics in the early Middle Ages' in D. Baker (ed.), *Medieval women: essays presented to R.M.T. Hill*. Studies in Church History, subsidia 1 (Oxford, 1978), pp. 79–100.

—— *Unification and conquest*. London, 1989.

Starkey, D. (ed.), *The English court from the Wars of the Roses to the Civil War*. 4th ed., London and New York, 1996.

Steegmuller, F., *La Grande Mademoiselle*. London, 1955.

Stephenson, W.H., 'An alleged son of Harold Harefoot', *English Historical Review* 28 (1913), pp. 112–17.

Stewart, M.A., *The kirk and the infidel*. Lancaster, 1994.

—— (ed.), *Studies in the philosophy of the Scottish Enlightenment*. Oxford, 1990.

Stones, E.L.G., 'The Folvilles of Ashby-Folville, Leicestershire, and their associates in crime', *Transactions of the Royal Historical Society*, 5th series, 7 (1957), pp. 91–116.

Storer, I., '"Johnny I hardly knew you". Women, wives and camp followers of the Napoleonic era', *The Age of Napoleon* 28 (1998), pp. 17–23.

Story, G., 'A true and impartial history', *Old Limerick Journal* 28 (1990), pp. 89–99.

Stradling, R.A., *Philip IV and the government of Spain, 1621–1655*. Cambridge, 1988.

Strauss, G. (ed.), *Manifestations of discontent in Germany on the eve of the Reformation*. Bloomington, Ind, 1971.

—— *Nuremberg in the sixteenth century: city politics and life between the Middle Ages and modern times*. Rev. ed., Bloomington, Ind, 1976.

Tomaselli, S., and Porter, R. (eds), *Rape*. Oxford, 1986.

Trexler, R.C., 'Infanticide in Florence: new sources and first results', *History of Childhood Quarterly* 1 (1973–4), pp. 98–116.

Unknown author, 'Passes to Irish soldiers, 1692–7', *Irish Sword* 15 (1982), p. 115.

Van Engen, J.H., *Rupert of Deutz*. Berkeley, CA,1983.

Van Houts, E., *The Normans in Europe*. Manchester, 2000.

Varey, J.E. and Shergold, N.D., 'Datos históricos sobre los primeros teatros de Madrid: prohibiciones de autos y comedias y sus consecuencias (1644–1651)', *Bulletin Hispanique* 62 (1960), pp. 286–325.

Vauchez, A., *Sainthood in the later Middle Ages*, trans. J. Birrell. Cambridge, 1997.

Walker, N.D., *Crime and insanity in England*. 2 vols, Edinburgh, 1973.

Walsh, L., 'Eye-witness and contemporary accounts', *Old Limerick Journal* 28 (1990), pp. 57–71.

Walsh, M., 'Some notes towards a history of the womenfolk of the wild geese', *Irish Sword* 5 (1961/2), pp. 98–106, 133–45.

Walsh, M. Kerney,'Irish Women in exile, 1600–1800', *O'Mahony Journal* 11 (1981), pp. 35–48.

Weisberg, D. Kelly (ed.), *Women and the law: the social historical perspective*. 2 vols., Cambridge, Mass., 1982.

Wemple, S.F., *Women in Frankish society: marriage and the cloister, 500 to 900*. Philadelphia, 1981.

Wheeler, J. Scott, 'The logistics of conquest' in P. Lenihan (ed.), *Conquest and resistance: war in seventeenth-century Ireland* (Leiden, 2001), pp. 177–209.

Whelan, B., 'Women and warfare, 1641–1691' in P. Lenihan (ed.), *Conquest and resistance: war in seventeenth-century Ireland* (Leiden, 2001), pp. 317–43.

Wiener, C.Z., 'Is a spinster an unmarried woman?', *American Journal of Legal History* 20 (1976), pp. 27–31.

Wiesner, M., 'Nuns, wives, and mothers: women and the Reformation in Germany' in S. Marshall (ed.),*Women in Reformation and Counter-Reformation Europe: public and private worlds* (Bloomington, Ind., 1989), pp. 8–28.

—— *Women and gender in early modern Europe*. Cambridge, 1993.

Williams, A., 'Some notes and considerations on problems connected with the English royal succession, 860–1066', *Proceedings of the Battle Conference on Anglo-Norman Studies* 1 (1978), pp. 144–67.

Williams, P., 'Lerma, 1618: dismissal or retirement?', *European History Quarterly* 19 (1989), pp. 307–32.

—— 'Lerma, Old Castile and the travels of Philip III of Spain', *History* 73 (1988), pp. 379–97.

Wingham, M.J., *The Irish Friends: a short history of the Religious Society of Friends in Ireland*. Dublin, 1992.

Wolfgang, M.E., *Patterns in criminal homicide*. Philadelphia, 1958.

Woshinsky, Barbara, *La princesse de Clèves: the tension of elegance*.The Hague, 1973.

Wright, E.R., *Pilgrimage to patronage: Lope de Vega and the court of Philip III, 1598–1621*. London, 2001.

Wright, P., 'A change in direction: the ramifications of a female household, 1558–1603' in D. Starkey (ed.), *The English court from the Wars of the Roses to the Civil War*, 4th ed. (London and New York, 1996), pp. 147–172.

Zanger, A., *Scenes from the marriage of Louis XIV*. Stanford, 1997.

Ziegler, G., *The court at Versailles*. London, 1960.

Bibliography

THESES

Edgington, S.B. (ed.), 'Albert of Aix, "Historia Hierosolomytaña"'. Unpublished Phd thesis, University of London, 1991.

France, John (ed.), 'Raymond D'Aguilers, "Historia Francorum qui ceperunt Iherusalem". Unpublished PhD thesis, University of Nottingham, 1967.

Gordon, D.S., 'Painting in Umbria 1250–1350'. Unpublished PhD thesis, University of London, 1979.

Guiral, María de los Ángeles Campo, 'Edición y estudio de la vigilia y octavario de San Juan Bautista de doña Ana Francisca Abarca de Bolea'. Doctoral thesis, University of Zaragoza, 1990.

Malcolm, A., 'Don Luis de Haro and the political elite of the Spanish monarchy in the mid-seventeenth century'. Unpublished DPhil thesis. University of Oxford, 1999.

Schenk, J.G., 'The use of rhetoric, biblical exegesis and polemic in Guibert of Nogent's Gesta Dei per Francos'. Unpublished M Phil thesis, Trinity College Dublin, 2001.

Contributors

MICHAEL BROWN is a Research Fellow at the Centre for Irish-Scottish Studies at Trinity College Dublin. Author of *Francis Hutcheson in Dublin, 1719–1730* (2002) and co-editor of *Converts and conversion in Ireland, 1650–1850* (2005), he is currently writing a history of the Irish Enlightenment.

PATRICK HEALY is an IRCHSS Government of Ireland Post-Doctoral Fellow in the Department of Medieval History, Trinity College Dublin specializing in eleventh-century ecclesiastical history.

LINDA KIERNAN tutors in early modern history at University College Dublin, where she is completing a doctoral thesis on 'Perceptions of power. The role of the royal mistress at the court of Louis XIV'. She is also working on the life of Louisa O'Murphy, the mistress of Louis XV.

CONOR KOSTICK is a history graduate of Trinity College Dublin and the holder of an IRCHSS scholarship; he is currently completing his PhD on 'The language of ordo in crusading chronicles, 1096-1184'.

CATHERINE LAWLESS obtained her PhD at Trinity College Dublin and is now a lecturer in the History Department at the University of Limerick, where she runs an MA course on art and design and is also curator of the university's art collections.

KIMBERLY LO PRETE obtained her PhD at the University of Chicago and is now a lecturer in the History Department at NUI, Galway, where she teaches medieval European history and the history of women.

ALISTAIR MALCOLM lectures in the History Department at the University of Limerick. He obtained his D.Phil. at Oxford and specializes in Spanish history of the reign of Philip IV, particularly the governing elite.

CHRISTINE MEEK is Associate Professor in the Department of Medieval History at Trinity College Dublin, where she specialises in late medieval Italian history and the history of women.

COLM Ó CONAILL obtained his PhD at Trinity College Dublin for a thesis on 'Divorce and civil society during the French Revolution, 1789–1803' and also worked at the Centre for Irish-Scottish Studies. He has published on Irish regiments in France and is now a Lecturer at NUI, Galway.

HELGA ROBINSON-HAMMERSTEIN is a Senior Lecturer in Modern History at Trinity College Dublin. Her research centres on the Reformation in Central and Western Europe and the history of universities in the Early Modern period.

MAIA SHERIDAN is a graduate of Trinity College Dublin, where she is currently completing a PhD thesis on Innocent III's distinction between heresy and orthodoxy. A trained archivist, she works for St Andrews University on their Special Collections.

RICHARD SIMS graduated in history at Aberdeen University, and specialized in Medieval History at Downing College Cambridge. His main interest is in the social and legal history of England, and this is his first publication.

CORDELIA WARR is Lecturer in History of Art at the University of Manchester. She has published articles on dress in *Art History*, *Journal of Medieval History* and *Arte Medievale*, and is completing a book *Physical and spiritual clothing in Italian art, 1215–1545*.

BERNADETTE WHELAN is Head of the Department of History at the University of Limerick. Her research interests lie in modern diplomatic history, Irish foreign policy and women and warfare in the seventeenth century.

Index